THE POLITICS OF SYMBOL IN SERBIA

Ivan Čolović, 1999. (Goranka Matić)

IVAN ČOLOVIĆ

The Politics of Symbol in Serbia

Essays in Political Anthropology

TRANSLATED FROM THE SERBIAN BY
CELIA HAWKESWORTH

HURST & COMPANY, LONDON

First published in Belgrade as
Politika simbola in 1997, and
published in a revised edition, from
which the English edition has been
translated, by Biblioteka 20 vek, 2000

This translation, by Celia Hawkesworth,
© C. Hurst & Co. (Publishers) Ltd., 2002
All rights reserved.

Printed in India

ISBNs
1-85065-465-4 casebound
1-85065-556-1 paperback

Contents

Illustrations	page ix
Author's Preface to the English Edition	xi
Translator's note	xii
Introduction	1

Part I. THE SERBIAN POLITICAL ETHNO-MYTH

1. Story	5
2. Time	13
3. Nature	21
4. Frontiers	29
5. Europe	39
6. Warrior	48
7. Pantheon	57
8. Identity	64
9. Bank	74
10. Criticism	80

Part II. FROM THE HISTORY OF SERBIAN POLITICAL MYTHOLOGY

1. Skerlić, 'Pan-Slavdom' and 'The Rotten West'	89
2. Skerlić and Serbian Political Myths	98
3. Town and Country in the Work of Tihomir Djordjević	112

Part III. CHARACTERS AND FIGURES OF POWER
(*32 case studies*)

1. The Spiritual — 125
2. The Politics of Time — 129
3. The Secret of the Balkans — 133
4. The Devil in Serbia — 137
5. Magic Mirror — 141
6. The Book of Preachers — 145
7. Serbian Lyric Verse — 149
8. Us? — 153
9. Hatred — 157
10. The Genes of the Tribe — 161
11. Relics — 166
12. Gauss — 171
13. Combat — 175
14. Theatre Town — 179
15. Tunnel — 183
16. Contemplation — 187
17. New Age — 191
18. The 'Other Srpska' — 195
19. Javor — 199
20. Mission — 203
21. At 'The Two Stags' — 207
22. Festival of Books — 211
23. Turbulent — 215
24. Enjoyment — 219
25. Everyone to the Sea! — 224
26. Piano — 228
27. *Gaudeamus* — 232
28. Service — 236

29.	Distillation	240
30.	Horseshoes	244
31.	Mantle	248
32.	Moloch	252

Part IV. THE AGE OF THE CROWD

1.	Football, Hooligans and War	259
2.	The Rhetoric of Peace	287
3.	Palm-reading and 'The Little Serbian Fist'	295
4.	Epilogue (November 200): Heavenly Serbia comes down to Earth	305

Appendixes

A. Key Characters and Concepts	309
B. Main Political Parties of Serbia	314

Bibliography 315

Index 321

Illustrations

Ivan Čolović, 1999	frontispiece
Monument to the Serbian hero Miloš Obilić in Obilić, Kosovo, destroyed after the withdrawal of Serbian forces, June 1999	4
The poet Matija Bećković in the charnel-house of Chilandar monastery on Mount Athos	19
Serbian fighter resting, eastern Herzegovina, 1993	23
Serbian coat of arms on a chain and tattoed on the arm of an American of Serbian Origin: 'Born in America, but my heart is in Serbia'	30
A young member of the armed forces of Bosnian Serbs at Pale, June 1992	47
Photograph from the front page of the paper *Vojska Krajine*, April 1993	50
A Serbian fighter in Slavonia, December 1991	56
Exchange of bodies from the war in Slavonia in 1992	73
Milošević playing the *gusle*, with the writer Dobrica Ćosić sitting on his knee	131
III Congress of the Socialist Party of Serbia	143

Dr Jovan Striković, director of the Saint Sava Hospital in
Belgrade, with nurses in Orthodox-style uniforms designed
by him, 1992 — 162

Radovan Karadžić participating in bringing out the relics of
St Vasilije Ostroški before their journey to Herzegovina,
10 May 1996 — 167

Cover of the first number of *Combat* magazine — 178

Mirjana Marković and Slobodan Milošević in 1998 — 221

Coat of arms of the Institute of Geopolitical Studies, Belgrade — 251

Caricature of bishops of the Serbian Orthodox Church,
Atanasije Jevtić and Amfilohije Radović — 254

Fighters of the Serbian Volunteer Guard in March 1992,
somewhere in Slavonia, reading the magazine of their favourite
football club — 277

'Look! The handful's on its way!', placard at the demonstrations
against the Milošević regime in Belgrade, November 1996 — 297

A rock-climber flashes the traditional Serbian three-finger sign on
top of the Belgrade City Hall as climbers remove the Communist
star, December 2000 — 303

Author's Preface to the English Edition

The Politics of Symbol consists of texts written between 1994 and 1997. The book was first published in Belgrade at the end of 1997, by the independent radio station B92. At that time it seemed that the then Yugoslav president Slobodan Milošević was stronger than ever before, because he had succeeded in holding onto power despite mass demonstrations by the citizens of Serbia against his regime. The demonstrations lasted nearly four months, from November 1996 to the middle of March 1997. However, later events, and particularly the war in Kosovo and the air attacks on Yugoslavia by the Nato Pact in the spring of 1999, fundamentally shook Milošević's government again. In the local and parliamentary elections held on 24 September 2000 he suffered a defeat of such proportions that no later tampering with the results could be concealed. But still that is just what Milošević tried to do. The united opposition (the Democratic Opposition of Serbia) reacted by organising large-scale demonstrations on 5 October in Belgrade, in the course of which the citizens occupied and set fire to the Yugoslav Parliament, the State Television building, several police stations and some other government institutions. The police offered surprisingly weak resistance to the demonstrations, and, despite Milošević's summons for assistance, the army remained in their barracks. So, after twelve years of rule, Milošević was finally brought down. He left behind him tens of thousands of dead and wounded, hundreds of thousands of displaced individuals, millions of impoverished and shamed citizens: the victims of the wars on the territory of former Yugoslavia, which he was largely responsible for causing to break out.

Serbia today faces a painful and probably lengthy confrontation with the truth about the regime of Milošević, his crimes and victims, but also about his allies and advisers. His legacy to Serbia and the Serbian people is also a rich arsenal of nationalist symbols, rituals and myths, out of which 'national workers' in the course of recent years constructed the building of the so-called Heavenly Serbia. This book may be described as a critical inventory of one part of that arsenal. Its author hopes that acquaintance with the content of this inventory is not merely a way of satisfying curiosity about one aspect of the recent past of Serbia and former Yugoslavia. Unlike Milošević himself, whose time, no matter what happens to him, has undoubtedly passed, it seems that the sell-by date of most of that arsenal of political symbols has not yet been reached. The new government in Serbia, which wishes to free itself from the mortgage of the former regime, must resist the obviously strong temptation of seeking elements of its symbolic identity in that rich store of nationalist stories, rituals, gestures, cults, symbols and images. That temptation is the subject of the epilogue to this edition of *The Politics of Symbol,* written two weeks after the fall of the Milošević regime.

My thanks for the appearance of an English edition of this book are due to Dr Gerlachus Duijzings, who recommended it to the British publisher. I was especially fortunate that Celia Hawkesworth undertook the translation. But for me the most important result of my working with them is not the book but their friendship.

Translator's note

The translation of this book has been both a pleasure and a challenge. I have endeavoured to retain as much as possible of the complexity and subtlety of Ivan Čolović's ideas. He approaches what are familiar topics in his own culture from an oblique angle, bringing them to new life. The text was originally written for a readership for whom the references are well known, and rather than overload the text with yet more footnotes we have provided a glossary of key characters and concepts. Items included in the glossary are marked with an asterisk the first time they occur. We have retained the diacritics of the original language. These letters are pronounced as follows:

Č - ch, as in church
Ć - tj, a 'softer' ch sound
Dj - similar to tj, a 'soft' sound

Dz - j, as in John
Š - sh, as in shuttle
Ž - g, as in Gigi

Introduction

The essays collected in this book are inspired by the idea that politics is in large part a matter of symbols. The use of symbols in politics is not merely a means (rhetorical, demagogic, promotional) of achieving and maintaining political power, manifested and practised on a different, non-symbolic, 'real' level of reality. The field of the symbolic is itself the greatest and richest empire which politicians and their generals, priests and poets conquer in salvoes of words, volleys, sermons and verses. The power to which they aspire, later to revel in it, is in fact power over symbol.

This is not an original idea. It has been familiar in political philosophy and political anthropology for a long time. In the modern age, we find it already in Rousseau, who said that even citizens' power has its profane— i.e. 'civil'—religion. In times closer to our own, to look at politics as a matter of symbols has become particularly relevant with the appearance of totalitarian political systems based on developed techniques of mass psychological manipulation. Today, as well, an insight into the symbolic nature of politics can further our understanding of contemporary offshoots of political totalitarianism and despotism. But more than that, we are also stimulated to reflect on the symbolic aspect of politics by difficulties involved in the development of a democratic model of society, particularly in the so-called 'countries in transition', such as the states which have come into being on the territory of former Yugoslavia. There is a widespread belief that some of the most significant obstacles in the path of democratisation in these countries are their exceptionally resilient nationalist cults and myths. The question arises as to what could oppose them. Should they be vanquished through rational argument or repressed by the promotion of other myths, appropriate to a democratic society? Is democracy, i.e. politics understood in a democratic way, simply the liberation of space for a debate about public matters, for what the French call *la mise en commun*, or does its survival require something else, its embodiment, its image?

These are some of the questions which will be encountered by readers of this book concerned with the symbols of politics and the politics of symbol in contemporary Serbia and Montenegro, and, far less, in some other former Yugoslav republics. I cannot promise that they will always find answers to these questions. More than searching for answers, I have endeavoured to justify raising these questions, which, at least in our country, are generally left on the margins of discussion about politics, as its 'folkloric' frill. I have been concerned to demonstrate the importance of the symbolic aspect of political power and its relevance for all serious reflection about politics, and about the social and political situation of this part of Europe.

The basis of the first part of the book, dedicated to contemporary Serbian political ethno-mythology, consists of texts on this theme published both in Serbia and abroad between 1994 and 1997, including 'Serbian political myths—time and space', published in 1994 in my book *Pucanje od zdravlja* (Bursting with health). They have all been fundamentally reworked and significantly expanded, so that they appear here as parts of ten chapters of a larger essay, also containing chapters published here for the first time.

The second and fourth parts of the book reproduce, unchanged, texts which appeared in the periodical *Republika* in January 1994 (Skerlić, 'Pan-Slavdom' and 'The Rotten West'); the collection *Srbija u modernizacijskim procesima XX veka* (Serbia in the Modernising Processes of the Twentieth Century), Belgrade, 1994 ('Skerlić and serbian political myths'); in *Glasnik Etnografskog instituta SANU* (Review of the Ethnographic Institute of the Serbian Academy of Arts and Science), XLIV, 1995 ('Town and country in the work of Tihomir Djordjević'); in the collection *Srpska strana rata* (published in English as *The Road to War in Serbia)*, edited by Nebojša Popov, Belgrade, 1996 ('Football, hooligans and war'); in the collection *Ka jeziku mira* (Towards a Language of Peace) edited by Božidar Jakšić, Belgrade, 1995 (The rhetoric of peace); and in the journal *Transit,* no. 13, 1997, published in Vienna (Palm-reading and 'The Little Serbian Fist'). The third part consists of texts published in the daily *Naša Borba* (Our Struggle) in the column entitled 'In Other Words', which I wrote twice a month from January 1996 to March 1997.

September 1997

PART I
The Serbian Political Ethno-Myth

'When we first heard people talk of political myths, they seemed to us so raw, so comical, so crazy and senseless that we found it hard to take them seriously. Now we know that this was a grave mistake. We must not make it a second time. For this reason it is necessary to undertake painstaking research into the origin, structure and technique of political myths.' (Ernst Kasirer, *The Myth of the State*, 1946)

Monument to the Serbian hero Miloš Obilić in Obilić, Kosovo, destroyed after the withdrawal of Serbian forces, June 1999. (Djordje Vukoje)

1. Story

In Serbia today, discussion of politics, the nation, the war and borders, Europe and the 'Serbian question', the church and the state, is largely reduced to a story. It is as though there were a prevailing belief that narrative is the most suitable form for discourse on important national topics. Politicians, journalists, academics, soldiers (not to mention writers and philosophers) readily, if not exclusively, discuss politics by telling stories. This can be explained by the advantage of the story over other forms of political discourse at a time when there is a need to reconstruct and strengthen, as speedily as possible, the image of the nation as an imagined community and to re-establish control over the symbols of political power, disrupted by the fall of the communist regime, the dissolution of the state and war.

Stories are indeed a suitable medium for this kind of renewal and reconstruction. Thanks to the procedures of emplotment, it is possible to establish apparently logical connections between what are otherwise unconnected, contradictory and ambivalent political events, ideas and figures. Transformed into sequences of narrative time, national history can develop without deviation or discontinuity. Thanks also to specific steps in the development of narrative time, it is possible to set up a direct, living connection with the past. The use of the historic present gives the impression that past events are unfolding before our eyes. Similarly, through the use of the traditional epic style (the epic perfect, for example), to tell the story of contemporary events, those events acquire the patina of a distant and glorious past. This in turn suggests that it is in the past that we should seek the key to their only correct interpretation.

Telling stories about national and political themes has an advantage over political analysis or debate also because that form of discourse does not pose, or rather because it easily solves, the problem of the credibility of the speaker and the persuasiveness of what is said. In the case of stories about the nation and politics, the generic convention according to which one accepts that the narrator is 'omniscient' makes it possible to claim a right to know the truth without evidence or argument, simply on the basis of the narrator's authority.

In addition to these inner, generic qualities, the story is recommended as especially suitable for discourse about 'national affairs', through the prestige it enjoys today as an exceptionally valuable means of handing down and maintaining Serbian culture. It is possible even to speak of a living cult of the story, developed above all around epic narration, which enables contemporary narrators, poets of epic narrative orientation, and writers in general, to play the role of important national figures. It is judged that they create works in which the spirit of the community, the spirit of its language, is shaped and expressed. That is why, when discourse about the nation and politics begins to abound in elements of story-telling, when it passes into the register of narrative, when it involves an abundance of literary embellishments, when it starts to teem with literary quotations—this does not at all mean that the speaker is renouncing serious things and indulging in an eloquence inappropriate to responsible discussion of the nation and politics. On the contrary, such political discourse is a sure sign that the speaker is treating a national question of exceptional importance and that he wishes, by the very narrative form of his presentation, to emphasise that importance.[1]

Discourse about politics and the nation in Serbia is today largely confined to story-telling also in the sense that in the majority of cases the skeleton of that discourse, its referential framework, even when

---

[1] In order to indicate the dramatic nature of the times and the importance of the themes he treats in one collection of poems about the war in Bosnia, Savo D. Vučić, a pensioner and amateur poet from Kneževo, gave his collection the title *Kada Srbin u stihu govori* (When a Serb speaks in verse) (Novi Sad: Educa,1995). Speaking in 1993 about Serbia under the burden of sanctions, the philosopher Mihailo Marković chose the register of poetic prose in a similar desire to emphasise the seriousness of the situation in which 'the world which considers itself Christian ... has condemned our entire people to collective imprisonment.' 'Nevertheless,' says Marković, 'it was unable to deprive us of our fundamentals, either natural or spiritual. The sun has continued to warm us, the rains still moisten our fields. From the depths of the soil our corn, grass and minerals continue to spring. This they could not take from us.' (Marković, p. 385)

it does not have a narrative form, consists of a series of more or less connected plots concerned with the Serbian nation, the Serbian state, the Serbian land and other important national themes. Because these plots have the role of being a credible and incontrovertible source of knowledge of the nation's first and last things and a model of correct collective thinking and behaviour, they may be called political mythic plots or simply myths. They hand down that specific kind of knowledge which Kerenyi connects with mythology, that is, knowledge attained by the answer to the question 'after what?' and not 'why?' (Kerenyi, 18). And in view of the fact that these plots are concerned above all with the question of the nation as the long-lost and almost re-found happy unity of ethnos, blood, state, territory, faith, culture and language, we can define them more precisely as Serbian ethno-nationalistic myths.

It is unrewarding and methodologically mistaken to present myths as a collection of clearly distinguished motifs and *topoi*, or a catalogue of unambiguously shaped ideas and concepts, because mythic discourse is characterised by fragmentedness, fluidity and ambivalence. But this *a priori* 'resistance' of myth to analytical interpretation may be reduced to a degree in the case of contemporary political myths. This is because they are the result of mythologisation, that is the re-working of 'original' mythic material (above all of that contained in traditional culture) from a specific perspective, and the scale of this mythologisation may be measured. With this in mind, I have decided to make a summary of the few most important *topoi* of Serbian ethno-nationalistic mythology. Of course, it is only here that they are separated *in vitro*, and logically connected into a text.

THE MYTH

The Serbian nation is the oldest nation in the world, all other nations originated from it, just as all other languages originated in the Serbian language. But it is at the same time the youngest and freshest nation, it offers the germ of universal, or at least European renewal. This is possible because this nation stands to one side of historical time, of the irretrievable loss of history. It lives in an eternal present, simultaneously old and young, in an eternal union of the dead, the living and the as yet unborn.[2]

---

[2] The Serbian word *narod* may be translated as both 'people' and 'nation'. I have used both possible English equivalents in different contexts, as I have felt it most appropriate and in the interests of clarity. (Translator's note—hereafter "Transl.")

The Serbian nation has lived on Serbian soil since time immemorial. That soil is its body. The river Neretva is the aorta of the Serbian bloodstream, the river Drina the Serbian spine or windpipe, while the Bosnian and Serbian mountains on either side of the Drina are its lungs. That soil has merged with its people into a living organism, the mother of every Serb.

The connection of the Serb with his motherland and the mutual connection of generations of Serbs, which is normally termed 'Serbdom', endures thanks to the preservation of this same connective substance—Serbian blood. It flows in a double bloodstream. Through one it is transferred from generation to generation, through the other, with the sacrificial blood of fallen heroes, it nourishes the body of Serbia, the native soil. That is why the places where this blood is spilled—battlefields, execution sites and pits, graveyards and graves—have exceptional symbolic value. They preserve the germs of national renewal, which implies initial sacrifice and death, and the roots through which the nation is connected to the ancestral soil. Graves are therefore the natural frontiers of Serbia.

The Serbs have remained as they are down to the present day, although other nations, more numerous than they are, materially richer and militarily more powerful, constantly endeavour to wipe them out biologically or destroy them spiritually. In this the enemies of the Serbs have always been assisted by their ungrateful and false brothers and neighbours, and by various traitors and degenerates among the Serbian people.

In the survival of the Serbs, that is of their spiritual vertical [sic], that which they are, despite everything and against everyone, one should see the finger of fate, the will of God, the Serbian cross. For the Serbs it is written that they should sacrifice themselves, unconditionally and unsparingly, for values which Providence has bequeathed them to defend: their name, the holy Cross, national freedom. This determination to defend their national identity in a merciless struggle with the tyrants of the world, was most clearly confirmed by the Serbs in the Battle of Kosovo, and this is why it is known as the Kosovo pledge.

The Serbs are today also the guardians of the rarest and most important civilisational values, the values of the heart and spirit. In the soulless world of modern materialism and rationalism, in a civilisation of false material well-being and cowardly pacifism, they prevail in the struggle for the ideals of the fighter, simultaneously dear to nature, and sacred. In that struggle they do not fear death, for without death there is no national resurrection. The suffering of the Serbs today and the dangers which have gathered over them, threatening their survival, may be compared only to the persecution and annihilation of the Jews in the Third Reich.

The Serbian struggle is directed against all forms of modern, anti-national life, against the merging of races, faiths and languages in unnatural mixed marriages, in degenerate and unhealthy towns with a cosmopolitan and democratic spirit, and in multiethnic states.

Serbia is today a thorn in the side of the extortionist-atheistic and demonic international community, which is driving peoples into the New World Order, just because the Serbs are a proud nation seeking to build their state on healthy, natural foundations, a state in which all will be together, on Serbian soil, where all will be one nation, one state, with one leader, where all will celebrate one Serbian faith, speak one Serbian language, write one Serbian script and think one Serbian thought.

This mytho-political framework is not manifested in any particular genre of verbal communication. The political mythic story does not exist as a particular kind of text. Given that it is a matter of a narrative structure, of a reservoir of plots, it is most at home in literary and folklore forms of story-telling. As has already been said, when it is realised in these forms, the political myth can count on their prestige as socially highly valued forms of symbolic communication. In addition, where it occurs in a folklore form, the political myth acquires also legitimacy as the 'voice of the people'.

But it can also adapt itself to other forms of discourse. For example, the mythic *topos* about the Serbian land as a territory defined by Serbian graves can be expressed in the language of 'newly-composed' folk songs, as, for example, in these lines: 'Where our forebears' bones now rest, there the Serbian frontiers stretch.'[3] It may also be displayed in the form of a literary essay: 'The frontiers were not drawn by Serbs, but by slaughtered Serbs. Wherever their heads fell, the frontier watch-towers were marked by those heads.' (Komnenić, 1989) It is possible to say that this essayistic version is not far removed from the folkloric. But grave-frontiers are discussed also in a scholarly tone, as, for example, in an article by an archaeologist: 'It was recently established that early medieval Serbian graveyards may easily be recognised as mounds on the surface of the earth. Their distribution designates our ethnic space before c. 1300 as lying between the waters of the Morava and Kupa rivers.' (Janković, 316)

---

[3]Dragutin Knežević Krunica, 'Gde su pale srpske glave', on the cassette *Srpska zora* (Serbian Dawn), Grafosund, Belgrade, 1992.

For this reason, the summary of some of the *topoi* in the Serbian ethno-nationalistic myth offered here is not only a list of commonplaces of the new national-political poems and similar narrative works about the Serbian nation and politics. It could serve also as a review of individual collections of scholarly and journalistic works on the same themes, a résumé of some patriotic-historical pamphlets, an overview of the subject matter of a number of political speeches, a brief contents-list of some history textbooks for elementary schools or an inventory of the stereotypes used by sports writers in moments of 'patriotic' exultation.

This weave of ethno-nationalistic mythology is manifested and realised only in fragments, in the form of the treatment of some commonplaces or plots (about rotten Europe, about graves as national boundaries, about the resurrection of the nation after death etc.). The whole remains as only latent, as the mainstream to which the scattered parts of the myth point, to which they flow. In fact, they function as synecdochic figures of the whole *(pars pro toto)*, i.e. as its embodiment on a small scale at the same time as codes for inclusion in a special programme of communication (in the computer sense), for entry into the mental space of ethno-nationalistic identification and participation.

This synecdochic function is particularly common in fragmented manifestations of the Kosovo myth, i.e. the ethno-nationalistic plots connected with the theme of the Battle of Kosovo in 1389. The very mention of Kosovo has become fixed as the clearest sign that discourse about the nation and politics seeks a point of support in the arsenal of what are for the Serbs, as an ethno-national community, self-evident and sacred tales. That is why one can say that the Kosovo myth, as a reference to that mythic point of support, has become a myth about a myth, that the so-called 'Kosovo option' means in fact opting for myth. But that does not mean that all those stories, that is the Serbian myths about the nation and national state as a whole, are nothing but variations on one central myth about Kosovo. The Kosovo subject-matter, together with other themes which make up the main weave of this ethno-nationalistic mythology, and which are historically linked to still older times or else to a time which is far closer to us, all combine in one constellation. No single one of these ideas may be found at the centre of this constellation, but what is there is the idea, or, as some philosophers would say, the phantasm of political power founded on the allegedly natural and divine right of the ethnic community to see itself as the only measure of all things.

In order to be included in this constellation, in this corpus of plots of Serbian ethno-nationalistic mythology, individual episodes in the tales about the Battle of Kosovo, like all other disparate elements of the material included in this corpus, must be adapted and stylised in keeping with the logic of its specifically focused organisation. There is no place here for confusing remnants of pagan cults and gods, for traces of classical ethical models and their Christian versions, for foreign literary influences, for everything that makes the Kosovo material such a significant part of the cultural heritage of the Serbs and other Balkan peoples. Kosovo, thus 'nationalised', has been transformed into a few tales, which, together with other similar ones, serve the symbolic legitimation of an ethnically centralised political order, that is its need to give an illusion of reality and continuity to its imaginary ethnic centre.[4]

For example, Prince Lazar's opting for the Kingdom of Heaven[5] is displayed in the political myth as the manifestation of a specific trait in the Serbian national character, as expressed by Radorvan Samardžić, the 'most deeply inscribed feature which marks the shared character of the Serbs' (Samardžić, 30). It has meant that the behaviour of Serbs at important historical moments becomes in a spontaneous way unique and predictable. The Kosovo option, in the opinion of A. Jevtić, 'has fatefully determined the whole people's behaviour at key moments of Serbian history' (Jevtić, 1989, 25). Or rather, as Radomir Lukić puts it, 'that inner strength has united the nation so that it lives for liberation, holds together and is not dispersed' (Lukić, 1989). In other versions, the Kosovo option is reduced to the repeated readiness of the Serbian nation to create, defend and strengthen

---

[4]The transformation of Kosovo into a nationalistic warrior myth was discussed by Zoran Mišić in 1961: 'Kosovo has become the warrior myth of a warrior tribe, in order, in its extremely distorted forms, to be transformed into the war cry of warlike tribal chiefs. It has become the state-forming myth of a state-forming nation, and then transformed into the aggressive and hegemonistic programme of one class. What Kosovo was and what it means, what the "Kosovo option" is at all—all this is completely forgotten. It was forgotten first of all by those who seized the Kosovo myth for themselves and decided to settle it in a pompous, imperial and imperialistic St Vitus Day temple [...]. The myth of Kosovo far transcends the borders of a national myth; in its essence it connects with those highest creations of the human spirit, collected in the Imaginary Museum of one single European culture.' (Mišić, 244)

[5]According to the oral tradition, on the eve of the battle Prince Lazar was given the choice of victory, if he opted for the 'Kingdom of Earth' or defeat, if he chose the 'Kingdom of Heaven', i.e. self-sacrifice in the name of eternal ideals. (Transl.)

its state through war, so that 'the brightest examples of its witness,' as Dragutin Ognjanović puts it, 'are the First Uprising, the Balkan Wars and the Serbian Golgotha of the First World War' (Ognjanović, 354).

In fact, the choice of the Kingdom of Heaven is transformed into a strategy of only temporary, necessary denial of the main aim, that of achieving the Kingdom of Earth, into an appeal to Serbian leaders never again to permit the defeat of Serbian arms. This about-turn has been most clearly expressed by Dragan Nedeljković: 'The holy Kosovo pledge is a pledge of the harmony and unity of Serbdom; this applies also to this historical moment, when the survival of the Serbian nation and its State is in doubt ... The Vidovdan[6] experience reminds us: disunity and conflict were the cause of our defeat ... at Kosovo. This must never be repeated. That must be known, like an immemorial prayer, by heart, by those who lead us.' (Nedeljković, 103)

These examples of the plots of the political myth which have come into being by adapting material about the Battle of Kosovo, like the examples of other plots of the mythic story of the Serbian nation and state discussed here, date from the last ten or so years. However, these plots were formed far earlier, largely during the nineteenth century. And what brought them together, during the 1990s, in one corpus of revived myths, their ethnically centred ideational or rather phantasmagoric framework, is also on the whole familiar. It represents a new version, a renewal of the political imaginary with the ethnic collective as the first principle and only horizon, which has come to the fore on several occasions in the political history of Serbia.

The history of these mytho-political plots and the individual forms of their crystallisation, that is their repetition and exploitation, is part of the political history of Serbia, that part which speaks of the creation, control and manipulation of the political imaginary. That history, whose foundations were laid above all by Jovan Skerlić, through his study of Serbian literary and national Romanticism, has not yet been written, although in recent times there have been several important contributions towards such a history.[7]

[6]St Vitus' Day, 28 June, the date of the Battle of Kosovo in 1389.
[7]Here one should mention particularly Radomir Konstantinović's studies, *Filozofija palanke* (The philosophy of the provincial town) and *Biće i jezik* (Being and language), not only because they are valuable contributions to the study of the history of political myths and symbols in Serbia, above all in Serbian literature, but still more because in these books Konstantinović offers an original philosophical foundation for this kind of study.

2. Time

One may often hear it said that one of the causes of the conflict and wars in former Yugoslavia is the fact that the warlike nationalists succeeded in imposing a cult of the past, in persuading people to turn to national history, in reviving old enmities and continuing wars that ended long ago—so that they lost interest in the real needs of the present and future.[1] This is only partly true. In some cases what was at stake really was an endeavour to seek and revive a connection with the distant past, to establish a continuity of certain ideas and projects from a contemporary perspective and for the sake of contemporary needs. However, in the course of the recent years of crisis and war, the Serbs, and by all accounts other peoples of our former shared state as well, in addition to the call to return to their history, listen also to the far louder and more authoritative summons to step beyond historical time. The discourse of warlike ethnic nationalism places contemporary events outside the present and future, but also outside the past, outside the co-ordinates of historical time. In other words, that discourse offers a mythic, anti-historical perception of time, in which time is in a way stopped, transformed into the eternal presence or eternal return of the same. In a temporality imagined in this way, the war waged in the 1990s by the Serbs in Croatia and Bosnia is only a continuation of former wars, or rather their repetition, and today's Serbian political and military leaders are in fact their reincarnated forebears. As the author of a new patriotic poem, inspired by the war

---

[1] For example, Paul Garde writes about the peoples of former Yugoslavia: 'Because the past returns to their spirit with a force that West Europeans would find hard to imagine.' (Garde, 244)

in Bosnia, puts it, the Serbian calendar is again at 1914 and Gavrilo Princip* is again lying in wait for Franz Ferdinand:

> *In Bosnia it's Vitus Day again*
> *The enemies there are both old and new*
> *'Fourteen approaches at the century's end*
> *Princip is poised to start it all anew.*[2]

Thanks to this mythic perception of time, in public communication, not only have fighters from the last world war, Ustashas and Chetniks, sprung up, or rather been resurrected, but also renowned forebears and heroes from all times, including legendary and mythological figures. Our political and military leaders have found themselves surrounded and protected by a retinue of the most important names of national history and folklore. This kind of aid is mentioned by Božidar Vučurević, a Serbian leader from Trebinje, who prides himself on it: 'We have enlisted the dead as well', he says, 'in order to preserve and defend the dignity of the living. That is why history is not only a teacher of life for the Serbs, but also a teacher of death. St Sava*, Prince Lazar*, Njegoš*, Karadjordje* ... they are all with us now, reminding us who and what we are.' (Mihović, 131)

Another means of attaining the epiphany of the ancestors consists in offering them an opportunity to be resurrected in the persons of our contemporary leaders and heroes. Tsar Dušan*, Obilić*, Karadjordje*, Hajduk Veljko* were able to choose in whose form to return among the Serbs, although of course—at least if one is to believe the most powerful media and the most popular singers—the most suitable vehicles for them are the biggest chiefs, from Milošević to Ražnatović*. In order that our heroic forebears should not be left with nothing to do in the present, political mythology will strive to find appropriate people for the reincarnation also of their eternal opponents, so that our television screens and newspaper columns resound with Turks and Latins, Musas* and Brankovićes.*

Epiphanies and the reincarnation of our renowned heroic forebears are not only commonplaces of contemporary trivial political propaganda and political folklorism—they are phenomena referred to above all by people who are supposed to be political, academic and literary authorities. Among the so-called national élite there is a widespread belief in the political mobilising value of the experience of extra-

---

*See Appendix: 'Key Characters and Concepts' (pp. 300–5).
[2]Djordje Nikolić, 'Mlada Bosna', *Vreme*, 3 July 1995.

temporality, that is the phenomenon of the epiphany and reincarnation of the ancestors. In addition, it is solicited as proof of the fact that ethnically centred plots about politics and war, as something based on the brotherhood of the dead and the living, have their foundations somewhere in the depths of the so-called national soul.

With this in mind, during the war years some politicians and political writers referred to the phenomenon of summoning legendary heroes in the course of a battle, which Veselin Čajkanović once described as 'the germination of our forebears'. Dragoš Kalajić arbitrarily limited this custom to the Slavs, regardless of the data quoted by Čajkanović to demonstrate its widespread use among other peoples.[3] 'The loyal Slav', writes Kalajić, 'feels himself to be a link in the chain of tradition and the bearer of the entire inheritance of thoughts and deeds, the duties and responsibilities of all the generations of his forebears. On the battlefield of such a feeling stands not only one man, but the whole people with him. Hence the ancient custom of Slav warriors—preserved and witnessed on many contemporary battlefields—of calling on their renowned forebears, by name, at the height of the battle, to join them in their attacks.' (Kalajic, 1993, 22)

The psychiatrist and poet Jovan N. Striković offered a combined, simultaneously neurological and psychoanalytical, explanation of the timeless sense of the unity of the ethnos and the phenomenon of the resurrection of the forebears. Striković concluded that Jung's theory of archetypes has a biological basis. He understands archetypes as the key historical events, and above all as representative personalities in the history of the ethnic collective, which remain in that collective once and for all, in the physical, biological sense, as part of the central nervous system of the individual, that part which, according to Striković's theory, belongs to the 'collective brain'. 'According to a philogenetic law', writes this author, 'the psychological structure of the personality consists of rungs on a mental ladder constructed by the forebears, like those which constitute his anatomical substructure. At a certain level of the emotional development of the nation, personalities appear who mark their time and epoch with their presence, and are no longer merely a metaphysical "substance" but a concrete physical substructure merged into the central nervous system of each individual of that nation, whose forebears survived that "psychological trauma

---

[3] Compare 'Klicanje predaka' (The Germination of the Forebears) and 'Nekolike opšte pojave u srpskoj staroj religiji' (Some General Phenomena in the Old Serbian Religion), in Čajkanović, 237 and 269. See Čolović, 1993, 34, for traces of the 'germination of the forebears' today.

and torture" in the form of the excitation of their own brain and the brain of the collectivity and created a mental engram in the form of a material imprint.' (*Politika*, 9 Oct. 1993)

The basis for an explanation of mythic temporality, the epiphany and reincarnation of the ancestors, and their high value is today most frequently sought in pseudo-scientific ideas about the biological-racial inheritance, in a kind of mythological genetics. According to this genetics, the same blood has flowed in the veins of the members of a nation from time immemorial and this immortal blood creates an ethnic identity and unity on the other side of the historical destiny of the people. The myth about ethnic and racial blood which came into being in Europe during the nineteenth century was spread in the not too distant past in the guise of physical-anthropological research, above all lobometrics, and today it has acquired the appearance of a rational and scientific basis through the pseudoscientific idea of genes. In this mythic tale, genes, as the bearers of inherited characteristics, preserve and transfer from generation to generation the qualities, talents and inclinations characteristic of a given nation. For example, what is called the 'Kosovo option' in the Serbian national myth is today explained also as a matter of genetic determinism. This explanation was offered by Rade Dačić, the author of a pamphlet about Kosovo. In his opinion, 'predetermination for the Option could be found already in the genes of the distant forebears of the Kosovo victims.' (*Politika*, 18 July 1997) Even love of the decasyllabic line and the *gusle*[4] is something that is preserved and passed on through the genes. This is something that the author of an article about the life of children in a camp for Serbian refugees near Benkovac in the spring of 1993 seeks to confirm. The administration of the camp had organised an artistic programme in honour of the journalists who had come to visit them; it was performed by the children, among them five-year olds. For this occasion they sang a song in decasyllabic lines, which begins like this:

> We have put on our camouflage clothing,
> We shall defend our native village,
> Smoković, native soil of ours,
> We shall defend you from the Ustashas.
> Ah, fascists, woe be unto your Gran
> You'll remember Dragan Kapetan ...

[4] Singled stringed instrument played to accompany heroic songs. (Transl.)

This inspired the author of the article to write: 'In all probability they do not know what a decasyllabic line is, nor did they use it consciously when they were composing their song, it is innate in them, it is imprinted in their genetic code.' (*Vojska Krajine*, April 1993)

What ought to ensure the success of the political and poetic undertakings of Radovan Karadžić*, guaranteeing them in advance, what both explains this success and at the same time legitimises it, is the alleged fact that he has inherited the patriotic and artistic genes of the great man with the same surname—Vuk Karadžić*. In a BBC documentary film, Karadžić can be seen in Vuk's house in his birthplace of Tršić demonstrating his skill in playing the *gusle*. But the strongest part of this film is a scene in which the Karadžić of our day points to a portrait of the old Karadžić, asking us to note a detail which discloses the miraculous working of the genes: a dimple in the chin of the old Karadžić which is identical to the one embellishing the chin of his professed descendant.

Those are the genes of the Karadžić tribe. In view of their crucial role in determining the direction and sense of the poetic and political path of Radovan Karadžić, an evaluation of what he achieved on that path can be presented only in the form of biography, and one that is concerned particularly with Karadžić's origin. This was the guiding idea of Djuro Zagorac, author of Dr *Radovan Karadžić, fanatik srpske ideje* (Dr Radovan Karadžić, fanatic of the Serbian idea). His portrait of the leader of the Bosnian Serbs is above all the story of his forebears, the Karadžićes of former times, in which the author is not content to link the origin of his hero with Vuk Karadžić, but goes back to 'the widely renowned fourteenth century'. That was the time of the Battle of the Marica* when the first Karadžićes began their great task, to which all the later generations of that tribe would dedicate themselves, the same one to which Radovan Karadžić was heroically sacrificing himself now. 'The fighting and dangerous confrontation of the Karadžićes with the Turks and members of the Muslim faith', writes Zagorac, 'lasted in that way, with intervals, right up until 25 November 1995, until the moment when at the Wright-Patterson American Air Force base, near the little town of Dayton, peace in Bosnia and Herzegovina was signed. It is easy to calculate: 624 years, one month and 25 days!'

But the *ethnos* does not reproduce itself and its best representatives do not succeed one another as incarnations of one immortal personality simply thanks to the miraculous work of genes, when the course of time is stopped and transformed into a kind of biological eternity. The mythic renewal of the *ethnos* is created also through the fertilisation of the native soil with native blood. This is a magic force, or rather, a sacrificial fertilisation by means of blood spilt in a war for existential space, that is for state territory understood ethnically. As is often said, 'every inch of our soil is soaked with our blood'. The soil which is made fruitful by the blood of those who fell for their fatherland has the role of an ethnic womb, while the wombs of individual biological mothers are reduced to transmitting and disseminating the fruits which come *ex terra*. In the case of this kind of sacrificial reproduction of the *ethnos*, time is not entirely frozen: it goes in a circle, and that kind of reproduction, unlike genetic reproduction, introduces an intermediary—the soil. The survival of the people develops in two directions, as the eternal exchange of two times, the time of death and the time of resurrection. In order to encourage their fighters, the propagators of war like to borrow from religion the image of the resurrection of the dead and to transform it into the propaganda slogan: 'There is no resurrection without death!'

The experience of the inclusion of the individual in the eternal present of collective endurance is linked by the mythic tale to the heat of the battle, to flights of enthusiasm and sacrifice, to outpourings of hatred towards the enemy. And also to abandoning oneself to the unified movements of the mass whose rhythm is set by the national leader. That experience is generally only a temporary illumination, a glimpse of national eternity, a miraculous sign of its existence. These moments of exultation are described with a vocabulary used in some religions to describe the mystic experience of the divine or the vocabulary with which poets describe the discovery of their vocation, which is one of the reasons why one may speak of political myths as also a para-religious and para-literary phenomenon.

But occasional insights into a national eternity may become more frequent and be interpreted as a sign that the end of historical time is coming: this is the final act of national eschatology, when the Serbian nation will at last gather together in time and space, discarding its history of suffering, betrayal, disharmony, fatal delays and premature anticipations—like a butterfly emerging from its larva. Such expectations were encouraged in Serbia from the moment when Slobodan Milošević took power. He was presented and honoured as the leader who would finally gather together and reconcile all Serbs, unite and

The poet Matija Bećković in the charnel-house of Chilandar monastery on Mount Athos. (Photograph published in a special supplement of the daily *NIN*, 15 January 1998)

connect 'all the Serbian lands' and so realise what more sober speakers call 'the national programme' or 'the national interest', and the less sober 'the eternal dream' or 'our forefathers' pledge'. The historian Gojko Desnica writes: 'The greatest contribution to the renewal of the Serbian state in our time has been made by the Serbian people, and its even greater role has been in having raised up, even if somewhat belatedly, out of its own milieu, its leader—Slobodan Milošević ...' (Desnica, 222)

The political realisation of Radovan Karadžić is described in the same way, for instance in the book by Dj. Zagorac: he apparently succeeded in triumphantly concluding the war with the Turks, begun more than six centuries earlier. He thereby put an end to the history of enslavement and suffering and led the Bosnian Serbs into an age they had been piously awaiting for centuries. What is more, Karadžić did not herald the beginning of a new age only for the Serbs, but for the whole of humanity. 'Radovan Karadžić', writes Dragan Nedeljković in one place, 'is one of the heroes of this end of the twentieth century;

he is opening up a new age—the era of the righteous.' (Nedeljković, 1997, 82)[5] So, parallel with the perception of national endurance as the repetition of 'always the same thing', including here the sporadic illumination of the extra-temporal being of the ethnic community, there appears also the idea of national time as a new beginning, which says to the history of the discord, suffering and sacrifice of 'the chosen people': 'Never again'.

---

[5] Analysing the eulogies heaped on Franjo Tudjman in the Croatian media after 'Operation Storm' (August 1995), Ivo Žanić drew attention to those in which the Croatian president was represented as a man who had restored to Croatia not only part of the state territory, but also the harmony lost in the eleventh century in the reign of King Zvonimir (1075–89). Thus Tudjman carried out an act which was described in the Croatian media as 'the closing of the Croatian historical circle'. 'The miraculous renewal', writes Žanić, 'of what had seemed a harmony lost forever, that providential reconciliation, means the end of Croatian history, a return to the Arcadia of before Zvonimir's slide into disunity.' (Žanić, 1996, 57)

3. Nature

Nature is the great goddess of all political mythology altogether, not only Serbian. The endeavour to step outside historical time and the construction of mythic space have in fact one aim: a return to natural man and natural society, to what the philosophers of the Enlightenment called the 'state of nature' (*l'état de nature*). In cutting peoples off from the golden age of life in harmony with nature, history did not spare the Serbs, although they tenaciously resisted that development for a long time. This struggle of the Serbs with history is recorded, in addition to local sources, by all those European travellers, philosophers and writers who over the last two centuries (and some even in our time) saw in Serbia a country whose people had retained their original connection with nature, despite the challenges of history.

Nevertheless, Serbia is today in history, and what is more in such a speeded-up and exhausting history that some Serbs find it insupportable. 'What is history if not naked violence?' complains the poet Rajko Petrov Nogo. 'We are all already bent, weighed down by history', he goes on, 'and we would gladly take a rest from it. But how can we rest when we have made our home on a main thoroughfare, and, in every dark time, it is into our house that adventurers and arsonists first throw their burning kindling. *But there—we are what we are.*' (Nogo, 7)[1]

[1] Many people before Nogo have complained of this violence of history against the Serbs, this 'what it is that we are', of the fact that others come along the highway like a drunken horde of plunderers into our peaceful harmonious house. There is an offprint of that stereotype also in an article by Vladimir Vujić about culture, published in the paper *Narodna odbrana* (National defence). Our culture is 'of a tragic nature ... in that it develops and starts its life on a borderland, on dangerous soil, over which the furious forces of historical invasion rage.' (Prpa-Jovanović, 16)

For the Serbs a stronger or weaker connection with nature, and thereby also a higher or lower quality of national life, depend on their distribution within their ethnic space. Fortunately not all Serbs live equally near to the highway over which History thunders. There are places where the people has preserved its authentic, God-given characteristics. They can be recognised according to a scheme of three spatial oppositions: rural/urban, mountain/valley and periphery/centre. Natural resilience and resistance, and therefore biological survival and, above all, the preservation of national identity, are more likely to be maintained by people who live in the countryside, in mountainous regions and close to the border, rather than those settled in multiethnic urban surroundings, in valleys crossed by international roads, and far from the border regions, that is far from the lines of first defence of the national territory.

Today's ethnically centralised political mythology in Serbia also brings to life images of the idyllic patriarchal village, representations of villagers —who are usually called by archaic, aestheticised names, such as 'rustic', 'ploughman', 'son/tiller of the soil'— as people who draw their physical and moral strength from their connection with the earth, with the culture and faith of their forebears, and do not mix with foreigners. Writing about the Serbs and the Russians today as harbingers and originators of the Slavonic revival, 'the Slavonic cultural revolution', Dragoš Kalajić expresses the opinion that this revolution means a return to the values of the 'traditional organic community', that is, 'it seeks also a great return to the soil and the village, the renewal of its vitality and fertility, joy and delight in living.' The nihilism of modern civilisation in the course of the last two centuries has meant, in the opinion of this author, the 'systematic destruction of the village and farming culture and the transformation of free farmers into dependent proletarians, uprooted and deprived of their soul, cramped into the vaults of the new Babylons.' (Kalajić, 1993, 24)[2]

---

[2] The myth of the restorative return of the nation to the soil and the country, which appeared in Europe at the end of the eighteenth century, as shown by the research of Raoul Girardet (Girardet, 97–137), has been most exploited in times closer to our own in order to legitimise extreme nationalist political ideas and movements. Nazism and Fascism used it as a simultaneously 'poetic' and 'scientific' cover for racist and anti-Semitic policies, so that it has had a bad name ever since, particularly in the form of the Nazi formulation *Blut und Boden* (Blood and soil) or Pétain's slogan *La terre, elle ne ment pas!* (The earth does not lie!). In the Serbian political mythology of the 1930s, an elaborate example of the treatment of this plot can be found in one place in Velmar-Jankvović's *Pogled sa Kalemegdana* (The view

Serbian fighter resting, eastern Herzegovina, 1993. (Kamenko Pajić)

Similarly, a redeeming return to nature is proposed also by the writer Momčilo Selić. He does not speak of a return to the countryside, but a return to natural man and natural human communities, from the family to the whole of humanity. 'Natural entities', according to Selić, are made up of the 'individual defined by God', the family, brotherhood, tribe, nation, the white race and humanity. The natural framework of all those entities is 'our blood', and it is also the main norm of ethically correct behaviour, for it implies 'mutual assis-

---

from Kalemegdan), in which the values of the soil and 'our man of nature' are opposed to false intellectualism, Europeanism and in general the 'so-called modern times'. The Serbian intelligentsia is here accused of aspiring 'neurotically and unconsciously to external Europeanisation', of having lost its 'life-giving contact with the soil'. The author ends his accusation with a real little hymn to the soil: 'Soil! With its indomitable spring and summer ripening, *it* raises a man, relativises his sense of suffering, teaches him the transience of pain; brings him closer to knowing the divine path, the unlearned, simply understood, but no less deep and comprehensible fate which is read in the stars and the grass, in the eye of man and the hoofprints of animals. Our intellectuals have neglected that life and the science gained from contact with ploughed land, lakes, the sea, forests, hills, with animals large and small, tame and wild, the life that gives our people who live with nature their broad understanding of life.' (Velmar-Janković, 138)

tance and support, regardless of the personal qualities of the members of that group (a brother is helped even if he is, perhaps, not the best sort of person, just as are the father and mother, uncles and aunts, etc.)' (*Duga,* 4 July 1992)

Warriors also live and behave in harmony with nature, they too are characterised by moral and physical health, for they have retained and reinforced their natural, instinctive capacity to hate and fight the enemy. The ideal of the natural man is best achieved by uniting the qualities of peasants and warriors in the figure of the peasant-warrior. Life in peacetime, like life outside the village, deforms man's natural vitality. That is why life on guard, filled with the expectation of an enemy attack, the life of a warrior, or at least that of the frontiersman, always ready for war, is preferable to a carefree life without threat. Drawing on her competence as a biologist, Biljana Plavšić* says in one place: 'The Serbs in Bosnia, particularly in the border areas, have developed and sharpened their capacity to sense danger to the nation and to develop a defence mechanism. In my family, we used to say that the Serbs in Bosnia are far better Serbs than the Serbs in Serbia ... I am a biologist, so I know: species which live close to other species which threaten them have the best powers of adaptation and survival.' (*Borba,* 28 July 1993)

The creation of an ethnically homogeneous—and in that sense natural—state is conceived as a return to an earlier state of natural harmony and order, to the time before the arrival of the Turks, when the Serbian state was supposed to be the ethnically homogeneous state of the Serbian people. The Turks damaged the Serbs not only by enslaving them, but still more because they opened the way for mixing peoples and cultures and thus caused the destruction of the original homogeneity which is preserved only in the countryside, particularly in the mountains. Parallel with this, the ethnically 'pure' Serbian state represents a utopian project, based on harmony with nature as well as the as yet unattained ideal condition of the state, still to be realised. In fact the state governed by the ethno-national idea has the task not only of preserving the so-called pure being of its people, but also of creating it. And on this point the Serbian myth about the mono-ethnic national collective does not differ greatly from the nationalistic myths of other countries. For instance, in Serbia and in other parts of former Yugoslavia we must recognise what the German sociologist Ulli Bielefeld said in speaking of the past and present of the concept of an ethnically homogeneous state in Germany. 'The ethnic state', he writes, 'was and still is able to construct ethnicity as

Nature

the natural culture; it seeks thereby to produce something that does not exist in modern societies: ethnic homogeneity; but its undertaking is today—just as it was in the past—doomed to failure.' (Bielefeld, 1993, 37)

This healthy, pure, resilient, popular and warrior nature has a dangerous opponent in its antipode, in anti-nature. Anti-nature appears in contemporary Serbian political mythology on three levels. The first is at the level of family life in the form of ethnically mixed marriages, which produce children who bring confusion into the natural order of affairs, i.e. into the mythic image of the fatal opposition and confrontation of Us and the Others, 'our own and alien blood', as it is usually expressed.

Ethnically mixed marriages are more frequent in towns than in the country. This is one of the reasons why in recent years mythic stories about politics are full of suspicion and open hostility towards urban centres. But in these stories towns are accused also of other betrayals of nature, deformation and artificiality: the coexistence of cultures, religions and races, comfort, democracy, cosmopolitanism, pacifism. Here too, as in the biblical destruction of Sodom and Gomorrah, cities are destroyed because of their corruption, but this fatal corruption is not presented as a specific characteristic of some cities in which evil holds sway and which are contrasted, as in the Bible, to examples of holy cities, above all Jerusalem—but as the destiny of urbanism. The destruction of cities in the recent conflicts in the former Yugoslavia is explained here as the inevitable result of their distance from nature, a product of the biological and moral corruption of their citizens. According to this myth, Vukovar, Mostar, Sarajevo and other cities devastated and plundered in the war were subject to the divine punishment they deserved because of the unhealthy, cosmopolitan, over-tolerant life in them, which was equal to unnatural debauchery.[3]

This mythic political naturalism also offered an image of Yugoslavia as an unnatural construction. Unnatural marriages and towns are not

---

[3]'Since the civil war began in former Yugoslavia', writes Sreten Vujović in his book *Grad u senci rata* (The Town in the Shadow of War), 'in the colourful arsenal of war propaganda, negative stereotypes about the town may be seen as an integral part of the war strategy. The lords of war and their apologists among the national ideologues in appropriate circumstances, publicly, through the means of mass communication, impart their judgment about the petulance and perversion of the town, about the unnaturalness of interethnic coexistence, about the rotten cosmopolitanism of towns, about the need to "Serbianise" the towns, and the like.' (Vujović, 89–90)

only the result of centuries spent under foreign rule, but, even more, the fateful consequence of the existence of that artificial state creation, that disgusting cocktail of peoples, faiths, languages and scripts. The downfall of Yugoslavia, like the destruction of some of its cities, was simply the fulfilment of the destiny of anti-natural human communities. 'To its peoples, gathered around their élites', writes Olivera Milosavljević, 'skilfully antagonised towards one another by a constructed hatred and always "righteous anger"', Yugoslavia was presented as an environment that held them linked in an unnatural communality which was dangerous for each of them.' (Milosavljević, 86–7)

Such a fate, according to the predictions of our new heralds of the Apocalypse, lies in store also for our current first world power—America. For it too is an anti-natural creation, the victim of supranational masters, who have made it—in the words of the writer Dr Petar Pavlović—'a den of injustice, a New Babylon, the most hated country in the world'. It seeks on unnatural foundations to establish an evil empire, that is a new world order, so that 'the whole world is forced into one unnatural mould'. (*Pogledi,* 20 August 1993)

The existential strength of a nation is reflected in its connection to the soil. But carried over into ethno-nationalistic political mythology, the ancient myth of invigorating contact with the earth has a confusingly morbid side, which is pithily expressed in the famous formula of Maurice Barrès, 'the earth and the dead'. People are connected with life, with the earth, above all through the dead. Dead forebears, their graves, their bones scattered over battlefields and execution sites, serve as an essential part of the foundation of the shared national home. In this one may easily recognise an echo of the beliefs and myths about immuring victims into the foundations or walls of towers and towns in order to pacify the supernatural beings which otherwise hinder their building.

However, in our political myths about the life and survival of the nation, it is most frequently presented as a body, as an organism capable of growing and spreading, but rooted to the soil, like a plant. And the roots of the nation are its dead. They enable the nation to survive on its own soil, to feel an integral part of that soil, to legitimate power in the name of a people on a specific territory, because, in the final analysis, it is natural. So, in the old metaphor which describes a people staying on their native soil as something that guarantees the maintenance of the natural order, that is 'rootedness', and the ostensibly unhealthy abandonment of the native soil, something alien to human nature, as 'uprooting', the basic image of the metaphor—the root—is completed by the image of the dead, that is of graves. The life-giving earth becomes above all that which conceals the dead, the land of battlefields, execution-sites and graves.

The symbolism of graves is two fold, following the double symbolism of the plant, which reaches downwards through its roots, towards the earth, towards the lower world, while its stem breaks out towards height and light. In political mythology, the graves of the heroic forebears symbolise simultaneously the roots by which a people is connected to the soil of its forebears and places which conceal the seed of national renewal. This is why it is said that the earth is *sown* with graves and that battlefields are *sown* with the bones of fallen heroes.

The symbolism of the grave as grave-root-seed has acquired a special meaning today, at a time of inter-ethnic wars over territory. This is because ideas about ethnic space and the right of the *ethnos* to be sovereign on its own territory have been revived, and these ideas are based on a kind of morbid geopolitics, whose key factor is the presence of the graves of the parents and ancestors. The idea that wherever there are Serbian graves, there is Serbia is repeated in various ways. In contemporary Serbian political mythology the dead determine where and how extensive our land is, and at the same time they conceal the answer to one of the questions at the centre of this mythology, the question of who we are. The Serbs are what their dead are, Serbia is where her dead lie. It may even be reduced to the morbid image of the holy soil of the Serbian *ethnos*, soaked in the blood of its ancestors and marked by the graves of its forebears, but without the presence of living Serbs. This could happen, according to Matija Bećković, in Kosovo. 'Must we, even on the 600 anniversary of the Battle of Kosovo', he writes, 'declare: Kosovo is Serbia and that fact does not depend on Albanian natality or Serbian mortality. There is so much Serbian blood and so many Serbian shrines there that it will still be Serbian land even if not a single Serb remains there.' (*Književne novine*, 15 March 1989)[4]

---

[4]One can find the idea of the fatherland as the land of the ancestors, individual parts of which may even remain without living descendants, in the political myths of other countries as well. In the book *Les Frontières de la France* (1864), the French historian Téophile Lavalée poses the question of 'whether France ought to reach towards its natural border to the north'. 'Without doubt', he replies, 'she should be within the borders which God's hand ordained, those which she had in her Celtic and Roman past, those which she restored at the time of her renewal in 1789; her territory must include the battlefield near Tolbiac and the grave of Charlemagne.' (Lavalée, 78)

For this reason what Denis de Rougemont said about 'political religion or totalitarian religious politics' is valid also for the political myths about Serbia as a natural mono-ethnic state. That is 'a religion of blood, a religion of the earth and the dead', open only to people of the same origin, so that others cannot 'convert' to it, because it does not recognise the possibility of 'spiritual conversion, which would mean that there are no longer either Jews or Greeks'. That is, continues Rougemont, a religion which 'does not ask what do you believe, what do you hope, but: where are your dead?' (Rougemont, 68–9)

4. Frontiers

In Serbian ethno-nationalist political mythology, the frontiers between peoples as ethnic communities are also 'natural'. And in keeping with the ideal harmony of the people and the state, which that mythology projects, the frontiers between states ought also to correspond to the 'natural' boundaries of peoples. This means that what are natural frontiers here are not the external geographical frontiers, but the boundaries which divide peoples as purportedly natural entities. This idea was put forward as early as 1807 by Fichte in his *Addresses to the German Nation*. 'The first, original and genuinely natural frontiers of states', writes Fichte, 'are undoubtedly their inner frontiers. Everything that speaks the same language was already linked in that fact of Nature, by a multitude of invisible threads, before any kind of human intervention.' (13th address)

Ideas about frontiers are based on one characteristic of the modern nation as an imagined community, that is on the fact that from the beginning, since the French revolution, it has been conceived as an individualised character, as an allegorical figure.[1] The way the nation

---

[1] The French historian Jean Plumyène observed that, with the appearance of the personified nation, ideas about the national collective and its territory, the familiar distinction between the artificial and natural borders of states, acquired a new meaning. Richelieu also gave himself the task of 'restoring to Gaul the limits ordained it by nature ... of making Gaul coincide with France and, wherever the old Gaul had been, of reconstituting the new one.' However, explains Plumyène, 'the "natural frontiers" proclaimed by revolutionary France are of a quite different kind from those which preoccupied the monarchy. They are less the expression of a realistic desire for security and power than the will to create a global *representation* of the national territory. France wants to see itself as an image, and this image requires for its construction a great gathering of allegorical figures.' (Plumyène, 60)

Serbian coat of arms on a chain and tatooed on the arm of an American of Serbian origin: 'Born in America, but my heart is in Serbia'. (Taken from the Internet during the Nato bombing campaign, author unknown)

has been embodied, its central images and the material used for their embodiment determine also the mythological presentation of what marks the limits of its extent, what and who lies on the other side of the border. This determines also the way the connection of the nation with its territory is presented. When it is a matter of representations of an ethnically centred nation, as is the case in our contemporary political mythology, national territory seeks to be identified with what is called ethnic or existential space, which does not coincide with the space limited by state frontiers. This makes the picture of the frontiers of the national territory exceptionally opaque.

For example, geographical elements often serve as material for portraying the national collective. But, even when it is a matter of such natural barriers as rivers and mountain ranges, they are rarely used in the mythic representation of the ethno-nation in the role of dividing lines between nations. It is far more common to stress the fact that the natural spread of nations is not halted by geographical barriers. In the myth, the nation has grown into its territory, it is rooted there, but its location and extent do not depend on the configuration of the terrain. They are ordained by God.

According to one view expressed during the war in Bosnia in the Banja Luka monthly *Zapadna Srbija* (Western Serbia, August 1993), Bosnia is land which was given once and for all to the Serbs: 'The Serbs have been here forever. The Almighty bequeathed them heavenly places on this earth.' But, precisely because of this transcendental motivation of its geographical position, the national community cleaves to its national territory in an ambivalent way, in the sense that this territory never has clear contours or established frontiers. In mythic geopolitics, the Serbian ethnic space has varying dimensions and varying boundaries. In one case the national territory stretches from 'Karlovac to flat Kosovo', in another from 'Vardar to the blue Adriatic'.

This fluidity of the borders in mythic discourse about the national community was observed by Anne-Marie Losonczy and Andreas Zempleni, the authors of a text dedicated to an anthropological investigation of the images of Hungarian patriotism. 'The fatherland', they write, 'is presented as a territory inseparable from the people and the land it inhabits. Nevertheless, its limits do not coincide with the frontiers of either the state or the nation, nor even with the limits of the geographical space inhabited by the people who call themselves and speak Hungarian. It cannot be reduced to either a geographical, or linguistic, or residential area, or to any political territory in the true sense. An initial question could therefore be formulated as follows: does the *fatherland* have borders at all, can it be identified with a territory and, if so, what marks its limits?' (Losonczy, 30)

There are two possible explanations of this vagueness. First of all, spatial limits of geographic origin enter into the myth in their fabulous meaning. If there is any geography here, it is imaginary. For example, so-called Heavenly Serbia could never fit into the profane frontiers of the earthly Serbia. Secondly, the presentation of the entirety of the national collective is dynamic, it is the presentation of its birth, suffering and tearing apart, of regeneration, liberation or renewal, that represents the growth and expansion of the nation. And consequently the borders of the state identified with the *ethnos* remain fairly vague and fluid. Their only constant feature is that only once in their past were they in their rightful place, while for us, in our time, they are always in some alien territory. In order to attain its natural borders, the territory of our state must be expanded ceaselessly, and this means that nature demands that the territory of our neighbours and enemies should be reduced. Explaining the concept of natural boundaries, Larousse in the *Grand Dictionnaire Universel du XIX siècle* (1866–7 edition) quotes these words of Saint-Marc Girardin: 'It is a curious thing that no nation has ever considered that, out of respect for natural boundaries, it ought to reduce its possessions and its frontiers, but rather every nation studies its natural geographical limits always in order to expand its territory.'

In order for this inevitable, natural course of development of the nation to be realised, geography itself will be changed, rivers will change their flow in order for our land to be expanded as nature demands. This motif is treated in a patriotic song in the folkloric style which came into being during the war in Croatia (written by Mirko Pajčin, known as 'Mali Knindža'): 'Tudjman thinks the Drina marks his land's extent. Now the Drina flows past Knin settlement.'

The best known and most widespread image of the nation represents it as an allegorical female figure, generally a mother, which has its basis in animistic notions of Mother Earth (*Terra Mater*), traces of which have been preserved in the traditional culture of many peoples.[2] Serbia has also long been most frequently referred to as 'Mother Serbia', and her devotees are her children, or rather her sons. More rarely she can appear as 'Our Little Sister' (*naša sela*).

Individual parts of the so-called Serbian ethnic space, when they are outside the frontiers of Serbia, can be represented as her children. In other cases, Mother Serbia is absent, as though it were a matter of a figure which belongs to the past, so that it is represented only through its descendants. Then the present-day Republic of Serbia becomes the daughter of Mother Serbia, as does Montenegro. And they are joined, like older sisters, during the war in Yugoslavia, by the new Serbian

---

[2] In Yugoslavia Petar Bulat wrote about this. He quotes examples which show that the cult of Mother Earth is transformed into patriotism as early as the Russian '*byliny*': 'For the singer of Russian folk songs, his fatherland is also his *matyushka* [little mother]. For example, he has a landlord say of Russia: 'I travel through the whole of Russia, my Russian mother land.' (Bulat, 8)

states. All of them together form the 'Serbian flock' in the poem of that name by Dragoslav Knežević Krunica:

> *One sister younger than the older*
> *Montenegro and Serbia,*
> *In peacetime and in time of war*
> *Krajina joins the Serbian flock.*

When the national community and its soil are embodied in the figures of a mother, sister or sweetheart, then the problem of national integrity and the problem of defending or altering borders becomes extremely traumatic and acquires the sense of defending one's mother's honour, and the honour of one's women in general. The motif of an attack on foreign soil in order to carry off maidens, which is very common in borderland folklore in Croatia and Bosnia, can acquire the meaning of desecration of the national honour. This is certainly the meaning of the book by Michael Lees, *The Rape of Serbia* (published in Belgrade in 1992).[3]

In political mythology, the connection between the soil and the character of the people is presented as mutual, not working in one direction only, that of the natural-scientific determination of a person's behaviour by his geographical origin. In some concepts of national territory, which includes both fauna and flora, that territory is imbued with the spirit of the people that inhabits it. France, Germany and Serbia are presented as catalogues of original national landscapes. This is true also of Hungary. In the 1930s the Hungarian statesman and patriot P. Teleki founded an Institute for the Study of the Hungarian Landscape and the Hungarian People. On the occasion of a celebration organised in 1991, in memory of Teleki, the Prime Minister of Hungary spoke of 'the soul of the people rooted in the landscape'. (Losonczy, 31)

'The Serbian land' is often imagined in the form of a giant figure, like Baudelaire's La Géante, in the shade of whose gigantic breasts the

---

[3] Rada Iveković thinks that the widespread custom of embodying ideas of freedom, nation, homeland and other similar concepts in the form of female figures 'does not mean that what is embodied here, the principle or mechanism displayed is—female. One must make a distinction between the bearers of the ideal and the ideal itself, Female incarnations of big ideas such as "Liberty", "Nation", "Wisdom", "The Motherland", "Purity" etc. often serve as an excuse for the concrete removal of women from these notions. This applies to both traditional mythology and contemporary politics.' (Iveković, 196)

poet would rest, 'like a quiet little hamlet at the foot of a mountain'. In this variant of the myth about Greater Serbia geographical elements, and especially rivers and mountains, become parts of the body, the spine, arteries, bosom or shoulders of such a personified Serbian national community. The title of an article about the river Neretva as a Serbian river, published in the Bosnian Serb paper *Javnost* (31 July 1993), is: 'The aorta of the Serbian bloodstream'. Another river, the Drina, which divides Serbia from eastern Bosnia, is described as the backbone of the Serbian national body. In that capacity, we find it, for example, in the poem by Milutin Savčić, 'As long as the Drina flows' (*Srpska vojska*, 13 May 1995):

> For centuries the Drina has flowed
> Through landscapes of the heavenly region
> It is the backbone, strong and firm,
> Uniting all the Serbian people.

Given that it has this role, that it has been granted such a function in the anatomy of the symbolic body of the nation, the Drina cannot be a frontier. The idea of 'cutting off' the Serbs on the Bosnian side of the Drina from those who are on its western bank then becomes a painful butchering, a severing of the body-Serbia.

Some elements which make up this image of the geographically embodied Serbia are more or less stable (the Drina seems irreplaceable in its role of backbone), while others (like the Neretva, which it would be hard to see as the aorta of Serbia today), are changeable. Among the changeable elements are those which acquire the role of the brain. Radovan Karadžić drew attention to these, concerned that the centre of Serbian thought and great deeds should be placed in Bosnia and Croatia, and above all in that part of Bosnia which he had at one point conquered. 'Destiny has ordained', he wrote, 'that the centre of events and upheavals, but also of the renewal of the Serbian nation, should be shifted to us. At one time it was in Serbia, at another in Montenegro, at one time on Kosovo, at another in Vojvodina. It moves, but it is in the same body and part of the same body the centre of which is now the Republika Srpska and the Krajina Republika Srpska.' (Quoted from Popov, 114)[4]

---

[4]Alexander Solzhenitsyn turns to the same reservoir of images in an interview published in the paper 'Arguments and Facts' (printed in *Politika*, 17 Jan. 1995). Explaining why, in his opinion, Russia has to recognise the indepenence of Chechnya, Solzhenitsyn says: 'When gangrene has affected a part of the body, it is obvious that

In some other cases also the Nation is imagined as a living being, the national corpus, the national organism, but not, as in the former examples, in the form of an allegorical figure or personified nature. Now what is foregrounded is a sharpened, close-up image of the 'biological substance of the nation', its 'tissue' and those parts of its fabric which are exposed to the greatest danger of attack, severing and amputation: the extreme, border regions of the national organism. Fear of such amputation is expressed in a text published in the Bosnian Serb paper, *Ognjišta:* 'The awareness that the act of division of the Serbian lands is almost inevitable and unavoidable penetrates the Serbian national being with fear and uncertainty, like a sharp blade cutting into the living tissue of the Serbian national organism ...' (February 1993) A similar feeling is suggested by the title of an article in the paper *Vojska krajina* (April 1993): 'Unparalleled dissection of the Serbian national tissue'.

According to some versions of the Serbian myth, Bosnia-Hercegovina is a part of the Serbian national tissue, and a part which has suffered the most severe wounds in the course of history, as witnessed by the ethnic picture of Bosnia of which it is said that it resembles the skin of a leopard. For the 'spots', 'freckles' or 'islands' on the ethnic map of Bosnia are in fact Serbian wounds. This correction to the metaphor about the ethnic map of Bosnia as a leopard skin was proposed by Veselin Djuretić, in a speech to the Second Congress of Serbian Intellectuals (Belgrade, 22–23 April 1994): 'One of my predecessors', said Djuretić, 'speaking of the on-going problems of the country, of Bosnia and Herzegovina, said that it was impossible to divide this region because its ethnic picture was like a leopard skin ... The "patterns" on the map referred to are in fact wounds on the body of the Serbian ethnic being.' (Djuretić, 208)

Losonczy and Zempeni suggest that a distinction should be made both between nationalism and patriotism and between nation and fatherland. They stress the imaginary, symbolic value of the 'fatherland',

---

that part has to be amputated in order to save the organism.' That fear of severing the body of the nation, of the penetration of a foreign body into the tissue of the national organism, also imbues an anonymous leaflet calling on the Croats to be wary of Serbs (published in *Duga,* 10 Oct. 1992). Here, among other things, is the following instruction: 'Do not associate with Serbs or be friends with them, because that will prevent them from entering into the Croatian national tissue.' Losonczy and Zempeni also quote examples of the same *topos* in Hungarian political discourse, and particularly in 'old irredentist laments' where there is much talk of the 'quartering', 'severing', 'amputation', 'wounding' suffered by the Hungarians fatherland. (Losonczy, 31)

which cannot therefore be reduced to one entity usually used by political sociology: nation, state, people, country. In the opinion of these authors, investigation of the 'fatherland' should be carried out by 'systematic study of *patriotic metaphors and rituals*.' (Losonczy, 29)

Research into the Serbian political myth demonstrates that here 'fatherland' represents only one of the images—or just one group of images—of the national collective. And this image of the national collective as fatherland, that is the land of the forebears, the fathers of the nation, preserves something of other images of the nation that have been mentioned, where it is a female, mother's body or a giant Mother or simply vulnerable tissue. The fatherland is also something physical, firstly because it has a bloodstream, through which the blood of the forebears flows into that of our contemporaries. In fact two bloodstreams, if we think also of that by which the blood of the forebears nourishes the soil of the fatherland.

For the image of the nation as fatherland, that second bloodstream, the one that flows through the soil, is more important because, together with the dust and bones of the forebears, which the soil preserves, it completes the image of the fatherland as a gigantic grave, which is one of the most obsessive phantasms of Serbian political mythology. The territory of the nation-fatherland stretches as far as the graves of the forebears, while the peripheral graves have the role of frontier markers.[5] We find this image, revived by many in recent years, also in a speech by Vuk Drašković in 1989, where it has the role of the starting point of national politics. 'Should it come to division and separation, where are the western borders of Serbia? This may be (strategically) confirmed. Those borders were, in truth, determined by Ante Pavelić[*]: they are wherever there are Serbian execution pits and graves. The obligation to mark those borders is in the Serbian national programme.' (Speech at the Extraordinary Meeting of the Serbian Writers' Union, *Književne novine*, 15 March 1989) There was not long to wait before the image of the grave-border 'entered into the people', to appear in a poem in the folklore style, written by D. Knežević Krunica:

---

[5]The grave as a frontier marker is not a discovery of the political mythology of nationalism. It is known in that function in the traditional culture of agricultural peoples. In Serbia it has become a custom to mark the boundary of a landholding (especially pasture) with a grave, or gravestone. The suitability of the grave and monument for this use comes from their sacral nature, their untouchability (taboo), which is supposed to deter the owner of the neighbouring land from any desire to extend his possession at the expense of his neighbour by shifting the boundary. (Bandić, 88–90, and Barjaktarović, 65)

There are numberless towers of bones
Strewn over the heroic expanses
Throughout brave Čaruga's* Slavonia
All through rocky Lika and Krajina.
Wherever the bones of our forebears lie
Those are the borders of Serbia.

But this does not prevent the fatherland as a land of the dead from being found also in the sky. In the other world as well, the Serbs, and especially the innocent Serbian victims, live organised into a state. That is Heavenly Serbia, the largest state in the sky. Among the first to have mentioned it was Jovan, Bishop of Šabac and Valjevo. On the occasion of the transference of the relics of Tsar Lazar, he published an epistle, in which, among other things, he wrote: 'Ever since Lazar and Kosovo, the Serbs have been above all engaged in creating Heavenly Serbia, which has by now certainly grown into the greatest state in Heaven. If we take only the innocent victims of this last war, millions and millions of Serb men and women, children and babies, murdered or tortured with the most terrible torments or thrown into pits and caves by the Ustasha criminals, then we can imagine the scale of the Serbian empire in heaven.' (Radić, 278)

The fatherland is not quite the same as the homeland, for this other word suggests an image of the national community as a spacious, warm home. 'Oh Serbia, warm roof', is a line in a new patriotic folk song. The inhabitants of the house, that is the locals, are linked by mutual respect and love like the members of some large family gathered around the hearth. Together they defend the hearth-home-homeland from the dangers of the outside world, above all from intruders. That is why, 'built beside the highway', the Serbian house is docile and idyllic within, while from outside it is organised like a fortress with well protected approaches and gates.[6]

Here, on guard, defending the homeland, stand her best sons— the frontiersmen. It is precisely in this place that they become the best, resisting dangers, steeling themselves in constant vigilance and

---

[6]Describing the dangers which frequently threatened France from its northeastern and eastern frontiers, Fernand Braudel evokes a mystic image of the French nation as a house whose doors are stormed by uninvited guests: 'Fragile, this northeastern and eastern frontier is more troubled than all the others, livelier, because it is always on the alert, just because of the danger presented by its aggressive and formidable neighbours. They have learned that it is here that the French home should be attacked, as there is a chance of its door being breached.' (Braudel, 298)

rebuttal of the enemy, sharpening their defence instincts. That is why, in Serbian political mythology, the so-called peripheral Serbs, the frontiersmen and above all the Serbs in Bosnia, are marked as the purest, the finest representatives of their people. They defy all enemies who lurk on the other side of the border, and that means more or less the entire world. The message they send to that hated hostile world is expressed in a poem by Predrag Pedja Pajović, 'The Serb no longer listens to anyone' (*Javnost*, 6 May 1995): the world will fare badly should it dare to cross the frontier:

> *Listen, world, to what I tell you*
> *Your boot will never cross my land*
> *For you will step at once on mines*
> *The world dares not defy the Serb.*

These are the basic images of mytho-political discourse about the national collective and its frontiers: the nation as a woman exposed to violent attack, where the defence of the borders is identified with the protection of a woman's honour; the nation as a living landscape, as a land-body, threatened with the danger of being dismembered; the nation as substance, as tissue exposed to the danger of injury and maiming; then, the nation as the execution-site and grave of the ancestors, threatened with the danger of profaning the dead; finally, the nation as a home with well guarded doors and intruders outside them. Hungarian, French and Russian examples, quoted alongside material taken from predominantly Serbian sources, suggest the presence of similar images in the discourse about the nation and its frontiers, the working of the same matrices in the political mythologies of various different peoples.

5. Europe

Among the figures of contemporary Serbian political myth, an important place has once again been occupied (as several times in the course of the nineteenth and twentieth centuries) by an evil divinity, a kind of fallen angel known by the name of the Rotten West or the Old Maid Europe. Facing this biologically and morally degenerate apparition stands the robust figure of Serbia, observing the monster before her with revulsion and shame. It stands there as its lost innocence or bad conscience and, at the same time, as a promise of possible salvation. Western Europe could restore its soul and return the blood to its sunken cheeks if it were to tread Serbia's path, to follow its example. But at present it stubbornly rejects Heaven, seduced and fettered by the Earth. In the words of Metropolitan Amfilohije Radović, 'The West is preoccupied and besieged by the Earth. That is why it does not think of Heaven. And that is why it is such an enemy to us today. There is no God among them. There is no heavenly kingdom there.' (Mihović, 56)

The Serbs have nothing in common with such a Europe. A Serb is, as Vladimir Velmar-Janković once wrote, a 'Non-European'. 'Of all the regions of Europe', in the opinion of the author of *A View from Kalemegdan,* 'the Balkans are the least European. And in the Balkans, of the Christian peoples, the Serbs and Bulgarians are least European of all.' (Velmar-Janković, 82) Similarly, at the end of the 1920s Vladimir Vujić also maintained: 'no, we are not Europe', explaining this by the difference between the 'sense of life' of the Serb and that which had been 'developed and brought virtually to impossibility by Europe'. (Prpa-Jovanović, 16)

According to some versions of the Serbian myth about Europe, it was not always as it is today. It has tumbled down the slippery slope of vice because it has betrayed its authentic sources. It is the sad fruit of decadence, decay, oblivion, corruption. We reject its vices today in the name of its former virtues. That is why it is possible that the Serbs, sometimes together with other Slav, Orthodox peoples, who have not been caught up in the degeneration of Europe, should be the guardians of authentic Europeanness. Velmar-Janković's Non-Europeans are in fact the only real Europeans, the only ones who deserve that name.

'Europe is not against us because we are not and do not wish to be Europe', wrote Metropolitan Amfilohije Radović in an article in October 1991, 'but because, not through our own deserts, but by the gift of God, we are the bearers and guardians of the genuine Jerusalem-Mediterranean Europeanness, which does not accept the loss of the balance of human existence in cross-bred centres, the loss of the horizontal and vertical of the Holy Cross. The West is turned too much to the material and to enriching its own works, to the expansionist impulse, to totalitarianism of the most perfidious kind. Lust and its earthbound mind are its religion.' (Radović, 279)

According to some contemporary versions of the myth, the sickness of Europe is of quite recent date. Predrag Milošević, teacher of physical education and author of a book, *Sveti ratnici* ('Holy warriors'), 1989, connects the sick state of Europe with 'the present age': 'the shadow of collapse', he explains, 'began to spread the moment people in west European countries lost their sense of real values, that is, when money, material concerns and economic interests took the place of philosophy, religion, history, politics. Opting for money and vulgar professionalism in sport and the army, the Europeans have cut off the branch on which they were sitting and in that sense this age resembles that of the eve of the collapse of the Roman Empire.' (Milošević, 169)

The fall of Europe into the material means also a kind of metaphysical amnesia, forgetfulness of being. Instead of continuity of being, Europe has accepted profane temporality, history understood as progress, history without a 'vertical' dimension, without a soul. This loss of being is a sickness which affects those peoples of the former Yugoslavia who have accepted the values of Western civilisation and its Western, unheroic, rapacious and carnal style of life. They have condemned themselves, as R.P. Nogo expressed it (*Duga*, 2 August 1991), 'to be nothing but tourists in history'. By contrast to them, the Serbs have preserved the continuity of awareness of themselves, their national identity, their sacred history. And these same

Serbs, apparently paradoxically, are at one and the same time Non-Europeans, because they are outside the main currents of profane European history, and the only real Europeans, because the deep history of the European spirit endures in them. In fact, Europe was born in Serbia. This idea is developed by Matija Bećković, who maintains, in an article written in 1989, that 'Europe has no deeper root than the one which, through Greece and Byzantium, springs up on our soil.' (Gojković, 387)

For this reason it is inappropriate to recommend to Serbia that she return to Europe. In fact, she is the best signpost for all who wish to turn towards the real Europe because, as Radovan Samardžić put it, 'that land and its people speak straight from the heart of Europe' (Perović, 1996, 124). This is also the opinion of the Russian writer Vladmir Volkov: 'The Serbs are offering the Europeans an example of how the national being, spiritual values and traditions, humanity and ethics should be protected. If the Europeans follow the Serbian example—they will be saved and reborn.' (Kalajić, 1995)

This *topos* of the Serbian political myth, in which Serbia is opposed to rotten Western Europe as the guardian of authentic European values, may be interpreted today as a polemical response to the equally mythic representation of the West as the embodiment of justice, culture and prosperity, in which the Balkans and Serbia take on the inglorious role of representing backwardness, primitivism and barbarity.

In recent years, in the political discourse of Slovenia and Croatia, one could observe an endeavour to justify the political and military actions undertaken there, and to legitimise them as actions which were in keeping with the values and interests of European culture. It is supposedly in the interests of Europe, for example, that a new border between its western and eastern parts be drawn and strengthened on the soil of former Yugoslavia—that is to say, between the 'modest, hard-working western-Catholic tradition' and the 'violent, perverted Oriental-Byzantine heritage', as the Slovene Minister of Science, Petar Tancig put it in June 1991. (Prošić-Dvornić, 295)

One study of the role of the media in the war in Croatia, quoted by Mark Thompson in his book *Forging War,* showed that, in reporting on the war, the Croatian media systematically stressed Croatia's place in European culture and the 'barbarity of the aggressor and its lack of culture' (Thompson, 1995). For Dubravko Jelačić-Bužanski, the author of an article 'Unworthy Opponent' (*Vijesnik*, 30 August 1991), the Serbs are a people who do not know the norms of European life: 'What has determined the civilisational and traditional norms of the life of the European peoples, simply does not exist on the side of our oriental opponent. To say that it is there that an Asiatic worldview begins would be insulting for Asia and its honourable countries. The example of our enemy is unique. It creates largely its own model of corruption. It is waging an unscrupulous, savage struggle with us, equipped with a Byzantine repertoire of perfidiousness and ritual crimes which will certainly enter history as an example of forgotten medieval cruelty.' (Knežević, 239)

Despite these images of allegedly irreconcilable differences between Serbs and Croats, portrayed as the consequence of their belonging to antagonistic civilisational circles, the Serbian and Croatian political myths about Europe and its culture contain much the same stories. These are, among other things, stories of a chosen people as a kind of cultural hero of European civilisation, which has the duty to fight in the world, even by fire and sword, for the victory of authentic cultural values.

In August 1995, immediately after 'Operation Storm', in which the Croatian army drove the majority of the Serbian population out of Krajina, the Zagreb paper *Arena* published a special edition (11 August 1995) dedicated to that event. In several contributions printed there, the war between the Croats and the Serbs was portrayed as a conflict between culture and barbarity. That was how one text described the entry of the Croatian army into Petrinja, a town of which it was said that while it was under Serbian control it was 'turned into a pigsty'. The uncultured and lazy Serbs had completely neglected Petrinja, so that even the clock on the main square was broken. 'The wretches', wrote the journalist, 'had not paid any attention to the clock.'

The *Arena* journalists were able to find inspiration for such a portrait of their uncultured enemy in articles published by the Bosnian Serb paper *Javnost*—on 22 July 1995, some three weeks before their own triumphant special edition—to mark the victorious entry of General Ratko Mladić's army into Srebrenica. In one of these articles the so-called liberation of Srebrenica is celebrated as the 'cleansing of a blot on the map'. This is the blot of the backwardness, primitivism and lack of culture of the Muslim population of Srebrenica and the restoration of the town to civilisation after the entry of Mladić's soldiers. Thanks to them, 'Srebrenica is being freely aired', explained a journalist, 'but the air is still heavy and unpleasant, imbued with the smell of backwardness. This was left by people who do not like wide-open windows or streets.'

Analysing the *topoi* of this myth on the Croatian side, the philosopher Boris Buden came to conclusions that can be applied almost in their entirety also to its Serbian variants. 'For Europe is not simply a place where we always were, but also an aim towards which we are moving. Its presence among us is experienced equally strongly as its absence. It is a region of the most sublime values of justice, freedom and equality, but at the same time a place where those values are perverted. It is as much the object of our devotion and desire as an object of disappointment and shame. As its chosen people who save it at one moment from its bitterest enemies, the next from itself, we are more European than it is, but also more anti-European.' (Buden, 193)

In both the Serbian and the Croatian versions of the myth or, as Buden puts it the 'phantasm' of Europe, there is one especially elaborated characteristic. That is ingratitude. Europe is ungrateful to those who today, as during the past centuries, allegedly guard its spirit and its frontiers. The Europeans forget that they owe their survival and peaceful development above all to Serbia, which defended Western Europe on the field of Kosovo from the Turkish advance. Slobodan Milošević reminded them of this fact in his speech at the celebration of the 600th anniversary of the battle. On that occasion he said, 'Six centuries ago, here on Kosovo field, Serbia defended herself. But she defended also Europe. She stood then on the rampart of Europe, defending European culture, religion, European society as a whole. That is why today it seems not only unjustified, but also unhistorical and completely absurd to question Serbia's belonging to Europe.' (*Politika*, 29 June 1989) The same theme, but in a far livelier and more dramatic tone, is taken up by *Politika,* in the special issue published on the day of the celebration: 'Today is the 28 June 1989, one of those days on which our thoughts fly back six hundred years into the past and alight on the field of Kosovo, among the clang of swords, in the clash of the Serbian and Turkish armies, on the 28 June 1389. The Battle of Kosovo. The Serbian army defending civilisation, for the defence of Serbian glory and the European cross. We could not defend Serbia, but we did defend Europe ...' (Nenadović, 604) Eight years after this jubilee, Rade Dačić, in a pamphlet entitled 'A view from Kosovo', also published in *Politika,* wrote about the echoes of the Battle of Kosovo in Europe: 'When everything is weighed up and compared, Europe did not celebrate a Serbian victory in vain. For themselves—the Serbs lost the battle. For others—they won.' (*Politika,* 12 July 1997)

In his reproach to Europe, the popular singer Savo D. Vučić mentions also more recent Serbian favours (Vučić, 13–15):

> We helped you in the Second War,
> As a brother helps his brother:
> Holding back Gerry divisions
> Keeping them from attacking you!
> ....
> But Europe is now deaf to that
> Saddling the Serbs with genocide.

In the same metre, Mile Krajina, a Croatian *gusle*-player and the author of new epic songs in the folk style, accuses Europe of not understanding how important the Croatian resistance to the aggression of Orthodox Serbs was for Europe and its security (Krajina, 42):

> Fierce war rages waged in Croatia
> While western Europe is silent ...
> Land of Europe, may you be damned
> For letting the Serbs commit crimes,
> Open your doors to Orthodoxy,
> Place a tight noose around your neck.
> Now you yourselves will lose your heads,
> The Thames and Seine will fill with blood.

The interpretation of Serbian political mythology and the myth of Europe would be incomplete, if not also wrong, if account were not taken of the fact that it did not develop independently of the political myths in other parts of former Yugoslavia and in its neighbourhood, or outside the broader context of the history of the European political imaginary. Parallel with this, it is exceptionally important for the interpretation of the Serbian myth about Europe to investigate its sources in the political and cultural history of Serbia.

One of these sources is the writings of some Serbian Orthodox theologians, where Western Europe is generally described as a space without real, living faith, in which both the dominant denominations, Catholicism and Protestantism, have succumbed to temptation and replaced Christianity with humanism. That is: they have installed their creation—man—on the throne of God. This fundamentalist position has been elaborated and defended with the greatest zeal by two Orthodox theologians, Nikolaj Velimirović (1880–1956) and

Justin Popović (1894–1979). The influence of their views can be felt today also outside the framework of theological debate. This is particularly true of their criticism of European culture and of those Serbs who succumb to the 'poisonous' temptations to which they are exposed by the seductive West. 'The central place in the thinking of these two spiritual leaders', writes the historian Radmila Radić, 'was occupied by criticism of humanism, European civilisation, the materialist spirit.' (Radić, 272) Velimirović maintained that 'the European school had departed from belief in God. That is what had transformed it into a "poisoner", and caused the death of European man.' (ibid.) Similarly, in a text from 1956, Justin Popović lamented that 'in our unhappy days, many descendants of St Sava had abandoned his path and hastened down the road of European culture, serving its idols day and night.' They had replaced St Sava by 'rotten European man, his humanism and relativism, his idolatry and his wardrobe.' (Popović, 187)

The influence of these two Orthodox thinkers on contemporary representatives of the 'national direction' in Serbian politics, who were trying, above all, to reconstruct the Serbian national myth, may be seen in the way in which a young historian presented Velimirović's and Popović's ideas: 'Their theological thought and accomplishment became the recognisable mark of theological thinking of the Serbs in our time, and the philosophy of the Son-of-God, the Orthodox Slav Pan-man, the historical and civilisational alternative to consumerist, spiritually impoverished and lost "Roman" Europe ...' (Subotić, 111)

The other important historical source of mythic images of Europe and Serbia, closely related to the first, is the Serbian version of the cult of the nation and the cult of heroic death on its altar.[1] Božidar Vučurević, one of the most prominent 'priests' of this cult among the Serbs today, responded to the question of whether he was a religious man (which he was asked by Dragan Mihović in his book *Rat su započeli mrtvi* (The war was begun by the dead) by saying: 'A heroic people is always moderately religious: it believes in God, but also in weapons. While a craven people is religious to the point of fanaticism. It spreads its arms, falls on its knees and prays to the Holy Virgin: "Help us, our Lady!". Our people has never called on the

---

[1] The basis of this cult was most pithily expressed in the middle of the nineteenth century by the French historian Jules Michelet: 'Let a man become accustomed in his childhood to seeing the living God in his fatherland.' (Girardet, 173)

Virgin. We took up our sabre and went to resolve our own destiny.' Vučurević is not a man who would follow Christ's path. He says that, had he by any chance been in Christ's place, he would not have allowed himself to be crucified, after Pilate's judgement: 'As an earthly sinner, I would have killed Pilate with that cross, and I would never have become the son of God.' (Mihović, 77)

This argument of Vučurević's in support of the untouchable nature of the cult of the nation was improved on by Vuk Drašković, when he maintained that the warrior impulse need not be out of step with Christian principles, that the Serb prepared for battle has not in fact abandoned Christ's path, because even the Son of God knew how to be angry with his enemies and, if necessary, to fight them. 'Christ could flare up with anger', said Drašković, in a speech in 1989, 'and even reach for a whip in the Jerusalem temple.' (Radić, 276)

The cult of the nation is a civilian and lay cult, even when holy figures participate in building and spreading it. At its heart, at least in the case of the dominant version of this cult in Serbia today, there are rituals of the ethnically founded nation, the glorification of its founders, remembrance of its holy sacrifices, celebration of its holy jubilees, emphasis on its emblems and symbols.

The values affirmed by this cult are blind loyalty to the leader, submission to the state, including readiness to die for it, and nurturing of military prowess. These values are opposed to the urban, cosmopolitan and democratic West European political culture. Not in the name of the true God, nor as something that would be alien to the secular, enlightened European nations, but with a sense of the God-given duty of the Serbs to remind Europe and the West as a whole that they are mortally sick, and to show them the path of redemption though their example of sacrifice and virtue.

Serbian political mythology, or at least its most active part, which represents a kind of ideological or imagological framework of the cult of the ethno-nation, offers two complementary images of 'rotten Europe'. In one it is declining because it has abandoned God in order unworthily to glorify man and the fragile creations of his power. In the other, which is far more frequent than the first, Europe is disintegrating because it has betrayed the authentic man and the only natural form of power—that which is embodied in the ethnically conceived nation.

The mythic opposition of the rotten, artificial or decadent, on the one hand, to the healthy, vital and natural, pleasing to God, on the other, appears quite early in European history: with Montaigne, and perhaps even earlier. In the course of the last three centuries many European politicians, priests, philosophers, poets or journalists have put their countries and people forward for the messianic role of guardian or restorer of the health, virtue and purity of the old Europe. The problem is that such pretensions have usually led to hatred and war. That is why democratic, civil Europe is today equally wary of those who offer to restore it to its old origins and those who wish to imbue it with new youth.

A young member of the armed forces of Bosnian Serbs at Pale, June 1992. (Miloš Čvetković)

6. Warrior

Serbia is best able to defend the Serbian nation and thereby authentic Europe, and altogether the interests of the national ideal, properly understood, through war. She has warriors always at the ready for that battle. They gladly sacrifice their male lives for her, while Serbia—that is, her authorities, secular and spiritual—gladly accept that male sacrifice. 'Blessings on your heroic wounds!' is a common cry, and 'Eternal glory to you, heroes!' even more so. Altogether, the battle for the nation is not only something patriotic but something very masculine.

Virility is one of the basic and most striking features of warriors as the heroes of mythic tales of war, at least those which came to life in former Yugoslavia in the course of the recent war. To be brave and to expose oneself readily to the dangers in which war abounds represents the greatest test and proof of masculinity. For instance, an article published in *Javnost* (12 Nov. 1994), talks about a part of Sarajevo which was dangerous for the Serbian fighters, accessible only to those 'who knew what they had between their legs'. War propaganda, and especially the call to the flag, is often based on that argument, on the identification of participation in war with initiation into the world of adult males. At the beginning of the war in Croatia, in front of television cameras, an officer of the Yugoslav People's Army encouraged his soldiers to set off across a minefield with the following words: 'Let anyone who is a man come with us!' (see Čolović, 11). In the magazine *Hrvatski vojnik* (Croatian Soldier), of September 1993, an article was published which bears witness to the fact that the Croatian army also reinforced its summons to participate in the battle with the 'male' argument. The main slogan was: 'Tiger, respond if you are a man'.[1]

---

[1] "Several new "tigers" are responding to the somewhat clumsy, but provocative

The same parallelism exists in a more developed form of this argument, in the issue of the disqualification of those who do not respond to the summons to participate in men's war. On both sides, such people are called 'mummy's pets'. 'In the final analysis', says one Croatian fighter, 'we are an army, and not mummy's pets.' (ibid.) At the same time, on the other, Serbian side, a duet by the 'Bajić Brothers' mocks a deserter who 'flees to his mummy'. (Čolović, 1993, 73)

The infantile nature of the unworthy hero is attributed to enemy soldiers. We find an example of this in the third warring faction in the last war, in an article published in the Sarajevo paper *Ljiljan* (2 Nov. 1994). It describes one of Alija Izetbegović's fighters chasing a young guard of Karadžić's over a mountain, to discover in the end that he was just a well-brought up and frightened mummy's pet: 'When he caught him, the guard raised his arms and mumbled: "Don't kill me, please, I've got thirty German Marks in my pocket".'

The phenomenon of the figure of the woman-warrior appears to oppose the masculine identity of the fighter. But it seems that her role is mostly intended to strengthen the appeal of war propaganda directed to men, letting them know that war may not be such a dangerous adventure after all if women venture into it, and, also, that this adventure, precisely because of the presence in it of young, attractive women-warriors, might even have its appealing side. And that is what women warriors are like: young, attractive and well-groomed. Serbian television used images of attractive young female volunteers for its propaganda for the campaign in Croatia. A statement by one of them, 'a very young woman in a soldier's uniform, the mother of two children', was quoted by Lazar Lalić in his book *Three Television Years in Serbia*. When she was asked what made her decide to go to war, she replied: 'Well, I watch television and see what's going on so I want to help and it's worth sacrificing one's life for this Serbia of ours.' (Lalić, 82)

The same issue of *Ljiljan* (2 Nov. 1994) published also a long illustrated report under the title: 'Beautiful women liberate the most beautiful of countries'. It speaks of 'the real pleasure of being in the company of blonde, brunette, red-headed, faultlessly turned out, discreetly made-up girls, holding rifles and machine guns firmly in their young girls' hands.' Similar to these attractive women-warriors of Izetbegović's army are two female volunteers of Martić's who look at us from the cover of the magazine *Vojna Krajina* (April 1993).

---

advertisement—"Tiger, respond if you are a man" which we see in our daily papers.' (*Hrvatski vojnik,* Zagreb, 10 September 1993)

Photograph from the front page of the paper *Vojska Krajine*, April 1993. (Zlatko Jejina)

Their sex-appeal cannot be disguised by either their uniforms or the hidden pain on their faces. One of them is clutching a machine gun in fingers with strikingly red nail polish, while we learn that the other has earned the affectionate name of 'Siki—the hellcat-woman'.

The phenomenon of women and women-warriors in the male fighters' world does not disturb the presentation of the essentially virile character of war, it may even confirm it. However, soldiers' virility is seriously questioned by certain feminised traits which endure persistently in the figures of what are at first sight the most masculine of fighters. I am not thinking here of the feminisation of which an example is offered by a war report published in *Duga* (December 1991), describing a drunken party of Montenegrin soldiers outside Dubrovnik, amusing themselves by dressing up in women's clothes which they found in Tito's villa in Konavle. (See Čolović, 1993, 74) What I have in mind is the old motif of the dual sexual identity of the warrior, who has the body and courage of a man, but the psyche, the soul of a girl. We find a trace of this motif in a sentence used by Pero

Slijepčević to describe the poet Aleksa Šantić: 'The blood of a hero, the soul of a girl'. In our time, the formula was used by Vuk Drašković in a speech at the funeral of Djordje Božović Giška, commander of a volunteer unit of the Serbian guard founded under the patronage of the Serbian Party of Renewal. Drašković said of the Serbian army: 'This is an army with the soul of a girl, the behaviour of a priest, and the heart of Obilić.' These qualities also adorned the figure of the commander Giška, who was, as the writers of a book dedicated to him put it, 'a tender man of strong build', who was even, 'in conversation with strangers sometimes known to blush.' (Mićković, 29)

A possible source of this formula may be the ambivalent character of the patriarchal Balkan warrior, who combines warlike activity which baulks at nothing, fearlessness in contact with the enemy and, on the other hand, restraint, sometimes real shyness in company, particularly that of women. Gerhard Gezeman called this combination of courage and restraint 'heroic timidity'. For the patriarchal Montenegrin warrior, in Gezeman's opinion, real masculinity has nothing to do with eroticism, love or attitudes to women. A man despises all that. What is considered masculine and heroic are the cult of battle, children, the ancestors and the community. (Gezeman, 146)

Such a restrained and negative attitude to sexuality, particularly in wartime, was attributed by Bishop Nikolaj Velimirović to Balkan peasants. In his book *War and the Bible* there is a chapter entitled 'Licence in war brings misery'. The author maintains that Balkan peasants continue to keep the commandment to refrain from adultery in war, given by God to Moses and his people: 'The avoidance of every evil thing in war', writes Bishop Velimirović here, 'especially adultery, represents a fundamental rule of the wartime morality of uncorrupted Balkan peasants right up to the present day.' (Velimirović, 1993) This is in keeping with what Matej Arsenijević claims that Dimitrije Ljotić thought about the moral character of the Serbian soldier: 'In his memoirs of the First World War, D. Ljotić writes that among the Serbian soldiers there was an unwritten rule that in wartime one must live monastically, ascetically and chastely in order to preserve an attitude of maximum personal purity and concentration on the soldier's duty.' (Arsenijević, 96)

If we follow this path, we can conclude that the warrior's 'soul of a girl' is a metaphor for unsullied sexual purity, for complete dedication to a sublimated eros. This is very different from the banal soldier's debauchery, with or without the company of sexually appealing women warriors, offered by contemporary war propaganda as its strongest argument. Now, however, we discover that the political myth of the warrior actually suggests, or seeks, something quite contrary to that on which the 'erotic' argument of war propaganda is based. That is liberation from sexuality and devotion to other activities of greater value to the collective. There is no doubt that the myth of the warrior seeks to complete the image of the brave, but also experienced, tempered fighter, with characteristics of sexual innocence or purity which are apparently at odds with that image.[2]

The need to give the warrior the soul of a girl, i.e. sexual purity and virginity, may be linked with his function of noble and honourable killer of the enemy, explained as a necessary condition for that function to be realised in what is in a religious sense a permissible and secure way. But, in my opinion, the innocent soul of a girl is required by the warrior above all because his main role in our warlike mythic story is the role of sacrificial victim and not victor. As we know, the gods seek the gift of an innocent victim.

In fact, the warrior, or the hero with the soul of a girl, is a less frequent metaphor for the innocence of sacrifice than the image which brings together the warrior and the child. Warriors also have the soul and face of a child or a boy. The journal of the First Krajina Corps of the Republika Srpska Army, *Krajiški vojnik*, which appears in Banja Luka, published several articles (in its February 1995 edition) about one unit of Martić's army which bore the nickname 'Vlasić Wolves'. Among these pieces is a poem with the following lines:

> *Who are these young lads who all bear*
> *The homeland's sorrow in their eyes?*
> *Warriors with boyish faces*
> *Who lie awake dreaming at nights ...*

Soldiers are most frequently referred to as our children, our sons, while the identity of their 'parents' remains unclear. It may be supposed, however, that at least one of them is the State which sends its children to war. Parenthood, particularly motherhood, is more familiar when soldiers are described as the children or sons of the Homeland, their country—Mother Serbia, for example. The soldiers are then no longer the mummy's pets of their biological mothers, but the favourites of

---

[2] Here we may recall Joan of Arc and her main feature, which is her chastity. She is not only a courageous warrior, but above all a virgin-warrior: *La Pucelle d'Orléans*.

their Motherland. She needs them precisely as innocent children, as boys untempered by sexual experience.

The warrior may be brought into a state of sexual purity and achieve the status of an innocent child and son of the Motherland through a kind of ritual which unfolds in the opposite direction from the direction of the ritual of the young man's sexual initiation. The scenario of this ritual of 'desexualisation' of young fighters is described in various accounts of departure for war, which above all means parting from wives and a halt to sexual activity. For instance, this theme is described in the following lines from an old Chetnik song:

> *Come on now, lads, the time is here*
> *for us to part from our sweethearts*
> *there's no more talk of love for us*
> *we must all go off to battle.*

The sexuality of the warriors is transformed into a substitution most frequently expressed as a fetish of weapons:

> *Instead of your sweet pale face*
> *My companion is my rifle*
> *Instead of your two slender arms*
> *My bride is now my cartridge belt.*

In one variation on this theme, also from Chetnik folklore, the once popular '*karabinka*' rifle is mentioned:

> *I took my rifle and grenade,*
> *Went to embrace the leafy woods;*
> *My mother is the green forest,*
> *My 'karabinka' is my love.*

The same theme of the weapon-fetish is contained in a war report about soldiers of the Croatian Army of Defence (HVO). 'Our curiosity is aroused', writes the journalist, 'by a young boy wearing a hat and improvised designer sunglasses. Juro Ivaković, a seventeen-year old fighter, who, instead of his first girl, embraced an "84", and instead of his first cigarette lit up a Chetnik tank.' (*Zmaj od Bosne*, 3 Nov. 1994)

This weapon-fetish bears witness to the fact that the myth of the warrior, in contrast to its apparent preoccupation with glorifying the potent virility of the man, speaks instead of a morbid eroticism, the real sense of which is abandonment to the instinct and cult of death.

The warrior is not only sexually immature or restrained and, as it were, ritually purified of sexuality, through regression to the pubescent phase, he is also entrusted with the task of fighting against the aggressive virility of the enemy, who is often shown in the figure of the rapist and abductor of 'our' women. Here, therefore, the enemy is made to personify untamed virile potency, the debauchery of licentious male sexuality, while our virtuous warriors are given the role of defending the honour of the Homeland, the nation and the national territory, which are, of course, in this mythology usually embodied as female figures.

In order for the nation to be defended from attack and conquest, from the penetration of the enemy into her body or tissue, there must be sacrifice, warriors must lay down their lives on the altar of the nation. Their task, as has already been said, is not so much to kill the enemy, as to perish, to shed their innocent sacrificial blood. This is confirmed by many examples. Sometimes the Fatherland is shown as a real primitive bloodthirsty deity, like the Moloch of national mythology, whose survival requires hecatombs of victims.[3]

The figure of the warrior often appears in retrospect, and this retrospective image of the warrior demands radical heroism, realised only with the sacrifice of his life. The warrior is the child of the Fatherland, then he is the holy warrior of the Nation, purified of carnal desires and deeds, but, above all, he is the dead hero. The innocence of the child, or the purity gained by oblivion and a brake on sexuality, are necessary in order for the warrior to achieve the status of innocent, pure victim, but also in order that he should be a credible dead body. The poem dedicated to 'The Vlasić Wolves' (mentioned in the

---

[3]The theme of the fatherland thirsty for sacrificial blood appears in Serbian patriotic poetry. For example, in 'Oh, my country' by Aleksa Šantić. Here the poet converses with his country and asks it:

> *Oh, my country, what pains you so?*
> *Why am I constantly shaken and oppressed*
> *By lengthy laments from your depths?*

And the land responds:

> *That is my heart expiring and perishing*
> *In hard frost, with no sun or dawn [...]*
> *I rouse the dead from their sleep with my sighs,*
> *For there are no living ready to die for me.*

preceding pages) speaks of 'warriors with boyish faces', but it also presents them retrospectively as dead heroes, for whom women in black weep, and whose deeds already belong to history:

> *And while their proud mothers,*
> *Sisters and wives*
> *Wipe their moist eyes with black kerchiefs*
> *Their gallants from the twenty second*
> *On Vlasić Mountain*
> *Are writing a new 'handbook of life'!*

Mircea Eliade observed that, unlike the ordinary mortal, the mythic hero continues to act even after his death. 'The mortal remains of the hero', writes Eliade, 'are filled with formidable magic-religious power. Their graves, their reliquaries, their cenotaphs act on the living down the centuries. In a certain sense, it can be said that heroes come close to the condition of the divine through their death: they enjoy a limitless post-existence, which is neither embryonic nor purely spiritual, but consists in a *sui generis* survival, because it depends on the remains, traces or symbols of their bodies.' (Eliade, I, 300)

This posthumous action of heroes explains the great concern which the survivors invest in bringing the mortal remains of their celebrated dead, and especially warriors who died or are even buried abroad, back to the homeland in order to bury them again in its soil. The same is true of the use of the clear and enduring marking of war graves and execution sites.

Dead soldiers and other victims of war, who have—as it is often said—laid down their innocent lives on the altar of the Homeland, represent the greater part of the active national collective, as it is portrayed in the national-warrior myth. The living Serbs are, as Matija Bečković formulated it, just the 'remnants of a slaughtered people'. A similar idea is contained in a poem entitled 'To Mother Croatia', published in *Hrvatski vjesnik* in Vinkovci (3 July 1994), in which Mother Croatia converses with Croatian soldiers killed at Bleiburg, a place which has a similar role in the contemporary Croatian national myth as Jasenovac in the Serbian one:

> *Croatian Soldiers in their thousands*
> *Call to their Mother 'Our Mother dear',*
> *Beneath the monument comes their voice:*
> *'The slaughtered Croats now call to thee.'*

A Serbian fighter in Slavonia, December 1991. (Zoran Jovanović)

All these examples show that the figures of contemporary Serbian and other Balkan warriors, as they are presented by the mythic war story, cannot be reduced to features of virility—however much this aspect has been stressed in some texts which have played a part in direct war propaganda. Those features in fact remain on the surface of these figures and are even in direct contradiction to other characteristics of warriors, those which make of them men with the soul of a girl or an innocent boy, sons of the Fatherland or at least men ritually brought into the status of soldierly celibacy. And these characteristics are 'underlined in black', because they are connected with the figure of the warrior as a dead hero. In this way, the explicit and superficial virile sexuality of the warrior makes way for a morbid image in which we see that, for the national warring Knight, Death is far closer than the Lady. The cunning of war propaganda lies precisely in the fact that it takes the call to give up one's life and sexuality as a symbol of the joy of life, in order to serve the insatiable Moloch of the nation state, and transforms it into the promise of something erotically attractive to men.

7. Pantheon

The Serbian warriors in the contemporary political myth have their models in the glorious war heroes of the past, those exceptionally respected inhabitants of the Serbian imaginary national Pantheon, in which the figures of other kinds of national heroes are also gathered, all those great Serbs whose brave, self-sacrificing exploits founded the nation and represent the object of a state cult. In the years of preparation for war and the war itself, the doors of the Pantheon are opened wide. The phenomenon of a new warlike mood and new warriors is accompanied by memories of the great models of heroism and patriotism, so that the figures of war heroes and other national heroes from the walls of museums and libraries come down into the streets, appear in the media and, thereby, enter every house. War propaganda is in large part the popularisation of heroic models.

However, the popularisation of national heroes has two meanings, it refers to two different, if mutually connected, procedures. On the one hand, it is a matter of a series of operations intended to give the fighters for the national cause a popular character. On the other, the popularisation of heroes means vulgarisation, the broad diffusion of myths about the valiant deeds of national heroes, through schools, for instance, or through the media. Of course, when national leaders and soldiers are shown as men of the people and the projects of building and strengthening the nation are described as the realisation of an idea which has been previously formulated in the popular tradition, then that is done precisely because it is expected that such representations will have a wide response among the people. And *vice versa*, the wide diffusion of the heroic deeds of the inhabitants of the national Pantheon leads in the end to their being transformed into figures from the popular imagination. Nevertheless, I think that it is not only possible, but methodologically important to distinguish between the qualitative and quantitative sense of the popularisation of national heroes and to discuss them separately.

To say that national heroes are popularised when popular features are attributed to them implies that there is a typological and historical difference between the popular and the national, for example, between the popular, folk, culture and national culture, between popular beliefs and rituals and the mythology of the nation, with its cult of the national, that is, if we mean the dominant political myth in Serbia today, the ethno-national state.

For the ideologues of the nation, who endeavour to define the legitimacy of the governments of nation states which appeared in Europe from the end of the eighteenth century, there is no question of any distinction between the popular and the national. On the contrary, the national élites endeavour to give their new government a popular base, to legitimise and justify their political and military undertakings by calling on the so-called 'spirit of the people' (today: 'ethnic identity'), that is by presenting the new political order—which no longer has a divine guarantee—as an order established in the name of the people.

This strategy is fruitful largely because this calling on the people may easily be duplicated by reference to nature, thus making the connotations richer, for in the neo-romantic view, now being imposed with surprising force, the people is connected with the natural world. As a result, the popularisation of the national here is the same as its naturalisation (in the sense Barthes gave to that term). The strategy of legitimating national authority requires the founders of the nation to be popularised and thereby naturalised. More precisely, popularisation is one moment in the construction of the national hero, the heroisation of prominent figures of national history.

On the basis of Serbian examples, it is possible to describe some of the most important steps in the process of this popularisation or construction of national heroes. The folklorisation of the national consists in painting the history of the nation and the portraits of those who fight for it in the popular, folklore style, thus transforming national history into popular literature and mythology. To present the undertakings of a political or military leader in a decasyllabic poem represents a simple and effective way of suggesting the idea that everything this leader does is in perfect harmony with the will of the people. When it is maintained that a figure important for the national cause is connected with some hero from popular tradition and when it is said that this new figure represents a faithful copy of the original, that he inherits and continues the deeds of his forebear, the folklore character is incarnated. Rooting is a process of popularisation in which the popular, peasant origin of some national leader or fighter is stressed: stories are told about his childhood in the village, about his connection with the land, his ancestors, popular traditions and customs, he is clothed in national costume and a *gusle* is placed in his hands.

It would be hard to identify the moment when historical figures from the first half of the nineteenth century entered the Pantheon of Serbian national heroes. What is certain is that they found there a group of heroes who had the honour of being accepted among the first: Saint Sava, Tsar Dušan, Prince Lazar, Obilić, Marko*, Starina Novak*, the Mother of the Jugovići* ... These first inhabitants of the Serbian national Pantheon originate in medieval history (from the twelfth to the fourteenth century), in folk poetry and in mythology and sometimes simultaneously in all three sources. But, in order to be received into the national Pantheon, they had to be subjected to a process of adaptation and embellishment. This process is 'nationalisation': their transference from folk memory and the popular imagination into a system of ideas which form the image of the nation.[1]

The character of the popular hero must be purified of any features which are ambiguous or unclear, and which are often traces of his mythic origin. For example, the image of the Mother of the Jugovici retains certain characteristics belonging to the figure of the *vila**, and is reminiscent of the Valkyries of Scandinavian mythology. She is

---

[1] In her work 'Serbian fascism and art', Bojana Vukotić quotes some examples of the nationalisation of Serbian traditional culture, and especially epic legend, which some ideologues of Serbian fascism tried to carry out, under the wing of the German occupation. Among other sources, the author quotes an article by M. Spalajković, 'The Serbian National Myth and Europe', published at Easter 1943, in the paper *Srpski narod* (The Serbian people). According to Spalajković, taken together the epic heroes, and other figures of the 'Serbian myth', 'represent various models which ought to enhance the standing of the nation, for as long as it endures.' However, here the nationalisation of the popular tradition runs parallel to its racialisation, if one can put it like that, because, as B. Vukotić points out, for Spalajković, 'Saint Sava and Prince Lazar are celebrated as the "personification of the innate racial idealism" of the Serbian people, Prince Marko and Miloš Obilić "represent the embodiment of a synthesis of popular militant decisiveness and purebred courage", the Mother of the Jugovići and the Maid of Kosovo are the best synthesis of the qualities of the purebred Serbian woman.' (Vukotić, 70–1)

not, therefore, an ordinary mother lamenting the death of her sons who died in battle. We owe this observation and an erudite account of the mythic layers in the figure of the Mother of the Jugovići to Veselin Čajkanović, who came to the conclusion that it is quite mistaken and unjustifiable to make this figure into 'a typical Serbian mother': 'but is this the grief of a Serbian woman and a Serbian mother?— Never and it never could be!' (Čajkanović, 11) And Čajkanović quotes the unusual lines with which the popular singer describes the death of the heroine:

> *The mother of the Jugovići swelled up,*
> *Swelled up, and then she burst into pieces.*

However, the author of a contemporary anthology of popular epic songs, intended for a broad audience and the patriotic education of the young, decided to include this song about the heroic mother in his collection, but in order to make the Mother of the Jugovići fit into the role of exemplary Serbian mother, he simply omitted these rough and ambiguous lines. (Djurić, V., 285)[2]

The places which the inhabitants of the national Pantheon acquired in it do not correspond to the meaning they have as heroes of popular legend and song. For example, Miloš Obilić is the Serbian national hero *par excellence*. 'He has a place on the national Olympus', writes Schmaus, 'he is like a god in the temple of a heroic-mythic religion.' (Schmaus, 317) Obilić's national prestige greatly exceeds that of Marko Kraljević, but in the context of the popular epic song (with the exception of the episode of the Battle of Kosovo), he remains in the shadow of his powerful friend and protector, who is the matchless star of this poetry. What prevents Marko from taking up a better place in the Serbian heroic *nomenklatura* is precisely his excessive popularity. This impedes any possible enhancement of his character in keeping with the needs of the national ideal and also, given that he crosses national borders, Marko Kraljević is prevented from being reduced to the embodiment of only Serbian national virtue. In addition, Marko is unsuitable for the role of personification of the national ideal also because of the emphatic 'realism' and the 'liveliness' of his character, which makes him too approachable, profane, insufficiently

---

[2] Vuk Karadžić also tried to justify the selection and adaptation of 'raw folklore material', starting from the observation that 'our people do not yet recognise the true worth of their popular songs.' For more on this, see Čolović, 1993, 86.

serious. Explaining why the 'Serbian popular tradition most values three figures from its past: Saint Sava, Tsar Lazar and Miloš Obilić' and why Marko Kraljević is in the background, Cvijić suggests that the main reason is Marko's too great attachment to life, the fact that he is without any inclination to 'great spiritual ideas', like Saint Sava, or 'conscious sacrifice', like Tsar Lazar, or 'knightly qualities', like Miloš Obilić. 'It is true', says Cvijić, 'that there are more stories and songs about Marko Kraljević than anyone else, because he represents life, with all the characteristics of life, good and bad; but he is not as well respected as the first three.' (Cvijić, 57) Cvijić does not distinguish between 'national' (political) and 'people's' (popular), because for him it was of primary importance to prove the rootedness of the political national project (Serbian, or Yugoslav) in traditional culture, in the 'popular tradition'.

The popularisation of national heroes (the diffusion of an image and a story) is a constant concern of modern states. However, it depends decisively on the historical and political context, it is different in times of peace or war, including 'cold war'. In keeping with this, it is possible to speak of two kinds of time and space in the popularisation of heroes.

In peacetime, when the danger of war, real or imagined, is removed, public evocations of national heroes develop in a slow and steady rhythm. Moments of these evocations are determined in advance in the calendar of national holidays, the anniversaries of historical events, and in the history curriculum of schools. Even less official forms of remembering national heroes—works of historiography, literature and film—are adapted to this rhythm.

When the country is going through a period of crisis and war, as was the case in recent years with Serbia and other parts of former Yugoslavia, the return to heroes becomes both more intensive and more frequent, transcending the temporal boundaries of customary ritual commemorations. There is an increase in the number of significant historical events whose anniversaries and other jubilees are marked. Current political and military events become also an opportunity for remembering glorious forebears, so that, for example, at mass political rallies, speakers call on 'our heroes'. Portraits of the heroic ancestors appear, together with pictures of current leaders, on placards carried by the participants in these rallies, and they are even mentioned in the political information and commentaries carried by the media.

The presence of national heroes in peacetime is generally discreet and confined to the public space. Their portraits and busts are found in museums and galleries, in official spaces and offices. Even the monuments to heroes erected in open spaces, in squares and parks, are almost unnoticed in peacetime. But, in times of war, they multiply and we see them more or less everywhere. They take over the work place and even the space of private life. For example, among the names which parents in Serbia have chosen for their sons born is recent years are often Rastko, Stefan and Nemanja, that is the names of members of the medieval Nemanjić dynasty.

In the middle of the 1980s in Serbia there began to be an upsurge of portraits of Saint Sava, Karadjordje and Njegoš and other pictures with themes from Serbian national history. At the same time, the popular music market saw a sudden growth in the sales of records and cassettes with newly composed folk songs dealing with events from the Serbian heroic past, legendary heroes and their successors in valiant deeds in the modern age. A private radio station, founded in Belgrade at the beginning of the war in Bosnia, broadcast exclusively this kind of song. The station itself had a heroic name: 'Radio Pride'. ('Radio Ponos', see Čolović, 1993, 117–21)

But the expansion of heroes in times of crisis and war is not confined within the borders of the traditional genres of folklore or, more accurately, folklorism. In order not to leave outside its influence a large number of young people who preferred international pop-culture to folk culture and especially songs in the folk style, the propaganda of heroes and heroism endeavoured to adapt to the taste, genres, behaviour and collective values connected with the international pop-scene. Such preoccupations inspired some attempts to express the theme of the war in former Yugoslavia in the language of the strip-cartoon and the so-called roto-novel.[3]

On the basis of these examples of the popularisation of heroes of the Serbian national myth, we can conclude that in peacetime these heroes remain within the boundaries of the time and space envisaged for ritual social commemoration, a clearly defined distance from the

---

[3] The authors of the cartoon strip 'Knights of the Knin Krajina' endeavoured to create a Serbian war hero who would be distinguished by characteristics appropriate to 'modern' cartoon heroes (karate champion, helicopter pilot, polyglot, charmer, etc.) and who would at the same time embody Serbian national values: he fights for his people, is called Sava and has the soul of Obilić. The same idea is the basis of cartoon strips with war heroes which appeared during the war in Croatia and Bosnia-Herzegovina: 'Superhrvoje' (*Slobodna Dalmacija*, 1992) and 'The Green Berets' ('Gorčin', Tuzla, 1994). See Čolović, 1993, 136.

rest of social life, and, above all, from the sphere of private life. At that time they are also mostly represented through individualised, recognisable canonical images. But, when the drums of war begin to sound, dead heroes emerge from the graves of their canonical pictures to appear in the figures of living political and military leaders. More exactly, they 'inscribe' themselves into them, because what is carried over through this transfer is in fact only the heroic name. The heroic name is a 'collective name'. This expression was used by the Yugoslav Minister of Defence Pavle Bulatović in a speech he made in March 1997 in Mojkovac, on the occasion of the eightieth anniversary of the Battle of Mojkovac and the unveiling of a statue of Serdar Janko Vukotić. 'The whole people was the army', said Bulatović on that occasion, 'and the priests carried a cross in one hand and a rifle in the other. We mention the Serdar now as a collective name for all those who have deserved our remembrance, but whom we cannot list on this occasion.' (*Politika*, 29 March 1997) In this way the popularisation of mythic national heroes represents a paradoxical process: it advances through the relative loss of individual heroic figures to the advantage of the expansion of heroic names. Serdar Janko, like other war heroes from the past, is not only a 'collective name' for the soldiers who fought alongside him, but also for all those who, if necessary, will continue his struggle today. It was they whom Bulatović was addressing.

8. Identity

Let us be what we are! That would be the briefest way of defining the main, if not indeed the sole aim of the national ambitions of the Serbs, their struggles with their external enemies and final reckoning with local adversaries, which feature in the Serbian ethnocentric political myth today. National identity has the greatest value here at present, the highest price is paid for it, it is more important than life, that is to say it alone can give life its true value. So that for individual Serbs and the Serbian people as a whole, death is better than a life in which they could not be what they are. This identity rhetoric, the central figure of which is a tautology, is based around two fundamental ideas.

According to the first of them, national identity is the basic, stable, easily recognisable and self-evident character trait of the member of a nation, which is expressed as a clear, specific difference between national mentalities and cultures and which is, in addition, the 'natural' foundation of the political sovereignty of the ethno-nation.[1] National identity is constant, not subject to change, it resists all pressures and foreign influences. It is so deeply rooted in every Serb that it is unchanged regardless of the circumstances and places in which Serbs live. 'But a Serb remains a Serb', says Gojko Desnica, 'wherever he is born and wherever he lives. For little Serbs can be born in a foreign state, but their consciousness of belonging to their people surpasses

---

[1] From the point of view of contemporary political philosophy, national identity is not a political concept. As the French philosopher Etienne Tassin puts it, 'with regard to the political community, the question posed is not that of identity, but of citizenship. And so the question is not: who are we? but: what do we do? The political question in the true sense of the word is not a question of communal identity, but of public action.' (Tassin, 97)

everything.' (Desnica, 212) This obviousness and constancy of national identity is described in a line of a newly composed folksong: 'I am a Serb, it is written on my brow'.[2]

Signs of the absence of Serbian national identity or symptoms of its weakening are also obvious at first glance. For example, Serbian nationalist contemporaries of Jovan Skerlić saw that he did not have 'Serb' written on his brow, but 'Parisian'. Later Velibor Gligorić also came to the 'unavoidable conclusion that Skerlić was not a purebred man of our race nor thoroughbred writer.' 'A purebred man of this land', wrote Gligorić, 'does not reject the sacred things of his past in favour of some sort of western ideology, nor does the need for Westernisation justify that rejection.' (Prpa-Jovanović, 25)

Thanks to national identity, individuals have a reliable yardstick in all situations in which they are faced with some moral and political choice. Given that this identity, 'what we are', is ethnically determined, what Radomir Konstantinović said about 'kin' is relevant for the relationship of the individual and that identity: 'I am enveloped in it as by the ultimately predetermining force, which may appear also as the power of an irrational "Avenging God", but which remains, predominantly, also a predetermination against every danger of the free-unpredictable, the un-kin chaotic, as the non-kin "beyond" (of the "world" that lies on the other side of the hill).' (Konstantinović, 236-7)

A Serb exists only as a branch of his tribe, and that means that he exists before his birth and even dies before his birth. This determining ethnic substance (blood, genes, tradition, ethnic archetype, being or something else), of which he is constructed, binds him at every moment to the whole tribe, to dead and as yet unborn Serbs, and he himself is insignificant, completely unimportant in his individual mortal existence. 'It was on Kosovo that I was born, I was on Kosovo before my birth', says Jovan Striković in traditional decasyllabic verse. (*Politika*, 9 May 1992)

This self-evident, innate, natural identity demands, on the one hand, that relations between fellow-nationals should be articulated on the basis of similarity, of kinship, and, on the other, that relations between nations should be regulated on the basis of difference, in the name of the right to difference and the right to self-determination. At the same time political myth focuses particularly on the terrain of culture, as a privileged place of particularity, the first and indisputably

---

[2]For national identity as a theme of political folklore, see Čolović 1993, 145–66.

'special' expression of the unrepeatable national spirit (being, mentality). The political myth becomes discourse about culture as an isolated, homogeneous, self-sufficient national community, threatened by others. This is discourse about the essential, profound and irreconcilable difference between peoples, which may be seen and defined, above all, in the cultural sphere.

However, the myth of national identity does not content itself with discourse about difference, nor is the problem of that myth reduced to the fact that it exaggerates the differences between peoples, bringing them into a state of irreconcilable antagonism. The demand 'Let us be what we are' goes further than that. First, it is transformed into a dream of complete separation from the world so that, as Konstantinović puts it, the specific character of the Serbian nation, its 'spirit-people', becomes a 'guarantee of the salutary separation of the Serbian world from the whole of the rest of the world'. (ibid., 352) The development of the idea of national identity as the centripetal force, which wrests the Serbian nation from the society of other nations, inspired the poet Matija Bećković to imagine Serbia as an autonomous heavenly body, with Kosovo as its equator: 'Kosovo is the equator of the Serbian planet'. (*Književne novine*, br. 722, 1989)

This separation from the world is, however, not as radical and final as it might seem at first glance. It is exemplary, and in this 'pedagogical' sense the Serbs separated from the world remain in contact with it or, more exactly, through their universally interesting dissension from the world, they attach that world to themselves. Serbia and its culture are something special, something apart, but not in the same way that every other nation is. Its special character is not relative, but absolute. It is more special than any other, because that original existence, which cannot be compared to anything known, is in fact today the only existence of one nation in the world. Serbia is the only country which is consistently true to its self, capable of shaping that self as original and unique. It is precisely because of this that in the political myth the national destiny of Serbia, always exceptional, always apart from the world, acquires a universal significance and is offered as an example to the world. As Nikolaj Velimirović writes in one place, 'That is why our people is the bearer of a progressive and salutary ideal, biblical and prophetic, which in the end the entire human race, now rent and ruptured through inflated notions of earthly greatness, will have to accept and adopt.' (Velimirović, 12)

True, authentic national identity, as the being of a people manifested in nationally 'conscious' politics and culture, is in the most profound harmony with nature and the divine purpose ('Nations are God-given' runs the myth)[3], but it is not given to all peoples or, more exactly, in other peoples it is more or less undeveloped, forgotten or neglected. Some, for instance the Americans, have no national identity at all, for they are an artificial community, without roots, without tradition, without collective memory, without soul. In the words of Dragoljub Jeknić, the political commentator of the paper *Javnost,* that country is 'a collection of adventurers, rootless individuals, barbarians, bandits, murderers from all corners of the world, a collection which history has punished by never letting them bear the attribute of a nation, let alone of a people.' (*Javnost,* 3 June 1955) With others, the national identity is in a bad, neglected state. Western Europeans, bogged down in materialism, humanism and cosmopolitanism, are left with a kind of sick, limp, rotten identity. They barely remember who they are.

Finally, a third group, for example Croats, Albanians, Macedonians, Muslims, Bulgarians and Romanians, have ersatz identities as nations, because they have abandoned their real, that is their Serbian, one and adopted a foreign or invented national identity as their own. Radovan Samardžić explained how this occurred over the past centuries. 'Throughout the Serbian lands, even those which had been so since time immemorial, foreign names, Albanian, Bulgarian and others, began to appear ... Serb shepherds and soldiers were called Vlachs, Serb frontiersmen Croats, Serbs of many occupations, starting with carters, Bulgars, Serb bodyguards, policemen and migrants in search of work, orginating from the heartland of their territory, Albanians.' (Samardžić, 1989, 67) As for the Romanians, their 'de-Serbianisation' seems to have begun far earlier. The expert on prehistory, Relja Novaković, finds traces of the presence of Serbs in present-day Romania dating from the fourth century BC, preserved particularly in toponyms. In this way, as Slobodan Jarčević stresses in his review of Novaković's book *Karpatski i Likijski Srbi* (The Carpathian and Lika Serbs), this scholar 'also raises the question of the origin of today's Romanians and their language. The Romanians adopted Christianity in the old

---

[3] It is interesting that the idea of the so-called divine nature of the nation, one of the 'truths' offered by the contemporary Serbian political myth, comes from Paul de Lagarde, the ideologue of the German popular (*völkisch*) movement of the 1870s. Lagarde 'defined the German nation as a spiritual entity distinguished from the state, as the soul is from the body, and, as such, charged with a divine mission.' (Plumyène, 285) This idea of Lagarde's found its place also in Rosenberg's *Myth of the Twentieth Century,* although here it is extended to race. (Lacoue-Labarthe, 57)

Serbian language, and, if this language was not their native tongue, then they are the only Christian people in the East to have been baptised in a foreign language, and not their own.' (*Politika*, 22 March 1997) This does not seem particularly likely, and it is more probable that the Romanians are descended from the Serbs, i.e. they are *in fact* Serbs. What is more, given that Novaković's book treats 'Serbian settlements or states from Great Britain to India', one can expect new 'revelations' about peoples who came into being earlier or later by abandoning their original Serbian identity.[4]

That could be good news for them, because for peoples descended from the Serbs the problem of the lack of an authentic national identity does not seem as hopeless as it does for others. They always have the possibility of returning to their former Serbianness, which they all carry somewhere in the depths of their soul. That identity has been preserved by contemporary Serbs also in the case of those who were once Serbs, in case they wish to rediscover it. By taking care of their own soul, they have at the same time cared for the soul of their 'renegade brothers'. 'By preserving Kosovo', says Amfilohije Radović, 'we are preserving not only our own soul, but also the soul of the Albanian people, because one should not lose sight of the fact that until yesterday they were Christians, and that tomorrow an Albanian will not be in a position to understand his historical being, if he loses contact with the monasteries of Dečani and Gračanica, and with the Patriarchate of Peć ... we are preserving our being, but we are preserving also the emblem for those others who live here and we are laying the foundations of their true future ... This emblem will one day serve as a reminder for these people to return to their own historical roots and discover the message of those emblems.' (Radović, 1992, 184)

A return to their original Serbianness would help peoples without a true identity return to the deepest roots of their national being and

---

[4]The same theme is developed also by the contemporary Croatian political myth, in which the widespread nature and ancient origin of the Croats are exaggerated to such an extent that the origin of all the other South Slav peoples, especially the Serbs, can be traced to them, although the Serbs for some reason do not accept this historical fact. 'Hence they do not accept', writes Vjekoslav Kaleb, 'even the historical fact that the only South Slav people from beyond the Carpathians at the time of the migrations of peoples were the Croats and that the Serbs (Servi) in the Balkans are descended from the Croats, who gave themselves over to the defence of Byzantium when they were able to snatch their freedom in the wake of the Avar defeat at Tsarigrad.' (*Danas*, 8 October 1991)

thereby, also, finally achieve the conditions for a just and peaceful end to the international conflicts and wars on the territory of former Yugoslavia. For example, the Macedonians would be able to rest from their endless search for their name. 'Are the Serbs to blame', wonders Nikola Poplašen, 'if the Macedonians, by not admitting that they are southern Serbs, cannot find a suitable, appropriate and acceptable name for the state, which it seemed to them it would not be a bad idea to construct?' (*Javnost,* 24 July 1993) Had the Catholicised Serbs (Croats) and the Islamicised Serbs (Muslims) been prepared to return to their Serbian roots, there would have been no war in Yugoslavia. It is not too late for them, they can always follow the example 'of the young Muslim from Mostar, who experienced a national and human transformation, by returning to his roots and his old faith' in a song recorded from an old peasant, also published in the Pale paper *Javnost* (7 October 1995). The young Muslim, in the song 'The Young Turk', sends this message:

> *It is known that my ancestors*
> *Were in the past Orthodox Serbs,*
> *And that they fought at Kosovo*
> *Just like the glorious Lazar.*
> ....
> *I shall no longer be a Turk,*
> *Nor gather up a Turkish band,*
> *I wish to go to Cetinje,*[5]
> *To bow before saintly Petar.*

In the opinion of Maksim Korać, a participant in the Second Congress of Serbian Intellectuals (Belgrade, 1994), the struggle of the Muslims in Bosnia-Herzegovina was not only hopeless, but also tragic, because it was a suicidal struggle. 'They cannot win a battle against themselves, against the Serbs in themselves.' (Korać, 335) The same is true of the Albanians in Kosovo. They are mostly of Serbian origin, and 'their greatest, fateful destiny is that they abandoned their Serbianness and became Albanians, thereby, as our blood brothers, they became their own greatest enemy and oppressors of their being.' (ibid., 338) However, in everything that they do and think today, for example in the affirmation of Dr Skender Razija that the Albanian language is more than 12,000 years old, in the

---

[5] The mountain stronghold of the rulers of Montenegro, including Petar Petrović Njegoš. (Transl.)

mass lighting of candles in the streets of Priština, in the slogan 'Kosovo—republic', Korać recognises 'the silent, badly articulated call of Serbian culture, Serbian literacy, Serbian Kosovo, Serbian Raška and the ancient state'. They can drive the Serbs from Kosovo, says Korać, but 'how can they drive the Serbian soul and Serbian blood out of their veins?' That is why he proposes the foundation of a general movement 'in order that we may once again, one day, with brotherly love and understanding, become one people with one faith, we Orthodox Serbs, Muslims, Montenegrins, Albanians of Serbian descent (Arnauts), Serb Roman Catholics (Catholicised and then Croaticised), and all Pharisees.' (ibid., 340)

An authentic national identity is characteristic of the Serbs and potentially accessible to all those who were once Serbs, while with other peoples it is forgotten or moribund, if not completely unknown, because the Serbs knew how to preserve it. What has remained latent in others, the Serbs have brought into being. That is the other key idea of the myth of Serbian identity.

It is the case that national identity is a gift from God, but it is only the Serbs who received that gift in the proper way and justified it by their heroic exploits. They understood the fact that it is more important than life and that it can be preserved only through sacrifice and confirmed only in death. In their readiness, proved several times since the Battle of Kosovo, to preserve 'what they are' at the price of the greatest sacrifice, the Serbs mark themselves off from other peoples and become gods, resembling a 'race of heroes'. 'And what is more valuable than life itself', says Rade Dacić, 'is found only by those who belong to a race of heroes—and perhaps the gods. And then: blackmailing life cannot succeed.' (*Politika,* 17 July 1997)

The history of the Serbs as an heroic nation is shown in the myth as an alternating series of ritual death and resurrection, testing and tempering through temptation, distillation and selection which gives the raw body of the people the purified substance of national identity. This technology of successive rites of passage from the banal life of a nationally unawakened people into the rank of a nation of heroes implies a great expense of material, measured in millions of human lives. According to one calculation carried out during the war in Bosnia, it was necessary to sacrifice around six million lives for 'what we are'. However, this price does not appear overly to concern the Serbian leaders and their advisers among the priesthood and intelligentsia. This is not only because they are not themselves threatened by any kind of danger, unlike the Serbian nobility which was wiped out six centuries ago on the field of Kosovo, but also because for them an ordinary unheroic human life, life without heightened national awareness, means nothing. It is not life in the true sense, but merely inauthentic, unconscious 'existence'.

Such a life has some value only in the eyes of the Serb 'intellectual' who, in the words of the poet R.P. Nogo, is 'a reed which often bends'. 'In the calculation of such reeds', Nogo explains, 'had we bent, bowed and knelt more often in our history—there would certainly be many more of us, and we would have had far fewer sacrifices! I confess that I do not understand this higher mathematics of hollow reeds. Because, would we than have been "who we are"?' (Nogo, 1995, 8) It would be better if such Serbs—those who model their lives on such 'reeds', for whom it is important to be, and not to be what they are—did not exist. This *topos* of the Serbian political myth, the *topos* of the identity gambit, was also most succinctly formulated by Matija Bećković: (Bećković, 1978)

> *Had there been not a single battle*
> *There would be more of us, but who?*
> *And it would be better, but for whom?*

Had they not unconditionally sacrificed themselves for their national identity, the Serbs today would be like the Czechs who, according to Mihailo Marković, have lost their freedom and courage because they systematically avoid battle and try only to make things easier for themselves without a struggle. The worst thing of all, if one is to believe Marković, is that the Czechs have an exceptionally low opinion of themselves. That is the fatal consequence of '"realistic" choices made by the Czech leaders in 1938, 1939 and 1968 ... seeking each time a solution which would incur the least damage, the Czech leaders capitulated three times in a row within a space of three decades. Physical damage was always avoided—but at the price of the loss of liberty, courage, self-confidence and self-respect. The first of these

---

[6] The idea of suffering and warfare as the only path to the preservation of national identity is not always met with approval, even among Balkan poets. One, the Romanian Mircea Dinescu, recently expressed the opinion (in an interview in *Politika* on 16 August 1997) that the exaggerated warlike behaviour of small peoples can be the cause of their loss of identity, that is that the pride and arrogance of small peoples is suicidal. 'Had Serbia and Romania and the other countries of the Eastern bloc not bent their necks a bit in the face of the great Empires, the Romanians would now speak Russian, and the Serbs Turkish.'

can always be replaced far more easily than the second.'[6] (Marković, 365) That first, physical, element, easily replaced, is the individual human life. In the political ethno-myth, as Marković's elaboration of that myth demonstrates, life is of little value in itself, and means nothing. Human life is here an easily replaceable value, a kind of biological coin of the nation, which patriotic men and women will easily forge in as large a quantity as the nation requires for war or post-war recovery. For the ethno-myth, all that is important is that the brand of identity should be preserved in order that each coin of the biological capital of the nation should be correctly marked.

But, fortunately, the Serbs are not Czechs, the choices of their leaders (for example in 1914, 1941 and 1948) were, in Marković's judgment, 'ethically exulted choices', and this means that they elected to have the spirit of a great people, regardless of the price to be paid by the national body. That was the origin of 'the spiritual tradition, which has enabled the Serbian people, regardless of its limited numbers, to become a great historical people'. (ibid., 366) Marković knows 'that our heroic choices have regularly entailed enormous sacrifices, suffering, destruction'. What is more, he has observed that heroic feats are followed by 'great falls'. But he mentions these falls only in order to make a contribution to the treatment of that often worn *topos* of the political myth which holds that the enemies of the Serbs achieve in peace what they were unable to in war. 'That is when our greatest falls occur', explains Marković, 'and then all those who hid in the deepest mouseholes when we were at our height, all those who are overcome by panic-stricken fear whenever it seems to them that we are coming to wake and stir them—then they do with us what they will.' In fact, Marković does not make a causal-consequential connection between the 'heroic choices' and 'great falls', he does not think that mass loss of life, persecution and suffering could be the reason for the 'falls'—they are for him just two historical sequences, which for some reason regularly succeed one another. The Serbian 'falls' are in fact unexpected and incomprehensible, they are 'long periods of feebleness, incomprehensible passivity, complete slackening'. (ibid., 367)

This passivity is incomprehensible to Marković also because for him personally, as for many other politicians, philosophers or poets, who have placed their narrative capacities at the service of reviving the myth of the heroic identity of the Serbian nation, the Serbian heroic drive has not declined at all. In their case, it resists the unfathomable fate which can be observed in the behaviour of the majority of Serbs.

Identity

In fact, from the perspective of the need for the enduring survival of the heroic identity, without unnecesary falls and lulls, it would be best to sharpen the criteria for defining those capable of preserving that identity. So that the only Serbs who remain alive are those who, consistently, in both war and peace, are what they are. If none such can be found, then all right. We shall not exist, but we shall know who it is that does not exist.

Exchange of bodies from the war in Slavonia in 1992. (Miloš Cvetković)

9. Bank

The interpretation of Serbian political myths, above all myths of ethnic nationalism, must be considered in the context of events in former Yugoslavia and in the broader regional, Balkan framework. Certain observations of the similarity between contemporary Serbian and Croatian political myths, only parenthetical here, show that they could be seen essentially as variations on elements from a common fund of plots, *topoi* and images.

It may be that this Serbo-Croatian fund is only a part of a larger arsenal. Such an assumption is suggested by what has been up to now rare comparative examination of the political myths of South-East Europe. It seems that all those allegedly autonomous and unique marks of the identity of individual nations in that part of Europe are in fact merely borrowings from a common Balkan bank of political myths. Of course, today's forgers of national symbols vouch for their autochtonous nature and do not acknowledge their debts. For them, even to discuss this subject is unacceptable, something which they leave to nationally unconscious, 'cosmopolitan' intellectuals. As George Konrad puts it—in a text about the citizens of Central European countries, who, in their desire to resemble the West as closely as possible, completely neglect their mutual similarities—'it is hard to make self-aware, proud subjects rejoice in the fact that we are going to compare them to one another. In their eyes, comparativists are impertinent types.' (Konrad, 83)

One of those 'impertinent' comparativists is certainly the Romanian anthropologist Vintila Mihailescu, who is particularly interested in the comparative analysis of the attitudes of individual Balkan countries to Europe and modernisation. In his review of that attitude he does not neglect the role of the great powers. 'In keeping with their current interests', he writes, 'the great powers support the demands of one or other nation and thus give the impression of encouraging now one now another identity discourse, supporting various "ancestor complexes" one after the other. "Great nations" (Greater Romania, Greater Bulgaria, Greater Albania, Greater Croatia, etc.) appear and disappear depending on the ebb and flow of the *Drang nach Osten* of various Western countries and the *Drang nach Westen* of the Eastern countries which have set out to conquer modernity.' (Mihailescu, 226) However, Mihailescu devotes most time to inner inter-Balkan affinities, to a shared Balkan fund of political assumptions, myths and symbols, thanks to which the ideological configurations of individual Balkan societies are to the greatest extent isomorphs.

For example, in all the Balkan countries the process of modernisation led to the appearance of an ambivalent identity discourse, 'in which the non-modern logic of the community's customary law was linked with the modern logic of the nation.' The similarity of the political imaginary of the Balkan countries is particularly striking when it appears in discourses which seek to deny that similarity, when the boundary between 'us' and 'them' is drawn as a boundary between Europeans and non-Europeans. 'The "struggle for Europe"', writes Mihailescu, 'is carried out through slogans, newspaper articles and political speeches in order to isolate, by erecting frontiers (not always symbolic ones), those who do or do not belong by right to the space of European modernity.' He quotes the words of a contemporary Slovene political leader who complained that the Slovenes 'cannot identify with pro-Asian and pro-African Yugoslavia, [because] of our character which we have acquired through a thousand-year history', and a similar speech by Tudjman's adviser Slaven Letica, who favoured the division of Yugoslavia according to the model of the difference between its 'oriental', 'Asiatic' model and its 'Western' one, which, naturally, characterises Croatia.

Mihailescu does not confine himself to just this example. 'A similar problem of a symbolic boundary occurs between Hungary and Romania in connection with Transylvania. In 1985 Jeno Szúcz revived the thesis of the protruding tip of the Ottoman Empire ending in East-Central Europe, notably in Hungary. The whole territory north-west of the Carpathians, including Transylvania, belonged therefore to Europe (that is to Central Europe), while the Orient began in the south-east, subjugated to Greater Turkey, and necessarily marked by a non-European way of life. Virtually the same discourse was cultivated by Romanian historians and intellectuals in general, with the "frontier of Europe" being the Danube rather than the Carpathians. And of course, according to them, the glory and heroism of having been the people on the "front line" belongs to the Romanians.' (Mihailescu, 225–6)

Contemporary Greece was also unable to resist the seductive Sirens of identity and other ethno-nationalist political myths. 'For a long time it was thought', writes the Greek political scientist Panayotis Elias Dimitras, 'that Greece, broadly speaking a democratic country, a member of the European Community since 1981, and of Nato since 1952, escaped that "Balkan destiny".' But such an expectation was unfounded and is based on an underestimation of 'the fact that the Greek people, like the other Balkan peoples, have been nurtured for a long time on historical revisionism and the spirit of intolerance ... The teaching of history in Greek schools and universities has not yet been modernised or adapted to contemporary theoretical analyses about the nation and nationalism. It is still dominated by the myth which has had the main currency since the end of the nineteenth century: that is, the myth of the continuity of Hellenism through three thousand years and implicitly, sometimes even explicitly, that of the superiority of the "Greek race".' (Dimitras, 62)

Dimitras thinks that an 'invitation to collective memory' is not in itself bad, and that the Balkan peoples will not find a way out of the present crisis by 'forgetting their history'. 'On the contrary', he explains, 'by re-learning the history of the last two centuries, in the light of the findings of scholarly research into the nation and nationalism and set in a regional context—which means learning the same history in all the countries of the region—collective memory may be "de-Balkanised" and "Europeanised".' (ibid., 64)

The 'wars of remembrance' and 'the ancestor complex', that is the conflicts between various Balkan versions of the myth of national identity and the national past, is also discussed by the Bulgarian philosopher Ivailo Dichev. 'Wars of remembrance in the Balkans', he writes in an article published in the Paris paper *Libération* in 1994, 'oscillate between the tragic and the comic. The Macedonians and Greeks fight over Alexander the Great and his star; the Serbs, Croats and Bosnians on the one hand, and the Macedonians and Bulgarians on the other, share their languages and literatures; the Bulgarians, Greeks and Macedonians claim Cyril and Methodius, the creators of the Cyrillic script, for themselves; the Albanians, Croats and Slovenes present themselves as the descendants of the Illyrians ... Do young nation-states on the road to consolidation suffer from an ancestor complex?'

Despite everything that could perhaps strike someone as 'barbaric', 'primitive' or merely 'exotic', the Serbian political myths, above all the myths of ethnic nationalism, discussed here, must sound familiar to our Balkan neighbours. But other contemporary Europeans may also recognise themselves in them. In order to understand them, they do not need to make the effort of anthropologists involved in field research into primitive peoples, to step for a moment outside the framework of their own culture in order to identify with some specific Serbian or Balkan mentality and so be able to describe and interpret it. The Serbian political myths may be quite easily understood when they are 'read' in the context of the political history of modern Europe. It is not a case of whether these myths correspond to some surpassed and no longer relevant aspect of European history, its belated echo, but of their belonging to the context of contemporary Europe.

It is often said that Europe has betrayed its political ideals by not energetically opposing the forceful creation of ethnic states on the territory of former Yugoslavia. The reasons quoted are the inertia, short-sightedness and irresponsibility of European politics, its inability to defend the vital interests of European democracy or a lack of interest in the fate of peoples and states on the periphery of Europe. However, the explanation of the hesitation by which European policy is contrasted to the warlike ethnic nationalism of the Balkans and its 'inconsistent' behaviour can be sought in the fact that, even in the most developed and largest states of Europe, ethnic nationalism, celebrated by the Serbian political myths described here, is not only not a thing of the past—it represents one of the central ideas of the social order.

In the opinion of Jean Baudrillard, presented in an article entitled 'Without Pity' carried by *Borba* (8 February 1994), the policies and practice in the armed conflict in former Yugoslavia of 'ethnic cleansing' were in fact just an expression of the contemporary spirit of the times throughout Europe. 'It is said', writes Baudrillard, 'that if we allow matters in Sarajevo to go on as they are, we will soon find ourselves in the same situation. But we are already there. All European countries are going the way of ethnic cleansing. That is the real Europe, which is quietly coming into being in the very shadow of parliament, while Serbia represents its advance guard. It is unnecessary to recall its passivity, its impotence to react, because we are witnessing a programme which is developing logically, and Bosnia is only its new frontier.'

Several contributions in the collection *Racisme et modernité* (ed. Wieviorka, 1993) discuss the importance of the ideology of ethnic nationalism in Western Europe and the political and social institutions founded on it in individual states. The contribution by Czarina Wilpert of the Institute of Sociology in Berlin contains data which demonstrate unambiguously that an ideology is in force in contemporary Germany, based on the inviolable value of ethnic identity. This ideology has institutional support in the discrimination that affects all those who are not ethnic Germans; the right to nationality is granted in the function of ethnic belonging. 'Unfortunately', writes Wilpert, 'the sacral character of the German nation, with its single inherited culture, is not questioned. This ideology permeates the institutions which decide who belongs to them and who does not.' (Wilpert, 235)

Uli Bielefeld, from the Institute for Social Research in Hamburg, agrees: 'The law about citizenship founded on the ethnos has survived into our time as the legal expression of an imaginary assumption of ethnic purity.' (Bielefeld, 1994, 204) In his opinion, 'Germany too is a country of the People [*Volk*], of ethnic nationalism or, in other words, of "the etatisation of ethnicity".' In this way, 'to be a member of the community in Germany means as it were "naturally" to belong to German culture. On the basis of this "natural culture", collective and individual, there develops a notion of homogeneity, seen as really existing. In this process others, as foreigners, collectively and individually, become irrevocably abnormal.' (Bielefeld, 1993, 31) Of particular interest for a consideration of the cultural-historical roots of Serbian and Balkan ethnically centred political myths—at a time when their role is to further the creation of ethnically homogeneous states on the territory of former Yugoslavia—is Bielefeld's judgment of the function of the concept of ethnic homogenisation in contemporary German society, because it is in large part also valid for the Balkans. Given that modern societies are not in reality ethnically homogeneous, says Bielefeld, 'the desire for homogenisation' is transformed into a view of heterogeneity as 'a problem which must be resolved', and hence there appear plans to 'transform the imaginary order into reality.' (ibid., 35)

Similar conclusions about the significance of ethnic nationalism in Great Britain, but also in other West European states, are reached by John Rex, of Warwick University. He writes of the 'ghettoisation of black and Asian communities'. (Rex, 334) In his opinion, anti-Islamism, widespread today in Britain and other West European countries, is similar to anti-Semitism. 'Europeans today', writes Rex, 'on the whole reject all Muslims as "fundamentalists".' He concludes that 'European political thought has great difficulty in accepting a truly pluri-cultural society.' This is true of Great Britain, where minority cultures can exist only in a subordinate position, of Germany, 'where the ethnic nationalism of the *Volk*, which excludes foreigners, still endures', of France, where 'the survival of minority cultures is felt as something directed against the state'. (ibid., 341)

Therefore an understanding and interpretation of the Serbian political myths which came to life during recent years, at a time of crisis and war on the territory of former Yugoslavia, requires the context of Balkan and European contemporary life. The greatest help in this is provided by the tradition of European humanistic criticism of political mythology, particularly of the nationalistic and similar myths of the modern age, and the experience of contemporary anti-racist movements. The scandalous, intolerable, extremist messages which these myths convey are only variants of similar messages with the same meaning formulated long ago in various European languages. These are conveyed in some parts of Europe perhaps with less sound and fury but their seductiveness and political usefulness are not thereby diminished. In the chaotic Balkan warfare at the end of the twentieth century and the myths that accompany and legitimate it we can clearly discern the madness of ethnic purity, so well known in Europe.

10. Criticism

The Serbian political ethno-myth does not date from yesterday. It consists for the most part of old stories. That is why it seems like something familiar, which we will understand best by going back into the past and looking for its origins. On the other hand, today's Serbian ethno-myth is a product of this age, that is the state of Serbia and former Yugoslavia during the last decade of the twentieth century. Often obscure and archaic, it is, nevertheless, focused on contemporary events, and its meaning becomes clearer when it is interpreted in the context of those events. Then it emerges that its obtrusive presence in almost all areas of public life, from popular music and sport to literature and the church, is a consequence of the instability of the former state since 1980, the crisis and abrupt collapse of the order, including the symbolic order, on which that state rested.

Our experience confirms the observations made by researchers in other countries about the correlation between the expansion of myths and periods of great social crisis. In the words of the French sociologist Roger Bastide, 'the majority of ethnologists today believe that myths are responses to phenomena of social upheaval, tensions within social structures, that they are screens on which groups project their collective fears.' (Bastide, 62) The historian Raoul Girardet also connects their appearance to social crisis, in the conclusion of a monograph dedicated to French political myths and mythologies. 'Among the mythological systems whose structures we have tried to determine, there is not one which is not in the most direct way connected with the phenomena of crisis: the brutal speeding up of the process of historical evolution, the sudden collapse of the cultural and social environment, the elimination of mechanisms of solidarity and complementarity which determine the life of a community. Analysis directs us constantly to Durkheim's concept of anomie or, more broadly, to the old distinction, widespread in French sociology, between "critical" and "organic" periods; in critical periods political myths are most clearly expressed, they are imposed with the greatest strength and show with the greatest force how attractive they can be.' (Girardet, 178)

Political myths are a phenomenon of crisis in so far as in critical periods of social life they occupy a far greater expanse of public communication than in periods of relative stability. However, they are not created by crisis nor do they disappear with it. They are constant, and perhaps also a constitutive element of the symbolic power of every political authority. Explaining the nature and significance of the 'social imaginary', the Polish historian Bronisław Baczko also refers to Durkheim, for whom 'one of the fundamental characteristics of the social fact (*le fait social*) is precisely its symbolic aspect.' (Baczko, 24) Baczko reminds us that contemporary researchers into society and politics—by contrast with the French students of 1968, who sought, among other things, that imagination should come to power (slogan: *Power to the imagination!*) —know that 'imagination is always in power'. 'The sciences of man', he writes, 'have shown that all power, especially political power, surrounds itself with collective representations and that for it the realm of the imaginary and the symbolic is a strategic area of crucial importance.' Baczko stresses that this is not a matter of spreading an illusion about the real strength of an authority, but of 'reinforcing effective domination through the appropriation of symbols' (ibid., 18), of combining 'physical and symbolic violence'. (ibid., 38)

Starting from an insight into the imaginary, symbolic dimension of political power, we may see the contemporary Serbian political ethno-myths as one way of expressing the ethnically centred political imaginary in Serbia and among the Serbs. It appears in the form of political rituals, such as various inaugurations and burials, political meetings and demonstrations, or of visual and musical symbols: emblems, crests, flags, anthems. More important, if we accept the thesis about the constitutive symbolic nature of political power, then criticism of our ethno-myths, like other similar forms of the political imaginary, cannot be reduced to the condemnation and rejection of all political myth-making and political symbolism in general. As the Italian political scientist Tiziano Bonazzi says, 'In sociological and historical research today myth is presented as a reality which must be analysed, not simply exorcised.' (Bonazzi, 365)

Undoubtedly political ethno-myths stand in the way of the development of a civil, democratic society in Serbia. In that sense, its criticism is today essential, but it is doubtful whether it can be reduced to the simple maxim 'Out of shadows and images into the truth'. And whether respect for the need to establish rational criteria for political and social life as a whole ought also to include the demand that the political arena should be freed from everything not connected with the rational and utilitarian resolution of conflicts.

For by all accounts democracy also has its stories and images and it is desirable that they should be borne in mind in discussions of nationalist myths and democracy. In the context of these discussions, a question emerges that is of particular interest to us here: does myth have a legitimate place in the symbolic representation and embodiment of democracy? Are there democratic myths? In the opinion of the French philosophers Philippe Lacoue-Labarthe and Jean-Luc Nancy, it is not enough for democracy to proclaim 'the rejection of all identification, constant self-examination as its greatest virtue ... and a kind of inner fragility, both avowed and justified, and which is undoubtedly exploited by the opponents of democracy.' However, these authors distinguish the problem of a figurativeness appropriate to democracy from the problems of political myth, for as they say, 'democracy poses, or in the future must pose the question of its "image"—which does not mean that this question should be confused with that of recourse to myth.' (Lacoue-Labarthe and Nancy, 12)

Focusing on the outcome of the Nazi myth, Lacoue-Labarthe and Nancy are uncertain whether to allow any myth at all into the space of democratic symbolism. Transplanted into politics, myth becomes a real danger. This is also the opinion of the German Slavist Reinhard Lauer, which he put forward in an article dedicated to the place of the Serbian national myth in the war in former Yugoslavia. Myths have their place in literature and art, in times of peace, but they are very dangerous when they appear outside that context, 'in real life', as happens in times of conflict. What happened earlier with national myths in Hitler's Germany is occurring in our time in Serbia. 'The myths which earlier flourished in the aimless garden of poetry have now come to life and begun to rage.' That is why Lauer directs his criticism above all to the application of mythology, carried out in political practice, because the 'literal transplantation of myth into action represents a general danger.' (Lauer, 7)

But he adds another argument to this one, affirming that a certain kind of myth, even when it is only in poetry, represents a latent danger even in peacetime. Thus his criticism of myths, after being directed to the peril that accompanies their being put into action, now turns to responsibility for preserving them and handing them down, even before they are put to any purpose. In view of the fact that, in his opinion, during the recent war the myths about *hajduks* served as a *vade mecum* for the Serbs' harsh settling of accounts with their enemies, the question emerges as to why and by whose fault the story of *hajduk* crimes remained among the valued texts of Serbian culture. Nevertheless, Lauer does not think that this story should be entirely eliminated, just that its negative message should somehow be toned down. 'It was fatal', he writes, 'that no one endeavoured to blunt the blade of inhumanity hidden in these songs. On the contrary, people delighted in them.' (ibid., 8)

With this second argument, Lauer adopts Plato's criticism of myths. In addition to the idea of the detrimental effect of the poetic treatment of Hellenic myths in the formation of virtuous and god-fearing citizens and in addition to the call for their creators to be reined in, Plato's criticism contains also the idea of the need for the state nevertheless to retain something of poetic mythic creativity, on condition that this is carefully selected and brought into line with the state's educational aims. According to Plato, and now Lauer, civic virtue requires that the godless or inhuman cruelty of myths should be toned down for pedagogical reasons. If they are at first dangerous, myths may in the end be useful.

The Zagreb anthropologist Ivo Žanić also favours some kind of constructive or, more exactly, reconstructive criticism of political myth. He is not suspicious of myth. He considers it to be one of the constitutive forms of political symbolic communication, and thereby also characteristic of democratic society. For him the attitude: 'Every society has its own mythology' derives from a somewhat more general attitude 'There can be no politics without symbol or accompanying rituals, nor is it possible to have a political system based solely on rational principles, i.e. freed from symbolic connotations.' (Žanić, 56) From this starting point, Žanić bases his criticism of contemporary Croatian political myths on the possibility of making a critical choice between them or between their different versions, so that nationalist mythology is rejected but those myths which give a symbolic foundation to Croatian democracy are fostered. For example, in his opinion, the myth about King Zvonimir of Knin can be interpreted in a democratic manner, as was apparently done by some leaders of the Catholic church in Croatia, so that it is 'no exaggeration to say that *good King Zvonimir,* for practical politics a symbol "only" of the right to an independent state vis-à-vis external aggressors, has grown into an equally valid symbol of the moral requirement that such a state should be internally legal and democratic.' (ibid., 62)

Looked at in this way, a political myth, if it is not acceptable for some reason—if it has become dangerous or superfluous, undesirable or outmoded—may be replaced by another. Sometimes, as in the case quoted by Žanić, it may be transposed from one plane of meaning to another, In the way that Aeschylus accepted the goddesses of vengeance, the Erinyes, into the *polis,* renaming them the Eumenides and making them goddesses of justice. Another way, that of creating new myths in place of old ones, was proposed by Svetislav Stefanović after the First World War, when the question was raised in Serbia of 'what to replace Kosovo with?' He wished the 'cult of the hero, that is the cult of the avenging hero' to be left to the past, 'for the sake of a higher and better one, the cult of mercy, the universal humanity of good will.' (Prpa-Jovanović, 9)

There is a problem with these various attempts at reconstructive criticism of political myth, which start from respect for the consubstantial symbolism and figurativeness of political communication. It lies in the fact that these endeavours presuppose the ability to recognise and distinguish socially useful and socially harmful myths and the possibility of forming citizens not only as individuals with a developed critical political consciousness but also as members of a community cemented by politically correct myths.

One must therefore ask whether the greatest danger from these myths does not appear precisely when, often for praiseworthy motives, they are subjected to stylisation, touching up, to what Lauer calls 'blunting their blade'. Freed of traces of primitive cruelty, the remnants of pagan cults and rituals, various ambiguities and confusing archaic elements, the myths of traditional popular culture become national deities, the object of a state cult and a tool of military training. They become usable for the propaganda of national intolerance and war only when they have acquired the appearance of a corpus of rational and socially respected ideas. They follow the path taken by the supporters of the 'Red Star Belgrade' football team recruited to form a voluntary unit: they are cleansed and prettified in order to be deadly.[1]

---

[1] This is why Marija Kleut is right when she objects to the way Lauer simplifies the meaning of individual themes of Serbian epic song. 'For that reason', she writes in a polemical review of Lauer's essay on the Serbian myth, 'even in Serbian oral heroic

In fact, what Georges Bataille, speaking of the social functions of literature, called 'hypermorality' is valid of myths, as it is of football hooligans. Like it or not, they are not 'innocent', nor should they try to be. On the contrary, they are guilty and should defend their guilt. It is only when they cease to be an anti-social bunch of hooligans, and are transformed into orderly soldiers, that football supporters have the opportunity of committing war crimes and crimes against humanity. It is only when myth ceases to scandalise with its mesmerising and terrifying images of violence and evil, when it is transformed into 'innocent poetry', when it is decanted into instructive patriotic reading matter, that it becomes a deadly weapon.

What remains for critics of contemporary political myths, in addition to their problematic attempts to discipline them, alter and tame them, in order to make them politically effective also in a democratic model of public communication, is the equally problematic possibility of radically questioning the mythic and mythopeic in politics. Here too there are problems of both a theoretical and a fundamental nature, for such criticism starts from the not all that convincing assumption that there are critics who are distanced from myth and independent of it, and that the prevalence of a critical spirit in society is not only a worthy aim, but also attainable. In addition, and worse than that, the adoption and practice of a radically critical attitude to national political myths presents the critic with a quite practical difficulty. 'To adhere to the truth', says Adam Michnik, 'and at the same time to follow the demand that everything around one should be analysed and that every idea of the powerful of this world should be put to the test—such an attitude means for intellectuals: you accept that you will become an object of disparagement; you must face the fact that people will spread malicious gossip about you—accusing you of despising your own country and betraying its national values.' (see Buden, 33)

---

poetry there are no unchangeable, once and forever given mythologemes, ideologemes, archetypes, nor is there any ethnic exclusivity from that point of view.' (Kleut, 402)

PART II
From the History of Serbian Political Mythology

1. Skerlić, 'Pan-Slavdom' and 'The Rotten West'

With ideas about the need for greater solidarity and firmer connections between Slav and Orthodox peoples and their united opposition to the West being revived on the Serbian political stage, it is useful to recall the fate of such ideas in the cultural and political history of Serbia. This is confirmed by an exceptionally interesting article by Latinka Perović about N. J. Danilevski's work *Russia and Europe* and its echoes in Serbia. Here for the first time there is documented evidence of the Slavophil ideas of Nikola Pašić*, their origins and meaning.

Readers of this article will discover, among other things, that, under the influence of Danilevski, Pašić accepted many ideas which appear today in the pages of our 'right-wing' publications: the conviction that the Slav East and the European West are two irreconcilably opposed worlds, 'in ceaseless cultural, religious, national and economic struggle', the fear that Serbia would lose her Slav specificity and be transformed into a 'little western state', the proposal to create a 'Slav empire' and to restore 'Byzantium'. (Perović, 1994, 9–10)

The relevance today of the theme of the Slavs and the West will surely increase the interest of the scholarly and broader public in other aspects of our political and cultural history in which this theme has been prominent. It is not hard to predict that among the first to which such interest will lead us will be Jovan Skerlić*. There are two reasons for this. The material which Skerlić the historian collected in his masterly monographs and studies is today one of the most reliable sources for studying the genesis of pan-Slav and Slavophil ideas in Serbian literature and politics. Secondly, the state of mind in Serbia in Skerlić's time, which greeted the new ideas of democratic and liberal Europe with mixed feelings of suspicion and enthusiasm, with great resistance, but also with the hope of a better future, in many ways corresponds to the circumstances in which we are living today. As a result, we can quite understand Skerlić's impulse to dedicate himself to a search for the historical roots of that state of mind, to an investigation and critical analysis of the history of political and social ideas in Serbian politics and literature, including ideas about the Slavs and the West and their mutual relations. For the same reason, the results of Skerlić's work have a new relevance and value for us today.

On the basis of Skerlić's research, it is possible to follow, through our political and cultural history, the main lines of the fate of the concept of the Slav peoples as a young, fresh 'race', which will take over the rudder of Europe from the weary, worn-out Westerners and so save it from destruction. On the basis of research by the ethnologist Matija Murko, Skerlić found the source of that flattering idea about the Slavs in Herder. 'He believes in the future of the Slav tribe', writes Skerlić; 'he is convinced that the Slavs will adapt to the conditions of civilisation, be strengthened by it and themselves strengthen it with their fresh, healthy blood. (*Omladina i njena književnost*), 'The Serbian — Youth Movement and its Literature', 139; hereafter *Serbian Youth*). The Slavophils were also influenced by Hegel and Fichte's conception of the Germans as the representatives of culture and the bearers of the development of the human spirit in the nineteenth century. As Skerlić explains, 'The Slavophils went logically further and maintained that this spiritual hegemony was being taken over by the rested, fresh Slavs, that authority in the spiritual world belonged to them, and that their culture was the greatest thing that the human spirit had created.' (ibid., 167)

Skerlić inherited the history of this idea from the 1840s, that is from the time when Slavophil ideas in general were encountered by Serbian students in Požun and Pest, where they were taught by the prominent Pan-Slavs, the Slovak Ljudevit Štúr and the Czech Jan Kollár. Skerlić established what was in his opinion a particularly important fact, 'that Slavophil ideas reached the Serbs from the Czech and Slovak Pan-Slavs, above all Kollár and Štúr, and not from the Russian Orthodox Pan-Slavs, Aksakov and Khomyakov, as might have been expected.' (ibid., 140) Štúr preached 'belief in Slavdom, that it was for the Slavs to resurrect enfeebled humanity, to replace the worn-out Latin and incomplete Germanic civilisation, to found a great Slav empire of full, humane and ideal civilization.' (ibid., 8)

On the eve of 1848, Štúr and Kollár's students and followers in

Vojvodina and Belgrade (founders of the Serbian Youth Society [Družina Mladeži Srbske], 1847) expected the rapid unification of the Slavs, 'Pan-Slav' education 'under the holy Slav lime-tree' (ibid., 20), and, like Sava, the hero of the popular story by Šapčanin, enthusiastically imagined the power of the multitudinous Slav community: 'You must be Slavs! Just think: a hundred million Slavs! A hundred million! A world! A universe!' Quoting these and other data, Skerlić concludes that Slav feeling among the Serbs at that time was so strong that 'in the first place they dreamed of a great "Slav empire", and only as a certain diminution of that ideal did they agree to "Dušan's empire".' (ibid., 143) Strong Slav feeling was one reason for resistance to Vuk Karadžić's linguistic reforms. For many Serbs of the time, the abandonment of the Russo-Slavonic language 'seemed like willing, planned alienation from Slavdom. Njegoš, whose play *Šćepan Mali* was printed in the new orthography in 1851 without his knowledge, said to Jovan Hadžić: "I am simply saying that the further we depart from Slavdom, the more we decline."' (ibid., 260)

In a poem, Jan Kollár imagined the Slavs, aroused and united, as a colossal statue of gold and silver, before which Europe would 'tremble'. The head of this statue would be the Russians, the Poles would be its breast, the Czechs its arms and the Serbs its legs. Skerlić found a translation of this poem in an issue of the magazine *Podunavka* of 1848:

> *Oh! If my spirit only had the strength*
> *To transform all Slavdom into gold,*
> *From that mass I would make such an image!*
> *From the Russians I would form the head,*
> *From the Poles I would mould the breast,*
> *From the Czechs the arms and shoulders,*
> *I would mould the Serbs into the legs,*
> *And the other branches of the Slavs,*
> *Lusatians, Wends and Slovaks,*
> *Would I form into weapons and clothing:*
> *And before this image of All-Slavdom*
> *The whole of Europe would have to kneel.*

This poem of Kollár's is of interest to us also because it reveals one of the oldest sources of the mythic concept of reproductive strength as a specific quality of the Serbian people. Together with the other Slavs, the Serbs are distinguished by their vital energy and resilience, freshness and naturalness, but in the Slav flock theirs is the role of guardian of the very essence of that vital force and freshness—

reproductive power, that is their male instruments and symbols. The shy Romantic Kollár and his anonymous translator give the ideally imagined Slavs only Serbian legs, but there is no doubt that this included also the main thing, lying between them.[1]

However, Skerlić's research shows that, from the time of its first well-known expression, in the middle of the nineteenth century, the myth of the Serbs as guardians of Pan-Slavdom and European potency and creativity has gone along with the complementary mythic assumption, also revived in our time, of the Serbs as an exceptionally old, if not the oldest, people in the world. Delighted with Štúr and Kollár's Panslav ideas, 'Slavicising' Serbian patriots 'see Slavs everywhere, in Northern Germany and Northern Italy, the Serbian people is for them the oldest Slav tribe, which gave rise to all the other tribes, between the Lusatian and the Balkan Serbs.' (*Serbian Youth,* 17). The thesis of the spread and age of the Slavs, and especially the Serbs, was backed up then, as now, with dubious etymological arguments. Thus Ljubomir P. Nenadović 'maintains that the word *Deutsch* comes from the Slavonic *tjutich,* '*ćutić*', German from Grmalj, while Neptune means a god who cannot drown [*potonuti*]'! (ibid., 145). These examples show that 'mythic logic' is not disturbed by contradictions, and that it is possible to attribute to the same characters (here, the Serbs) both the greatest vital freshness and the creative power associated with it and, at the same time, primeval age.

Tracing the destiny of Panslavism in Serbia in the 1850s and '60s, Skerlić notices that at that time people 'Slavicised more cautiously than in 1848, but still with conviction and constantly'. (ibid., 144) 'Like their parents', he wrote, 'the younger generation were convinced of the great cultural abilities of the Slavs, they too held that young and uncorrupted Slavdom was called to resurrect the "rotten West" and old "Gotho-German Europe".' (ibid., 145)

But the writer of *Serbian Youth* revealed that in Serbia in the 1860s the Slavophil conception of the differences and inevitable conflict between the languishing West and the life-giving Slavs was increasingly acquiring nationalistic colour, so that the remaining vitality of the world and the hope of its renewal was gradually becoming exclusively connected with the Serbs. And among the peoples from whom the

---

[1] The far less shy Danilo Kiš came across this old representation of the Serbs—as guardians and priests of the cult of fertility in contemporary Serbian literature and described it as 'elephantiasis nostras': 'Genitals are a national seal, a racial brand; other peoples have good fortune, tradition, erudition, history, *ratio*, but genitals are ours alone.' (Kiš, 58)

Serbs were seen, from this point of view, to be different and omnipotent were all the other Slav peoples. Skerlić finds the best evidence of this change in the writings of Vladimir Jovanović, lecturer at the High School in Belgrade. He too 'started from statements which should not be questioned, that the West showed all the signs of degeneracy and decay, that the Slavs represented the rested, fresh energies of humanity, its youth and hope.' According to Jovanović, 'of all the Slav peoples, the Russians have contributed most and the Serbs are those from whom most is expected.' In order that those expectations should be fulfilled, the 'rotten West' reborn and 'putrid humanity' saved, the Serbs—as Skerlić puts it, explaining Jovanović's ideas— 'must first of all be Serbs, as pure as possible, without any foreign admixture. Everything that is good in the Serbian people is there by nature, everything bad is "an alien spirit", "foreign influence".' And he quotes Jovanović's words that 'the only salvation for both the Serbian people and humanity lies in the greatest possible care of Serbian culture', and his division of Serbian society into two groups. In one were the 'parasites', 'those who represent foreignness and decay', who included not only the 'Parisians', 'Schwabians' and 'Tsarigraders' but also the 'Russomans', while the other group consisted of 'men of the people, useful, ideal—real Serbs [*Srbende*].' (ibid., 170)

Skerlić finds other examples of these 'voices of rebuke against the West and the conviction of the ideal purity of Serbian national qualities' constantly recurring 'in the writings and speeches of the Youth Movement'. (ibid., 171) Some other stereotypes of our contemporary political mythology may be recognised in these examples as well, which shows that it would be very worthwhile to look again, not only at Skerlić's work but also at the material he is examining. It would be interesting, for example, to research the traces of the prejudice about the special lack of resilience of the town and urban culture to the allegedly detrimental influences of the West, which Skerlić discovers in a story by the Bulgarian writer Ljuben Karavelov about the pathetic state of Belgrade, where the 'gentlemen's culture of Vienna has already begun to cut the wings of the old customs and rituals.' (ibid., 171)

Studying the 'national and literary romanticism of the Serbs', that is the history of political and literary ideas in Serbia between 1848 and 1871, Skerlić came across ideas about the conflict between the Latin and Germanic West and the Slav East, and between the West and Serbian popular culture. He followed them in their Pan-Slav nationalistic versions, but his work is particularly important because these ideas are considered and interpreted as parts of a complete picture, containing other elements as well. In the conclusion of a chapter devoted to 'Youth Movement ideas', he stresses their 'complexity'. This means that ideas about the West and the Slavs are not reduced to an image of unbridgeable antagonism. 'For all its "Slavonic" and nationalistic character, for all its fantasies about national culture and the "Serbian spirit",' writes Skerlić, 'the Youth Movement had something that connected it with the general liberal movement in Europe.' (ibid., 187)

In support of this observation, he quotes data about the influence of the European democratic and republican movement, particularly of the Italian and French republicans Mazzini and Garibaldi, Hugo, Gambetta and Laboulaye and the Spaniard Emilio Castelar, on the work and ideas of United Serbian Youth. Among those of its members who tried hardest to bring republican and democratic ideas closer to the Serbs was Vladimir Jovanović, the author of the theory of the damage of foreign influences on 'real Serbs', which Skerlić refers to as 'an interesting contradiction'. Jovanović himself tried to avoid this contradiction by separating 'Young Europe' from sick, 'rotten' Europe, saying that 'waves of that sea of injustice and vice in which old, demoralised Europe was drowning' were breaking on 'the healthy consciousness' of the Young. (ibid., 195)

In his monograph about Svetozar Marković, which came after *Serbian Youth* and *Srpska književnost u XVIII veku,* (Serbian literature in the eighteenth century), 1909, as the third part of his masterly panorama of Serbian political and literary history from the beginning of the eighteenth century to the 1880s, Skerlić devoted quite a lot of attention to the ideas of German and Russian socialists about the Slavs and the influence of these ideas on Svetozar Marković. He paid particular attention to 'the antipathy towards the Slavs' of some German socialists, particularly Engels and Lassalle, 'who proclaimed the Slavs a lower race, justified Turkish rule and hampered the liberation of the Serbian people'. (*Svetozar Marković,* 180)[2] But he

---

[2] In the same place, Skerlić also accused Marx of 'not caring for the Slavs at all', of 'defending the Hungarians against the Slavs', of discrediting the Slav movement of 1848. In Skerlić's opinion, it was only in an article in 1853 that Marx 'had tempered his Slavophobic chauvinism a little'. (*Svetozar Marković,* 175–6) However, in the same year that he published his monograph on Marković, 1910, the socialist magazine *Borba* published Marx's article 'What will become of Turkey-in-Europe?' with a commentary from the pen of N. Ryazanov. This inspired Skerlić to publish a piece in *Srpski književni glasnik* (Serbian Literary Herald) (1910, no. 8), entitled 'Karl Marx on the Serbs', a kind of indirect correction of his opinion of Marx as expressed in the

also stressed that individual Russian socialists had not let them down, especially Bakunin, who called Marx and his supporters in the 1872 International a 'German-Yid gang'. (ibid., 179)

In this matter, says Skerlić, Svetozar Marković 'followed the Russians'. There is no doubt that of all the Russian socialists the closest to him was Chernishevsky, whose writings he translated and popularised. He described Chernishevsky as 'opposed to the Slavophil conception of the liberation of Slavdom "under the shadow of the wing of the Russian eagle"' and believing that 'the liberation of the South Slavs did not mean the creation of Russian provinces in the Balkans'. (ibid., 184)

Skerlić's literary-historical monographs read today as exceptionally modern, thanks to the attention their author paid to picturesque details, descriptions of what is today called 'the spirit of the age' and its 'mentality', and to literary and journalistic 'second and third-rate works', more 'documents than monuments'. In them, Skerlić endeavoured above all to give as complete as possible an account of the development of ideas and the fate of individual political and literary movements in Serbia, to come as close as possible to them, as it were from the inside, to understand them as fully as possible. In the introduction to *Serbian Youth* he writes: 'Starting from the attitude of the French historian that "empathy is the soul of history", I endeavoured to stand on the same ground as these people, to enter into their souls and to live their inner lives.'

Skerlić shows far more critical and polemical zeal in his articles and critical reviews dedicated to political and literary events in the Serbia of his own time. Here he repeatedly mocks outmoded Panslav and Slavophil ideas. In one article he roundly rebukes Stjepan Radić for 'railing against *phoney German culture* and glorifying *Russia the Protector*, almost to the point of our hearing the banal refrains of the Moscow Slavophils and Belgrade reactionaries about the "rotten West".' 'Radić knows many things', Skerlić went on, 'but he forgets that the West is the source of light and the hub of life on the earth; that there are two paths for new peoples, either to accept Western culture, like the Japanese, and live, or to oppose it and be crushed, like the American Redskins and the Australian Blacks; that Slav culture

---

monograph on Marković. 'As in so many other aspects of his complex doctrine', wrote Skerlić, 'in this question too Marx has been misunderstood and popularised. The idea of Marx as hostile to the Southern Slavs does not correspond to the truth.' (in *Feljtoni, škice i govori*, 'Feuilletons, Sketches and Speeches' 254)

is an empty phrase, that German culture, the culture of Goethe, Hegel and Wierhof, should not be confused with the culture of semi-feudal and clerical Austria, and, finally, that the prospect of losing the Slav rivers in the Russian sea is not at all appealing, and if we are fighting it is not in order to change the yoke, but to achieve the full liberation of humanity, in the definitive victory of Democracy'. ('The Youth Congresses, 1904' in *Feuilletons,* 95)

Some years later, Skerlić again criticised 'romantic Panslavism' and condemned particularly fiercely the 'brutal and backward Slavophilism', which had 'gathered together only the dark elements of Russian society, for whom Orthodox and Slav nationalism was an excuse for the religious, political and national oppression of non-Russian, non-Orthodox and free-thinking elements in Russia itself'. But now he was doing it in order to welcome the phenomenon of a new, modern idea of Slav solidarity—'Neoslavism', which did not wish to count on hazy dreams about the past, which had put aside all thoughts of dominance over this or that faith, this or that tribe, but which had set itself the task of achieving the 'autonomy and federation of all the Slav tribes on an equal basis.' It is clear, nevertheless, that while Skerlić writes about Neoslavism he has before his eyes what was for him at that time a more urgent and important idea, the idea of Yugoslavism, because, he wrote in 1909, 'it is as clear as day that, as Neoslavism is for all Slavs, so Yugoslavism is for us South Slavs not only the most ideal and best but the only rational and only possible *national* policy.' ('Neoslavism and Yugoslavism' in *Feuilletons,* 233–7)

In both his historical and literary-historical monographs, and in his studies and polemical and critical articles, Skerlić tried to distinguish in the main ideas prevalent in Serbia in the eighteenth and nineteenth centuries and in the dominant political and literary ideas of his own age—what he called 'chimeras', 'illusions', 'fog', 'the cult of force', the 'clumsy idol of the fatherland', 'clericalism', 'prejudice, fetishism and intolerance', 'dogma', 'mouldy phrases', 'boiling enthusiasm', 'orgies of heated imagination', the 'mania of the past'—from well-founded, rational and sober contemporary ideas, or, in his favourite phrases, 'realistic and positive', 'healthy and progressive' thoughts, deeds and programmes. What Skerlić, writing about the poet Šantić, sought from renewed patriotic poetry, he expected also from modern Serbian society as a whole, that is that it must free itself of chimeras and illusions, from myths, as we would say today, and acquire 'a realistic base and positive content'. ('The Renewal of our Patriotic Poetry' in *Odabrani kritički spisi* [Selected critical writings], 380)

This programme had many weak points and critics have already highlighted some of them, above all Skerlić's intolerant, harsh and misguided judgment of some of the finest Serbian poets (Kostić, Dis, Pandurović). Both his 'positivism' and his 'realism' and his educational and rationalistic ideas belong to the past and many of them look today like mistakes and illusions which Skerlic shared with his age, with his teachers and models, and with his followers.

Nevertheless, we respond today to Skerlić's unshakeable determination, confirmed by his diligent work. We recognise his trust in the power of reason and faith in a better future for humanity, and particularly for the South Slavs and Balkan peoples. We see his choice of the example of the enlightener Dositej Obradović* and Svetozar Marković—for him the model of a 'man of action'—as familiar. Because these choices represent Skerlić's determination to fight against our numerous and omnipresent (ineradicable?) illusions and chimeras, including various traces of the old romantic, slavophil myth of 'rotten Europe'. All this strikes one today as something close, recognisable, acceptable, at least as a moral position, if not as a political programme.

2. Skerlić and Serbian Political Myths

Jovan Skerlić did not use the expressions 'political myths' or 'political mythology'. However, as he wrote about the political ideas of his time, tracing their origin and describing their history, he paid particular attention to concepts and beliefs which we could today call mythic. For example, ideas about the 'rotten West', about the Serbs as the freshest or the oldest people, about returning to the 'glorious past', about the 'natural' or morally superior life of the 'simple people', about the unstoppable progress of humanity led by reason and learning. Although he did not talk about political myths, Skerlić generally considered these concepts and beliefs as a kind of para-religious or pseudo-religious phenomenon, as is confirmed by his choice of terms to indicate them: 'religion', 'cult', 'idol', 'fetishism', 'Messianism', 'mysticism'.

Skerlić came across the majority of these phenomena as he studied Serbian political and literary history in the period between 1848 and 1871, which he described as a time of 'national and literary romanticism among the Serbs'. In his historical studies and in his literary-critical and political work he was concerned with political 'cults', 'idols', 'fetishes', which he called 'romantic'. In this way he identified their origin, the fact that they appeared in Serbian literature and political journalism under the influence of European romanticism, above all French and German romanticism, 'as a weak, sometimes almost distorted echo of the great movement in the West.' (*Serbian Youth*, 312)

In the abundant material about Serbian romanticism, which consists more of 'documents', that is 'second or third-rate works', rather than 'monuments' (ibid., xv), Skerlić was above all looking for constants, characteristics of the 'romantic spirit', or 'features of Serbian romanticism'.

In this way he confirmed that the political ideas and beliefs of Serbian romanticism amounted to no more than a few commonplaces. Skerlić described their repertoire as a series of cults, whose subjects, that is their idols, were Serbdom, Slavs, the simple people, the pure Serb, the historic past, oriental poetry, traditional poetry, the *gusle*, traditional customs, the fatherland, *hajduks**, Kosovo, Montenegro, Serbian culture and Vuk Karadžić. Contemporary researchers into collective ideas and beliefs must be impressed by Skerlić's simultaneous historical and typological account of these 'mythological constellations' as Gilbert Durand would call them.

All these individual cults spring from the central general cult—the cult of the people, the adoration of the nation, understood in the romantic sense of an ethnic community imbued with a unique and unchangeable 'spirit'. 'The love of the people has become the idol of the new generation', wrote Skerlić, 'the only god, before whose altar they burned incense and fell on their knees.' (ibid., 165)

In the nature of things, these cults also have a negative side, Serbian romantic idol-worship is inseparable from anathemisation of the enemy and those who defile the holy values embodied in the idols. As a result, it is possible to find in Skerlić also a repertoire of anti-idols of Serbian romanticism, that is objects of romantic anathema and hatred. This runs parallel to the repertoire of romantic idols, so that each of them is duplicated by its antithesis. Thus, for example, Serbdom is opposed by profiteering Europe, or, alternatively, by the 'Asian plague', the Slavs by the rotten West, fresh Serbian culture by putrid Western civilisation, popular customs by foreign ways, traditional poetry by artificial poetry, ancient glory by the poverty of the present, the healthy simple people by the estranged upper class, 'the true Serb' by the 'parasite', the mountain *hajduks* by urban merchants.

Skerlić found another series of political concepts and beliefs with a para-religious meaning in the writings of the Serbian realists and socialists of the 1870s, above all Svetozar Marković and his followers. This was a time of the 'renewal of rationalism and reaction to the earlier romanticism', on the basis of the 'unprecedented progress of the natural sciences'. (*Istorija nove srpske književnosti* [A history of new Serbian literature, hereafter *History*], 357) These were also the years when Russian students brought socialist ideas into Serbia. Using the methods he had applied in his analysis of Serbian romanticism, here too Skerlić revealed the phenomenon of a cult attitude towards renewed or newly instituted values.

Reason and science became the new idols, while socialism was the new religion. A wave of the adoration of reason arrived from Russia: 'All these people are rationalists, and they hold that all evil comes from the fact that reason is hampered and disparaged, that a person still does not know how or dare to think, that happiness will come to earth when all ideas and institutions are placed on a rational basis.' ('The "destruction of aesthetics" and the democratisation of art' in *Kritički radovi* [Critical Works], 62) The great new idol is science. It is the 'new faith, the redeemer of mankind'. (*Svetozar Marković*, 234) 'Mankind, which has waited for centuries for its salvation, has today acquired its liberating Messiah in science.' (ibid., 222) 'The works of Auguste Comte, Spencer, J. S. Mill, Darwin, Buckle are being translated and becoming a kind of gospel', while 'Buchner, Fogt, Meleschot and Feuerbach are becoming the deities of the "new science".' (*Serbian Youth*, 221–2)

Interpreting the socialistic ideas of Svetozar Marković, Skerlić observes that they do not contain any of the 'fetishism of the worker, which endures from the time of the Revolution of 1848' (*Svetozar Marković*, 127), but that they do reflect an idealised picture of the socialist as an 'apostle of the new society'. (ibid., 129) In order to show that Marković 'magnifies them lyrically as the saints of the new religion of humanity', as 'prophets of the new social religion', Skerlić quotes his words: 'Without them the earth would stagnate and stink. They are the "salt of the salt of the earth", as it is written in the Holy Bible of the Prophets.' (ibid., 129)

This repertoire of rationalistic and socialistic idols is also accompanied by a parallel repertoire of anti-idols. The new society of social justice is opposed to the 'hateful and humiliating past' (*History*, 352), sober realism to romantic elation, enlightenment to religious fanaticism, scientific history to national legends. The historian Ilarion Ruvarac used scientific methods to 'refute many deeply rooted and beloved traditions, legends about the eternal freedom of Montenegro, the death of Tsar Uroš*, the treachery of Vuk Branković at Kosovo, the authenticity of the Despot Djordje Branković-Hebski*.' (ibid., 358)

But the main opponent of the cult of the new science and new society is the Christian religion, which the Russian progressives about 1860 describe in the same words as those used before them by the Slavophiles of the West: 'an old worm-ridden building, which is still standing only because it has not occurred to anyone to lean on it.' (*Svetozar Marković*, 232) Under the influence of such ideas, Svetozar Marković concludes that faith is 'the same as superstition, except that it is superstition officially recognised.' (ibid., 233)

Skerlić takes a critical attitude to both series of mythic political ideas and beliefs, that is both to the romantic and to the rationalistic-positivistic cults. Largely because of that fundamentally critical attitude towards established traditional values, he was one of the most open representatives of Serbian modernism of the beginning of the twentieth century. However, his critical position oscillates considerably, depending on several factors.

First of all, it is striking that Skerlić takes issue far more often and with greater zeal with romantic, nationalistic myths than with positivist and socialist ones. This is quite understandable since he saw himself, above all, as continuing the enlightenment, rationalist and realist tradition in Serbian literature and politics, a follower of Dositej Obradović and Svetozar Marković. There is no doubt that for Skerlić the most difficult and dangerous errors and delusions of Serbia at the end of the eighteenth and beginning of the nineteenth century were those which he connected with the cults of romanticism, just as it is indisputable that he judged them in the main, although not exclusively, from the point of view of reason, science and progress.

From this point of view he explicitly condemns or describes in an ironic way myths about the patriarchal, natural and pure life of the people and its antithesis—rotten, distorted European civilisation. Skerlić is particularly caustic about echoes of these romantic myths in his own day. This is seen in several early articles, which lead one to assume that he later embarked on systematic research into the history of Serbian political and literary ideas above all in order to make the most successful and well-founded case against what were for him contemporary offshoots of some of these ideas.

'There are many people in our country', he wrote in 1902, 'who declaim against the "rotten West", and who talk with exaltation about some "Serbian" and "Slav" culture. They have taken from the "rotten West" their clothes, and habits, and institutions, and appetites, but not that which makes the West so great, in which it really is a great teacher: a sense of individual dignity, liberty, initiative, that serene, enterprising, sober spirit which has built all civilisation ... and for us there is only one cure: to open wide our doors to the West and its ideas, the West which thinks, which acts, which creates, which lives a full and intensive life, the only one worthy of being called human life.' ('Education abroad', *Feuilletons*, 66–7) Three years later, Skerlić was again moved to say that 'only limited people can repeat the old and stupid phrases about the "rotten West", "Slav" or "Serbian" culture.' (*Omladinski glasnik* [The Youth Herald], *Feuilletons*, 89)

Later, in his study of Svetozar Marković, Skerlić sees such 'limited people' among the ranks of the radicals, among the 'so-called "men of the people"'. 'The fate of Democracy in Serbia', he writes here, 'depends on uprooting that patriarchal conservatism and reactionary demagogy, which leads to all that is bad not only in radicalism but in the whole of our political life. And from this point of view, it is possible to say with complete justification: democracy in Serbia will either be European, or it will not be at all.' (*Svetozar Marković*, 264)

However, Skerlić is not always a consistent critic of romantic myths, nor is his criticism always consistently universalistic and rationalistic. Sometimes one finds unexpectedly in his writings political and literary stereotypes which he himself describes and rejects in other places as constructions of the romantic imagination. The fact that he spoke ironically several times, and in particularly great detail in *Serbian Youth*, about the 'cult of the simple people', 'the natural Serb', 'the true Serb', about the way the so-called life of the people is idealised and transformed into a subject of reactionary demagogy, about 'the conservatism of the unenlightened and primitive country people' (*Svetozar Marković*, 264) did not prevent Skerlić from sometimes himself enthusing about the natural, virginal virtues of the simple Serbian peasant.

In the character of Vuk Karadžić, for example, he stressed the 'natural acuteness and sharp wit of the Serbian peasant' (*History*, 272), and in another place he even attributes an almost superhuman dimension to that acuteness: 'The Serbian peasant is sharp, one could say gifted, and he often displays extraordinary kinds of intelligence.' ('Serbia, her Culture and her Literature', in *Critical Works*, 504) Skerlić defends the simple people, that is the 'herd' from Ljubomir Nedić's attack, with the argument: 'they are without spiritual selfishness, they have retained a freshness of feeling, they always have the precious capacity to be enthusiastic, their soul has remained virginal.' ('Dr Ljubomir Nedić', *Selected Critical Writings*, 90) In an article written in 1904, he expresses belief in the 'simple people who look on life soberly, with their own eyes, and not through books'. ('The Youth Movement Congresses', in *Feuilletons*, 93) Skerlić also values highly the qualities of the healthy men of the people described by Marko Miljanov, he is 'impressed by all these people with nerves like steel cables and a simple life of the soul which consists entirely of will and activity'. ('Marko Miljanov', *Selected Critical Writings*, 290)

Describing the revolutionary and liberational zeal of the 'generation of 1860', its 'patriotic impatience', Skerlić dwells on 'the cult of

Montenegro' and its antithesis 'hatred of the Turks'. He endeavours to understand 'those impulsive people ... the exaltation of national feeling', but at the same time lets it be known that he does not consider particularly valuable and effective 'that intoxication with words, that paroxysm of patriotism, that waking dream of freedom and Serbian unification'. (*Serbian Youth*, 185–6) He mentions the historical and contemporary causes of the 'hatred of the eternal enemy, "Mujo",* "the Asian plague", "Turkish beasts", and whatever else the Turks have been called' (ibid., 180), but he does not refrain from painting expressions of that hatred with ironic distance. 'Whatever black colours could be found,' writes Skerlić, 'they were used to paint the Turks, and there were no vices or crimes which were not attributed to them ... the Youth Movement poets were cannibalistically disposed towards the Turks'. (ibid., 181)

Skerlić opposes romantic idols and anti-idols, prayers and curses, loves and hatreds, by supporting a balanced and realistic judgment of the Serbs' several centuries of enslavement to the Turks and Serbo-Turkish relations in his time. This may be seen in his explanation of the very widespread 'cult of oriental poetry' among the Serbian romantic poets, so that our poets 'Turcophobes such as one can only imagine, paradoxically became rapturous devotees of Islamic poetry'. (*Serbian Youth*, 296)

However, Skerlić knows that the paradox is only apparent and that the success of oriental poetry and poems with oriental themes in Serbia has a cultural-historical basis. 'Several hundred years of enslavement to an oriental race', he explains, 'the immediate proximity of Muslim Turks, meant that oriental poetry was far closer and more comprehensible to the Serbs than to the Germans. The Bosnian *sevdalinke* poems, with their Arabic melodies and music, were the product of that encounter of Slavonic and oriental poetry.' In the same place he mentions, as a commonly known fact, the 'affection for the Bosnian "sevdalinke" which every Serb carries in his heart' (ibid., 299), and when he writes of the Serbian writer Borisav Stanković's play *Koštana,* he calls those Bosnian *sevdalinke* 'our popular songs'. (*Književne Studije* [Literary Studies], 106) In the Bosnian *sevdalinke* and in Stanković, there is, in Skerlić's opinion, 'something sensual, ardent, left over from the Turks' poetry 'intoxicating as an oriental aroma', 'intoxicating oriental poetry of the senses and flesh'. (ibid., 114)

But in Skerlić's writing, these oriental aromas can be transformed into a poisonous stench and foul odour. Talking of the Belgrade landscapes in Milan Rakić's poetry, he feels in their blurred and muddy greyness, in the melancholy emanating from them, the 'stench of the miserable East'. (*Selected Critical Writings*, 393) In his desire to bring as close as possible to Serbian youth the cultural and political models of West European democracy, he sometimes speaks, particularly in his shorter journalistic pieces, with the greatest contempt, almost in the style of romantic 'hatred of the Turks', of the features of the oriental mentality in the character of the Serbs. 'Four centuries of enslavement to a fatalistic and barbarian race'—he writes in 1902, in an article 'Education Abroad'—'have not passed without leaving any trace on us. Orientalism has entered our blood, like a kind of poison ... and that festering, drowsy, repulsive East is still constantly around us and within us ... We are stifled by that passive, stagnant, oriental spirit, and for us there is only one cure: to open wide the doors to the West and its ideas ...' (*Feuilletons*, 67) Skerlić repeats this condemnation of 'orientalism' in his articles 'Popular Libraries', 1906, 'Personal and National Initiative', 1910, and 'Bright days', 1912.

Skerlić's attitude towards the romantic cult of the *hajduk* is also ambivalent. He maintains that the source of this cult, like the cult of traditional literature and the cult of oriental poetry, is West European and literary. He mocks the poet Djura Jakšić for painting in his story 'The Russian Woman' the portrait of a *hajduk* 'at the very end of a prosaic century, in the still more prosaic little provincial town of Belgrade ... with a flat near the "Balkan" Hotel'. (*Serbian Youth*, 318) In another place, he sees in the 'atavistic instincts' of shepherds and *hajduks*, who still live in 'great rural masses', a brake to the progress of Serbian society and obstacle to the organisation of a modern Serbian state. (*Svetozar Marković*, 264)

By contrast, in Skerlić's characterisation of the figure of Ante Starčević*, those same 'atavistic features which he inherited from generations of his *hajduk* and *uskok** forebears' are judged differently. Here they are used to support the opinion that the father of Croatian nationalism and 'embittered Serbophobe', the author of a book entitled *Pasmina Slavoserbska u Hervatskoj* (Slavo-Serbian Stock in Croatia) is in fact 'one of us, with all the faults and virtues of our race'. Although these are the 'characteristics of our race in its primitive state', and although they consist, above all of 'untamed energy, a rebellious spirit, impulsiveness, stubbornness, haste, ardour, malice', Skerlić writes about them with a kind of warmth and affection, even with romantic overtones. In his judgment, Starčević 'retained the strong soul of his forebears'; he is the 'descendant of the old *uskoks* ... he sprang from the hard ground of this blood-spattered Krajina' . (*Eseji o srpsko-hrvatskom pitanju*

[Essays on the Serbo-Croatian question], 63) Delighted with the victories of the Serbian army in 1912, he described the strength of the Serbian soldier, countryman and townsman as 'the old dormant *hajduk* spirit of our forebears coming to life on the battlefield'. ('Bright Days' in *Feuilletons,* 278)

These and other examples of oscillation in Skerlić's attitude to some of the *topoi* of Serbian political myths, and particularly to the 'romantic cults', may be partly explained by the differences between the research method he applied in his literary-historical monographs and studies and the interpretative procedure he used in his critical articles and essays. There is no doubt that he was aware of these differences and that in this respect he followed the recommendation of his teacher Georges Renan, who asked that the historian be as objective as possible, but encouraged critics to be subjective. ('Georges Renan's scholarly method of literary history' in *Kritički radovi* ['Critical works'], 600–1) However, Skerlić did not understand objectivity as taking a neutral, distanced stance towards the subject of his research, but, on the contrary, as the endeavour to see things from the point of view of the actors of history, to 'stand on those people's ground'. (*Serbian Youth,* xv)

In addition, an explanation of such inconsistencies in Skerlić's attitude towards Serbian political myths may be sought in the fact that he took from French moralists a dynamic model of morally correct and socially valuable intellectual commitment, in which the imperatives of strict critical thinking are reconciled with the demands of human tolerance and solidarity. Skerlić wrote about this model in his study of Chamfor, the French moralist of the eighteenth century, in whom he saw the forerunner of an 'intellectualism' that was close to him and whose basic ethical stance was expressed by Lamartine: 'In thinking, one should separate oneself from the mass; in action, one must join with it.' In support of this attitude, Skerlić quotes the words of two lesser known French thinkers, E. Thiaudière, who wanted one 'to think like a sceptic, but to act like a believer', and B. Malon, who thought that 'the greatest wisdom of this age consists in a man thinking as a pessimist ... but acting as an optimist.' ('Chamfor' in *Critical Works,* 592, 598) This may explain Skerlić's readiness in some texts and some moments to forget his ironic, distanced attitude to romantic national myths and passions, and, reconciling himself with his opponents and merging with the 'mass', to participate in the loves and hates of the national collective, in their hopes and disappointments.

Nevertheless, the explanation of the inconsistency and oscillation in Skerlić's attitude to literary and political myths must, above all, be sought in the ambivalence at the heart of his critical position and his project of a modern Serbian literature, and, altogether, a modern Serbian society. It is difficult to connect his main literary-critical and socio-political ideas into a coherent whole, but nevertheless one may carry out a rough division into two groups. One would consist of ideas of rationalistic, positivist and universal provenance (reason, realism, progress, science, man), and the other of elements of relativist and vitalist notions (national energy, the 'race', health, will, work).

In keeping with this, it is possible to find in Skerlić elements of two models of the criticism of political myths. One is based on the identification and demystification in Serbian literature and politics of irrational and unrealistic ideas, concepts and beliefs unsustainable from the point of view of modern education and the criteria of universal values. The critic confronts the remnants of romantic delusions and the conservatism of his outdated environment, deeply convinced that the time has come for science to become 'both the school and the tool of justice', when it would 'completely liberate people, not only from material chains, enslavement and poverty, but also from their passions, that is from ignorance'. ('Political and Social Problems at the End of the 19th century', *Feuilletons*, 52) Education based on reason and science had the task of preparing the citizens for a genuinely democratic society, for—Skerlić wrote in a review of Gabriel Seaj's book *Education and Revolution*—'there is no true and pure popular rule, if the people do not have enough sense to lead themselves: Democracy would betray itself if it were to wash its hands of the education of the people.' (*Feuilletons*, 125)

Reason and culture are universal values and in several places Skerlić takes a stand against the romantic idea of a special 'Serbian culture, whose content no one ever defined or explained' (*History*, 101), against 'a naïve belief in Serbian culture' ('The Renewal of our Patriotic Poetry', *Critical Works*, 488), or against the 'theory of Serbian culture' or 'Serbian popular culture'. (*Serbian Youth*, 167, 169, 171)

That myth about Serbian culture and the fear connected with it of foreign cultural influences acquired comic dimensions in the 1860s, at least with some romantic poets. In support of this idea, Skerlić quotes the prologue written by Laza Kostić for a production of 'King Richard' (*sic*) given at the celebration of the 300th anniversary of Shakespeare's birth in Novi Sad. Here Kostić praised Shakespeare, or rather 'Willy', but he also gave him a warning. 'In an address', writes Skerlić, 'he invites him to make no mistake about the significance of this celebration. The Serb wants "heavenly treasure", he wants to revel in his immeasurable poetic beauty, but "Willy" will be much mistaken if he thinks that, greedy for his treasure, the Serbs will betray "the dear name of Serb", and "so much of Dušan's spilled blood" will glisten in the foreign land of England:

> *If you think thus, then we regret it:*
> *Be patient until Judgment Day!*
> *If you do not—then become a Serb!'*

In another model of Skerlić's criticism of Serbian political myths, they are not called into question or condemned for their divergence from reason and positive reality, or because they betray some universal values, but because they are outmoded, surpassed, 'fetid', lifeless, because these 'cults' hamper the flowering of national energy, stifle the will of the people to affirm itself and develop, lulling them with stories about the glorious past and holy traditions. In Skerlić's opinion, one of the main mistakes of the generation of the Romantics was that 'their patriotism was too historical and archaeological; it built a building of the future on the graves of the past ...' It is true that he opposes to this 'real, immediate and material needs', but these needs are transformed in the same place into the not exactly pragmatic necessity to speak 'strong words of life, initiative, energy, faith in the future, manly impulse to work, such as those which the clever Hungarian reformer Istvan Szeczenyi spoke to his fellow-countrymen: "Let us not dream about the past; let us work for the future ... There was no Hungary, Hungary is yet to be!"' (*Serbian Youth,* 160)

In this vitalist and activist model of Skerlić's criticism of political myths, he criticises the act of bowing before 'an idol of nationality', 'patriotic mysticism', and 'national messianism', which places the Serbs—or, in Starčević's eyes, the Croats—in the role of a chosen people, the saviours of humanity, not so much from the point of view of reason and enlightenment but more in the name of renewal and strengthening of national vitality. It is because of outmoded romantic myths that 'the great reservoir of strength and energy which is called the people', or 'the great river of national energy, a river which no dams can hold back', remains unused. (*Feuilletons,* 124, 272) Skerlić contrasts romantic dreamers, lovers of the legendary past, the sleeping East, the *gusle* and traditional poetry and the 'false modernists' and pessimists in Serbian poetry to the example of Njegoš, 'a poet of national energy and strength' (*History,* 186–7), and that of Marko

Miljanov, and his 'rare book, full of life and health, both physical and moral, in an age of insipid aridity.' (*Selected Critical Writings*, 290) Seeing Aleksa Šantić and Veljko Petrović as the rejuvenators of Serbian patriotic poetry, he expresses particular satisfaction that they introduce 'spiritual and emotional health, sincerity and life'. ('The Renewal of our Patriotic Poetry', *Critical Works*, 489)

For the criticism of romantic concepts of Serbdom, the nation and national, ('Serbian') culture, the most important thing is not that these concepts are out of step with universalistic premises of European democracy and modern civilisation but that they give an inadequate and dispiriting image of national physical and intellectual potential and prevent their full exploitation. Skerlić mocks the 'exalted chauvinism' of the writer Jakov Ignjatović and quotes places where he gets carried away, among them this judgment of Ignjatović's about Serbian blood: 'If a physiologist were to analyse the blood of a Serb, and of someone who eats more cabbage and spinach, he would probably find that Serbian blood is at least two thirds heavier and keener, and so the blood of, for instance, five million Serbs, would outweigh that of some other fifteen million.' (*Jakov Ignjatović*, 65) But, judging by those places where Skerlić speaks about the Serbian, South-West, Serbo-Croatian or Slavonic 'race',[1] about the 'national soul', the 'popular' or 'national character', even about 'the healthy blood of the people' (*Critical Works*, 504), one can conclude that he rejects exaggerated, comical chauvinism, such as Ignjatović's, mostly because it confuses the idea of the true virtues characteristic of the Serbian, or the Serbo-Croatian, nation.

Although he knew that 'nothing is more difficult than to determine a national character and how sceptical one had to be towards that science invented by the Germans, ethnopsychology, *Völkerspsychologie*' (*Feuilletons*, 214), nevertheless, on many occasions, Skerlić wrote about the virtues and shortcomings of 'our race' and valued highly those writers who were able to affirm the specific values of the national climate and spirit. Thus he stressed as Njegoš's greatest service the

---

[1] In keeping with his age, Skerlić accepts the idea of 'race' as more a cultural than biological entity. It is true, as M. Begić says, in the introduction to Skerlić's *Selected Critical Writings*, 'that Skerlić's concept of race does not at all have the character given it by racism.' Skerlić himself wrote that 'today in scholarship the theory of race is worth little.' (Begić, 59) His appeal to the 'race' may be connected with Renan and Taine's 'racialist' (Tsvetan Todorov's term) concepts, according to which the human 'races' differ on the basis of cultural and linguistic criteria, because of which, in Todorov's opinion, it would be better to call such concepts 'culturalism.' (Todorov, 156)

fact that the poet of *The Mountain Wreath* 'gave expression to the whole Serbian race ... characteristics of the Serbian national spirit ... the soul of the people'. (*History,* 186–7) In his opinion, Šantić was preordained to renew Serbian patriotic poetry, because he was Herzegovinian, 'born in that proud region where the well-spring of our entire people lies, in that land of stalwart men and powerful emotions, where our finest traditional songs were born, in that region which was the seedbed of our whole race ...' (*Critical Works,* 482) Ante Starčević could also be considered 'one of us', because he had the 'characteristics of our race', albeit 'in a primitive state'. (Essays on the Serb-Croatian Question, 63)

Sometimes Skerlić goes in for lists of the virtues and shortcomings of 'our race'. His judgment in some texts is very severe. In one article, he says with disappointment: 'We are a feeble, delicate, fatalistic race.' ('Before the Work Begins ...', *Feuilletons,* 85) Our 'South-West race' has other faults as well: an individualistic spirit, lack of discipline, lack of socialisation, unpolished wildness, and 'there is something destructive and anarchic in the Serbian character.' ('Serbia, her Culture and her Literature', *Critical Works,* 504)[2]

Nevertheless, Skerlić's judgment of 'our race' is as a whole positive, for 'that bold and rebellious race, created by a kind of revolutionary selection, has some very good qualities', and what is more 'the robust Serbian race has some rare qualities'. Most importantly, 'positive qualities make up the essence of the national character and do not change, while these negative qualities, which are in fundamental and irreconcilable disharmony with modern life, with the social spirit of our time and contemporary society, are visibly and progressively weakening and disappearing.' (ibid., 503–5)

It is important to note that the faults of 'our race' mentioned here in fact amount to elements of cultural and economic backwardness, to 'atavisms' with which education in a contemporary democratic and European spirit will easily deal. Faults of the national character understood in this way match the choice of its virtues that Skerlić places in the foreground. Although they are the product of relative and 'ethno-psychological' factors, there is no doubt that they are in perfect harmony with the universal demands of the modern age, as Skerlić understands it. Among the Serbian national virtues, pride of place goes to 'the healthy common sense of the people' (*Feuilletons,* 93), that is intelligence, or various qualities connected with it. 'The Serbian peasant is acute', says Skerlić, 'almost gifted, and he manifests a remarkable intelligence. Hence there is in the Serbian race and in Serbian literature so much sobriety, intelligent innovation, breadth of vision, liberalism of ideas, sharp wit and correct judgment, so much reasonable criticism and fruitful positivism.' (*Critical Works*, 504) Along with acuteness go the qualities 'of those cheerful, zealous and ambitious people in Šumadija, who are the salt of the salt of our earth.' (*Feuilletons*, 175)

These examples lead us to the conclusion that Skerlić sought doubly based arguments for his critique of political myths and for his political and literary project. On the one hand, he referred to those values, and options which he recognised as the fundamental levers of modern European democracy and which he wanted to introduce, and affirm in his own country. On the other hand, he sought a foundation for those modern European values and options in 'our', 'home-grown' qualities—in the national character of the Serbs. That is why for Skerlić 'untraditionalism', 'broad horizons' and 'rational criticism' had to be both the values of the new civic, liberal and democratic Europe and characteristics of the 'Serbian race'. In this way they were not simply elements of a foreign, Western ideology, which Skerlić and 'Parisians' like him sought to transplant onto the soil of national history and culture, but virtues already deeply rooted in that soil. They were thus naturalised and legitimised as something simultaneously universal and particular, European and local. In addition, they became psychologically and sociologically necessary and not theoretical voluntarism.

The oscillations in Skerlić's critical position and the ambivalence of his political and cultural project may then be interpreted, above all, as the consequence of his endeavour to connect and reconcile several contradictory ideas. The contradiction lay in two fundamentally exclusive criteria: universal or relative, rational or irrational. The two models of his criticism of political mythology have been constructed and described here separately, but in fact in Skerlić's work there is only one complex model. Its components give rise to friction, sometimes more and sometimes less. In this model, criticism of Serbian political myths is connected with their reconstruction: Skerlić destroys them, but at the same time renews them on new, firmer foundations.

This too makes Jovan Skerlić a representative of European modernism. The oscillations and ambivalence in his critical position have their main and deepest source in a dualism which characterises the development of the modern age from the beginning of the nineteenth century, a dualism whose classic formulation was given by Ferdinand Tenies, when he described it as an opposition between society (*Gesellschaft*) and community (*Gemeinschaft*). 'To speak about the modern age,' writes the contemporary French sociologist Michel Wieviorka, 'means to accept the principle of duality of reference, and to accept the existence of tensions that simultaneously link and mutually oppose, on the one hand, progress and reason, and, on the other, the subjectivity of culture, nation and identities.' (Wieviorka, 10) Like other thinkers of the modern age, Skerlić also endeavoured to present a modern project of society, based on the aims of enlightenment and republicanism, as a collective ordered according to the international laws of reason and progress, as something resulting from the nature of the community, that is to say from the collective marked by a specific ethnic identity.

3. Town and Country in the Work of Tihomir Djordjević

Differentiating between the town and the country is one of the basic methodological postulates used by Tihomir Djordjević in both his ethnographic writings and his research into the social and cultural history of the Serbs and other Balkan peoples. Starting from that fundamental distinction, he endeavoured to create a comparative and contrastive picture of the qualities and values of life in rural and urban settings at various times of Balkan and Serbian history and, in addition, to establish the nature of relations between those two environments in the past and in more recent times.

The greater part of Djordjević's comparative study of town and country refers to conditions in Serbia immediately before and during the first period of Miloš Obrenović's rule (1815–39). This was the focus of his major two-volume work *Iz Srbije Kneza Miloša*, I : *Kulturne prilike*, 1922, and II: *Stanovništvo—naselja, 1924* (The Serbia of Prince Miloš, I : Cultural Conditions, and II: Population and Settlements). In addition, in several places, Djordjević considered briefly the period of the arrival of the South Slavs in the Balkans and, among them, the Serbs (between the seventh and ninth centuries), examining their settlement in the towns that then existed in the Balkans and also, briefly, the relations between the urban and provincial population during Turkish rule in the Balkans. Finally, the town-country distinction appears in Djordjević's texts dealing with the state and tasks of research into national culture in his own time, that is during the early decades of the twentieth century.

Djordjević finds manifestations of the difference between the town and country in several important areas of social and cultural life. In his opinion, they are not only two kinds of settlement, but two kinds of social community. The last chapters of the second volume of his study of Prince Miloš's rule are devoted to a comparative analysis of the village and the town as social communities in Serbia in the time before the uprisings against the Turks. At that time, writes Djordjević, 'the village and the town were two quite different social communities', and that difference is threefold: 'in occupation, in organisation and in the origin of the population.' (*The Serbia of Prince Miloš*, 305)

The main urban occupations—commerce and trades—were barely known in the villages. What is more, if there were trades in the village, they differed from those in the town. Djordjević's article 'Our Village Trades' begins with the sentence: 'Ever since anything was known about our people's involvement in trade, there has been a clear difference between urban and rural trades.' (*Naš narodni život* [*Our national life*], I, 38) When he considers the differences that appear on the level of organisation, Djordjević means that the towns, which were entirely in the hands of the Turkish authorities, were unfamiliar with the kind of autonomy enjoyed by the Serbian peasants thanks to the 'territorial self-administering totality' known as the '*knežina*'. (*Serbia*, 220) Finally, he particularly stresses the fact that there were few Serbs in the towns, as they were inhabited predominantly by Turks, or, in any case, by people of foreign origin (Greeks, Tsintsars, Armenians), while the villages were populated almost exclusively by Serbs. (ibid., 304)

The existence of a long-established and enduring difference between town and country is the reason why, in Djordjević's interpretation, two types of culture and two types of art came into being on the territory of the Balkans and among the South Slavs, particularly the Serbs. This is how he explains, in his article 'Our Popular Art', that from the time of the formation of the first South Slav states, between the seventh and the ninth centuries, 'all the culture, and therefore also the art, of the South Slavs falls into two main types, which are still today clearly discernible, and those are the *urban* and the *rural* type.' (*Our national life*, I, 54)

In Djordjević's opinion, the most important aspect of the manifestation of the difference between town and country is the loss of national individuality and the lack of interest in its preservation among the Serbian urban population, especially in towns under Turkish administration. By contrast, he identifies a high degree of preservation of the national character and heritage of national culture in the Serbian villages and a developed consciousness of the importance of preserving those values. At the time of the uprising against the Turks in

1804, there was in the towns, alongside the Turks and other foreigners, 'also a Serbian, alienated, population', while the rural population was 'beyond the influence of the towns ... with an undisturbed national consciousness'. (*ONL*, III, 177) That rural population, he says in another place, 'preserved its full individuality, its undisturbed old historical consciousness, its national feeling.' (*Serbia*, 302)

Djordjević suggests two reasons for the 'estrangement' of the urban population under Turkish rule. The first is the fact that in the towns 'the Turks had a privileged position and sometimes Serbs converted to Islam and called themselves Turks.' (ibid.) The other was the fact that the Serbs in the towns became members of an inter-ethnic and super-ethnic community. 'There were few Serbs in the towns, in some none at all', writes Djordjević, 'and the few that there were adapted to the urban occupations, urban organisation and foreign nationalities with whom they lived, so that they felt that they formed a community with them. They all lived from the same occupations: commerce and trades; they all lived under one organisation, the "*čaršija* order", as it was called, which, preserved by tradition, was passed down the generations; they all submitted to one urban administration; they all had houses in one style and clothing of one cut; they all felt like urban dwellers and were all equally proud of their urban nature.' (ibid., 304–5)

The preservation of national individuality among the Serbs in the countryside and the 'estrangement' of those in the towns resulted in an unequal degree of vitality of the Serbian rural and urban population, particularly under Turkish rule. In fact, according to Djordjević, it was only in the countryside that 'the life force of the people' (ibid., 301) was preserved, it was only there that one could still find 'the fresh and wholesome national spirit', 'the sharp spirit', 'the fresh and vital spirit of our people', 'the healthy rootstock of our national tree trunk'. (ibid., 302)

Djordjević devoted a great deal of attention to the description and interpretation of the different relations that were manifested in the framework of the country–town contrast in the periods of Balkan and Serbian history with which he was concerned. The weakest links between town and country in Serbia were, in his opinion, in the times preceding the Serbian uprisings against the Turks. Then they were mutually *isolated*, like 'two separate societies, two separate worlds' (ibid., 304), and 'the only connection between the town and village was the Muselim from the *nahija* centre, who was a kind of supervisory authority over the *knez* ...' (ibid., 227)

The same period is characterised by *antagonism* between the townspeople and villagers. Drawing on Vuk Karadžić and Jovan Cvijić, Djordjević expresses the opinion that there was between the inhabitants of the towns and the villages 'as almost everywhere in the Balkan Peninsula, a strong antagonism'. 'Urban dwellers', he continues, 'considered villagers uncouth, low, while the villagers saw the townspeople as parasites, renegades and degenerates.' (ibid., 305) That antagonism, according to Djordjević, was motivated not by social, but by national reasons. During the uprisings against the Turks, the Serbian people from the villages attacked the towns because they were the embodiment of foreign authority and foreign culture: 'Thus they rose precisely against the towns, against their Turkish administration and their oriental character, captured them and settled in them *en masse*.' (ibid., 302)

In several places in his writing, Djordjević returns to a far older period, to the time when the South Slavs, including the Serbs, arrived in the Balkans and first came across towns, capturing them and settling in them. This first encounter of the South Slav and Serbian population with towns led to that population accepting the model of life and values of the old Balkan urban culture. However, in one place Djordjević describes that process of urbanisation as *assimilation* and in another as *adaptation*.

In the first case, he is discussing those Serbs who, having accepted urban culture, neglected the characteristics and values of their national character and lost contact with the people in the country. 'The new Serbian population', writes Djordjević in the chapter of his *The Serbia of Knez Miloš* devoted to the town as a social community, 'having settled in the towns, entered into them as it were into new moulds, to which they had to adapt. With time they did adapt, and they themselves became true urban-dwellers, preserving a heritage of urban tradition and living under an inherited urban administration, which, of course, differed fundamentally from the national administration in the villages.' (ibid., 303)

By contrast, in 'Our Popular Art' Djordjević maintains that the new Slav arrivals in the old Balkan towns simultaneously accepted 'the role of bearers and guardians of the old urban culture and art'. But the South Slavs did not accept this cultural and artistic tradition passively, rather they 'adapted it to their spirit and needs, developing it and advancing it according to their abilities.' (*Our national life,* I, 57)

Accepting here the possibility that the heritage of urban culture should be adapted to specific ethnic or national requirements, Djordjević arrived at the model of a *complementary* relationship between town and village, between urban and rural culture, between urban and rural art. Both could have a national character and in that sense be 'of the people'. The concept 'our national art' includes the two types, urban and rural. In the course of history, both types of Serbian national art developed under the influence of 'foreign art', but they retained their specific character. 'The South Slavs', writes Djordjević at the end of this study, 'brought their own spirit and their own taste into everything that they borrowed from other peoples, they gave it their own forms, their own proportions and their own arrangement of colour, they reworked it in their own way and imprinted their own character onto it, so that Yugoslav national art is distinguished as something independent, typically and specifically Yugoslav.' (ibid.)

After the withdrawal of the Turks, some urban centres in Serbia, such as Ražanj, Batočina, Bagrdan, Tekija, Rudnik and Brza Palanka, lost their urban character and became *ruralised*. As Djordjević puts it, 'as villagers settled in them, they became villages.' At the same time, other towns became provincial towns, which 'represented a kind of middle ground between town and village. The villagers in them only gradually became townspeople, and for a long time they could not reach the point of continuing fully the old urban economic production and traditions, which had been interrupted with the departure of the Turks. Loznica is a good example of this process.' (*Serbia*, 301)

Nevertheless, the most important political, economic and cultural changes that took place in Serbia during the first rule of Miloš Obrenović were connected with the rapid development of towns and the urban way of life. The towns were the centres of Serbia's renewal. 'Without going into details', writes Djordjević, 'I shall say at once that the strongest upsurge was felt in our towns.' (*Our national life*, III, 186) 'In their rapid rise, our towns became the most progressive places in our country. It was in them that the first seeds of the economic and cultural advance of Serbia were sown and where they flourished, and those are the facts which gave rise to the whole vitality not only of Serbia, but a spiritual and national refreshing and reinvigorating of our whole people beyond her borders as well.' (*Serbia*, 301)

Djordjević sees that his survey of the restorative role of the Serbian towns is surprising, in view of the fact that, in his often repeated judgment, the sources of national consciousness and national energy were to be found exclusively in the villages. He himself posed the question as to where the towns found the energy to carry out the renewal of Serbian society: 'How was it that our town had this honour?' The answer is simple: 'That energy did not come from them, but from our villages.' (*Serbia*, 302) By this Djordjević means the influx of Serbian rural dwellers into the towns, but, above all, of the ability of that population to retain its national character even in the conditions of urban life, and to adapt to it the modern urban culture which was brought into the revived Serbian towns by Serbs who settled in them from Austrian and other European towns.

Here Djordjević returns to the same model of the town-country relationship, which he used, in 'Our National Art', to describe the conditions in which the South Slavs lived in the medieval Balkan towns, adapting to their needs and to their national character the heritage of urban culture that they found in them. Now this model of adaptation is described in more detail and presented more eloquently. The new population, which came from the countryside, gave the Serbian towns 'the strength to accept what was progressive, to rework it and nationalise it.' (*Serbia*, 301)

'Here, in the towns', writes Djordjević, 'the Serbian villagers became that healthy rootstock of our national tree, onto which the new and the useful has been grafted through doors open to Europe. Those grafts have continued to grow and they have become ours. Here in the towns, we see a mingling of town shoes and peasant shoes, sheepskins and overcoats, the fez and the town hat, a sharp mind and schooling, the *gusle* and the piano, traditional song and written history, the yokel and the merchant, our local produce and the European trader, Serbia and Europe. Here the fresh and vital spirit of our people accepted the grafts, coloured them with its own national colour and gave them its national character. From there, from the towns, they were carried ever further and deeper among the mass of the people. This encounter of our urbanised villagers with high culture, its Serbianisation and its continued role is a great event and an interesting problem of our recent history.' (*Serbia*, 302)

By means of this extended model of the adaptation of urban culture to national needs—that is, its Serbianisation—Djordjević is apparently trying to reconcile two contradictory demands: the demand that forms of modern urban culture should be accepted and that, at the same time, the main values which he attributes to traditional village culture should be preserved: ethnic, i.e. national individuality and vitality. However, in the solution which he proposes, urban culture is in the background, while his basic, almost his only preoccupation is the endeavour to salvage the values of village culture even in conditions of urban life, and particularly from the perspective of the gradual but certain disappearance of the traditional village and its culture.

It cannot be said that Djordjević does not attribute significance or devote attention to the various legacies and achievements of European culture which, after 1815, began to alter the appearance of Serbian towns and the quality of life in them. He describes in detail the growth of the towns, their organisation according to European standards, the development of commerce and trades, education and health, the appearance of the European urban style of life. However, in Djordjević's model of the new Serbianised urban culture, European urban culture appears as its non-essential, formal, organisational or technical, even material aspect. What he sees as essential, as he puts it—its 'being', 'character', 'spirit'—comes from the village and retains the quality it had in the village, when it enters the new culture developing in the Serbian towns after the Second Serbian Uprising, that is the culture of the urbanised Serbs.

In fact, although he offers solutions for reconciling urban and rural contradictions, traditional and modern culture, Djordjević does not abandon the mythic idea of the fundamental and fatal antagonism of the two cultures. He accepts the fact that in this clash of cultures, the modern culture is stronger, even that it represents a higher level of culture. That is why he speaks with understanding of the endeavours of the Montenegrin rulers and tribal chieftains during the eighteenth and nineteenth centuries, and of Karadjordje and Prince Miloš, to repress and eradicate many popular customs. 'Time itself has diluted and weakened them', writes Djordjević about popular customs in Serbia and Montenegro since the liberation from the Turks, 'but there were nevertheless so many that were sufficiently and so well maintained that very serious measures were taken against some of them.' Djordjević mentions particularly the directives of Karadjordje and Prince Miloš 'against the abduction of women and girls, informal social administration, village punishments, revenge, the disinterment of vampires, the persecution of witches and so on.' (*Our national life*, I, 32)

Similarly, he sympathises with the authorities in Austria who prohibited the 'primitive and superstitious customs of our people' and with the Serbs living there who 'had access to high culture, and also raised their voices against national customs, particularly those which were damaging.' (ibid., 31) Djordjević even agrees with the opinion that the struggle for culture implies the repression of customs which comprise the essence of the traditional national culture in the countryside. 'A great part of the hard cultural work of humanity is used in the struggle against customs which have acquired deep roots in all their manifestations', he writes in 1909 in the introduction to volume 14 of *Srpski etnografski zbornik* (Serbian Ethnographic Papers), which contains a study by Savatije M. Grbić, 'Serbian National Customs from Srez Boljevački'.

Nevertheless, Djordjević's sympathies are undoubtedly on the side of traditional national culture, on the side of folklore and customs, on the side of what he called 'our national life'. He sees national culture as the victim of an undesirable, but inevitable trend. Traditional rural Serbia was not hurrying to meet modern culture, it was not interested in it, but that culture was 'constantly encroaching on us'. (*Our national life*, IV, 8). Still worse, national culture was being overcome and squeezed out by 'foreign, alien culture, which was encroaching on it'. (ibid.) In his article 'Our National Costume', Djordjević notes with regret that in his lifetime national costume was rapidly going out of use. 'The rapid advance of modern culture is burning it up like a flame.' (ibid., 63)

Reconciled to the inevitable repression of various forms of national culture, as something which was 'quite natural and against which it was impossible to fight' (ibid.), Djordjević asked only that this culture should at least be saved from oblivion, that specialist scholarly and cultural institutions should be concerned with collecting, preserving and studying it. For instance, he asked that people should not permit 'our national costume to die out before all its best examples, from all our regions, were placed in ethnographic museums and before every aspect of all of them had been carefully described and sketched.' (ibid.)

However, the study 'On Serbian Folklore' shows that, in Djordjević's opinion, scholarly concern with traditional culture has exceptionally important, indeed primary social and national functions. Being involved with folklore was a way of doing 'a service to one's people'. We were obliged to study folklore by 'the contemporary needs of scholarship', but also by 'our national aspirations'; it was essential 'if we wish to be ourselves'. In other words, he placed the study of folklore in the service of preserving, or building the national identity.

Here Djordjević distinguishes the ethical, educational, political and aesthetic significance of folklore. 'Folkore is good for instilling in the young soul a childlike love of the fatherland, God, birthplace, charity, etc.' (ibid., IV, 19) 'Our folklore has also a POLITICAL SIGNIFICANCE for us', he continues, 'because it is a powerful means of determining national borders. It has enabled the national concept to draw itself a national boundary. We do not know what an identical thing expressed in the same language and in the same way from the Adriatic Sea to the Balkan mountains and from the White Sea to Budapest could signify, if not that it is a product of the spirit and aspirations of one people.' (ibid.)

The task of folklore research is the renewal of music and literature in the Serbian national spirit. Traditional music is the 'basis on which the melody to which the Serbian musician gives a voice should be based, and out of which it should spring, if he wishes that his artistic musical creation should bear a Serbian mark and Serbian spirit. We shall acquire a Serbian opera only when the Serbian poet stands on Serbian soil, when he draws his material and inspiration from Serbian life, and when a Serbian musician clothes it in sounds which are in indivisible harmony with that life.' (ibid., 15)

Similarly, Djordjević believes that folklore research will bring us 'the definitive rebirth of our literature, which will only begin to create great works, when Serbian writers stand on Serbian soil, when they cease to nourish themselves from foreign, non-national, sources.' (ibid., 23)

These examples show that Djordjević sought a solution whereby the negative consequences of the inevitable withdrawal of traditional and advance of modern culture could be not only mitigated, but removed. He saw it in the conscious, organised, institutionalised cultivation of the national spirit, of Serbian national individuality through modern cultural, educational and artistic work. If traditional culture had ceased to exist in a spontaneous way as the culture of a society at a primitive level of development, it is possible in the modern age, thanks to appropriate scholarly procedures, by means of a kind of distillation, to collect and save sufficient material in which the substance of that culture, its spirit, its character are preserved. It is then possible to introduce that culture, salvaged and cleansed by methods of selection, into education and into forms of modern art and literature. That is how it is possible for an 'imported' modern culture, initially foreign, in the end to acquire a Serbian national character.

In this way scholarship and, particularly, ethnology and folklore studies have an exceptional national importance, because they enable the transfer from primitive to modern culture without the loss of national cultural individuality. That leads us to the conclusion—which remains implicit in Djordjević—that, thanks to appropriate methods of scholarly work and education, the national individuality, the 'character', 'spirit', 'being' of the people, may be distinguished from traditional culture, which in its original manifestations (rituals, customs) may and even must be suppressed and replaced by models of modern life.

Such a mythic and metaphysical, originally romantic, conception of national individuality, which is conceived as a timeless substance or energy, is the reason why Djordjević did not attribute any greater value to the political and cultural heritage of the life of the Serbs in the old Balkan or Austro-Hungarian towns. He did write very precisely, on the basis of documents, about the life of townspeople of Serbian nationality in Austria, and particularly about the urban religious communities of the Serbs living there. These writings enable us to conclude that these communities, led by prominent townspeople, far surpassed the framework of strictly religious institutions and were important forms of cultural and administrative autonomy.

But by all accounts Djordjević considered the experience of maintaining and developing national individuality in a multinational milieu, the experience of a multicultural society, as belonging to the past of Serbia and the Serbian people. He looked towards the future of Serbia and, potentially, a Yugoslavia, which he envisaged as the definitively established rule of one national principle or spirit. His ethnographic and cultural-historical research, and particularly his study of the urban and rural settlements in Serbia at the beginning of the nineteenth century, their population, social organisation and economic and cultural life, represent an important contribution to a scholarly understanding and interpretation of the time in which modern Serbian society came into being. He belonged to the generation of Serbian scholars at the beginning of the twentieth century who established the foundations of scholarly research into Serbian and Yugoslav history, culture and society. He and the other representatives of that generation (Cvijić, Dvorniković, Skerlić) share, on the one hand, a readiness to preserve the documents of national tradition and history and subject them to objective critical analysis, and, on the other, a liking for certain ideas of European and Serbian romanticism, above all the myth of the national character and the national spirit. This was being renewed— in the form of nationalistic, racist or vitalist doctrines—in European philosophy and political thought at the time when the scholars we are considering were developing their ideas.

PART III
Characters and Figures of Power
32 case studies

1. The Spiritual

A few years ago I read an advertisement in a Belgrade daily saying: 'The Orchestra Ballet Studio announces the opening of a Spiritual Workshop in the form of a three-month seminar. Leader: Mrs Janja Todorović. Promotional evening 23. 3. 1995 at 8 p.m. Free entry.' The organiser did not mention the venue, but gave a phone number.

I cut the advertisement out of the newspaper and kept it, but I was not interested in the fate of the Spiritual Workshop. For me the phenomenon of 'the spiritual' in a ballet studio, as something that could be treated and learned in a 'workshop', 'in the form of a seminar', was just one bizarre example of the penetration of the words 'spiritual' and 'spirituality' into virtually all areas of public discourse in Serbia. It seemed that there was nothing in our country that had not been said either to be or not to be 'spiritual'. One does not need a long memory or great lucidity to observe that 'spiritual' has come to mean 'ideological' as a sign of the times and a vague but respectable symbol of authority.

The greatest impetus and contribution to this transition from 'ideological' to 'spiritual' have been made by our writers. Many of them harnessed their talent to the project of making 'the spiritual' one of the most frequent and almost compulsory figures of our literary, journalistic and political language. For example, we owe to the poet M. Bećković the expressions 'spiritual property', 'spiritual suicide' and 'spiritual honour'. This last was, in the poet's opinion, saved by the Serbs at Kosovo. (Bećković, 1989, 59)

Bećković's colleague I. Negrišorac favours the 'formation of a quite new spirituality', the organisation of a 'spiritual movement', with the aim of furthering 'the spiritual evolution of the Serb'. He foresees that on that road the Serb will be confronted by various 'spiritual challenges', but that he will be saved from temptation by the fact that he will read that 'spiritual practice' with 'an eternally watchful spiritual eye', that is that he will rely on the rich experience of Orthodoxy, which is the 'spiritual backbone' of the Serbian people. (Negrišorac, 428)

In his book *Otažbinske teme* (Fatherland themes) Professor Nikola Koljević entrusts 'spirituality' with the main task: to ground and connect his thoughts on Serbian culture, faith and fatherland. He is on the whole satisfied with an already threadbare repertoire of metaphors: 'spiritual horizons', 'spiritual models', 'spiritual level', 'spiritual sources', 'spiritual measure', 'spiritual physiognomy', 'spiritual breadth'. Nevertheless, in one place he deviates from these well-worn paths to call 'the sources of Serbian culture' 'spiritual threads', but this deviation ends unhappily with the announcement that these threads 'have become so firmly interwoven that even when one is not in the foreground, it is nevertheless present implicitly or in a detail.' (Koljević, 31–46)

Among the metaphors of spirituality that Koljević uses we find also 'spiritual space'. In contemporary journalistic discourse, this metaphor, the expression 'Serbian spiritual space', has acquired a far simpler function: that of being one of the ways of designating territory that the Serbs consider their own. For instance, in one newspaper report from a conference on the writer Ivo Andrić, held in Višegrad, we find that the conference was held 'with the participation of writers from the whole Serbian spiritual terrain.' (*Politika*, 10 March 1995)

Entering the vocabulary of the discourse of newspapers, trivial literature and political journalism, 'the spiritual' and 'spirituality' have acquired at the same time broader and more banal meanings. Everything that is not entertainment, money or the West may now be 'spiritual'. Our Orthodox neighbours have become our 'spiritual kin'. Among the new literary prizes, there is now a distinction between their 'financial' and 'spiritual' parts. If the newspapers are to be believed, last year's winner of the Dučić prize, R.P. Nogo, announced that 'he would bear the spiritual part [of the prize] with pride, and give the financial part away ...' (*Politika*, 9 April 1995) At the initiative of Abbot Glikerija, the 'Father Justin' Spiritual Library was founded last year in Valjevo, and at the opening of this 'spiritual institution' at the Association of Writers of Serbia, the functionary of the Association, P. Bogdanović Ci, 'agreed with the opinion that it was necessary to found a centre which would spiritually edify young people who were increasingly abandoned to foreign influences and amusement in cafés.' (*Politika*, 18 Feb. 1995) This spiritomania goes so far as to suggest that there may even be something 'spiritual' about amusement in cafés, but that then it is a question of bad 'spirituality'. We learn from the author of a newspaper article that 'local folk kitsch represents the only spiritual experience of a large proportion of the population of Serbia.' For that population, it seems that better days are on the way, for the news has just broken that the writer D. Bokan (otherwise an admirer of the work of the popular poet Baja Mali Knindža*) is preparing to publish his 'spiritual testament'. (*Naša borba*, 9 Jan. 1996)

For writers, journalists and politicians 'the spiritual' is a conveniently ambiguous but still intelligible sign by means of which they align themselves with something that is a little to do with belief, to an extent ascetic, moderately devout, in fact healthy, in a certain sense intellectual, nearly artistic, fairly national, almost romantic, apparently innocuous, obviously deep, quite learned.

Clerics have made a contribution to this endless spiritualisation of things, although a lesser one than might have been expected, and very small in comparison to that of writers and journalists. There are even examples of Serbian Orthodox priests speaking about 'spirituality' in a quite profane and trivial sense. Thus one priest from Kraljevo explains, in a statement to a newspaper, that in his town, in order to defend themselves from various religious sects, people have engaged in 'a real spiritual war'. What kind of war they mean becomes clear when one reads the priest's reprimand to the state for tolerating religious freedom, because 'it is not yet aware of the danger that threatens it from sects, that they threaten to destroy it from inside and turn young people away from the army.' (*Politika*, 13 July 1994)

Orthodox theologians are also sometimes ready to give 'spirituality' and 'spiritual life' a predominantly, if not exclusively, national and political meaning. This may be seen in an interview with the theologian and historian of art Slobodan Mileusnić given last year to a state paper, on the subject of Serbian monasteries. Mileusnić calls the monasteries 'spiritual classrooms of St Sava-dom' and the 'primer of our spiritual and cultural heritage', but the only lesson he mentions that may be found in these classrooms and primers is: 'awareness of national self-determination and authenticity.' (*Politika*, 21 April 1995)

It is hard to believe that people in the Serbian Orthodox church are not aware of the danger to Orthodox belief and the church posed by this enormous wave of popular, literary-political 'spiritualism', this dilution of the Christian and, particularly, Orthodox understanding of 'the spiritual'. I am the last person to want to take on other people's concerns, but it would not surprise me if among our Christians, and above all among Orthodox believers and clerics, there were not only resistance to the vulgarisation and profanation of the spiritual, but a summons to fight for the protection and defence of the neglected and forgotten material world, for the affirmation of the abandoned human body! For even those of us who know little about Christian and Orthodox teachings recall, now that we are being offered spiritual hills and valleys in all directions, that among the holy things it celebrates the Christian religion does also celebrate the holiness of the human body. Christian teaching tells us that as long as the body is forgotten the spirit will not soar up to the heights, but will remain a quite worldly and often cheap story of 'spirituality'.

2. The Politics of Time

During a recent visit to Bosnia and Herzegovina, President Clinton voiced the opinion that the war in Bosnia was not a battle between the Serbs, Muslims and Croats, but 'a conflict between those who want peace and those who want war', that is 'between those who wish for a better future and those who are the slaves of the past'. In this way he repeated and—with the authority of the power which he represents—reinforced the widespread idea that the wars in the Balkans at the end of the twentieth century broke out because of the fatal connection of the Balkan political élites and fighters with the past, because of the kindling of ancient hatreds and the mad desire that old scores should be settled and old dreams realised. In keeping with that idea, the end of the war and return to peacetime life in former Yugoslavia imply a reorientation of temporal perspective. Instead of seeking the sense and aims of present-day life in the past, full of wars and suffering, one must turn to the future, in the hope that it will be better than the past.

It is hard to see that this idea—that the Balkan warriors of today and their chiefs and advisers are 'slaves of the past, and that the 'forces of peace' consist of people who are rushing into the twenty-first century, freed from ancient hatreds—will offer a convincing explanation of reality for anyone who evaluates and criticises that idea from a historical, sociological, ethnological or any other expert angle. But that does not concern us here. Clinton's pronouncement is no incidental philosophical or academic observation of wartime and peacetime, but a political statement, a statement about an important aspect of politics, that could be called the politics of time.

Much has been said about the wars in former Yugoslavia, and people are still talking about the politics of space, about territories, about borders, about corridors, about geopolitics. Political mythology has offered an image of the national collective linked inextricably (by its roots) to the 'ancestral soil', to 'ethnic space'. In this mythology, the nation has been embodied in the landscape, individual rivers and mountains have become the aorta, the spine, the lungs or the lap of the nation-body.

But political battles and wars are fought also for the conquest and control of time. In addition to geopolitics, there is tempo-politics, the politics of time. The main aim of the wars in Croatia and Bosnia, the creation of ethnically pure states, has a temporal dimension as well. That is the ethnic cleansing of time, which is carried out by means of a reworking of 'collective memory' in political speeches, in popular historiography and history textbooks, in linguistics and literature or through the destruction of 'foreign' cultural-historical monuments. The myth of ethnic nationalism seeks the most homogeneous and exclusive possible space, but also homogeneous and exclusive ethnic time.

The authorities in Serbia have for years been building their legitimacy and popularity on the politics of reviving the mythic national past, on slogans about the final realisation of the 'centuries-long' or 'historical' aspirations of the Serbian people. An accurate and concise description of such a politics of time is offered by a caricature by Corax published in *Borba* in December 1992, in which we see (opposite) Slobodan Milošević playing the *gusle* and telling a little Dobrica Ćosić, who is sitting on his knee, how things used to be.

However, for some time now Serbia has been obliged to revise its politics of time, and to do so in keeping with what Clinton said in Bosnia. Anyone who follows political life in Serbia at all may observe that the Serbian authorities took the obligation to turn to the future seriously, as though it were a matter of an unwritten but compulsory clause in the peace treaties.

The regime propaganda is today building an image of Serbia and its government in the colours of a peace-loving and hard-working future. Milošević is here leading his people into the twenty-first century. In the media, in the news of projects, investments, buildings, the future tense is used, and all future successes, income, revenues and wealth are already calculated and presented precisely, in percentages, tonnes, kilograms and billions of dollars. And, while Karadžić continues stubbornly to hang on to his *gusle,* Milošević is increasingly enamoured of symbols of progress and the future: computers and

The Politics of Time

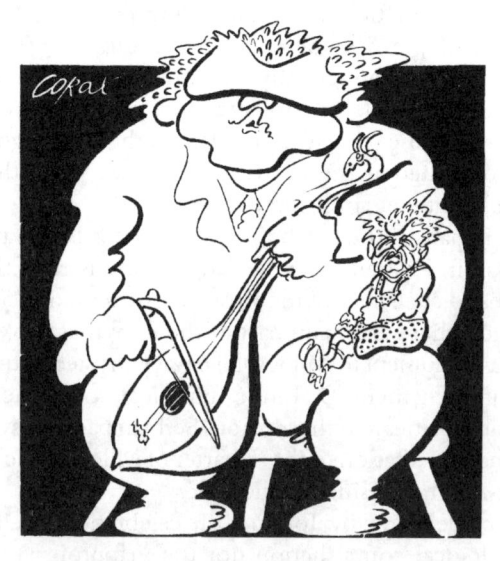

Milošević playing the *gusle*, with the writer Dobrica Ćosić sitting on his knee (Caricature by Predrag Koraksić Corax, published in *Borba*, December 1992.

mobile telephones, not to mention high-speed railways—his greatest peacetime love.

But the Serbian government has not forgotten and will not so easily forget the past. That dimension of the politics of time is no longer in the foreground, but this does not mean that the government is prepared to abandon it to its political opponents. The government wants to retain a monopoly on summoning, ordering and controlling the past, although intensive exploitation of that past is now no longer essential.

There is no doubt that in 1995 the leaders of the governing party studied the calendars of historical anniversaries and religious holidays of acknowledged or potential national significance as first-class political material. Not one historical jubilee (from St Vitus Day* to the Day of the Warriors*) was marked without their participation, patronage and speeches. Nor was one monument to celebrated ancestors unveiled, if we discount one segment of history towards which the present government still has reservations—Draža Mihailović and the Chetniks of the Second World War. State television has continued to wish its viewers happiness for both the 'international' and the 'Serbian' New Year.

A prominent functionary of the ruling party, R. Bogdanović, was in charge of the celebration of the 190th anniversary of the Battle of Ivankovac. The recently instituted celebration of the 80th anniversary of the Battle of Mojkovac was an opportunity for the authorities—in whose name the president of the federal government, R. Kontić, officiated at the festivities—to 'take over' that page of Serbian and Montenegrin history as well.

In 1995, as part of the celebration of St Vitus Day, a monument to Tsar Dušan in Prizren was unveiled by a minister of the Serbian government and chairman of the Kosovo District Council, A. Jokić, and in Obilić, where the main part of the festivities took place, the unveiling of a monument to Miloš Obilić was entrusted to the president of the Serbian Parliament, D. Tomić. The close connection between the Serbian authorities and the glorious Serbian past was symbolically marked by the presentation of the 'Charter of Miloš Obilić', instituted for the occasion, to President Milošević.

The speech delivered by Tomić at the celebration in Obilić shows that neither logical contradiction nor the inappropriateness of his speech to the character of the celebration interfered with his using it to signal the current political message inviting the Serbs to turn peacefully to the future. 'Remembering the Battle of Kosovo and its heroes', said Mr Tomić on this occasion, 'we remember the past, and, feeling respect for its victims and their devotion to the fatherland and to liberty, we turn more than ever towards the future. The greatest interest of the entire Serbian people is to live in peace.' (*Politika*, 29 June 1995)

The fact that it was a question of evoking the memory of an event six centuries old and a monument to the greatest Serbian war hero did not prevent Tomić from speaking about the future and peace. What is more, his party's propaganda team probably judged that the desired effect would be strengthened if a speech about the peaceful, industrious future was inserted precisely into the scenario of the celebration of the most important date of the Serbian warlike past. Today St Vitus Day and Obilić serve to provide the authorities with legitimacy for their political future and peace, just as—only yesterday and with apparently more logic and appropriateness—those Serbian national holy relics were necessary in order for the war in Bosnia to be begun in their name, as though it were the continuation of the Battle of Kosovo.

3. The Secret of the Balkans

Recently, the second edition of *Tajna Balkana* (*The Secret of the Balkans*) was published. The title might lead one to the erroneous conclusion that it is an historical adventure novel along the lines of *The Secrets of Paris*. No, it is a collection of essays by some twenty local and foreign authors devoted to geopolitics, edited by Branislav Matić and published by the Students' Cultural Centre in Belgrade. The secret discussed here is the secret of geopolitics.

If we discount Cvijić, who is given the role of distinguished forebear and whose presence is meant to ensure a scholarly aspect to the volume which it would not otherwise have, the authors of the collection offer roughly similar answers to the questions 'what is geopolitics', who are its creators, to whom and how can it be of use? As a result, it is possible to describe briefly what *The Secret of the Balkans* has to say about geopolitics.

One can describe as geopolitics the endeavours, since the beginning of the twentieth century, to take old philosophical, historical or literary observations about the dependence of the historical destiny of individual peoples and states on geographical conditions and base them on natural science. Such 'scientific' observations can then be placed at the disposal of political leaders and military strategists.

Geopolitics reached its peak of scholarly respect and eminence in political and military circles in Germany between the two World Wars. The greatest input was made by the German officer and geographer Karl Haushofer (1869–1946), who founded in 1923 the *Journal of Geopolitics*. The geopolitical ideas of Haushofer and his colleagues were particularly prized in Hitler's day and served the Nazis as a theoretical base for important diplomatic and military strategic decisions. That was the reason why Haushofer was to be found in 1946 among those accused of war crimes at Nuremberg and the probable reason for his suicide in that year. (The editor of *The Secret of the Balkans* does not mention this inglorious end of one of the most important authors in his collection.)

After the Second World War, geopolitical ideas, at least in the form given them by the German school, lost the status of scientific thought and they remained politically exploitable only by the extreme right. The collection *The Secret of the Balkans,* the contributions to which are on the whole in the Haushofer tradition, bears witness to the limited, marginal validity of this geopolitical school. Among the contemporary authors chosen to represent it in this collection are Robert Steuckers, one of the leaders and ideologues of the Flemish extreme Right; Alexander Dugin, the main representative of the Russian 'Eurasian' school, which preaches the renewal of world politics on a 'sacral' basis; and the Canadian of Greek origin Dimitrios Katsikis, the author of a project for the renewal of Europe on Orthodox foundations.

Of local authors in the collection there are representatives of the so-called New Serbian Right, writing for the journal *Naše ideje* (Our ideas) (D. Kalajić, M. Knežević, B. Matić), and, judging by the texts published here, their sympathisers (A. Miletić, M. Stojković, D. R. Simić and R. Radinović). Miletić distances himself up to a point, as he rejects the German geopolitical school and its social Darwinism as a Nazi 'abuse of geopolitics', but nevertheless in his analyses he does not go beyond the framework of its teaching, for example when he speaks dramatically about the fact that 'we are once again at the epicentre of a Balkan, and wider, European and world geopolitical earthquake' and that we must 'harness' all our energy so as not to be swallowed up by a 'Balkan black hole'.

The main idea of geopolitics as it is presented here is that states are 'living organisms'. As Katsikis puts it, 'to think geopolitically means to think organically', or, in Steuckers' words, 'to get to know the geopolitical programme of a nation means to get to know its organic, deep-seated instincts'. The main instinct is the 'struggle for survival', and since the state is an organism in space, that is 'a struggle for living space'. One of those who particularly liked this idea was Hitler, as may be seen in his pronouncement 'that all politics that do not have a biological foundation or biological aims are blind.'

When one starts from biological and geographical realism, international politics is reduced to a merciless struggle, a ceaseless conflict of 'existential interests'. Alliances are possible, if they are also founded on biological-geographical determinism. Thus, in the opinion of B. Matić, the Balkan peoples 'belong organically to Eurasia'. There are also false alliances, but a geopolitician recognises them. Such a false alliance is the 'new world order', in which the great powers are formally partners, but in fact bitter rivals, so that international relations create, as Simić puts it, 'the trite image of a contemporary menagerie'.

In addition to this scientist tradition, geopolitics as it is represented here is connected with various trends of the esoteric and mystic interpretation of politics. Among these is the widespread opinion that the 'struggle for survival' among states and peoples is carried out above all by means of secret, occult, para-religious means, in various Vatican, masonic, satanist circles and spies' kitchens. In addition, the struggle between states or continents, open or behind the scenes, is simply an echo of an all-encompassing mystic struggle between opposing sacral values, mystic principles, matter and spirit, earth and heaven, water and dry land, etc. This tendency in geopolitics is hinted at in the title of *The Secret of the Balkans*.

In the volume particular attention is paid to endeavours to found Serbian geopolitics. This is elaborated in the contribution by D. Kalajić. He is presented as 'a painter, writer, publisher, culturologist, one of the best experts on the traditional doctrines of East and West, classical philosophy and European Christian civilisation'. According to Kalajić, Serbian geopolitics is founded on differentiating 'the space of obstacles' (mountains) from 'the space of passes' (valleys). This division is important in times of attack by superior conquerors: the best part of the Serbian people seeks shelter in the world of obstacles, the worst, avoiding struggle for the sake of convenience, remains in the world of passes. Then comes the process of natural selection. 'On the one hand, the world of *obstacles*, through its difficult conditions of life over the centuries, carried out a biological selection of the species, rejecting genetic material which was incapable or too weak for the harsh struggle for life. This was where the first-class human element was tempered and is still being tempered. On the other hand, those who remained in the world of *passes,* underwent a centuries-long negative selection of the species and genetic contamination, through the occupiers' custom of mass rapes ... To put it in the most concise but also the crudest terms, the subjugated population no longer gives birth to children inclined to freedom, but to slavery.'

Kalajić attributes important pedagogical and political aims to a science based on such analyses. It should be the foundation of 'a new system of upbringing and education, directed at forging Serbian people according to the models of classical *andragathis*' (Vujaklija translates this as 'masculinity'). It seems that Kalajić and his collaborators on this project have the support of the educational authorities in Serbia. As one reads on the first page of the book, the publication of *The Secret of the Balkans* was supported by the Ministry of Education of the Republic of Serbia—the department for school and university standards (!). Furthermore, the editor stresses in several places that the book 'is included in the compulsory university curriculum', that it will be 'part of the required reading in a series of subjects of the regular university programme in Belgrade' and that one can expect that a Department of Geopolitics will soon be established. This information is reinforced at the end of the book by a copy of a facsimile of an official act whereby the Dean of the Faculty of Political Science(M. Stojković, one of the authors of *The Secret of the Balkans*) informs those interested that, because of its value and 'the needs of the educational curriculum in the Faculty of Political Science, the book has been included in the bibliography for both undergraduate and postgraduate studies in the fields of International Relations, External Policy and Diplomacy and Diplomatic History.'

4. The Devil in Serbia

Has some Devil got into the Serbs? The assumption that something of the kind has really happened is, at one and the same time, rejected and taken seriously in the media. It is rejected when it comes from foreign commentators on Serbian politics and the Serbian actions during the war in Croatia and Bosnia. No, the Devil does not live at a Serbian address. Such situating of Satan is usually described as the 'demonisation of the Serbian people'. But, it is also accepted as possible that the Devil has somehow found his way into today's Serbia. What is more, alarming warnings arrive from various directions suggesting that there is a great danger of his power spreading, particularly among younger people. In that case, the Devil is described as a foreigner from the West, infiltrated into our country.

In this century his place of permanent residence is allegedly in the West, that is in the countries which are developed materially and technically at the expense of their spiritual life and moral values. There the Devil has built himself a luxury dwelling, full of white, electronic and other technology, based on the devilish calculation that two and two make four, but it is a dwelling without a soul or a heart.

In the recently published opinion of the special needs expert Jasmina Milašinović, it seems that the old Serbs knew that the twentieth century would be given to the Devil to manage. In support of her opinion, she quotes a Serbian traditional tale, in which it is said that God, on the day that he made the world, promised the Devil: 'To you I will bequeath the twentieth century.' (*Politika*, 21 January 1996) Our forebears knew this, but their descendants forgot. This is particularly the case with the younger generation today, who do not know how to resist the temptations of computers, electronic mail, microwave ovens and other colourful lies by means of which Satan tries to win them over.

For the Devil today is not content with rampaging through the West. He is exploiting the opportunity offered him by the collapse of communism in order to extend his work also to the east of Europe, and signs of his presence have thus become frequent also in Serbia. Harbingers of the Devil in Serbia are, above all, religious sects. They are, as one daily paper wrote recently, 'the dark forces of evil'. Members of sects 'lurk in the streets', 'frequent places where large numbers of people assemble, like bus and railway stations, clinics, libraries, fairs, discotheques, coffee bars'. (*Politika*, 22 January 1996)

When the Devil takes control of people through such sects, then, in the words of Ljubodrag Petrović, elder of Aleksandar Nevski Church, 'their lives have painful, tragic ends or they live burdened by various spiritual deformations.' (ibid.) Among the most widespread spiritual deformations are illnesses of dependence, alcoholism and drug addiction. AIDS is similar. This notion is based on the conviction that a person is not a duality of body and soul, but a triad of body, soul and spirit, and that, therefore, illnesses may also be categorised as bodily, spiritual and of the soul. When one perceives the spiritual nature or at least the spiritual causes of the illness of dependence, i.e. that it is a question of dependence on Satan, then it becomes essential that priests, 'spiritual leaders', should become involved in their treatment.

It is interesting that this revision of the definition and treatment of illnesses of dependence and other psychiatric illnesses is more favoured by doctors, particularly special needs experts and psychiatrists, than by priests and theologians. J.Milašinović, who works in the Centre for Illnesses of Dependence in Belgrade, is one of the most persistent in endeavouring to engage priests in the therapy of psychiatric illnesses. She is mentioned as one of the main organisers of a conference entitled 'Spiritual Health', which was held in Belgrade in 1996.

With the announcement of the conference, the paper published information about the recent initiative of successful co-operation between doctors and theologians. We learned that 'in some hospitals, a priest visits the wards every morning with a cross, an icon and sweet basil.' (*Politika*, 10 January 1996) The director of the Centre for Illnesses of Dependence, Dr Milutin Nenadović, also stresses the good results of the 'complementary work of psychiatrists, theologians and priests'. (ibid.)

Doctors themselves are sometimes involved in treating spiritual illnesses, that is in driving out the Devil. The attention of our media was recently drawn to the alleged successes in the practice of exorcism of a psychiatrist in the town of Vršac. 'In the Vršac Psychiatric Hospital, while not neglecting the rules of contemporary psychiatry, the director Milan Bešlin succeeds in treating even the most aggressive states in patients of this kind with the figure of the White Angel of Mileševo, harbinger of human salvation.'[1] (*Politika,* 21 January 1996)

Bešlin's colleague, Dr Jovan Striković, Director of the 'Sveti Sava' clinic, an institution which is in the forefront of eradicating illnesses of devilish provenance with the help of priests, proposes and even tries out on himself various methods of treating the spirit, that it would be hard to fit into the framework of scientific psychiatry or Christian theology. He believes in the healing power of stone: 'My power, if I have any', says Dr. Striković, 'comes from stone. Not only its concrete, physical touch, which I apply even in my clinic, but from the very thought of that cruel but at the same time also warm "creature".' (*Politika,* 3 February 1996)

A contribution to investigating and testing miraculous balms for the body and soul was recently made also by Željko Simić, the President of the Water Polo Association of Yugoslavia. Quite in keeping with his function, he finds healing and solace in water. 'My love of swimming, of water polo,' Mr Simić confesses in a sports paper, 'was born of a totally irrational inclination to water, which still heals me and strengthens me spiritually today.' (*Vreme,* 3 February 1996)

Among the methods which may be effectively used for defence against the Prince of Darkness, words are at a special premium. As Dr Striković puts it, words are 'the weapons of the spirit'. Priests engaged in the treatment of dependents on devilish drugs and other possessed people make use of the miraculous power of the cross and sweet basil, but they rely above all on the de-satanising effect of the holy word. J. Milašinović spoke in a newspaper interview 'about some concrete effects which the word of clerics has produced on patients in the Centre for Illnesses of Dependence. Proverbially impatient and known as listeners whose attention can rarely be held for more than ten minutes at a time, patients of this centre have listened attentively, without pressure, for more than 90 minutes to the words of clerics about love as the essence of life and belief.' (*Politika,* 21 January 1996)

In view of the significance of well composed words for curing spiritual illnesses, doctors and priests seek the co-operation of artists of the word, writers. By participating in the treatment of the diseased spirituality of psychiatric and special needs patients, writers would

---

[1] A famous fresco in the Orthodox monastery of Mileševo. (Transl.)

only be accepting their part of responsibility in this area, for, as J. Milašinović says, 'literature and art are very much responsible for people's spiritual health'. (ibid.) That is why it is anticipated that among the participants in the conference on 'Spiritual Health', in addition to psychiatrists, priests and theologians, there will also be some Serbian writers.

They are all involved in the search for the best cure for the spiritual faltering of the Serbs who have succumbed to the devilish temptations of a life without true belief and a reliable national compass. And the one against whom the above-mentioned interdisciplinary movement has been launched would be able to react to all of this mockingly, as only he knows how, and with a shake of his head to say: 'Psychiatrists, priests, poets ... this all sounds somehow familiar. The only thing lacking are soldiers, above all artillery, for this to be a devilishly strong team.'

5. Magic Mirror

There is no doubt that of everything that could be seen and heard at the Third Congress of the Socialist Party of Serbia held in Belgrade on 2 March 1996, what attracted the greatest attention was the gigantic video screen behind the working presidency. The journalists who attended the congress informed us that this installation, as yet unseen in Serbia, was called a 'video wall' and a 'video bin', that it had 96 monitors and a total surface of 50 square metres.

According to the journalists and delegates, this video screen was constantly in operation throughout the congress. There were two kinds of images on it. First there were magnified pictures of the television broadcast of everything that was happening in the congress hall. In that case the video screen functioned like a gigantic mirror. The participants in the congress thus had the opportunity not only of seeing the congress, but at the same time of seeing themselves at the congress.

In addition to these reflection-pictures, the video screen showed also fictitious-pictures, that is, images of the future Serbia, the Serbia of the twenty-first century. There was also a film, *Serbia 2000*, which, according to the newspaper *Borba*, 'illustrated, in a very vivid manner, everything that will characterise Serbia on the eve of the third millennium—Serbia as a modern, European, rich, prosperous country of free, equal and happy people.' In the same way the speeches of the delegates from the interior were accompanied by film images of the bright future of individual regions of Serbia.

The role of these video films cannot be considered merely as illustrating and supplementing a propaganda document about the development of Serbia which the Socialists had prepared for this congress and called *Serbia 2000—Stepping into the XXI Century*. When one reads carefully and compares everything that the delegates and journalists present at the congress said about these fictitious pictures, one comes to the conclusion that their character and function—and thereby also the character of the gigantic screen on which they were shown—were far more important and interesting than it might seem at first sight.

The first thing to strike one is that the fictitious pictures of the future Serbia, including those shown at the SPS congress, were regularly referred to by party chiefs and the party media as 'visions'. On the eve of the congress, the SPS spokesman, I. Dačić, made an interesting statement to Radio Belgrade, which was carried also by the paper *Politka Ekspres,* in which he said openly that the Socialists had decided to turn their congress into an unusual kind of video séance, in which the screening and experience of 'visions' of the future would be the main event. 'In his words', the newspaper reported, 'what they had in mind were up-to-date media techniques with scenic effects, because this was not simply a political manifestation, but a meeting which would lay the foundations for our development with a vision for several years ahead.' On the day of the congress, there was an enormous headline in the evening paper *Večernje novine*: 'A Vision of the Development of Serbia'.

The course of the congress confirmed the significance of the visions hinted at during this meeting and persuaded me that I would have a better understanding of what the Socialists had done that day in the 'Blue Hall' of the Sava Centre if I took their pronouncements about their visions of the future seriously, that is as the pronouncements of people who really had seen the future, who really had been to the future. A 'vision' is above all what one should call the apprehension of something which is otherwise inaccessible to the senses, something supernatural (divine) or something that belongs to the past or the future.

The delegates at the Socialists' congress not only had the feeling that they were seeing the future Serbia with their own eyes, but, they said, it even seemed to them that they were already in it. Their experience could almost be compared with the 'state of clear vision of the blessed' in the Heavenly Kingdom about which Pascal wrote. They were able to experience this above all thanks to the video screen, which evidently did not serve here simply as a large mirror, but had the role of a specific magic device. It showed, in addition to reflections of the delegates in the hall, also pictures apparently coming from the twenty-first century, of the future Serbia, as an exceptionally

III Congress of the Socialist Party of Serbia. (Draško Gagović)

beautiful, progressive and peaceful land. And more than that, the apex of the congress séance represented stepping into that future Serbia, the passing of the Socialists through the screen into the world on the other side of the mirror.

The organisers of the congress announced the event and described it accurately. One needed only to read. They did not promise a step 'towards the twenty-first century', but 'into the twenty-first century'. Equally, they put forward unambiguous evidence of the experience of the congress's stepping out of the present. 'I think', announced Gorica Gajević, 'that today in this hall, we were in that new century both technologically and in terms of creativity, intellectual potential, ideas and people—today we have already been in the new century.'

Because the organisers of the congress did all they could to organise, at least for one day and in one hall, a collective vision of a different Serbia—a more beautiful, happier and richer vision than we see today, the reproach voiced after the congress is quite out of place. Notably, that what they had experienced on the other side of the mirror did not at all resemble the gloomy reality of contemporary Serbia, our misery and despair. When Goran Perčević announced that it was 'essential that the vision of Serbia 2000 should be realistic', what he meant was that it was important that it should be psychologically realistic, truly experienced, and not that it should correspond to the real state of the country.

The magic character and wizardry of the congress of Socialists was well observed also by the *Politika* journalist, R. Petrović. He praised the presentation of the party with the help of video-technology, which 'part of the membership judged euphorically, in its first statements, as though we had "already entered the twenty-first century".' Petrović went on: 'The impression we took away from the Sava Centre is all the more significant in that the congress had little connection with the present ... It was illusory to expect that the Socialists should publicly concern themselves, at such a carefully organised political meeting, with what troubles and oppresses us.'

Gazing into the magic mirror installed at the Sava Centre, and passing through it as though in a trance, the Socialists announced joyfully that there were Socialists on the other side, but far more beautiful and happier than they are today. Their political calculation is quite clear. They stepped into the future in order to reassure us and tell us: we have been there, don't be afraid. The most reliable multi-media magic—an enchanted mirror measuring 10 by 5 metres—enabled us, for your sake and as your advance guard, to visit the next century. It is wonderful. It does not at all resemble this sad reality which our enemies have imposed on us.

Undertaking their journey into the future, the Serbian Socialists were far more cautious than the Belgrade *dahias**. They made every effort to ensure that they would have no unpleasant experience like the one the *dahias* confronted when, bending over a basin full of water from the Danube to read their future, they saw the far from cheerful image of the end of their power.

6. The Book of Preachers

'My sermon is bleak,' writes Dragan Nedeljković in one of the speeches he collected and published in his book *Reči Srbima u smutnom vremenu* (*Words to the Serbs in a turbulent time*). And even without the author's explicit indication of the genre to which his speeches belong, it is clear that these *are* sermons or homilies. Nedeljković is trying to speak in the language of the Biblical prophets. He says: 'I keep constantly repeating, from the depths of my soul, shouting *De profundis* ...' He compares his words to 'a voice crying in the wilderness'. Disgusted and grieved by scenes of the evil, 'turbulent' times through which we are living, he exclaims: '*O tempora, O mores!*'

Words to the Serbs are sermons, but sermons of a lay preacher, someone who teaches literature, which is Dragan Nedeljković's profession. The classic themes of religious sermons—the transience and vanity of earthly life, sin and redemption, salvation in God and faith— have been transferred from the religious to the national-political plane also. What is the purpose of the sermon? Why has Nedeljković chosen it out of all the possible forms of political engagement? The answer lies in Nedeljković's understanding of so-called national affairs as something which in essence is not and should not be the business of politics and politicians, but exclusively of the rare visionary leaders of the people, national apostles, whose task is to preserve the holy relics of the ethnic community: its myths and rituals.

According to Nedeljković, Serbia was left without visionary national apostles precisely when she had the greatest need of them, over these recent years of crisis and war, in this 'turbulent time'. 'Apostles did not appear', he writes; 'what appeared were politicians, sowing, division, discord and hatred in the name of democracy.' Here, modestly,

Nedeljković omits to say what his book clearly suggests—that he is indeed just one of those rare people, and perhaps even the only apostle of Serbdom, who has hastened to the aid of his nation with his teaching and encouragement.

And the apostle's work, even when it is a matter of national business, is above all the work of the prophet: the language of faith, reproach and hope. It cannot be the dry discourse of figures, proof, arguments, debate, analysis, the dull, calm language of every day, with its petty calculations and assessments. 'Turbulent times' call for something stronger. 'When the destiny of the individual or the nation confronts its greatest test, the struggle for life and death', Nedeljković explains, what is needed is 'the exalted language of poetry, which is borne heavenwards, merging with prayer.' When he wishes to explain 'to his dear fellow countrymen' the circumstances in which they are living, he chooses 'the language of the parable, metaphor and symbol', for he is 'aiming at the truth'.

Fulfilling his national apostolic task, Nedeljković directs his sermonising messages and instructions to all the Serbs, although for the most part they came into being as speeches for a specific occasion and a specific audience. On several occasions he addressed the Serbs in Germany, where he 'gave the neglected consciousness of our honourable workers injections'; he spoke often to Serbian intellectuals and writers, but he also gave sermons to the political leaders in Kruševac, the citizens of Ruma, Leskovac and Vranje, members of the Serbian Geographical Society, villagers in Prislonica, the wounded and refugees in Ribarska Banja, dispensers of humanitarian aid and soldiers in Republika Srpska. Some of his sermons were broadcast on television.

The primary function of the religious sermon—spreading the word of God—becomes in Nedeljković's speeches spreading faith in Serbdom, that is propagating the cult of the Serbian ethnic community, embodied in his poetic sermons in the figure of the Serbian people. This is 'a heroic, an honourable, an exceptional people', which stands out among other peoples for its historical and moral greatness. 'Do not for one moment forget', Nedeljković exhorts the Serbs, 'that you belong to a great people among small peoples, historically and morally tall and among the great.' The Serbian people are particularly great from a moral viewpoint, because they are a people chosen by God, a righteous people; they are, 'like the Old Testament Job, on the right path.' And in his sermonising rapture he cries: 'Raise up your heads, you carry God within you!'

The Serbian people resemble Job also in their undeserved, innocent suffering, for, Nedeljković explains, 'just because they are the better part of the human race—they are often victims of their noble sensitivity, 'which is why evil forces rush to destroy them', and why they are 'the victims of violence and lies'. The most vicious and merciless of the enemies of the Serbian people are neighbours closest to them in language and blood, especially 'as the Serbian people treated their brothers in language and blood, their neighbours, with greater self-sacrifice and generosity, nobility and honour.' Those neighbours and brothers are 'our Cains'.

But Nedeljković's *Words to the Serbs* would not be sermons if they did not contain homilies, that is the kind of reproaches, reproofs, warnings, accusations and reprimands which it seems that preachers, especially patriots, prefer to words of comfort and encouragement. 'I know the other face of Serbdom', says the author, 'and I frequently chide it publicly.' And it is a long list of failings and weaknesses that Nedeljković ascribes to the Serbian people—their quality is 'low', they are 'spiritually the most impoverished people of Europe', 'the most backward from the point of view of faith', 'very superficial', 'morally feeble', 'unenlightened, badly brought up', 'with an old-fashioned and self-satisfied turn of mind', 'insufficiently supportive', 'inclined to be forgetful', 'living in the shallows'; and they like 'vulgar music sung by tastelessly dressed women singers'. But the greatest, the fatal weakness of the Serbian people is disunity, division, and 'the evil fate that has dogged us from the quarrel of the Nemanjić rulers up to this day'. Today, in Nedeljković's judgment, those who are to blame for the schism, for the 'de-Serbianisation' of their blood are 'renegades, traitors, destroyers of Serbdom, new converts, Turks and Uniates, all kinds of weeds and scum'.

Of course, all is not lost, there is salvation and 'there is always hope'. 'The Serbian people will survive', they will overcome their 'fatal sickness, which is the evil spirit of disunity', they will be reborn, they will cure and restore the national spirit, they will pull up the poisonous weeds from out of their corn. 'The heavens will open as soon as we find a common, pan-Serb language', Nedeljković promises.

Does the war of sermons bought by the apostle Dragan Nedeljković for the salvation of the Serbian people, for their unification and purification, for a return to their growing traditions, the faith and courage of their forebears, mean a new affirmation of the fundamental direction of the Serbian national myth, its orientation towards the role of innocent victim like Abel or Job, whereby the evils of this world are redeemed and in return the Serbian people are granted

God's mercy and the glory of suffering deeply in a righteous cause?

It appears that the moral lesson of Nedeljković's sermons is not always reduced to a demand. In some places he permits the possibility that the Serbian people could stop playing simply the role of innocent victim, allocated them by the long-established scenario of the national myth. Let them continue to be Job, but 'let them also be Solomon the wise.' And to be as wise as Solomon, according to the example offered by Nedeljković, means for the Serbs to accept 'the implacable will of nature' and to co-operate once again with their neighbours, but with a clear calculation. 'We must trade with the Slovenes', Nedeljković advises, but '*only* if they are significantly cheaper than the Germans, Austrians, Italians, that is, if it is clearly in *our* interest.'

An excellent piece of advice, and if we ignore the word 'significantly', quite sensible. The question only remains whether Nedeljković's Serbian people, when that 'Solomon-like' characteristic is added to them, will be able to retain the 'Job-like' trait in their character, and any other heroic quality which the Serbian national myth attributes to it. Do the serbs in that case have any need at all of apostles and prophets, in addition to those in the church, do they need poetic discourse in addition to that of poetry? For if, with Nedeljković, we are to imagine the Serbian people trading, calculating interest rates and profit, then for that image we need merchants, economists, bankers, accountants, correspondence in foreign languages, and all of that in prose. It is a boring picture, I know, but, for a change, soothing.

7. Serbian Lyric Verse

It is impossible to govern Serbia without poetry. In order to present what they do as not only acceptable, but as the only possible course of action, the political authorities rely almost more on poetry and poets than on state, economic, social and other national interests. The explanation of this interest of Serbian politics in poetry must be sought in our very lively romantic conception of poetry as the deepest, most authentic manifestation of human, and especially, national aspirations. To be with poetry, to have at one's side the dead and living giants of poetry, means to have an unbreakable connection with the people. Political power cannot wish for a better image of itself. On the other hand, it could not be said that Serbian poets find it hard to play the prestigious and often well rewarded role of the generators of the righteousness and legitimacy of national politics, including even the worst.

But it is not only that politicians—and especially those in power—refer to poetry and seek its support, they also aspire to present politics itself as a kind of poetry. Politicians poeticise their discourse, which is one of the procedures for creating what Adorno calls 'the jargon of authenticity'. In that way, speaking politically becomes the same as speaking poetically. For Serbian politics that means, above all, speaking in the folklore-epic style. The proximity which was long ago observed between political jargon and popular epic singing in former Yugoslavia became very striking during the years of crisis and war. The propaganda of hate and war gladly exploits epic motifs, evokes memories of mythic and legendary events and heroes, and often uses the form of the decasyllabic traditional epic song.

The change of political colour of the government in Belgrade, which is today presented as the main actor in the so-called 'peace process' in former Yugoslavia, has led also to a change in the dominant style of political discourse. The discourse of power has not severed its links with poetry, it has not abandoned the poeticisation of its messages. But, instead of speaking in the style of the heroic decasyllabic verse, which has been squeezed out of the foreground although not entirely abandoned to the opponents of the regime's new policies, the authorities today prefer to strike a lyric note. Hence, after several years of politics in the style of the famous 'Serbian epic', the time has come for Serbian politics to sing in a calmer, sweeter, lyric voice, it is the time of the 'Serbian lyric'.

The most prominent representative of the new Serbian peace-making political lyricism is Mira Marković, the president of the Yugoslav United Left (JUL) party. She has developed a recognisable lyrico-political jargon, through diligently writing her popular diary for the magazine *Duga*. M. Marković's diary enables one to observe some qualities of the political poeticisation achieved by predominant reliance on lyric means. It is striking, for example, that, by contrast with the so-called 'epic vertical', here we find something which could be called the 'lyric horizontal'. That is to say, what is characteristic of Serbian politics in the epic style is the endeavour, on the other side of historical changes and the passing generations, to strengthen the axis of the eternal life of 'the whole of Serbdom', that is all the dead, living and as yet unborn members of the Serbian national community. By contrast, the lyric politician seeks to establish a link between himself and the world, the world of nature and the world of 'the whole of Humanity'.

Instead of the epic 'we', lyric political discourse is dominated by the lyric 'I'. In we-discourse, the individual is merged with the collective and only through it with nature, experienced as a part of the collective (for example, Serbian rivers are the bloodstream of Serbdom). Whereas in political-lyrical I-discourse the individual is separated from the mass, raised above it, filled with a sense of personal power accompanied by a sentimental experience of the loneliness of great spirits. Over the heads of the primitive, violent crowd, which he despises and of which he is a little afraid, the lyric politician establishes contact with Nature, with Humanity, with the Future. This relationship is well illustrated by numerous places in the daily notes of M. Marković, in which she describes her solitary meditations on the stirring beauty of nature, summer heat, icy rain, or frost which makes 'white, icy arabesques on the panes of the windows in our house.' (*Duga*, 16 February 1996)

Politics in the lyric key does not wish to be politics, it rejects the name of politics and transforms itself into the cultural-artistic endeavour of building an ideal world of love, liberty and happiness. In that sense, the lyric strain of political discourse does not differ greatly from epic. Both epic and lyric politics are hidden politics. But, in the first instance, concern for the people and dignity serves as a screen, while in the other it is anxiety about man and his happiness.

When politics is carried out like poetry, the chronicle of political life is transformed into a cultural and literary chronicle. Here too epic and lyric politics meet, but they differ in their choice of poetic-political perspective. In the first case, attention is directed to cultural history, to the celebration of great historical dates, above all battles, and honouring great people, above all warriors and leaders of men. In the second, when the lyric strings are played, politicians are more interested in nature and youth. The local JUL committee in the town of Leskovac had an entirely lyric inspiration when on 21 March it organised the celebration of a significant date in the life of the whole natural world—the arrival of spring, under the unambiguously apolitical title 'Spring Greeting'. The presidential directorate of JUL and other guests were treated to an artistic programme by actors and the choir from an elementary school, which did not after all change its epic name of 'Karadjordje' for the occasion. (*Politika*, 22 March 1996) On the same day, this party organised public meetings in other parts of Serbia as well, where people spoke about culture, music, 'creation and creativity', 'a nicer, better society', 'the spiritual life of the citizen', and everything beautiful and poetic, but 'without politics'.

The main editor of *Borba*, Dr Živorad Djordjević, also realised that the authorities in Serbia had discarded the *gusle* and picked up the lyre. He endeavoured to count and identify the lyric-political aims of the present regime, which he calls 'the left option' for short. In the first place, writes Djordjević, is 'the battle for the good of man'. Then, the leftists 'do all they can to make young people look forward to tomorrow', 'they open their doors to young people who are bubbling over with knowledge'. They are particularly concerned that citizens should experience real love, that is, that they should 'affirm love with emotion instead of the misuse of love for the sake of easy and brutal acquisition of money.' In a word, the authorities 'of the left option' in Serbia work hardest to make people happy, as Djordjević explains, they 'protect nobility of soul, happiness', 'they aim at a society at peace, human happiness, the prosperity and nobility of the human being'.

In its concern for man and his happiness, the 'left option' goes so far as to determine which places are suitable for the gatherings of citizens imbued with the noble and joyous emotion of love. These are stadia because, as Djordjević says, people 'need to gather and be joyful at sporting events instead of displaying their primitivism at political demonstrations and destroying what it has taken years to build.' So it turns out that to be opposed to the Serbian left today means to trample on love, to despise youth, threaten peace, destroy happiness, and to favour and organise 'nationalistic self-indulgence and street brawls'. According to Djordjević, that is what our 'home-grown right' does, 'threatening peace and tranquillity, the functioning of the legal state and the desire of the left for our people to be happy'. (*Borba*, 7 March 1996)

It is clear that in political lyricism, the figure of the traitor is important. But its 'Vuk Branković'* is not a national freak, a bad Serb, a Muslim convert or a Western toady, but an antisocial, primitive type, an uncultured drunkard, who mocks everything beautiful and poetic. And so, yesterday with the *gusle*, today with the lyre, (tomorrow with the *gusle* again?), the government in Serbia is trying to convince us that its song is better than all politics, that dubious activity unworthy of decent Serbian people.

8. Us?

Vojislav Djordjević, general manager of the Soko-Štark factory, published a newspaper article about the economic situation in Yugoslavia today, which began with a reminder of 'what has happened to us'. 'After everything that has happened to us, and need not have done', writes Djordjević, 'we are in the situation of deciding our fate for ourselves, and that ought to be an additional motive for us in our endeavour to find our own way out of the crisis and thereby join European economic trends.' (*Politika*, 9 April 1996)

What does this 'us' refer to? Which plurality does this author represent? To whom did something happen which need not have done? Who is it that ought to resolve our fate? The uncertainty does not last long. As the article goes on, it becomes clear that the author is not resorting to the plural in order to talk about the collective of which he is the director, nor in the name of the confectionery industry in which his factory is involved, nor even because he wants his voice to be understood as the voice of the Yugoslav economy and producers as a whole. His 'we' is even more comprehensive and in fact stretches to include all of 'us' and each of 'us'. It is the national 'we'.

The fact that Djordjević's 'we' is national may be seen in the poverty of the 'grammar' to which it belongs, where there is space only for the third person plural—'them'. And 'they' are those who are outside the borders of our national collective. In this article, 'they' are the former Yugoslav republics and other foreign states. We, those included in Djordjević's 'us', declare that 'they' betrayed us, and that we have settled our accounts with 'them'. 'Those with whom we spent years building what was once called a brighter future have betrayed us, although we have held our own,' writes the general manager of Soko-Štark.

Assimilated along with Djordjević and all our other compatriots into one national 'we', I shall distinguish among foreign states 'our centuries-old friendships', but I shall have to recall that I am currently disappointed in those friends and that I am basing my future relations with them on naked interest. 'We must understand', says Djordjević in my name and that of all of 'us', that 'there has always been friendship between states, and there will be in the future, in direct relation to economic power and economic interest.'

The example of this article may be used to identify a rhetorical strategy which is the basis of the functioning of the national 'we'. The undesirable phenomenon of the reader's 'I', and thereby of a critical attitude towards what the text offers, is forestalled by the author himself, who rhetorically gives up his 'I' and places himself at the service of the expression of would-be communal, national ideas and feelings. Djordjević's only aim, he says, is 'to open up a rational path for our thinking and thereby avoid illusions.'

The same rhetorical procedure is used by many other participants in public communication who seek to present their messages as *vox nationis*. Thus the journalist Goran Kozić, writing of an American plane crashing near Dubrovnik, offers his readers the rhetorical national 'we', in order to share with them a sense of alleged relief, in fact malicious gloating, which that incident must, according to Kozić, awaken in the breasts of all Serbs. 'We were afraid it would turn out to be us who were to blame again', writes Kozić, 'that it would emerge in some dispatch that the plane was hit from somewhere near Trebinje or Hercegnovi. We trembled lest it should be revealed that a bomb had been loaded by some airport official—a Serb. We were justifiably fearful, because they had given us a good fright.' (*Politika*, 7 April 1996) In other circumstances, the functioning of the national 'we' is reinforced by a picturesque conception of the national community, most frequently by the image of the nation as an organism, as a body. Then 'we' refers to a figure of flesh and blood, 'our' flesh and 'our' blood. It is writers in particular who strive to breathe corporeal life into 'our' nation, to supply it with skin, tissue, bones, a back, lungs, a bloodstream, nerves, even if for the most part this is in order to describe at length 'our' wounds and torments.

One of the most recent examples of this incarnated national 'we' is a speech by the writer Antonije Isaković. 'Much skin has been flayed from our backs', said Isaković, 'down to our very bones. But, although we have been crucified like Christ, we have held out, the substance has been preserved.' (*Politika*, 31 March 1996) In other words, the national skin has paid the price in order that the national skeleton and substance should be saved. When the result of the last Serbian warfaring is presented like this, then the question of the victim of that warfaring becomes not only politically out of place, but almost senseless: shall 'we' who had the role of flayed skin find solace in the fact that 'we', in the role of bones and substance, were saved?

The Serbian national 'we' is easily deepened and broadened: on the one hand, it seeks to embrace also 'our forebears', and, on the other hand, it wishes to stretch to all Slavs or at least all Orthodox ones. 'What we need', writes the journalist Gordana Petković, the author of the TV series 'A Treasury of Belgrade Spirituality', 'is to return to the language and culture of the Slav spirit which is in us and which links us with past times.' (*Politika*, 7 April 1996) In order to serve the business of expressing that distant Slav spirit of ours, she offers the sacrifice of her 'I', her author's personality, and attributes the authorship of her work to her forebears: 'In that sense, I do not consider myself the creator of this work. Those are generations which existed in the past and which are now speaking through us.'

In the rhetoric and aesthetics based on the national 'we', the destiny of 'I' is to disappear, by being assimilated into the national plural or accepted as an instance of the humble and penitent declaration of the individual announcing that in his fragile and ephemeral 'I', he has recognised and submissively accepted the eternal, potent national 'we'. National politicians and artists accept this apparently humble and self-effacing role of medium of the national will and national spirit, encouraging us not to see anything individual and personal in their works, but to accept them and celebrate them as examples of 'our' wisdom and 'our' glory.

The national rhetoric will not hear of 'I', while the society whose communication it dominates is full of conceited autocrats and great poets. In fact, the only 'I' which is really questioned here is the 'I' of critical distance and non-acceptance. Since it resists national assimilation and homogenisation, it excludes itself. The customary nature of that exclusion is the condemnation of the individual critical voice as a false 'I', for it is only a disguised 'we', and an alien 'we'. In national rhetoric generally, 'I' is therefore the pronoun of deceit and betrayal.

For example, the fact that I am now going to quote the words of the Bosnian Croat Ivan Lovrenović about 'we-speech' in Bosnia and Hercegovina and announce that in them I recognise reflections which are close to me will be proof to some that my critical 'I' in Serbia is nothing other than a hidden Croatian 'we'. Lovrenović writes about the 'ease with which people, so-called intellectuals (writers, scholars, academicians ...), abandon in an instant what was certainly a fragile, risky and isolated critical voice, but irreplaceably individual, and slip into "we-speech", falsely, inadequately, justified by exceptional circumstances (war, the suffering of the people, the interests of the nation, the needs of the homeland). It is not only Bosnia that is the setting for such a form of mental destruction, the Croatian intellectual milieu is equally undermined, while there is no need even to mention Serbian populism and collectivism, which is where it all began.' (Lovrenović, p. 40) We should not doubt for a moment that in both Bosnia and Croatia people will be found who will condemn this critical 'I' of Lovrenović's as a disguised Serbian 'we'.

9. Hatred

Mobile telephones, Chinese verse, the 'Moonlight' Sonata, the Belgrade marathon, the return of ambassadors to Belgrade, the reception in the White House garden, dressing the police up for Vrbica,[1] the Twenty-First Century, science and women, Europolis, return to the world, Cran Montana, the Internet, sunrise on the First of May, renewal and peace, peace, peace. These are just some of the images and words used by the designers and programmers of the regime in Serbia in recent weeks in order to embody as vividly and richly as possible the present politics of that regime, the so-called 'politics of peace'.

But in this symphony in praise of peace and the joy of life, there may often be heard, quite distinctly, the drums of war. The funereal voice of revenge howls, hatred sings, contempt grimaces. Where do those warlike notes in the peace-loving music of the Serbian government come from? Have the orchestra and choir which perform such music been infiltrated by disobedient players and singers, disinclined to peace without an alternative, hoodwinking their conductor and continuing in the old vein? Or are these, perhaps, the last echoes of 'Echoes and Reactions',[2] those ever weaker outpourings of sound and fury which precede the final and complete stilling of the warmongers?

---

[1] Vrbica is a religious feast day, probably of pagan origin. Parents dress their children up nicely and take them out for a walk. They buy them little yellow tin bells, to hang on ribbons round their necks. The expression 'dressing oneself up for Vrbica' means dressing up nicely.

[2] An exchange of views of readers of *Politika*, in which on the eve of the wars in former Yugoslavia and while they were in progress, a large number of texts were published whose authors, including some well-known Serbian intellectuals, gave their contribution to the propaganda of nationalism and war.

Several means are in use to send messages of hatred and intolerance through the main Serbian media, which now devote most of their space to the propaganda of peace and tolerance, i.e., where warlike messages apparently have no place or justification. One of these means is the adoption and inversion of anti-war messages. For example, in an article by Sandra Gucijan published in *Politika* (14 April 1996), on the occasion of the third anniversary of the death of Boško Brkić and Admira Ismić, a young man and girl killed on the Vrbanje bridge in Sarajevo as they attempted to cross into the part of the city controlled by the Bosnian Serbs. That tragic event, one of the most widely quoted examples of the horrors of the war in Bosnia, was described in such a way that two mutually contradictory conclusions could be drawn from the description.

On the one hand, the article offers a clear anti-war message, in which it is said that the tragic death of these two young people is 'a memorial which will remain as witness to Balkan madness and to a love which remained on the empty space between two hatreds'. Such a message is reinforced, among other things, by the detail that 'where the snipers' bullets originated remains a secret today'. Death could have come from either side, and perhaps from both.

But this anti-war message is mirrored by a message of hatred; later in the article, not caring much for consistency, the journalist accepts the opinion of the 'Serbian soldiers of Grbavica' that Boško and Admira were in fact killed by Muslims. Accepting that opinion, she endeavours to express it as suggestively as possible. 'Even the main Japanese television station, NHK, broadcast this moving tale,' she writes, 'showing clearly that the bullets came from the Muslim side, probably because of Admira's joyful leap as she approached Serbian territory—which, one supposes, annoyed someone who had a light finger on the trigger.' In this case, Boško and Admira are no longer an example of the innocent victims of war in which hatred and chauvinism do battle with love and togetherness. Their death becomes an illustration of alleged Muslim fickleness and cruelty, which can only arouse the anger of the just and engender a desire for revenge. Because who can be indifferent to these lines: 'So, in each other's arms, in no-man's land, they remained for a full six days and nights, while from the Muslim side, there was constant firing and a succession of bottles filled with petrol and set alight.' Death could have come only from that side. Curse it.

Of the various forms of the language of hatred which came into being on the eve of the wars in former Yugoslavia and during them, those which have most easily survived the new peace-loving trend of the Serbian regime are the manifestation of contempt and belittling of others in a clowning style. Thanks to the fact that the most direct and offensive manifestation of racist and chauvinistic hatred, when it is expressed in an ostensibly joking tone, with clowning grimaces and winking, may be considered rude but essentially frivolous and innocuous, the regime media are most willing to give space today to the clowning language of hatred. Such a language does not undermine the 'serious', official rhetoric of peace. While on the front pages of *Politika* Serbian officials write at length about the rapid establishment of economic and other co-operation with Croatia and the other former Yugoslav republics, in the column 'Cultural Corner' the journalist Dragana Bukmirović can write: 'I am overcome with panic at the idea that Zagreb pop, rock and other groups could come back. I have only just managed to rest my soul from their lovely song.' (*Politika*, 16 April 1996)

The clowning style of hate-speech in *Politika* is best illustrated by the ostensibly joking commentaries of Goran Kozić in his column 'From Week to Week'. Presumably believing that jokes and derision should not yield to anything, especially if it is a barb against our hated enemy, Kozić greeted the news of the stroke suffered by the Bosnian Federation President Alija Izetbegović with the following remark: 'In principle a person should not wish others ill, but there are cases when God would forgive such thoughts.' (*Politika*, 25 February 1996)

Kozić's favourite clowning trick consists in anticipating his reader's possible indignation at his heedless and primitive expression of hatred by ostensibly accepting in advance all the worst that the reader could think about his clownish grimacing. After passing on with delight the news that 'our former brothers are having a really hard time', because again this year 'no one wants to go to either the Croatian or the Slovene coast', Kozić pauses over what he has said in order to confirm that the reader has properly understood what he has read: 'This might sound as though we were gloating over someone else's misfortune. Which, in fact, we are.' (*Politika*, 3 March 1996)

Because why should a patriotic Serb today not be delighted and laugh heartily at the misfortunes of his former brothers, who had hoped that they would live better without him? It is harder to comprehend why that same Serb should gloat also over the misfortune of blacks in America. But Kozić, who likes to shock his reader with jokes at the expense of the 'coloured', wishes here too to liberate him from self-restraint and encourage him to join the author in enjoying his racist humour. He found his most recent cause for such a kind of amusement in the news of the judgment which ended the several years long trial of Bernard Getz, a white man who shot at four black youths when they tried to rob him in the New York subway. Kozić's attention was caught by the information that one of the wounded youths had suffered wounds which upset his mental development. This inspired him to write that insistence on this consequence of the wounding called into question the outcome of the trial, which had ended by condemning Getz. 'So the blacks clobbered the whites,' writes Kozić, 'although towards the end they nearly ruined the whole thing by maintaining that one of the attackers (30) has the brain of an eight-year-old, which is nothing unusual for someone born in the Bronx who had spent his youth there playing basket-ball and stealing cars.' Racism? Returning to his well-tried clowning trick, Kozić hastens to confess that there may be some in his text. 'Has it occurred to you', he asks his reader, 'that this part contains some uncivilised racist elements? Well, it does a bit.' (*Politika,* 28 April 1996)

It is hard to explain these and many other everyday examples of the presence of a warlike note in the media which otherwise propagate the so-called peace policy of the Serbian regime as remnants of a time that has in fact passed, which survive thanks to the power of political and psychological inertia. The fact that the language of war endures tenaciously in the media over which the government has complete control and that it coexists calmly with the language of the regime leads one to conclude that the strategists of Serbian politics do not believe that it is possible to govern Serbia in peacetime without recourse to fury, contempt and hatred directed above all at 'our' enemies, as at all of those (Jews, Blacks, Europe, America) who long since showed themselves suitable targets for maintaining hatred at a working temperature. I hear them saying: it is possible to govern without war, but not without hatred; you've deprived us of war, at least leave us hatred.

10. The Genes of the Tribe

In a newspaper announcement in which the employees of a Belgrade firm recently expressed their sorrow at the passing of their director, they ascribed his virtues to the 'genes of the tribe which had engendered him'. This is just one example which confirms the notion, very popular in Serbia today, that a man is governed by the genes of his community. Among those who are credited with popularising this idea, one of the most prominent is Dr Jovan Striković, manager of the 'Sveti Sava' hospital in Belgrade. His articles and speeches, collected and published in his book *Doba ravnodušnih* (*The Time of the Indifferent*), are linked above all by the author's effort to give a scientific and philosophical basis and popular expression to the idea that a person acts, thinks and feels exclusively the way the genetic code of the community to which he belongs determines.

At first glance, Striković's explanations seem to offer something more than mere biological determinism. He often calls on authors whom it is hard to connect with such a simple idea of man (Kant, Hegel, Nietzsche, Cassirer, Freud, Jung and Lacan). However, Striković's 'reading' of these great minds of the past and present amounts to the fact that, in one way or another, they reached the same position as the author of *The Time of the Indifferent* arrived at even without them. That is, what he allegedly knows at first hand from 'the people's philosophy'—that a man is governed by instincts inherited from his forebears and shared with other members of the ethnic community. It is enough for us to 'contemplate reality', writes Striković, to see that the teachings of Hegel, Frankl and Nietzsche 'have a biological foundation *par excellence*'.

Striković reduces the majority of psychological phenomena to a

Dr Jovan Striković, director of the Saint Sava Hospital in Belgrade, with nurses in Orthodox-style uniforms designed by him, 1992. (Draško Gagović)

biological foundation. This includes the concept of the archetype, to which he is glad to have recourse. Archetypes, he says, 'must be transmitted exclusively by a genetic path', while they are created 'on the basis of concrete etiology'. For him the genetic code and the archetype are the same: a reservoir of inherited and biologically predetermined ideas, images, figures, feelings and behaviours characteristic of the members of an ethnic community. These can be such things as melancholy, treachery, paranoia, Obilić, Kosovo, credulity. For example, in Striković's judgment the Montenegrin people 'does not have the idea of suspicion in their archetype, in their genetic code' and 'the credulity of this people is its characteristic and characterological feature.'

Archetypes and genes are the same, 'spiritual and mental needs', just as instincts are. It is always a matter of some 'imperative' older than the individual and consciousness. This imperative is what Striković relies on when he forsees that the Montenegrins will, willy nilly, restore the chapel on the peak of Mount Lovćen.[1] This will happen because of 'spiritual and mental needs which have priority over every prohibition and are stronger because they have the specificity of instinct'. 'The restoration of Njegoš's tomb to its original state', he continues, 'is no longer a matter of someone's will, nor a conscious activity, but an imperative which will be realised—whether anyone wants it or not.'

Biology does not make Striković's man close to other people, for him it is not a universal on which a general human identity rests. On the contrary, biology connects a person fatefully with his ethnic community and separates him from members of different communities. The archetypes, myths and instincts which are genetically 'encoded' are above all nationally coloured. 'Each individual member of a nation carries the sediment of that nation's experience in himself, in the form of archetypes or myths.' They are the stuff of the *ethnos*, understood as an animal species, and incomprehensible and inaccessible to another *ethnos*. People are fatally divided by ethnic (national, tribal) differences, for it is only within the framework of the same ethnic community that we feel the 'empathy which may be defined as the capacity to transfer to oneself the thoughts, feelings and actions of others'. Those who are outside do not understand anything, they do not participate in anything of 'ours'. As the writer of *The Time of the Indifferent* explains, 'some Yugoslav political leaders have not grasped or felt the pain and suffering of the Serbian people ... because of a diametrically contradictory way of thinking. They reason in different categorical forms, which is a consequence of belonging to a different ethnos in which people not only think but also feel differently.'

Different genes—different faiths. Striković's biology of the *ethnos* leads one to conclude that there are unbridgeable religious differences between peoples. Neither their gods nor their beliefs can be shared. The Serbs and the Montenegrins believe more in Obilić and St Sava than in a Christian God. 'It would even be possible to say', he writes, 'that in the Montenegrin national being the archetype of God

---

[1] The original small Orthodox tomb of the Prince-Bishop and poet Petar Petrović Njegoš was replaced by a grandiose mausoleum designed by the renowned Croatian (Catholic) sculptor Ivan Mestrović. (Transl.)

is fairly suppressed,' and that 'Obilić has taken His place'. Everything begins with him. 'It is not from Christ, but from Obilić's act, that we calculate time,' says Striković elsewhere.

National genes are not mutually comprehensible. One *ethnos* does not understand what another tells it. They are divided by untranslatable symbols. That is why Striković reduces psychoanalysis to investigating the national soul. For example, the five-pointed star is, he says, 'for our ethnos, strange and unacceptable as a symbol.' In the same way, it is mistaken to interpret the symbol of the weapon, which appears in Njegoš's *Gorski Vijenac* (The Mountain Wreath) in Knez Bajko's dream, as a universal *topos*, i.e. as 'sexual symbolism'. It is mistaken because 'weapons in Montenegro, then and today—but especially then—were the symbol of manliness.' Striković evidently does not perceive any sexual connotation in the word 'manliness'.

The instinctive, tribal man is not tormented by problems brought by civilisation. He is true to his genetic code, that is to instinct and tradition, he does not forget his origins. At every moment he knows what he has to think and do. This raises him above 'the state of general hypocrisy, degeneration and moral corrosion in which contemporary civilisation is choking.' While the tribe engendered 'epic man', civilisation creates a monstrous 'test-tube man'. Epic man says: 'I want to know who I am and of whose blood.' When that question is posed by 'test-tube men', continues Striković, 'I believe that this is their greatest existential dilemma, and perhaps an unmanageable torment.'

All in all, both as a doctor and a writer, Striković advises us, even today, to cling to our tribe, to 'that umbilical cord through which men of this region acquire far more of the good and human than the bad.' One should return to the earth and instincts, cherish the biological inheritance of the tribe. 'Endeavour', the writer of *The Time of the Indifferent* recommends, 'to restore to yourself the reflex of the animal, that biological gift, to react to offence with greater offence. Draw the fluids of life out of the earth, in order to be cured of sickness, of sick civilisation.'

When the national identity is determined by the biology of the *ethnos*, the genes of the tribe, the reflex of the animal, then a man can have only one identity. For instance, he can be either a Montenegrin or a Serb, or say that they are the same thing. It is precisely on this point that Striković's model does not satisfy even himself. Because he evidently wishes to preserve for himself a double national identity, Serbian and Montenegrin, which is a common and in many cases successful identity strategy in the Balkans. But it cannot be explained by Strikovič's 'genetic' determinism. That is why the author of *The Time of the Indifferent* constantly contradicts himself. On the one hand, he writes that the Montenegrins are 'part of the Serbian people', that 'Montenegrin melancholy is part of Serbian sorrow', and that Njegoš is 'the most Serbian Serbian poet', while at the same time, he talks of 'the Montenegrin national being', and the 'Montenegrin *ethnos*', maintaining that 'Montenegro is a planetary phenomenon, a miracle in the earthly pattern'. In truth, the fact that someone is both a Serb and a Montenegrin, and at the same time one or two other things besides, is simply a banal way of living today in a civilised society. Instead of satisfying himself with that, Strikovič torments himself with the question of 'whose blood' he belongs to. In seeking an answer to that impossible question, a great deal of blood has been taken, and not only from people's fingers.

11. Relics

In recent weeks the attention of the media in Serbia has been preoccupied with the earthly remains of ancestors. The Serbian Orthodox Church organised several spectacular rituals dedicated to the earthly remains of two saints, Sava and Vasilije Ostroški, and a dignitary of the church, Bishop Nikolaj Velimirović. The Church calls these remains relics, *'mošti'*, a Church-Slavonic word which, the dictionaries tell us, originates in Old Slavonic. Its etymology directs us to the main characteristic which religion attributes to the earthly remains of saintly forebears, because at the root of the word *mošti* we find the Germano-Slav lexeme *Macht*, that is *moć* (power). The Greek word for 'relics'—*dynamis*—has a similar etymological origin.

In the eyes of the church, the earthly remains of saints, martyrs or prominent priests and reliquaries (the boxes in which these remains are kept) like their graves and parts of their clothing, have supernatural, miraculous power. Most frequently, they are endowed with miraculous healing action. They heal sickness of the body and spirit. This is the power, for instance, of the *sanctorum reliquiae* of Saint Vasilije Ostroški. When his relics were carried recently in a religious procession through Nikšić, it was conceived and carried out as a kind of collective therapy. The organisers explained that through the miraculous power of the holy relics they wished to influence the spiritual state of the inhabitants of that Montenegrin town, where over the last few years there had been an exceptionally large number of murders and suicides.

The lawful keepers of the relics, the announcers, directors and interpreters of the miraculous events brought about by them, have at their disposal an exceptionally important instrument and symbol of power. That is why from earliest times the church and priesthood

Radovan Karadžić participating in bringing out the relics of St Vasilije Ostroški before their journey to Herzegovina, 10 May 1996. (Photograph published in the paper 'Pravoslavlje', 1 June 1996)

have endeavoured to preserve their monopoly of care for all kinds of relics. Their possession represents a traditional source of authority for the church, while the ritual manipulation and exhibition of relics serves the spread of belief. But control of relics may also be important political capital. The priesthood can use them to achieve political influence. On the other hand, political regimes are also interested in placing the cult of the relics of the forebears at the service of strengthening and legitimating their own power. In some cases they do so in co-operation with the church authorities, and in others independently of them or even contrary to their will, on their own initiative.

The procession bearing the relics of Vasilije Ostroški on 10 and 11 May through Montenegro and Hercegovina, from Ostrog to Tvrdnoš and back, is an example of the co-operation of the clerical and secular powers in the use of religious relics for political purposes. This is borne out by three pages dedicated to this event in the paper *Javnost* (18 May 1996), one of the organs of the regime in Pale. A report entitled 'Miracle in Hercegovina' describes the miraculous events which accompanied the procession. It says that 'the night before they set off', Patriarch Pavle, Metropolitan Amfilohije and Bishop Atanasije 'removed the cover from the miracle-worker'. Metropolitan Amfilohije observed that the body of Saint Vasilije was exceptionally well preserved and later described 'how the Saint's arms bent, as though he wished to help us more easily clothe him for the long journey'. The second miracle—proof of the saintliness of Vasilije Ostroški—occurred just before the procession set off: 'Those who had the good fortune to approach his relics before they left, as they kissed the cross on his breast, smelled the divine aroma which came from the Saint's breast.' Finally, along the whole length of the journey of the relics of the miracle-worker from Ostrog, there was a miracle of joy among every living thing: 'The birds, flowers, even the animals rejoiced wherever the procession with the relics passed.' Particularly striking was the joy of a dappled horse: 'The horse ran for a long time in the column of cars, as though he too wished to show his joy at being alive on the day when the greatest Serbian son of Hercegovina was passing through his holy, Biblical Homeland.'

Nevertheless, according to the words of the author of the report, and according to the statements of the organisers of the procession, 'The Lord directed the relics of Saint Vasilije Ostroški, the miracle-worker' to Hercegovina 'on 10 May of this year', with the aim above all of having the miracle-worker help towards its salvation from the suffering and torment provoked by its enemies. 'Alas, help us, Holy Hercegovinian', wailed Bishop Atanasije over the relics of Saint Vasilije. He did not refrain from making a predominantly political speech and on that occasion named the external and internal enemies of Hercegovina, a country 'wounded from outside and from within', a country where 'the foundations of Orthodox Byzantium' and the 'foundations of Serbdom' were situated. He complained to the miracle-worker Vasilije of 'foreigners' and 'occupiers from the wide world', the United Nations, the European Union, the Spanish 'who are a little gentler than the others', and most of all of 'the false promise-givers, who said that we would not bow our heads, while today they crawl before foreigners and occupiers, you know who I mean.'

Speaking over the relics of his holy forebear, trusting in their miracle-working powers, and even more in the authority and power of the words of the authorised keepers and demonstrators of those relics, Bishop Atanasije called on the Serbs gathered there to pledge themselves to a decisive showdown with their enemies, to war to the last man: 'Brothers, let this be our pledge to Saint Vasilije, that we shall stand tall and straight, that we shall gladly perish, rather than sully our honour.' At that moment, the speaker was joined by some of the highest representatives of the government and army of Republika Srpska. One of them, Božidar Vučurević, ended his reflection on Saint Vasilije and Serbdom, which he confided in the journalist from *Javnost*, with the message that 'everyone who votes in the next election for any other party than the SDS bears responsibility for the future of the Serbian people, but also responsibility towards the dead, who gave their lives for this state.'

The regime of Slobodan Milošević has now to satisfy its need for an appropriate number of forebears and their holy relics on the whole independently of the Serbian Orthodox Church, which does not wish at this moment to place its supply of that strategic symbolic material at his disposal or to share it with him. As a result, the government in Serbia endeavours to compensate for its lack of relics and reliquaries of saints and clerics through the earthly remains and graves of national heroes, above all warriors. In the course of the last two years, the greatest number of celebrations of the anniversaries of glorious battles and other episodes in the life of national heroes was held within the organisation of the government and with political leaders in the main roles. The last such event was the commemorative ceremony before the mausoleum on the island of Vid and over the Corfu 'blue graveyard', with the Serbian Prime Minister Mirko Marjanović in the role of the main priest. As *Politika* wrote, in a lengthy account on the first two pages of its edition of 24 May 1996, on that occasion Marjanović particularly stressed what is expected above all from every ritual involving relics—a manifestation of miraculous power, that is, as the Prime Minister put it, 'the proud feeling of strength and self-confidence at the moment when we evoke the glorious epic of the Serbian army of eight decades ago.'

Nor can the police reduce its authority to physical power—it has to draw its strength and prestige from the cult of nationally acknowledged forebears. It too bows to the relics of its miracle-workers. Thus the State Security Service recently proclaimed the former ministers A. Ranković, S. Penezić and S. Lazarević as its founding fathers—and introduced a ritual of bowing before their graves. The same kind of preoccupation of the government may be seen in the controversy over the preservation of Tito's earthly remains in Belgrade. The question of whether the contemporary state needs Tito's tomb or whether it ought to be handed over to Croatia, which, it seems, knows what to do with it, is in fact a question about the destiny of something that is currently an underestimated but potentially powerful weapon of the government. Tito's relics are perhaps in a better state than is judged today. Perhaps they too have the power to bring joy among the people and animals, the power once embodied in Tito's baton?* Why hurry to hand them over to Croatia?

Given that the government and the majority of the opposition in Serbia are hastily filling up their ranks with dead forebears and endeavouring to hold the largest possible number of graves, chapels, monuments, reliquaries, epiphanies and requiems in their control, it may be anticipated that political conflicts in Serbia will in future take place increasingly under the sign of a war of relics, in which the winner will be the one who has the greatest number preserved in the best state.

12. Gauss

Gauss is the only name mentioned in a speech by the President of the Serbian Academy of Science and Arts, Aleksandar Despić, about Kosovo as 'the most significant strategic problem' of the Serbian people. Despić refers to Gauss in the part of his speech devoted to a kind of scientific description of the Albanians. 'The Albanians,' he said, 'like any other people, are a people in which, if one follows the Gauss distribution statistically, there is a wide spectrum of human characteristics, from the very bad, producing murderers and drug-dealers, the good ones which constitute a hard-working and honourable people of patriarchal upbringing who must be respected, to people of fine minds and creative abilities, true intellectuals.' (*Naša Borba,* 10 June 1996)

I am one of those who had to look at the encyclopaedia to see what it said under 'Gauss'. That was how I discovered that he was Karl Friedrich Gauss (1777–1855), a renowned German mathematician, physicist and astronomer. The Prosveta encyclopaedia explains also 'the Gauss distribution', which 'occurs in statistics, external ballistics and technology', and which is also known as 'the normal distribution'. In Despić's portrait of the Albanians, the judgment that the characteristics of this people correspond to the Gauss distribution means that they are normal. Hence they include both the worst and the best, but most of all ordinary, simply good people neither too terrible nor too outstanding.

It seems that Despić thinks that in Serbia there are doubts and reservations concerning the human characteristics and even the normality of the Albanian people. He sees nothing strange in the fact that in a discussion of the problem of Kosovo he should start by clearing this up, that is by expressing in the Academy of Sciences the realistic and competent judgment that the Albanians are indisputably real, normal people. On the basis of that judgment, Despić arrives at the conclusion that the Albanian people are in essence sufficiently qualified for the Serbs to 'live harmoniously with them and share the administration of the state'.

But what is Gauss doing here? If Despić has already concluded that it is necessary today to say that the Albanians are neither worse nor better than other people, he could quite easily have said so without recourse to the Gauss distribution or any other scientific argument. We would have believed him even without that. There is no doubt that in Despić's speech Gauss does not have the role of a scientific authority necessary for a credible account of the actual state of affairs, but rather that he serves here as a rhetorical figure. He is a figure of that kind of political language which seeks to be accepted as discourse from the other side of illusion and error, myths and mystification, as 'the discourse of reality'.

In our contemporary political language, 'the discourse of reality' most frequently creates the impression of conviction with the help of scientific or pseudo-scientific references. 'Gauss', as a rhetorical figure in Despić's speech, is an example of that 'realism' of political language equipped with the stamp of the scientific. Through the figure of 'Gauss', the speaker is letting us know that what he is saying is something that is in the greatest measure (i.e. scientifically) real, objective and rational, far from any kind of prejudice or myths, unsullied by emotions. He acknowledges that he is motivated by a feeling of great anxiety, but that he is responding to that impulse sensibly, soberly, controlling his heart, and above all on the basis of scientifically confirmed facts. Emotion, he is saying, should not 'blur our vision so that we cannot realistically perceive both our contemporary situation and our perspectives'. This is an important point in the rhetorical strategy of Despić's speech.

But the originality of this strategy and of Despić's rhetorical skill generally lies above all in the fact that he is endeavouring to present a realistically and scientifically based solution of the Kosovo problem, which he evidently believes to be completely unacceptable to the Serbs, leading them straight to ruin. By pointing out, broadly and in a tone of distanced scientific objectivity, with reference to Gauss, all the good sides of one of what he sees as the 'two possible paths' leading to a solution of the Kosovo problem—i.e. the path which leads to the preservation and strengthening of a common state of

Serbs and Albanians—he, apparently paradoxically, only wishes to increase the conviction of the political message that the Serbs absolutely must not follow that path. Despić describes it 'realistically', one would say impartially, he conjures up all its good sides, but only in order that the rejection of that path to solving the Kosovo problem should appear to be the result of a mature and scientific assessment of the Serbian national interest.

In this speech Despić is in fact trying to prove that a common state of Serbs and Albanians, 'a country of ethnic duality', is not in the Serbian interest. Such a state is acceptable only 'in principle'. Of the two ostensible paths to resolving the Kosovo problem, one is, as Orwell might say, more possible than the other. That is entering into talks in good time 'about civilised separation and delineation, so that the tragic experiences of the immediate past should not be repeated.'

Despić tries to present this second solution as scientifically based as well, strengthening it with rhetorical figures à la Gauss, that is with figures from the arsenal of the 'discourse of reality' based on an arsenal from science. Thus in Despić's speech data appear about the demographic recession of the Serbian people and expansion of the Albanians, more as rhetorical figures of 'scientificness' than as scientific facts important for his thesis. In the whole search for the 'rational basis' of the problem, there follows a discussion, in a scientific style, about the 'categorisation' of the Albanians as a minority and about the 'nature of the process of merging'.

However, in this part of his speech Despić also has recourse to other rhetorical devices. The explanation he gave for the first possible road to solving the Kosovo problem, which would in fact be fatal for the Serbs (a shared state), remains in its entirety within the borders of the rhetoric of the 'discourse of reality', put forward in a tone of measured description. By contrast, the explanation he offers for the second and in his opinion only correct solution to this problem—the timely and peaceful separation of Serbs and Albanians)—is based mostly on achieving agreement by means of provoking emotional and irrational solidarity. For example, the rapid increase in the number of Albanian inhabitants of Kosovo is here not described only as 'demographic expansion' but, far more suggestively, as a 'demographic flood' and 'explosion'.

And the most important and 'weighty' argument in the whole of Despić's speech also belongs to this kind of rhetoric, which exploits feelings of frustration, threat, fear and hatred. The Serbs should on no account decide in favour of continuing to live with the Albanians in the same state, above all because that would allegedly suit the enemies of Serbia. It is precisely the proven enemies of the Serbs who 'very decisively insist that the Albanians in Kosovo ought not to imagine that they could become an independent state.' Despić advises that it is worth reflecting on this and grasping the fact that it conceals an underhand conspiracy of certain international circles, whom it suits to have the Albanians stay in Serbia and subjugate the Serbs by means of a demographic explosion. They 'wish in this way to bring about a kind of occupation of Serbia from within'. The Germans excel in this. 'The German government', explains Despić, 'has just decided to assist this ethnic transformation of Serbia and speed it up by sending back to Yugoslavia 120,000 mainly Albanian "asylum-seekers"'.

In an endeavour to make his view of what should be done to solve the problem of Kosovo as convincing as possible, Despić calls on old Gauss only in order to give the impression that he was being quite correct in his presentation of something that he did not accept. What he does accept and proposes should be generally accepted—the separation and fencing off of the Serbs and Albanians—he reinforces with something which, by all accounts, he considers far stronger: the age-old fear of the Germans.

13. Combat

How did it happen that the 'Laser 21' exercise took place before the eyes of the Supreme Defence Council of the Federal Republic of Yugoslavia? Where is the French army going? How does one become an agent of the CIA? What makes invisible warships invisible? How is Albania armed? What are the emblems of the squadron which bears the sign of the tiger in some Western countries? Do women fighter pilots have sexual problems? Are we on the threshold of an age of robot war? These are some of the most important questions to which answers are offered by the new magazine for military issues, *Combat,* recently founded by the company that publishes *Politika* and edited by the journalist Miroslav Lazanski.

According to the intention of the editor, described in the editorial of the first issue under the title 'Competence', this magazine about war and weapons will write about the 'geo-strategic aspects of the modern world, about foreign armies and their problems', but above all about interesting features of military technology. It is to open up space 'for expert, objective and absolutely professional concern with military issues ... for a modern approach to military questions.' There will be 'critical analysis', but there will not be any discussion of ticklish questions about our army and its recent past. 'This is not a time for gloating', explains Lazanski, 'regardless of everything that happened, and even when it is a matter of our own army.'

Judging by the first issue (June 1996), *Combat* intends to consign 'everything that happened' to salutary oblivion. There is little mention of the war in Croatia and Bosnia and its consequences, and then only in passing, as something that has a distant, indirect connection with present-day Yugoslavia and its army. There is no trace of the horrors of war, war devastation and war crimes and their protagonists. Not a word about the hundreds of thousands of people killed, dispossessed and persecuted. The war in Croatia and Bosnia is mentioned only as 'a military flare-up in the neighbourhood'. In one article it is reduced to a 'circumstance' which meant that our army was more tired than usual because of having to keep watch, and military technological resources were used up faster than usual. 'This demanded considerable exertion on the part of the Army', writes the author of this article, 'but also in this recent period in many ways military technology reached the limits of its capacity.'

The first issue of *Combat* hints that the magazine will not only avoid writing about the recently concluded war in Croatia and Bosnia, but will also leave aside any other real war, or real aspect of war. It is as though competent and expert writing about an army is limited to its peacetime activities, to the time when the soldier is ironed, fed, rested and when all members of his family, all his comrades and all his limbs are in place.

Young readers of this magazine—and it is intended above all for them—are offered a picture of the army as a kind of sports-recreational and educational-scientific organisation. Reading *Combat,* they will not for a moment think that shiny aircraft and their pilots with Ray Ban goggles, powerful tanks and their multi-barrelled mortars, polished boots and moustachioed officers have anything whatever to do with devastated towns and torched villages, with scattered intestines and mass graves. On the contrary, they will think that all these images of devastation and misery are only malicious, spiteful propaganda against the army and its noble work. For in *Combat,* a competent, professional and modern magazine intended for young people, they will find that the army and warfare are a kind of permanent Olympiad of knowledge and talent, especially in the area of electronic games and comradely contest in elegance and fine manners.

In this magazine, war exists only as a theme of military exercises and games, where it is conjured up in the form of so-called virtual reality, that is, as it is explained in one text, as 'simulation of integrated battle in real time'. Of course, what is meant is real chronometrical time and not real historical time. Because the presentation of the army and war outside real historical time is one of the fundamental characteristics of this magazine. This is best illustrated by the fact that in the longest text in the first issue (written by Lazanski), an image of future war is conjured up. It is quite mistaken to expect, on the basis of the shameful experience of the latest Balkan warfare, that in some future war the main role will belong to hordes of murderers and plunderers led by false national saviours and prophets. That is not a competent and professional judgment. In a future war, Lazanski assures us, an important role, if not the decisive one, will be played by a herd of robots led by engineers and technicians.

This is how it could look: 'The year 1999. Tank columns of the "blue" advance over the plain while at the same time the war planes of the "red" appear on the horizon. The anti-aircraft guns of the attackers automatically aim at the sky, from where a real rain of special anti-tank missiles falls, on little parachutes. In the thunderstorm of explosions which follows, aircraft are brought down, tanks immobilised and abandoned. Losses of the conflicting parties, dead and wounded? There are none! The tanks and aircraft have no human crews, they are directed and led from a distance.'

Thus, 'regardless of all that happened', which must, evidently, be ascribed to some mistake and confusion that has nothing to do with real soldiers and military experts, the soldier has no real reason to be afraid of a future war. He certainly does not have any reason to shrink from the army and military calling in peacetime. In its very first issue, *Combat* offers in support of this attitude what is a very important argument for a young man: the army is full of beautiful women, and some of them have nothing against demonstrating their beauty. As a result, Lazanski is in the fortunate position of being able to show in his magazine just how good women look in colour photographs in uniform, and even better without it. They are there to illustrate one place in an article on 'modern Amazons', which describes how 'several female members of the American armed forces were recently dismissed, because they were photographed nude for *Playboy*, which scandalised their commanders, but delighted their male colleagues at headquarters and in the units.' Although this refers only to beautiful women in foreign armies, there is no doubt that the surroundings in which our officers move also abound in beauties. This is suggested by an advertisement for the Military Academy of the Yugoslav Army, published in this magazine: a pair of male legs in officers' trousers and beside them a pair of female legs wriggling in the air, for their owner is evidently hanging round the neck of her 'commander'. Caption: 'Be an officer and a gentleman'.

This example shows that there is a paradoxical distribution of symbols between the regular and voluntary military units in Serbia. One would expect that the latter, composed often of people of dubious origin including former criminals, would correspond to models from

Cover of the first number of *Combat* magazine.

American films and fantasies about beauties from *Playboy*, while the regular army and its academy would maintain military traditions and their symbols and images. But, it seems that the logic of symbolisation can hold surprises. Thus it has happened that the figures of Obilić, Karadjordje or Hajduk Veljko* are connected exclusively with people such as Giška, Kapetan Dragan and Arkan*, while the Yugoslav Army has opted to look for symbols of the identity of the military profession in the field of contemporary popular culture.

There is no less of a paradox in the fact that the editor of *Combat*, the magazine for military questions, mentions only one name in the editorial of its first issue, namely that of one of the fiercest opponents of armies and war: Mahatma Gandhi. Should we see in this a sign that the shame and disgrace the recent bloodbath in Croatia and Bosnia have dulled the salt of war even for its most cynical 'expert commentators'? Or is it rather the old propaganda strategy of the army and warfare, which presents them as the only possible means of dedicated service to peace?

14. Theatre Town

In the Montenegrin coastal town of Budva, on 1 July 1996, there was a change of local government. It was carried out non-violently: the representatives of the previous government and their followers withdrew from the town without a fight. Entering into Budva, its new leaders did not encounter any resistance. That same evening, they summoned a meeting of the citizens in the main town square. The occasion was the ceremony of handing the keys of the town over to the new leader. Those gathered there were informed of the first decrees of the new authorities, including the decision that the name Budva should be changed to Theatre Town. By the same decision, the main town square would now be called Poets' Square. The next day, 2 July, the citizens were again invited to gather and hear their new commander. In a lengthy speech, punctuated by applause, he particularly warned any remaining adherents of the old regime that war against them would be continued. 'We shall carry on', he said.

The newspapers wrote at length about this event, so that everyone knew that Budva had not really fallen to a new power, but had done so only in play, according to the scenario of the town's summer festival. Government was handed over only symbolically, for a specified time (fifty-one days) and into the hands of masters of a particular kind—artists. As the President of the Federal Republic of Yugoslavia, Zoran Lilić, said in the speech with which he opened the festival, Budva 'was opening its gates wide and handing over the keys of the town to new masters, masters of creativity, masters of talent, masters of skill and masters of artistry.' (*Politika*, 1 July 1996)

In the procession of these new symbolic masters of Budva the most notable were the theatre director and writer Vida Ognjenović, the author of a programme with the poetic title 'City of Sun and Games', which was performed at the opening of the festival; then the conductor Darinka Matić-Marović, with the 'Krsmanović' choir, which has also recently begun to use its maiden name, and is now called the 'Obilić-Krsmanović' choir; the writer Borislav Mihailović Mihiz, and the Metropolitan of coastal Montenegro and member of the Writers' Union of Serbia, Amfilohije Radović. Before them all, in the role of their leader and symbolic Commander of the Theatre Town, was Academician Matija Bećković, who was referred to in the report in *Politika* about the change of authority in Budva by the title of 'the Prince of Serbian Poetry'. 'We shall carry on' was the title of Bećković's comic verse which he read on the Poets' Square.

When masters of art take power, everything that can only be dreamed about under the authority of ordinary political leaders suddenly becomes realisable, miracles happen before our eyes, constraints are shattered, horizons of thought and spirit stretch to unimagined borders. The pitiful reality of everyday life gives way to another, finer reality. Even President Lilić, when he speaks of this, appears to become obsessed by an irresistible power, which drives him to express himself with an inspiration which is absolutely unexpected from him. 'Under the clear summer sky, everything is possible', said Lilić, 'and even miracles become natural and expected and experienced. All this is reality, that other reality which makes life meaningful and worth living.' (*Politika,* 3 July 1996)

The masters of Theatre Town were given a mandate to govern in that other reality. Their job was not to change or possibly correct actuality, but temporarily to chase it ritually from the town, in order for the town to forget it as long as the festival lasted and rest its soul from it. That was required of them also by the actor Svetozar Cvetković, who, in the costume of the renowned nineteenth-century writer and citizen of Budva Stevan Mitrov Ljubiša, symbolically handed over government of the town to the artists, with the words: 'Let reality behind be suspended these ramparts for the next fifty days and nights.'

The festival change of government in Budva was carried out according to a scenario that reminds one in many ways of what we knew, thanks to research into old and traditional societies, about the temporary symbolic deposition of legal authorities during orgiastic and carnival celebrations. These celebrations were also characterised by a controlled and time-limited suspension of the legal authorities, and their symbolic replacement by the institution of rule in the name of unlimited freedom, madness and dream, that is in the name of a principle contrary to those which real authority has to represent and defend. The titles of Master of Theatre Town and Prince of Poetry are similar to the medieval ones of King of the Madmen and Queen of the Carnival.

The festival transformation of Budva into Theatre Town reminds one of the medieval feast days of the Madmen and the Innocent mostly in the fact that now too the new symbolic provisional government is presented as a parody of real government. And the artists establish their regime just as it is done by real military and political authorities today. First of all, they occupy the territory, leaving no small area outside their control. 'When the banners are unfurled on the masts and when the fanfare echoes from the town ramparts', explains Lilić, 'the actors, musicians, painters, sculptors, writers ... will occupy every smallest corner under the clear sky, suitable for and in harmony with their expression and creativity.' Then, imitating contemporary politicians, they too endeavour to homogenise the population and to that end offer the ideal of the parliamentary state as a living organism, as one body. For, still according to Lilić, 'for 51 days the whole of Budva becomes one single body—a Town of Theatre.' Just as the Serbian state is the state of the Serbian people, so the Theatre Town is the town of a 'theatre people'. Statesmen and military commanders devote their lives to the Serbian people, and the masters of the Theatre Town, according to Lilić, 'bequeath to the theatre people gathered here the fruits of their inspiration.' (*Politika*, 2 July 1996)

The specific nature of the symbolic renunciation of power at this year's summer festival in Budva lies in the fact that it was carried out three times, each time in a different way. First, the surrender of the administration of this Montenegrin town by the authorities to artists and its transformation into Teatropolis was announced by the President of the Federal State himself. Then it was carried out as part of a dramatic programme at the opening of the festival, as a game within a game, in which an actor in the role of Stefan Mitrov Ljubiša gave the town into the hands of the artists on the stage. Finally, the role of those who were symbolically surrendering their authority to the artists was played by the highest functionaries of Montenegro (M. Bulatović, S. Marović, M. Djukanović) and the most important local dignitaries. Sitting among the guests at the opening of the festival on 1 July, they accepted calmly and without a word the fact that their authority in this part of the Republic was suspended and, as a result, they did not appear the following day, when the Prince of Poets read his comic verse.

In fact, the Montenegrin leaders seemed convincing in their roles of power-holders only when they withdrew before the masters of the game, the spirit and the pen. They gave the impression that they were abandoning power reluctantly. It was only thanks to them that the proclamation of Theatre Town had something of a real revolt, resembling a little summer putsch. President Lilić did not help greatly. On the contrary, instead of accepting the role of defeated political reality along with the Montenegrin leadership, he hurried to join the side of the artists, masquerading as one of them. This is borne out by the poetic style of his speech, and, still more, by his effort to approach the Prince of Poets. Unlike the Montenegrin President and his suite, the Yugoslav President appeared on 2 July in the square of poetry in order to hear Bećković. Stepping altogether outside the role of the defeated power of the politicians, whom the Prince of Poets had 'driven' from the town, he even struck up a friendly conversation with him, whose Ionesco-esque beginning was carried by the newspapers. 'At the end, when the audience was still crowding round Bećković', writes the reporter for *Politika*, 'President Lilić came up to him and said: "It was exceptionally pleasant to listen to you." Academician Bećković replied: "I am delighted that you enjoyed it."' (*Politika*, 4 July 1996)

The fact that Lilić, either as a game or as a joke, did not feel like enjoying the role of retreating authority may have been the reason why, after the opening ceremony, his Montenegrin colleagues could no longer be seen in Theatre Town, and why, as reported in *Naša Borba* (3 July 1996), Bećković spoke on the second day of the festival 'in the noticeable absence of republican and local officials'. Seeing that Lilić had left them and joined the masters of Theatre Town, among whom was one artistic figure they knew well—Amfilohije Radović—the Montenegrin leaders must have thought that the dividing lines between game and reality, between dream and waking, between theatre and politics are often illusory.

15. Tunnel

On the basis of one of his war reports, the journalist Vanja Bulić wrote the first version of the scenario of S. Dragojević's film *Lepa sela lepo gore* (Pretty Village Pretty Flame). He also wrote a novel on the same theme, entitled *Tunel* (*Tunnel*). After the report and the scenario, Bulić's novel also talks of the suffering of a group of Serbian fighters, as they endured several days of siege by Muslims in a tunnel on the Višegrad-Foča road.

In a note printed on the book's jacket, the author says that he was inspired by the 'moving story of the curse of civil war'. However, that inspiration is only partly recognisable in the novel. The 'moving' quality is there, but not the 'curse'. It is evident that the author has striven to paint the most barbaric possible picture of the horrors of war, to describe the atrocities and agony to which people are exposed in war. And to do so without sparing the sensitivities of his reader. But in the novel these horrors are not ascribed to some curse, not even to the curse of civil war, they are just the high price of the noble battle of the Serbian fighters for survival and freedom. Not one of them doubts the sense and justification of this struggle and the sufferings that it entails. As far as the Muslim fighters are concerned, they are there only to torture, wound and kill the besieged Serbs. Their own possible suffering, essential if it is to be at all possible to speak of the 'curse of civil war', is barely mentioned.

In fact, Bulić's image of the war in Bosnia is reduced to the repetition of several platitudes reflecting the way this war is widely seen in Serbia today. He too subscribes to the cliché of Bosnia as a land of hatred. Thus in *Tunnel* too the alleged supreme witness of that fatal Bosnian hatred is named as Ivo Andrić.[1] In Bulić's book, the war began when Muslims killed a Serbian guest at a wedding in the Sarajevo Baščaršija. In the war everyone suffers, but the Serbs most of all; the worst people in Bosnia are not the old settlers, but the newcomers from the Sandžak. The war here also has a good side: it drove people to grasp the truth which they had tried to hide from themselves, according to which they are what they are by nationality. 'I am a Serb', rejoices one of the Serbian fighters in Bulić's novel. 'I have realised who we are, and who you are,' a Muslim officer announces proudly.

But, as a result, *Tunnel* is not only a patriotic or war-propaganda novel. In it the story of the causes, aims and message of the war is nevertheless in the background, while the war itself is less a theme than décor for the main thing—the 'moving' story. That décor should not draw the reader's attention to itself. That is the reason why Bulić prefers to stick to a quite conventional picture of the Bosnian war as a heroic Serbian revolt and resistance, avoiding involving himself in thematising the far more complicated idea of its 'cursed' nature.

Equally, concentration on the 'moving' and the generic consequences of such a focus of his novel are the reason why Bulić does not pay much attention to the literary aspect of his novel either. In order to stimulate the emotion with which he wishes to stir up the readers of *Tunnel*, he does not need what are in the true sense artistic means. Indeed, they would only get in his way. That is why the characterisation, the motivation of the action and other requirements of the narration of the novel rely exclusively on a repertoire of clichés from para-literary and trivial genres.

The main character Milan is described as 'a machine that walks, shoots and burns'; professor Petar is 'a quiet teacher', he has 'passed through life quietly'. The former criminal Velja is 'a lover of life', he 'lives on his memories of thieving and whores' while 'he talks with the calm of a poker-player'. The villagers of Ljigo 'dream of the green uplands of Rudnik'. They all have the same soul. They are 'somewhat eccentric people, warriors, stubborn, but essentially—tender and vulnerable'. The dead doctor is remarkable for her 'large eyes like an unreal flower blooming in the dark', while Petar's wife has 'large, gentle and anxious eyes'. The children are 'little devils'. When the

---

[1] One short story by the Yugoslav writer Ivo Andrić (winner of the Nobel Prize in 1961), 'A letter from 1920', in which the war-traumatised narrator describes Bosnia as 'a land of hatred', was used by Radovan Karadžić and many other nationalist Serbs in the course of the war to justify their actions. (Transl.)

nurse Milena 'enters a room, she brings in the sun.' She 'looks like a frightened little girl', while Milan has 'the soft profile of a prematurely grown-up boy'. And so on.

These rudimentary characters, or cardboard cut-outs, placed in the décor of the war in Bosnia reduced to a few conventional lines, are supposed to enable Bulić to realise his idea of a moving war novel. And in his interpretation what is moving is above all horrific and disgusting. That is why he tries to move his reader by describing, for example, 'intestines scattered round a beech tree', 'part of the brain splattered on the tree trunk', 'pieces of Velja's brain and locks of his hair on the tyres of the truck', 'the appalling stench of spilt intestines'. The episode in which the besieged fighters drink their own urine is also this kind of revoltingly moving scene. Equally disgusting are the 'flies on the corpses' and the cockroaches in the military hospital.

Another and more important aspect of what is 'moving' in Bulić's novel is more salacious and profane. Swearing is the main means the author uses to affect and upset the reader from this point of view. Almost without exception, his heroes are most eloquent when they swear. In fact, their way of swearing is the characteristic of Bulić's heroes by which they are most fully individualised, most obviously distinguished from each other. The main hero, a villager by birth, does not go further than the basic verb, using it to attack the flaming sun, mothers and other more or less standard objects of the Serbian national repertoire of curses. He inherited some of that from his father Miloš, to whom Bulić also gives the opportunity of cursing the 'flaming sun'. Lazar and Gavra, villagers from the region of Šumadija, bring local colour into their swearing, and their objects include 'your grandmother's granny'. The school teacher Malina also curses the name of the mother—but, as Bulić specifies, 'artlessly'. The Belgrade style of hooligan swearing is admirably represented by Velja, whose entire discourse is reduced to swearing. And the phrase 'Chetnik cunts' is the way the Muslims announce their presence to the tunnel.

Swearing in *Tunnel* is moving because the most blasphemous and disgusting expressions are used by exceptionally sensitive, noble and patriotic young men. They curse only because they are caught up in war, because the horror of war drags crude language with it. As the narrator explains, 'The war drove them all to use a different kind of language. They express themselves roughly even when they ought logically to be using tender words. Most often they swear.' Since swearing is the language of war—which is presumably what Bulić thinks—it is not only appropriate, but also essential that in a moving war novel people should swear. With this reference to the psychology of the warrior and demands of the genre, he places the following words in the mouth of his main character: 'And why are you asking us about tears, you *balija* cunt![2] Ask your Allah. He knows everything, bugger him, the all-knowing. If he doesn't know, ask our God. They probably know each other. They must have gone whoring together.' Moving?

Endeavouring to write an exciting and readable novel about the war in Bosnia, and at the same time to avoid the trap of reflecting on that war and taking trouble over its artistic literary transposition, Bulić relied most of all on the effect that a succession of revolting scenes and swearing could have on the reader. Starting from my own experience as a reader, I can bear witness to the fact that anyone reading Bulić's book would really find it difficult to avoid the impression of disgust and nausea. In that sense, the author has achieved his desired aim. But is there anything really moving in that disgust? And is that remorseless disgust enough for *Tunnel* to be considered a new genre, the first Serbian trash novel about the war in Bosnia?

---

[2] '*Balija*': offensive name for 'Muslim'. (Transl.)

16. Contemplation

A new name has recently appeared in the list of those accused of the defeat, suffering and shame with which the Serbian war in Croatia and Bosnia ended, that of Vuk Stefanović Karadžić. The accusation against him was brought in the weekly journal *NIN* (19 July 1996) by the writer Svetislav Basara. Vuk's reform of the Serbian language and alphabet in the first half of the nineteenth century is described here as a 'sleight of hand' against the Serbian people and its state. And the Serbs have been dealing with its fatal consequences for almost two centuries, from time to time, as during recent years, facing the prospect of complete downfall.

Vuk's anti-Serbian work remained on the whole concealed, even falsely represented and scandalously glorified as a victory. But here at last is a courageous writer, Basara, prepared to bring the truth of Karadžić's damaging activity to light, to deconstruct and condemn it. 'The confusion into which the Serbian people has fallen', he writes, 'has at its root a strategic blunder, which has not been identified as a blunder, and which, defended with incomprehensible stubbornness, survives tenaciously as something quite opposite, as a great advantage. I see the crucial, but hidden, cause of our present misfortunes and misunderstandings with history as lying in the domain of linguistics— in Vuk's reform of the language and alphabet.' And Basara quotes some of the worst contemporary troubles of the Serbs, whose origin lies in Vuk's work: defeat in war, the disintegration of the national corpus, the decline in the birth rate, moral and material misery. All of this came upon the Serbs because they followed 'a strategy of dull-wittedness, the foundations of which were laid by Vuk and those who thought like him.'

What is it in Vuk's reform that makes it an old and inexhaustible well of Serbian misfortune? In order to answer that question, Basara refers to an extremely simplified version of ethnolinguistic determinism, according to which the history of a people moves within borders determined in advance by the nature of its language. 'Language', he writes, 'is what determines the reality of a people and its historical achievements.' That means that a people has the kind of history its language deserves: like language, like history. If the language has weak expressive potential, if it is imprecise, crude, full of loan-words— and that, in Basara's judgment, is what the Serbian language was like after Vuk's reforms—'then the people that speaks it is condemned to languish on the margins of history.' That is all the more true of the Serbs in so far as they live, Basara reminds us, 'in a geopolitically exceptionally sensitive place; a place in which precise thinking is more pressingly needed than guns.'

But Vuk left the Serbs without a language appropriate for precise thinking and reflection. Hence the chaos in their heads. That is why they have no philosophy, or rather, if they are real philosophers, they have to write in a foreign language, as Branislav Petronijević did. Through Vuk's 'profanised' language, the Serbs cannot reach God. For the same reason, world history also passes them by. That language, a language of peasants, practical, concrete, crude, has made 'Serbian thought' hopelessly earthy and provincial.

It did not need to be like that. Had the Serbs not followed Vuk, if they had heeded the wise opponents of Vuk's reforms, 'our material and spiritual history would have been richer in every way.' And another path was available to them: imperial, sacral, Byzantine. Was that not the path by which 'we had stepped into civilisation', 'into the circle of cultured peoples'? But Vuk forcibly separated the Serbian language from the linguistic treasury of its early literature, where 'there existed Slavonic words for the majority of concepts which, in our poverty, we now replace with Latin and German words.' Today that treasury has historical value, because it contains only the remains of a 'murdered language'. Among those remains is a word, which Basara holds especially dear: the word '*sozercanje*' — contemplation.

Whoever spoils a language also ruins the history and character of the people which speaks it. That is why, in Basara's judgement, Vuk is to blame also for the appearance of many negative traits in the Serbian national character. 'Opting for simplification, which later became a national characteristic', he explains, 'choosing easy victories which are transformed after a certain time into defeats whose real cause is unknown, all of this is a consequence of the absolute irresponsibility, incompetence, improvisation which Vuk put into practice.'

The faults and shortcomings mentioned here are so great and of such a kind that Vuk's accuser believes that there will be no objection if he calls him 'an uneducated adventurer', 'an ignorant amateur', 'a semi-talented and vainglorious man' with 'a primitive feeling for language', while his reform is a 'sleight of hand', 'an amateur and pretentious experiment', which is worth no more than a game indulged in by 'little adolescent girls who imagine secret letters'. But Basara's condemnation is written, above all, in the style of an erudite tract with appropriate pretentiousness. In addition to linguistics and history, there is here also a bit of national characterology, a noticeable admixture of geopolitics and theology, rather more philosophy, represented by pieces of substantial calibre ('ontological emptiness', 'inner emanations'), and somewhat lighter weapons from the repertoire of the postmodern ('simulation of history', 'a virtual people'). There is also a review of the sociological 'doctrine of the insurgent mass' and other things whose origin it is more difficult to confirm, such as, for instance, 'a pseudo-mythic milieu' and 'historical graphics'.

Nevertheless, with a little effort, one can make out that the main current of Basara's erudite argumentation is based on the so-called 'sacral' or 'mystic' geopolitics developed within the frame of the European extreme Right, which has reached our regions thanks to a group of journalists gathered round the magazine *Naše Ideje* (Our Ideas). In his reflections on the sacral tradition, the Slav linguistic being, authority and the hierarchical order—in other words, on the values from which, through his fatal reform, Vuk allegedly distanced the Serbs—one feels the strong influence of the political mysticism of the extreme Right, European 'traditionalists' and Russian 'Euro-Asians'. The main part of his accusation against Vuk, where he says that his reform is 'anti-traditional and anti-sacral', that it is 'the expression of a rebellion against authority, against the principle of hierarchical order', is written in the spirit and language of radical rightwing mysticism.

Basara interprets the misfortune brought upon the Serbs by warlike nationalism as the consequence of the inauthenticity of that nationalism, too pragmatic and simple, too populist and profane, an inauthenicity whose hidden but still vital spring lies in Vuk's reform. He seeks an alternative to that peasant and folklore nationalism in another model of anti-democratic and anti-modern order, according to which the principles of elitism, authority and social hierarchy would rule. Serbian culture and politics based on folklore and populist myth-making should give way to a sacral order based on authentic thought, what was described in pre-Vuk language as 'contemplation', '*sozercanje*', on the myth of the mediaeval Serbian elite, the Slavonic being and Byzantine civilisation. In other words, Basara rejects rightwing populism in the name of right-wing elitism.

His text about Vuk deserves attention as yet another example of the unreadiness of Serbian intellectuals, in their justified resistance to contemporary folkloristic and ethnic nationalism and in a welcome deconstruction of its cults and myths (including here the cult of Vuk, his perfect alphabet and the annual state-party ritual dedicated to it in his native village of Tršić). It really does step outside the obsessions, frustrations and phantasms characteristic of nationalism. To anyone who, like Basara, is disappointed by the return to epic Kosovo it recommends a return to Byzantium. No one, not even Basara, recommends a return to the United Nations, but on the other hand many, including certainly Basara himself, expect that Serbia will tomorrow regain its membership of an alternative international order of spiritually prodigious and spiritually similar nations which, as is well known, is called the Byzantine Commonwealth.

17. New Age

The anti-Christian religious movement known as the New Age is the main source and cause of drug-addiction, alcoholism, criminality, superstition, pornography, sexual deviance, AIDS, the collapse of the family, the decline in the birth-rate, the crisis of national identity and the other evils and trials that have recently descended on the Serbs, and especially the young people of Serbia. This is the main conclusion of the report of an inquiry into the state of Serbian youth submitted to the Holy Archiepiscopal Assembly of the Serbian Orthodox Church by the Elder of the Church of St Alexander Nevsky in Belgrade, Archpriest Ljubodrag Petrović and a group of his colleagues. The report, entitled 'Serbian Youth in the Temptations of the New Age' with the subtitle 'Sketches of Serbian Orthodox Youth and Possible Ways of Protecting its Spiritual-National Identity', was published in two issues of the journal of the Cetinje Metropolitanate, *Svetigora* (nos 50 and 51, 1996).

The report about the so-called religion of the New Age is based on American sources. The basic idea is taken from American conservative Christian journalists—above all Tex Mars, to whose books the authors of the report refer. That idea is that many apparently unconnected phenomena in contemporary culture and politics (interest in eastern religions, astrology, tarot, spiritism, homeopathy, rock and roll, science fiction, films about extra-terrestrials and horror films, drug abuse, sexual freedom, political and social movements based on ecology, such as the Greens and Greenpeace, or on transnational connections such as multinational companies, and ideas about the so-called New World Order) represent different manifestations of a planetary anti-Christian movement. That movement is reputedly inspired and led by demonic forces, preparing the ground for a definitive showdown with Christ and Christianity, whose domination, according to the beliefs of followers of the New Age, will come to an end with the end of the astrological age in the sign of Pisces, that is the end of the twentieth century, giving way to a new dominant religion in the sign of Aquarius, that is, in the power of Satan. For this reason New Age believers are also called Aquarians.

The authors of the report, relying on American literature, pay particularly careful attention to showing the sophisticated methods whereby the Aquarians secretly realise their influence over innocent children's souls. While still in their mothers' wombs, the children are exposed to the influence of special New Age music. 'Subconscious messages are built into it', which are broadcast, among other outlets, by the famous musical television station MTV. Beguiled by the musical items of that station, a seven-year-old girl from Texas refused to go to church with her mother: 'Mom,' she said, 'I don't want to go. I don't like Jesus. Lucifer is my god.'

No more innocent are the picture-books which teach children 'to use the snake's energy of the spine'. Various magic messages await them also on the pictures in chewing-gum packets, on heavy-metal T-shirts, on toys and video-games with occult symbols, and in the texts of special Aquarian lullabies. The demonic propaganda of the New Age is especially developed in strip cartoons and films about magicians and witches. For this reason the film directors Lucas and Spielberg enjoy a great reputation among Aquarians. They apparently call Spielberg their new Joseph. 'Cartoons are also used', report Petrović and his colleagues, 'as a polygon for spreading New Age propaganda. In the cartoon about the Mighty Mouse, the main character sniffs cocaine. In "The Smurfs" the Great Smurf draws pentagrams and speaks magic words; smurfs levitate and have tails.'

After the 'Spiritual Fathers' had given a detailed account of the danger which, in the form of the religion of the New Age, had spread over the whole Christian world, especially in the West, the authors of this report dwell on what is for us the most interesting question: 'What connection does all of this have with the situation in Serbia?' Their answer is: 'Close, as close as it could possibly be.' For, through occult literature, sects, television programmes with MTV spots, pornographic and horror films, astrological cards, rock music and the like, the devilish New Age is spreading rapidly and unhindered 'through the lands of St Sava', calling into question the spiritual and physical health of the young and the very survival of the Serbian people.

New Age

The allegedly detrimental influence of the New Age may be seen in the all-embracing 'brutal and uncompromising re-paganisation of Serbia', managed, Petrović and his colleagues suppose, 'from some centre with an interest in the complete spiritual, emotional and moral ruin of our people'. In addition to foreign Aquarian products, which are being spread throughout Serbia by irresponsible or recruited publishers of books and magazines and distributors of films and video-cassettes, the report mentions also examples of autochtonous Serbian Aquarian paganism. Among them the so-called 'turbo-folk' is stressed, which the authors of the report see as 'one of the most successful channels through which the new pagan messages are transmitted'. This is reinforced by quotations from songs of that genre: 'We are witches, best friends', 'Deceit, adultery, that is my life', 'For you a nymph would lose her wings and a saint would fall, so why not me?' But the spread of new paganism, and hence the penetration of the devil under the sign of Aquarius, are assisted also by some works of respected and at first glance well-intentioned public figures.' The authors of the report mention 'one of these, who often refers to Orthodoxy and the Byzantine literary tradition' and has published a novel under the name of Aleister Crowley, 'which contains a complete set of allegedly Byzantine tarot cards for reading the future'.

Thanks to the unhindered propaganda of the Aquarians, in Serbia the signs of Satan's presence are ever more numerous. Many murders, according to Petrović and his colleagues, have a 'demonic foundation', they are the consequence of 'devil-immanence'. The same is true of drug-addiction and 'sexual licence', the blackest examples of which are pornographic video-cassettes including male and female prostitution, incest, bestiality and the like, which are accessible to children. These are all signs of the strengthening of 'the forces of Hades which prevent little children and young people coming to Christ'.

At the end of the report, the authors enumerate the steps which, in their opinion, the Church could take in order somehow to respond to the challenges of the devilish New Age: increase their religious work with the young, work more decisively on introducing religious study into schools, publish popular religious literature, demand frequencies for a radio and television station of the Serbian Orthodox Church and seek advice and funds from the Greeks to this end.

This report on the state of Serbia, Serbian youth and the role of the Serbian Orthodox Church in connection with it can be criticised in view of its barely sustainable thesis that this situation, described as miserable, even desperate, should be blamed on the demonically inspired religion of the New Age, which, coming from the West which was indeed inclined to the Devil, has poisoned many souls here as well. This and other similar ideas about the distant and mysterious causes of the catastrophe that has beset Serbia in recent years serve most of all to avoid a general public debate about the role in the instigation and deepening of that catastrophe played by the ambitious and warlike Serbian elite, including the Serbian Orthodox Church.

But the report of Petrović and his colleagues will have to be exposed to criticism also from those who accept its basic thesis about the decisive influence of an Aquarian conspiracy on the shaping of wretched Serbian reality. They will observe that the authors, proudly sure of themselves and the untouchable virtue of the Serbian Orthodox clergy, do not pay any attention whatever to the possibility that Aquarian paganism, with its magic tricks and devilment, has penetrated also into their ranks. What would they say, for example, about the frequent political use among the clergy of miracle-working relics, about treating the mentally ill with the help of basil, icons and the cross, about belief in the epiphany of the forebears? Finally, the question also arises as to whether the authors of the report on the temptations of the New Age have not themselves to a degree succumbed to these temptations. Is not the methodology of their report, whereby they first describe the state of mankind on the eve of the age of Aquarius, and then move on to the circumstances in Serbia and the actions by which one should defend and save oneself from the New Age, in fact based on the philosophy of the Aquarians? According to Petrović and his colleagues, this is best summed up in their favourite slogan 'Think globally, act locally'.

18. The 'Other Srpska'

Of all the events accompanying preparations for the forthcoming elections in Bosnia and Herzegovina,[1] what has attracted the greatest attention of the media in Serbia is the endeavour of the current followers of Milošević to drive his former followers from power in Republika Srpska (RS). What is particularly interesting for a reflection on political marketing or, as it is often called today, 'electoral engineering', is the fact that, in their attacks on the ruling SDS party, the opposition close to Milošević (the Union for Peace and the Patriotic Democratic Bloc) make use of exactly the same arguments used by the civil and anti-war opposition in Serbia in its revolt against Milošević himself, particularly at the time when he was achieving and strengthening his power on a wave of war-mongering populism.

The regime in Pale is accused of ruling by spreading hatred towards the alleged external and internal enemies of Republika Srpska, by inventing conspiracies and traitors and keeping the people in a state of war psychosis. According to Dr Branko Dokić from Prijedor, its leaders do not understand 'that the Serbs have acquired sufficient experience to know that it is not possible to solve the national question through war.' (*Politika,* 8 August 1996) That is to say, as Milovan Stanković in Lopari put it, 'whoever pushes the incomprehensible and unacceptable war-mongering option can only help the general damage to the Serbian people.' (*Politika,* 27 August 1996)

Borislav Mikelić, who joined the pre-election campaign on the side of the Socialists, explains that the SDS is one of the extreme

---

[1] The general elections in Bosnia and Herzegovina of 14 September 1996, the first after the end of the war.

nationalist parties, 'produced by the difficult civil war in Bosnia and Hercegovina', because 'they did not wish for any kind of tolerance,' In his opinion, the current occupant of the presidency in RS, Biljana Plavšić, represents 'a blatant example of a representative of the Chetnik option.' (*Nezavisne novine,* Banja Luka, 28 August 1996) With her and similar politicians at its head, Republika Srpska has 'quarrelled with the whole world', been left without any friends, like Albania in its time. At the meeting in Zvornik, Ljubiša Savić Mauzer spoke about this, saying that in RS people 'waved black flags with deaths-heads on them and threatened the entire world.' (*Politika,* 25 August 1996)

This extreme nationalistic and war-mongering policy of the SDS also has the support of intellectuals. As Dr Mićo Carević says, 'This war has shown that the consciousness of many intellectuals is still focused on nationalism.' (*Nezavisne novine,* 28 August 1996) Many of them transformed themselves into 'professional patriots', Serbs by profession. As the leader of the Socialist Party of RS, Živko Radišić, put it, they spread stories of 'the exclusive bastion of Serbdom on the left bank of the Drina.' (*Politika,* 20 August 1996) They would like the Serbs in Bosnia to enter the third millennium to the sound of the *gusle.* They are responsible for the fact that the innocent popular dialect, *ijekavica,* has been driven out of the official language of Republika Srpska, the old names of towns have been changed—even that of Foča, which, according to the writer Ranko Risojević, is 'older than the Turks'—and 'the adjective "Serbian" has been scattered in all directions, relentlessly and without measure.' (*Politika,* 9 August 1996)

The Socialists and their allies warn that the government in Pale is maintained through its absolute control of the main media. Serbian Radio-Television has been transformed into a real Bastille TV. 'The state papers *Glas srpski* and *Oslobodjenje'*, says Nebojša Radmanović, leader of the SMP list for Banja Luka, 'participate in the information violence.' (*Politika,* 17 August 1996) In such circumstances, in RS, as Živko Radišić puts it, 'totalitarianism and unanimity rule, and every other opinion is proclaimed treachery by the ruling party.' (*Politika,* 18 August 1996) That happens, he believes, because Republika Srpska is in fact in the hands of war profiteers, i.e. 'people who have acquired great wealth through the blood of their nation'.

Instead of such a government, the Socialists in Republka Srpska and their allies offer the rule of peace, reason, tolerance, prosperity and well-being. As Milorad P. Ivošević, leader of JUL in RS, promised: 'We will bring the Serbian people there into harmony with our age, because it must be a modern people.' (*Alternativa,* Doboj, 28 August

1996) 'We do not wish to be either "heavenly" or underground', says Milovan Stanković, 'we wish to be a nation on this earth and of this time.' (ibid.) The Socialists will do all it takes, adds Tihomir Gligorić of Doboj, to 'carry out democratic renewal as the aim of a modern civilised people and society'. He also promises 'love and laughter for people confident of a better tomorrow', and the undertaking 'that children will feel happy and not like the victims of a failed time.' (ibid.) This idea is expressed also by the slogan launched by Živko Radišić in Šamac: 'Our future lies in new Teslas'.*

The political rhetoric of the current followers of Milošević in Republika Srpska, in which the promotion of peace, tolerance and prosperity has such an important place, is in accord with the so-called one-and-only policy of peace, which the authorities in Serbia embraced two years ago. However, it is one thing to celebrate peace, reason and tolerance—and anything else—when you are already firmly in power, roaring and hitting out to left and right, and quite another thing to drive someone from power by celebrating peace, reason and tolerance, even if it was you yourself who put him there in the first place.

There is no doubt that the creators of the strategy of the Socialists and their allies for the elections in RS had this problem in mind. That is why their promotion of law and order, unlike that of the current rulers, is not reduced to criticism in the name of reason, tolerance and progress. The Socialist project of an alternative Republika Srpska, their Other Srpska, is after all fundamentally different from the one which the civil and democratic opposition in Serbia called the 'Other Serbia'.

The Socialist Other Srpska is not only a modern, democratic and peace-loving alternative to the nationalist and anti-modern regime established in Pale. It contains also far more robust material. It is a project for maintaining and consolidating the political and military achievements of that regime, called into question only in the time immediately following the withdrawal of allegiance to Belgrade. The main sin which the Socialists attribute to the SDS is nevertheless not primitive and aggressive nationalism, for in the matter of the national question, in the words of the Socialist leader Živko Radišić, 'globally our programmes are the same.' (*NIN*, 30 August 1996) That is why he does not condemn the leadership in Pale because it waged war for an ethnically homogeneous state, but because, in turning its back on Milošević, it began to lose the war and everything that had ostensibly been gained, because 'it heedlessly lost the purest ethnic spaces and centuries-old hearths'. As Milovan Stanković reminds them, they lost even 'that most Serbian of all towns, Drvar'. (*Politika*, 15 August 1996)

The greatest fault of the regime in Pale is neither extreme nationalism nor the Chetnik ideology, nor clericalism, nor favouring the *gusle* over the computer, but the fact that its Serbdom failed its exam. That is why, as Mladen Ivanić put it, what are needed are 'better people with the same national aim' (*Alternativa*, 28 August 1996), i.e. better Serbs. And he is one of those better ones. That is the opinion of Ivanić's electoral ally Milorad Dodik. 'We are convinced', says Dodik, 'that we have round us better Serbs than those in the SDS. For example, Dr Mladen Ivanić is a better Serb than Momčilo Krajišnik ... Živko Radišić is a better Serb than Biljana Plavšić'. (*Politika*, 20 August 1996) Hence it is quite possible for us to call the Socialist Other Srpska also a 'More Serbian Srpska'.

19. Javor

On 7 September 1996 the Deputy Prime Minister of the Serbian government, Ratko Marković, climbed to the top of Javor mountain. At this celebration of the 120th anniversary of the First Serbian-Turkish war of 1876, the Deputy Prime Minister made a speech about the heroes of that war and what it makes us think of today. After his speech an appropriate cultural-artistic programme was performed, orchestrated by Milovan Vitezović.

The celebration on Javor is one of a series of ritual evocations of the national past which confirm the great interest of the Serbian authorities in such evocations, when they are carried out under their control. The best illustration of this is the fact that the celebration on Javor was graced by the presence of three Serbian ministers in addition to Marković himself, (M. Stamatović, A. Milosavljević and D. Dragojlović), as well as the chairmen of two county councils and several municipalities, and representatives of the Yugoslav army. They all climbed the mountain so that the political gesture of the celebration of the 120th anniversary of the First Serbian-Turkish war should have the maximum impact, i.e. guarantee success for the main aim of political celebrations of this kind: *marking a date*.

Really, the main political function of celebrating important dates of national history corresponds to the fundamental meaning of the verb 'to mark': to place a stamp, a mark on something, to brand it. Celebrations of historical jubilees, commemorative ceremonies, speeches, wreaths and memorials enable the authorities to place their stamp on the most important moments of national history, to connect them with their name and paint them with their colours, in order to show that they are their only legitimate heir and protector.

Marking the 120th anniversary of the war of Javor under the direction of the Serbian government, as it was described in the newspapers, is a good example of the ritual evocation of the national past in real space, that is in the place where the events evoked occurred. The identification of the place of the celebration with the place of past events certainly makes it easier to establish the ritual communication of the participants in the celebration with the past, to 'bring it to life'. A mountain peak, reaching to the sky, up to which one has to climb, from which views stretch on all sides, is a particularly suitable place for ritual communication with one's heroic forebears. The reporter from *Politika,* aware of the importance of the fact that the jubilee of the Javor war was being marked on Javor itself, dated his report from the celebration: 'Javor Mountain, 7 September'.

According to the scenario for the celebration on Javor, the people from the nearby villages and towns, who assembled on the mountain, at a place made glorious by a great event of national history, symbolised the nation. But the nation brought on to the mountain was far calmer and more contented than that which had been brought out onto the streets some eight years earlier. The people on Javor were assigned the completely passive role of listening to what the authorities had to say to the nation, and at the same time of standing in for the descendants who were carrying on the work of their glorious forebears of 120 years before. This is called 'a great national gathering' or 'an assembly of the people'.

The harmonious nation, gathered around its leaders, appeared also in Deputy Prime Minister Marković's speech. In his opinion, Serbian history is the history of always realising the same political aspirations of always the same nation to create always the same thing, that is a national state. These aspirations are a constant of Serbian history because they are natural. The Serbian people did realise them once long ago. That happened in medieval Raška, where, as Marković said, 'the Serbian people, in its long history, created the greatest aim of every people—its own national state'. At that time 'some trans-Atlantic states did not even exist', while 'Serbia was a European power'. And much later the Serbo-Turkish wars of 1876–7, were 'the expression of the natural aspiration that the Serbs should live an independent life in their own national state.'

The same natural aim to achieve a natural state of all the Serbs confronts the Serbian people today as well. That is why a government which respects the will of the people—and the present government in Serbia maintains that it is such—has only to assist Serbian national history to follow the natural path long ago marked out for it. Its policy comes down to a search for the most appropriate ways to affirm and perhaps realise the first and always the same 'national interest' in contemporary conditions. But, according to the judgment of Deputy Prime Minister Marković, the prospects for that today are not as good as they might be. 'Today', he said, '120 years after the beginning of the First Serbian-Turkish war, dark clouds hang over many of the national aims of our people.'

What then? Here too, said Marković, history can help a great deal. Remembrance of great historical events, such as the Javor war, serves not only to emphasise the basic line of Serbian history and Serbian politics, but also for us to learn from our forebears how the Serbian great national ideal was fought for in hard, even 'stormy' times. The message they send to present-day Serbs is above all: be united and make a strong state. 'History has already taught us enough lessons', said Ratko Marković, 'about the fact that only a united and strong Serbia, which relies on its own strength and not on outside help, for such help is not offered without important calculations, only such a Serbia can resolve questions of national importance enduringly and righteously, given that it had the misfortune not to have resolved them at the proper time.' Marković particularly stresses the value today of the recipe of Knez Milan Obrenović, according to which Serbia ought to establish relations which were 'wise outside, and strong within'. That recipe ought to be accepted also by those for whom civil liberties are dear, for 'without a strong state, there are no civil liberties either.'

The other message of the heroic forebears directed through Ratko Marković to the present generation of Serbs goes: Be self-sacrificing and courageous in war and carry out the orders of your wise leaders obediently. The Deputy Prime Minister of the Serbian government sees 'a significant result' of the first Serbian-Turkish war, in which Serbia otherwise suffered a heavy defeat, in the fact that 'the Serbian national army, which then encompassed a sixth of the population, survived a fierce battle for four months, which was more than the military circles had expected.' To go gladly into a war which resembles 'madness', to bear military struggle and sufferings without grumbling or question represents, for Ratko Marković, a rare virtue for a people who, since time immemorial, have striven tirelessly for their great ultimate aim. They are closest to that aim when, in addition to heroes ready to die for them, they also have wise leaders capable of organising that heroic death. The Serbian nation had such leaders in the past, and it has them now. They are the ones who recommend to the people that they should be 'worthy of the heroism of their grandfathers', and themselves endeavour to have 'the wisdom of their leaders'.

The celebration on Javor and the speech made there by the Deputy Prime Minister justify those who are sceptical about hints that the present government in Serbia is seriously abandoning the so-called 'national project', the revival of which has been its main political trump card up to now. Under the regime of Slobodan Milošević popular gatherings with a cultural-artistic programme (and promotional party meetings, organised according to the same scenario) are a far more acceptable form of political activity than a multiparty national assembly and debate within it. For the assembly, unlike the dignified and magnificent gathering of the people on Javor, may be transformed into a stage for quarrels, conflict, ill-mannered attacks by deputies and other ugly things unworthy of glorious Serbian history, which only blur and compromise the clear aims of the national struggle, disturb national harmony, break up the power of the state.

20. Mission

The clinical psychologist Dr Ratibor M. Djurdjević (born in 1915 in the neighbourhood of Vranje) lived in the West, mostly in America, and returned to Serbia in 1992. God Himself sent him back, he says, to help the almost extinguished ancestral Orthodox faith flare up again among the Serbs, who had been de-Christianised and paganised under communism and lived like wild creatures. In 1996 Djurdjević published a book of more than 400 pages entitled *Srbin povratnik medju Novosrbima* (A Serb returnee among the Newserb), in which he described the missionary work he had been carrying out till then in Serbia.

The returnee found a Serbia not remotely like the country he had left fifty years earlier, when, as he recalls, 'Christian refinement adorned the honest Serbian peasant and householder.' The Serbs of today have 'irrationally accepted the amorality and degeneration of Western secular culture', they have 'fallen into the slavery of the Judeo-American and Judeo-European way of life', unaware that the 'Europeans and Americans are morally sick people'. The symptoms of the infection to which the Serbs had succumbed are speech full of blasphemies and utter shamelessness. People swear in books and films, 'the sexual act is openly shown in regular television programmes', couples live together unmarried and 'copulate like monkeys or dogs', women wear 'shameless swimming costumes', and 'some do not even wear the top half at all'.

To call on the Serbs, above all the young, to liberate themselves from enslavement to the sick mentality of the godless West, to reveal the anti-Christian Satanic conspiracy directed above all against the Serbs, to help them to return to the wholesome spirit of St Sava, this is the God-given mission of the patriotic returnee, worthy of his efforts and his American savings. For we too, Djurdjević explains, like the non-Christian countries of Asia and Africa, 'need missionaries for these wild creatures of ours, the so-called Serbs'.

In the balance-sheet on his three-year missionary work, Djurdjević stresses one positive paragraph: successful work in publishing his books about the 'anti-Christian conspiracy'. In four years he published some thirty books in Serbian, including the following: *The Contemporary Faces of Satan; Abortion; Intruders Govern America and the World; Karl Marx, Servant and Victim of Satan; Freud's Phoney Science; Adventurers of Hades; Superbankers, Vampires of Contemporary Humanity; The Gay Brigade; Monsters and Lies of American Democracy.* The same story recurs, with variations, in all of them: Western Europe and America are today governed by 'Judeo-bankers' or 'Judeo-masons', descendants of the Pharisees who over three centuries (the 18th to the 20th), have succeeded in dividing the West from Christianity. They inspired two revolutions (the French and the Russian) directed against the Christian world. For their anti-Christian, worldly aims they make equal use of communism and secular democracy, and the 'hidden forms of Pharisee-Talmudic teaching'. In the present day, the Judeo-Masonic conspirators have taken Orthodoxy between their teeth, because it is 'the only remaining island of Christianity in the world'. That is why they did all they could to provoke wars in the former Soviet Union and former Yugoslavia.

To avoid the accusation of anti-semitism, Djurdjević has invented a distinction between the Jews, descendants of Moses, and the Judeans, descendants of the Pharisees. In one instance he even says that 'the Jews are mistaken in counting the Judeans as their compatriots'. But he often forgets this caution, and attacks the Jews without beating about the bush: 'the Jews are the ancient enemies of Orthodoxy and all Christianity' and 'a rightly persecuted nation'.

Djurdjević is more than satisfied with his publishing work. Not only has he published books in Serbia which, as he says himself, 'could not be printed and sold in book-shops in America', but one of them was praised in several papers as first-class patriotic material, and lengthy interviews with him were carried in many newspapers. Voices speaking out against this unimpeded spreading of anti-semitism have been few, notably the president of the Association of Jewish Municipalities (A. Singer) and the president of Serbian-Jewish Friendship Society (Lj. Tadić).

But Djurdjević's missionary work in the narrower sense, the engagement of priests, theologians and the laity in religious work with the young, the creation of a mass Orthodox youth movement, the training of missionary groups, was completely barren. In several dozen pages of his book, *A Serb Returnee,* he analyses the causes of this failure. Few people signed up for the work of the St Sava Youth and Student Movement, which Djurdjević founded in 1992. His young colleagues proved inadequate to the great task; although they were paid, they did not even try to earn their pay. Ostensibly chaste Orthodox believers, they smoked and drank in the office of the Movement, reproducing 'the stinking air of a village inn'. They stole everything they found: seals, books, pencils, copying-paper ... They held on to money from the sale of the Movement's publications. Using the office telephones for private conversations, they ran up gigantic bills.

Struggling with the indifference, lack of discipline and irresponsibility of the Orthodox young people he had gathered around him, Djurdjević spent months trying to talk them into respecting at least a minimum of order. He introduced rewards according to achievement, sick leave and promotion, and regulations about the way the office should be used, determined the budget and the way it should be spent, wrote manuals for organising missionary work, put padlocks on the telephones.

So his work with the young Orthodox Serbs was increasingly transformed into an endeavour to familiarise them with certain norms of behaviour and social values characteristic of societies which appreciate rational and efficient work, and respect the individual and property, i.e. the West. Unexpectedly, his mission took on a new meaning and a new direction. He completely forgot how much he had loved the Serbian 'almost childlike emotion and spontaneity' before his experience with the ungovernable 'Newserbs', how hateful he had found the 'more organised, but obtuse Westerners' and how pleased he had been that Serbia has more artists 'than many other European rationally oriented nations'. He no longer thought that the Serbs had acquired technological progress but lost their soul. When he heard that his associates had allowed some poor student to phone his mother in Ukraine from the office telephone, he did not so much admire such Serbian feeling as coldly respond: 'We are not a richly endowed humanitarian organisation that can afford to do good in this way. I see this as typical Serbian carelessness and impudence.' He raised his voice against inefficiency, sluggishness and laziness. He complained that 'it was all disorganised, unsystematic, at the African level. He began to speak nostalgically about life in America and to hold it up as an example. America became a 'normal country', in which a person's individuality, and even more his time, were respected. 'Our people', writes Djurdjević after three years of living among the 'Newserbs', 'could learn a great deal from Euro-Americans in respect of politeness in relations, keeping promises, orderliness in correspondence, keeping primitive narcissism under control, carrying out accepted obligations and avoiding unscrupulous, fickle aspirations.'

It did not do any good. The mission failed. The movement fell apart. The financial police intervened, there was nearly a fight. In the end Djurdjević took some of his associates to court and they paid him back in equal measure. At the same time, they accused him to the church dignitaries of trying to introduce 'Western, non-Orthodox discipline among the members' and of 'using certain Protestant ... sectarian methods of work'. In the end this accusation was reduced to Djurdjević's own well-known formula, which he could never in his wildest dreams have imagined being used against him. It was being said that 'Rajko is a mason'.[1]

There is a hidden message in this story about the adventures of the so-called missionary Dr Ratibor Djurdjević in Serbia; namely that those propagating antisemitism (and many other mad things) can expect substantial success, while anyone spreading ideas about responsible, organised and effective work—even if it is work aimed at spreading Orthodoxy—can expect to face considerable difficulties.

---

[1] Rajko is a the familiar form of Ratibor. (Transl.)

21. At 'The Two Stags'

'How wonderful it is to be freed from the stale civilisation of Europe!' This was the conclusion arrived at by the English traveller A. W. Kinglake (1809–91), author of *Eothen*, one summer night in 1835 in some Serbian village a day's walk from Belgrade on the way to Istanbul. Kinglake enjoyed that evening among the 'natives' who spoke 'some Slavonic dialect', and particularly the dinner and his sound sleep on the earth floor. Enjoyment of the simple and natural beauty of 'eastern scenes' drove him to reflect upon 'people tied to luncheon tables, or crushed into ballrooms, or brutally crammed into church pews'. He was delighted that he was not one of those 'poor devils who live in a state of complete conventionality', that he had summoned the courage for this 'wonderful escape' to the East.

In recent years Serbia has again been attracting travel writers from the West. In their eyes it has acquired once again, as in Kinglake's day, something of the exotic. More exactly, it has become again part of the imaginary exotic East. Today as well, European writers looking for exotic sensations—which are apparently those we feel in an encounter with a world different and better than our own—do not need to travel, in their thoughts or in reality, further than Belgrade and its environs. Word has got round that one can find everything needed for literary or philosophical exoticism: real, naked, authentic life, not remotely like that in the West. Here the traveller may be reborn, re-awoken, shaken out of his lethargy, freed from constraints, made aware of the vanity and malice of Europe.

On another summer night, more than a century and a half after the one enjoyed by Kinglake—to be exact, on 20 August 1992—the contemporary travel writer Daniel Salvatore Schiffer dined among the Serbs. He described this dinner in his story 'Travelling on Hot Coals', which he published in *Politika* (6 October 1996). This 'Italian of French culture, philosopher, writer and journalist', as he is described in the note accompanying the story, found himself in an exotic ambience far sooner and more easily than his distant predecessor: from the Intercontinental he went straight to the Skadarlije district, to the well-known 'Kod dva jelena' (Two Stags) restaurant. That place, recently restored and decorated in keeping with a certain notion of the demands of tourists, immediately struck Schiffer as a haven in which could be found all that was ancient, original, heroic, passionate, wild, innocent and aromatic, which the West has forgotten and trampled underfoot.

The exotic story is not much concerned with plausibility. Its writer asks one to believe his word that in Serbia, and in Skadarlije particularly, he has discovered the authentic virtues and values which Europe has allegedly lost, and can only regret or dream about. The exotic story of the European traveller must be appropriate to that nostalgia. In it there is everything that cannot be found in Europe. As Tsvetan Todorov says, exoticism 'is not so much the description of a reality as the formulation of a certain ideal.' (Todorov, 257)

When this is borne in mind, it becomes clear why Mr Schiffer saw that things and happenings are exceedingly improbable, especially for someone who really knows the place, which had become 'a luxurious restaurant from the end of the nineteenth century made of old wood of warm colours ... soaked with the aromas of spices'. In it Schiffer found expressions of authentic humanity, unknown to Europeans. One of these was the 'outpouring of emotions accompanied by some Gypsy truth' to which 'only the South Slavs know how to abandon themselves'. This outpouring comes about when the South Slavs sing, 'souls brimming with inexpressible nostalgia, their songs simultaneously courageous and melancholy, songs filled to the brim with heroic epic as popular as it is deathless, incredible exploits and binding customs, contents imbued with the sound of time and the whisper of the soil'. These songs are, of course, 'ancient' and 'authentically popular', 'with harmonies fashioned to condemn your spirit to torment after they have driven you to tears and torn at your heart-strings'; in them, quite in the spirit of oriental exoticism, 'Slavonic longing and Arab sorrow' intertwine. The titles of the songs included *Djelem, djelem*; *Djurdjevdan* (St Vitus' Day), *Moj, Milane* (My Milan), *Volela me jedna Vranjanka* (A girl from Vranje loved me), *Ima dana* (There are days) and *Tamo daleko* (There, far away).

But the enthusiastic exclamations—'O, lovely Serbia on that night' and 'How I fell for it! Passionately! Madly!'—were coaxed from Schiffer by the Serbian women, those 'tender and beautiful gazelles', when 'with their hands on their hips and their hair loosed over their shoulders, barefoot, but still dignified ... they began to dance on the tables'. They were 'more wild than provocative', and their lips were red 'like half-open wild strawberries above teeth whiter than lily petals'. So at the heart of Schiffer's travel story there appears one of the *topoi* of exoticism, typical in its primitive and orientalist variants, the *topos* of the 'barefoot contessa', the noble, passionate Oriental or untamed women. The main symbols of their erotic or seditious (vis-à-vis insipid Europe) charm are their bare feet and loose hair, and dancing on café tables. Their male companion is Zorba the Greek.

Among the barefoot contessas at 'The Two Stags' was a young Serbian girl from Sarajevo, 'a being whom nature had endowed with such rare charms', who, fleeing from certain death, had to leave her native city and her Muslim husband because, as she confided to our traveller, Izetbegović's fanatical Muslims 'drove out every Serb, sometimes also Croats, who refused to submit unquestioningly to the laws of the Koran'. However inappropriate and illogical her appearance among the half-drunk, singing café guests seemed at first, she fitted into the morality and logic of Schiffer's exotic tale because her innocent suffering, together with other scenes from the lives of the innocent and simple-hearted Serbian locals, served only to emphasise the evil and malice of the civilised West. The heartless Westerners, 'people called civilised', had decided to imprison even her, along with the other barefoot contessas and the nostalgically singing Slavs at 'The Two Stags', and all Serbs in general, 'a whole people so full of life and so beautiful'. They are 'exposed to mockery', says Schiffer, and disdained by 'the civilisation to which I myself belong', which calls them 'barbarians', thus 'revealing the worst sadism'.

The exotic Serbs who live a full and uncorrupted life and suffer innocently have in Schiffer's story the function of the ideal opposite of the depraved and heartless Europeans. If one is to believe Schiffer and other travel writers who make their way into our part of the world with guides and interpreters, contemporary Serbs may once again be described as a people radically different from the civilised Europeans, in another place far removed from Europe and its civilisations. In exotic tales this radical difference is judged as to the Serbs' advantage, which ought to flatter them, since they are better than the civilised Europeans, and not worse, as they are portrayed in the texts of European chauvinists and racists. But this cannot conceal the essential similarity of exoticism and racism. Both mean the radical exclusion of the Other. Their demonisation, as is often said today—or their angelisation, as could also be said. Bad or good, the figures with which Daniel Salvatore Schiffer peopled 'The Two Stags' are nevertheless barbarians. And when he returns to France he will be able to say what was said by the best-known friend of noble savages, Jean-Jacques Rousseau: 'In the depths of my heart I am all too aware how hard it would be for me to cease to live with people as corrupt as I am myself.' (Quoted in Todorov, 269)

22. Festival of Books

In recent weeks in Serbia the book has been hailed and celebrated on all sides. Its cult has been renewed and included in the shaping of the official picture of life in Serbia as being directed towards peace, knowledge, beauty and progress. Serbia is a land of the book. The book is its holy object and its oath. If anyone attacks Serbia with a stone, she will respond with a book. For Serbia the book has no substitute.

The renewal of this cult was promoted by the recently concluded Book Fair in Belgrade. This exhibition always had an expressly ceremonial and political-propaganda character, because it is not organised by publishers and booksellers themselves, but by the state-party bureaucracy under the label of a so-called professional association. This year, as before, the Fair was opened 'in the presence of prominent guests', with fanfares, television coverage and formal speeches. And as on all earlier occasions, the journalists recalled that the Book Fair was a 'holiday of the spirit' or 'a holy day of the written word'. However, this time there was a noticeable effort to give the usual ritual praise of the book greater symbolic weight than before. Its cult has shifted towards the foreground of that mixture of various para-religious adorations, supplications and prostrations which constitutes a kind of 'profane religion' at the heart of the present movement in Serbia.

This new, magnified importance of the cult of the book is well expressed in the headline of an article in *Politika* about the opening of the Book Fair: 'The book is our destiny'. That is, in fact, a quote from the opening words of Ognjen Lakićević, director of the Association of Publishers and Booksellers of Yugoslavia, where it is possible to find also the thought: 'The book has kept us going, praise be to it!'. It is true that in Lakićević's speech this apparently fated connection to the book remains ambiguous, because it can be understood as something that not only refers to publishers and readers of books, but is also the destiny of all Serbs. 'Not even the most difficult moments, which are behind us', said Lakićević on that occasion, 'were able to discourage either the publishers or us, admirers of the book, in the noble pursuit of dreaming of beauty and the future. Those who did not understand us then will, I believe, understand us now: the book is our destiny. Your loyalty to the book is more than love, it has determined us and given us the strength to carry on. The book sustained us, praise be to it!' (*Politika*, 23 October 1996)

But in a newspaper headline across three columns 'The Book is our Destiny' there is no ambiguity, and readers are invited to recognise themselves as best they can in the new symbol of national identity and dedicate themselves to its cult. Equally, the sentence 'The book has sustained us, praise be to it' is not to be understood in a material and essentially erroneous way, as a statement of gratitude to the book by someone who lives from it, but correctly, as the slogan of a new Serbian national cult. 'When it is a matter of books', writes the journalist from *Borba* about the opening of the Fair, 'they have always had a cult place among us. Through the book (written or oral) we have held together as a people, through history our rulers and bishops were writers, in our dwellings it is a great disgrace not to have a book' Here one may clearly see that the new cult is being introduced by reference to the old, to tradition, as the celebration of something sacred that is long established and deeply rooted. That is why, in the *Borba* article, the book has always been a Serbian sacred thing, and why it can exist paradoxically also in oral form; that is also why our renowned forebears, already known for using spoons and forks before other Europeans, now had to take up the pen as well and become writers. The same logic of making the new 'ancient', with the aim that its implant should support the authority of the alleged tradition, can explain the otherwise harmless lie that it is a disgrace for our people not to have a book in their homes.

Like the myth about spoons and forks, the renewed cult of the book has its place in Serbs' symbolic assessment of their place in the world, their conflict and reconciliation with it. This is hinted at by Lakićević when he calls on those 'who have not understood us' to 'grasp' that the Serbs are, above all, a people who nurture 'something stronger than love' for the book. The same meaning, but in an even more specific and exalted fashion, was conveyed by the main speaker at the opening of the Fair, the French writer of Russian descent, Vladimir Volkov. To the hatred and lies of the world the Serbs responded with books. 'Against such dishonesty paid for with dollars from oil', says Volkov, 'against such murderous power directed against a people who have no other desire but to live in liberty, against an international conspiracy of such dimensions, what do the Serbs fight with? With a Book Fair, a festival of books, books!'

The message about the Serbs as captives of the book and writing, and about their leaders who, in keeping with the book-loving traditions of their people, are themselves men of the pen, has recently reached America—and at the highest levels too. According to a news item from Tanjug, carried by *Politika* on 27 October, in Washington Mrs Milanka Karić, president of the Karić Brothers Foundation, gave Hillary Clinton a personal gift from Professor Mirjana Marković*: the American edition of her book *Night and Day*. From one writer to another, one could say.

Here the question can be raised as to whether the cult of the book brings to the people to whom it is allegedly dedicated anything more than the respect of the well-intentioned. Two more or less mutually coherent answers to this question have been given. The first is Lakićević's. Referring to Shakespeare, he sees the book as 'the stuff that dreams are made of', and in keeping with this he calls the Book Fair 'a great magic spell among books'. That is, he explains, 'a magic place where you gather and pursue your dreams under the domes of the Belgrade Fair'. Is that all? Are we linked by destiny to the book only because of our dreams? Is it dreams that have sustained us? Praise be to them?

But to offer a dream along with a book does not seem at first sight to offer much. Only the ungrateful, those Serbs desirous of earthly joys and hollow material values, those who are maddened by politics and endless strikes, demonstrations and elections, do not know how to assess the value of dreams among the books under the domes of the Belgrade Fair. But they fail to understand that it is in those dreams that true wealth lies, the wealth of the inner life, the 'spirituality' so valued today; that it is dreams which raise us up above a century mired in materialism and preoccupied with financial worries, shield us from the brutal struggle for power, and cleanse our souls, poisoned with war and politics. In a word, the book offers happiness. This is the thought arrived at by the President of the Federal Republic of Yugoslavia, Zoran Lilić. It inspired the oration given by the President at the ceremonial symposium on the occasion of the 150th anniversary of the founding of the National Library in the town of Negotin. 'Lovers of books say that reading is a form of happiness,' said Lilić on that occasion (*Politika*, 26 October 1996). It is interesting that he did not refer to his own personal experience in this connection: has he not shared that happiness?

The cult of the book is closely linked to cultural policy: it is being spread at its expense, and stands in inverse proportion to real concern about books. The more the book is a sacred object and a name to be reverenced, the less it belongs to the real world. The less it is read and the more it is worshipped, the more inaccessible it becomes as a fundamental medium of education and culture and the more easily it is offered as an excuse for festivities.

23. Turbulent

Two decades after the publication of the novel *Smutnoe vreme* (Turbulent Times), by Mladen Markov in 1976, the expression 'turbulent times' has become one in which we recognise the rhetoric of so-called Serbian national workers. For example, we find it in the subtitle of a book by Atanasije Jevtić, *Znak preporečni. Razgovori u vremena smutna* (A Sign of Disagreement: Conversations in Turbulent Times) published in 1994. In 1996 'turbulent times' appeared on the covers of two newly published books. Dragan Nedeljković called a collection of his political speeches, *Reči Srbima u smutnom vremenu* (Words to the Serbs in Turbulent Times) and a book appeared was published by Prosveta with the title *Intelektualac u smutnom vremenu, A* (The Intellectual in Turbulent Times) consisting of the answers of some forty Serbian academics, writers and artists to a questionnaire drawn up by the journalist Rada Saratlić about the place of intellectuals in 'the storm of history'. It had previously been published from July and August 1994 in *Politika*.

What is it about the expression 'turbulent times' that makes it so attractive to some writers today? It seems that in political matters the use of words such as 'turbulent', 'convocation', 'schism', 'disconsolate', 'discord' and the like is above all characteristic of those Serbian 'national workers' who like everything to have an ancient and biblical note, breathing an ancestral and prophetic wisdom, which is always 'bitter' and often 'admonitory'. This is in keeping with the tendency of conservative and nationalist intellectuals to renew an allegedly authentic language of Serbian national ideas and translate into it various contemporary 'ideological' discourses, in order to renew on the linguistic plane the foundation of Pan-Serb accord and 'convocation', to heal the painful 'schism' in the Serbian flock and clan.

The majority of the contributions published in R. Saratlić's book bear witness to this endeavour to enable authentic Pan-Serb ideas to emerge from the sediment of contemporary history and politics into the light of day, if only in words. However, this is not by any means a search for terms that would be more suitable than others for the formulation of some specific Serbian political programme, but a search for a suggestive and cherished sound. This may be seen in the fact that neither the author nor the participants in this questionnaire about 'turbulent times', apart from Jovan Ćirilov, are interested in the dictionary meaning of the adjective 'turbulent', but generally reduce it to the sense of 'troubled', 'disturbed', 'impure', satisfied with their pleasure in its archaic melodiousness.

Nevertheless, the texts published in Saratlić's book allow one to identify some other political-rhetorical functions of the image of 'turbulent times'. One of these is the fact that any discussion of the real causes and consequences of the unenviable situation of present-day Serbia, and of the responsibility of our political and cultural elite for that situation is replaced by philosophising lamentations over the fate of our epoch and its inhuman laws, for it is there, in the malice and brutality of the age, that we should allegedly find the source of all our woes.

In the opinion of most of the authors represented in this book, 'turbulent times' are a global, planetary phenomenon. The misfortune that has beset the Serbs and Serbia is just one aspect of the general wretchedness that has overwhelmed the contemporary world. That is why they mostly ponder globally about mankind, the world, the epoch, the planet, the destiny of civilisation. They come to the conclusion that 'the planetary spirit is evidently on a downward slope' (A. Vukadinović), that 'planetary chaos' has overcome us (S. Vuković), that what is striking today is the 'planetary agitation' which has been 'manifested precisely in the Balkans, the site of international fetters', as one of its most sensitive spots (B. Jovanović). They also, find, that 'the world has fallen on hard, pivotal times' (D. Medaković), that 'it sometimes seems that the whole of humanity is on the *Titanic*, heedlessly dancing and singing on the deck while the ship slowly sinks.' (A. Despić)

The causes of the coming of 'turbulent times' in the world today are obvious for many authors of this book. They see them in the 'planetary totalitarianism' (T. Mladenović, C. Popov), through which the famous New World Order has been established—in other words the 'international extortionist empire' (R.P. Nogo), whose interests are protected by 'global ideological police' (M. Perišić) and powerful electronic media. But although it has easily recognisable historical and political causes, the 'turbulent time' in this book on the whole indicates a fatal state of affairs. History is following its course, laid down long ago, a course of 'continuity of horrors and crimes' (M. Belović), while historical events most closely resemble events in nature. This is particularly true of war, which is 'an elemental tempest, typhoon, flood—and in that flood, it is impossible to make out the river-bed.' (R.P. Nogo) Man finds himself suddenly in war, beyond his will, as in some marvel. 'I know', writes R. Jovović, 'that we were not in favour of war, God forbid, but since we are already in that marvel, we have no other choice, but, like men, to wage and conclude that accursed war, so that our people should once again regain its name, space and time.'

The hard, chauvinistic variant of the image of the planetary and fatal 'turbulent times' is also well represented in the book. That is the image through which the Serbs are presented exclusively in the role of innocent victim, which they allegedly took over from the Jews. 'Yesterday', explains M. Šobajić, 'Catholic Europe, organised in the Third Reich, brought about the liquidation of the Jews with well-known consequences. Today it is enough for Europe to unite in a new Reich, created at Maastricht, for the annihilation of the Serbian people to be immediately instituted.' Why the Serbs? In case you have forgotten, T. Mladenović and R. P. Nogo will remind you: we live in a house in the middle of a thoroughfare.

When 'turbulent times' is a metaphor for planetary chaos, the evil fate of humanity, by which everywhere, except in our country, international extortionists and the international media have come to power, then it is possible to reconcile two apparently contradictory things: the critical function of intellectuals—which, according to the unanimous opinion of the authors represented here, is their main social function—and the contribution of intellectuals to strengthening the power of prevailing political ideas. The intellectual is 'by nature a heretic' and his 'mission is to cast down idols', to destroy fetishes and sacred cows. But since these idols are today mainly offered by the West, the so-called 'free world' and so-called 'democracy', the task of our intellectual is to fight courageously against them (D. Nedeljković) and to stand up in defence of the regime in Serbia, that is to be 'on the side of one's people', as it is euphemistically called in the language of Serbian 'national workers'.

When the intellectual understands his task in this way, he becomes a merciless critic of foreign intellectuals who spread untruths about 'us', and even more an opponent of local critics of the regime and the political ideas of the elite who support it. For they are those who 'simply prostitute themselves ... prepared casually to cast off both their nation and their state, in order to ingratiate themselves with the powerful abroad.' (V. Krestić) They want to 'destroy and besmirch everything around them, mock everything, and even vilify the people they belong to, only because they refuse to think like them'. (S. Vuković) They dare 'to vilify the people and the army because it is not to them that they come for a blessing on their decisions'. (R.P. Nogo)

With the exception of a few contributions—among which are texts by Z. Trebješanin, O. Jančić, M. Savić and R. Putnik—*The Intellectual in Turbulent Times* bears witness to the fact that in Serbia in 1994 a particular kind of discourse by prominent intellectuals was well represented and widely propagated in the media (through the influential *Politika,* but not only there). This was an ostentatious, tedious and grandiose discourse about the state of the nation, a discourse allegedly open to the future and to international horizons, but in fact limited to anachronistic and provincial cogitation about the 'turbulent times'. Among the few serious and noteworthy texts in this book are the aphorisms of A. Baljak. Printed at the end of the book, they act as its somewhat unexpected satirical epilogue. Some of them could have been written after reading the patriotic thoughts presented in the book about the 'turbulent times'. For example: 'The further Serbia stretches, the more remote abroad becomes. [...] They spilled a sea of blood. Their act will nourish future generations. [...] What is the use of democracy being at the door when we are not at home?'

24. Enjoyment

After the local elections in Serbia, Milošević's government looks far smaller and less secure. It has been reduced and unsettled by the very fact that a good part of the local political administration has passed into the hands of the opposition.[1] But its reduction in size is not confined to that loss. The impression has been created that Milošević's political potential as a whole has declined, that not only has the scale of its manifestation been reduced, but also its intensity, the very core of that power has suddenly softened. We could even be witnessing an evaporation of power that may be hard to stop. Defeat in the local elections is hard for the President of Serbia not so much because it has weakened his authority in particular places, as because it has suddenly and as it were spectacularly disclosed its general weakness, and just at a time when it appeared that this authority was greater and firmer than ever before.

For in recent years Milošević's political power, measured by the number and importance of the so-called levers of power which he controls—such as the army, police, media, the economy, international support—has shown signs of steady growth. But, nevertheless, it must be that this power has been constantly seeping away through some other channels, so that now it seems that it cannot meet (at

---

[1] This refers to the local government elections of November 1996. The ruling Socialist Party was dissatisfied with the results of those elections, which brought the opposition coalition 'Zajedno' (Together) to power in Belgrade and in many other towns in Serbia. The government then tried to change the results in its favour, which provoked four months of protests by the citizens and students (November 1996–February 1997).

least not by legal means) even the basic needs of the government's survival. Today in Milošević's political capital there gapes a large and, it seems, irretrievable shortfall. His regime increasingly resembles a ruined plutocrat's house which still lives lavishly, receives in grand style, keeps servants and a conspicuous fleet of cars, while the debts pile up vertiginously and creditors besiege him.

What has happened to Milošević's authority? Where are that skill and that shrewdness which even his fiercest opponents acknowledged? Is it possible that he, this player, of whom it was believed that in the political chessgame he was able to calculate ten moves ahead, should have failed to foresee the loss in the local elections of several important figures? Could even he have been taken by surprise? In the reports from those elections the assessment recurs that the authorities were 'amazed' by the loss of the big cities, that the Socialists were 'shocked' by it, that they were 'caught off-guard', that the ruling gang was 'showing signs of real hysteria'. The first commentaries agree that the authorities were 'rocked', that they had not properly 'taken the temperature of the people', that Milošević had been 'intoxicated' with the epithets of peace-maker and crucial factor for peace and prosperity, that he had 'overestimated his ability'.

These commentaries analyse Milošević's misguided moves, list the mistakes he made in his endeavour to maintain and strengthen his rule. They list his mistaken investments of political capital, mentioning, for instance, the shortcomings of his appointments policy, the loss of standing of the bearers of power and leaders of the ruling party, the unpopularity of 'little local dictators'. There will certainly be more such assessments and analyses of the regime's political tactics and strategy, and also those of the opposition. However, the weakness of Milošević's power, as it was manifested in the local elections in Serbia, raises the question also of how far it is a consequence of having spent political capital which is by its very nature unproductive, or of simple waste and squandering, i.e. the mere enjoyment of power.

The political economy, at least that which considers political capital, the capital of symbolic power, just like any other property, knows that a good part of that capital does not go on reproduction, but is irretrievably spent simply for the sake of spending. Power is sought and it is coveted, certainly not only because of what is undoubtedly true—namely that the need to protect what has been acquired brings nothing but anxiety and fear—but also because it is enjoyed. And the Eros of power—its sweetness, as is usually said—lies less in accumulating power and more in its arrogant, pretentious and exhibi-

Mirjana Marković and Slobodan Milošević in 1998. (Photograph published in the album *The Heart is also on the Left*, Belgrade, 1999)

tionistic squandering. This has induced many important sociologists (Max Weber and Torsten Veblen, for example) to make a distinction between power and prestige: the desire for prestige is often realised by the ostentatious expenditure of power.

When such a pleasure-seeking, consumerist 'use' of political power is borne in mind, then the assessment of the situation in which the regime in Serbia found itself after the local elections cannot be reduced to the enumeration of misguided, unintelligent acts by that regime, its mistakes in calculation. One should also take into account everything on which in recent times the chief of that regime, so to speak consciously plummeting, sinfully revelling, in fact spent his otherwise valuable political property, painstakingly acquired and until now on the whole carefully preserved.

He spent it most of all on his wife. I hope that the reader will not be offended by my saying this so directly and crudely. In fact, I am only repeating the widespread opinion that the political literary activity of Mira Markovic has inflicted great harm on her husband's regime, that the loud propaganda of JUL in the regime media, its pioneer performances, party seminars and 'leftwing' and 'progressive' ideas have turned many of its most dedicated supporters away from the government. This opinion is borne out by, among other things, the extremely modest results achieved by JUL in the local elections. Its programme—filled with visions of progress, European integration, general (and especially women's) emancipation, postmodern science and philanthropic culture—met with approval in only five municipalities: Lebani, Žagubica, Crna Trava, Ada and Čoka.[2]

My interpretation of the role of Mira Marković and the parasitical past she played in the economy of Milošević's power differs somewhat from opinions expressed up to now, insofar as I think that this is not so much to do with any mistaken judgment by Milošević of the benefit he could have from his wife's intensive political activity. We would have seriously to underestimate him and to forget all those agile, well-calculated moves thanks to which he achieved power, and so far maintained it, if we were to believe that Milošević is really convinced that he can be helped in reinforcing and strengthening his power by his lovelier half, with her sub-party, which seeks to unite in one as yet unseen whole socialist humanism (personified by Ljubiša Ristić and reduced to an arid idea) and the material prosperity of capitalism (represented by the figure of the plump and jovial Hadži Dragan Antić).[3] There is little doubt that he has no illusions in that regard. But, even so!

But, even so, Milošević allows it all to go the way it is going. Why? I think that he does it out of pure enjoyment. And, say the enthusiasts, there can be no pure enjoyment without pure cost. That is why moments of abandon to enjoyment are at the same time moments of the greatest weakness; the greater the expense, the greater the sweet shudder, the intoxicating vertigo of enjoyment. If power could not be spent heedlessly and at extreme risk, it would not have such a high price. It would be transformed into a boring and passion-less bureaucratic administration. Milošević's example confirms this, for the President of Serbia evidently enjoys watching the way his wife spends his political property. At the beginning it appeared that he was going to squander it on war. Nevertheless, he did not go to the end. Will he now know how to stop before it is too late? But, even if it is late, there are good prospects that the same play about

---

[2] The municipalities in which Mira Marković's Yugoslav United Left (JUL) won in the local elections.

[3] The first is the President of the Directorate of JUL, and the second the director of the *Politika* company.

the diligent acquisition and crazy expenditure of power will be performed on the Serbian political stage, but with different protagonists. For by all accounts Milošević's main opponent and candidate to be his heir, Vuk Drašković, enjoys watching the way that everything he and his political friends have somehow earned and saved is blown away in an instant by his wife.[4]

---

[4] An allusion to the damage done to the civil protest and Drašković's SPO Party by Danica Drašković's invitation to the demonstrators to take on the Milošević regime more energetically (she mentioned even 'bombs').

25. Everyone to the Sea!

'It is all unfolding according to an organised scenario.' This 'assessment' of the demonstrations in Belgrade and other large cities of Serbia that have lasted for several weeks now is repeated in almost every one of the short and, one would say, extorted reports which the regime media devote to these events. Why? Why has the image of an 'organised scenario' acquired such an important place in the repertoire of picturesque expressions with which the regime propaganda endeavours to blacken and discredit the mass protests against the usurpation of local power in Serbia?

It is not hard to understand why the very word 'scenario' is a suitable means for a certain type of political propaganda. When an event of general interest, and particularly a political event with a large number of participants, like the demonstrations in Serbia now, is described as unfolding 'according to a scenario', it suggests that the event is being used to bring about something which was planned beforehand and in another place, that participants in the event are only the misused ('manipulated') executors of someone else's will, actors and extras in a film thought up and directed by someone foreign and far away. That someone is in fact their enemy, that is an enemy of the people. That is why in *Večernje novosti* (10 December 1996) one article about the demonstrations in Belgrade acquired the headline 'Scenario against the People'.

But when the word 'organised' (or 'familiar', 'tried', 'usual' etc.) is added to 'scenario', then the propaganda value of such formulae is enriched by a new sheaf of implied concepts. At their centre is the suggestion that the events which the propaganda condemns do not represent anything new, they are simply the repetition of something that has already happened once or several times, and consequently they are not events in the true sense. This hint refers at the same time to three temporal levels, which may be separated—only, of course, for the purposes of this little analysis.

First of all, it is a matter of creating the impression that day after day what is happening at the demonstrations is the same thing, that there is no progress of any kind, that the first day and the twenty-first day are the same, that this is just a boring, monotonous and in fact senseless walking in a circle, or stamping on the spot. The demonstrations are therefore unfolding 'according to an organised' or 'an everyday scenario', 'in a practised manner'. It is stressed that the demonstrators move 'along the usual route', at the 'usual time', in 'the usual way', that it is a matter of their 'usual passing'. As a Tanjug report puts it, it is 'an endless repetition of the same, on the whole peaceful images'. It is important that it is a question of 'an already established practice', 'a repetition of the old demands', that it is going on 'as usual', 'as in previous days'; 'they repeat their earlier position', 'repeating their abusive shouts', 'their familiar slogans', 'their already familiar rhetoric'. The aim of all these formulae is to present the demonstrations as a false movement and thus symbolically to put an end to them.

This image of a daily, tedious and barren repetition of the same is then incorporated into a broader picture of the equally fruitless repetition of demonstrations by the opposition in Belgrade over the last six years. 'Demonstrations like these were organised after all the elections,' reported I. Dačić, 'regardless of whether there were objections or not'. Therefore, 'what is happening in the streets of certain towns is nothing new' (*Politika*, 4 December 1996). And in the document which Dačić's party sent to its members, instructing them how to behave towards the on-going demonstrations, it says, among other things, that the opposition had put into practice 'a scenario practised earlier—students, workers, refugees, etc. are summoned' (*Nasa borba*, 7–8 December 1996). I. V. Jovanović, the Federal Minister of Internal Affairs, made his contribution to the idea that the opposition is repeating itself: 'We have already seen and encountered this several times.' (*Naša borba*, 11 December 1996)

Besides going round in circles every day for all these years, repeating sterile attempts to beat the ruling Socialists, the Serbian opposition, as it is painted by the regime propaganda, represents a vain return to something already seen also in the broadest historical context. For example, it offers scope for the renewal of the Chetnik and Ustasha movements. Lj. Ristić saw Chetniks at the demonstrations in Belgrade, while fascists were seen by the director of *Borba*, Živorad Djordjević ('pro-fascist hysteria'), and the president of the Parliament of Serbia, D. Tomić. The latter emphasised in his report that the protests of the citizens of Serbia were 'destructive, violent demonstrations, with all the hallmarks of pro-fascist groups and ideologies'. Tomić also revealed the real author of the 'scenario'. 'Just remember Hitler's assumption of power', he said, 'in the period before he came to power and after he had come to power, the same scenario.' (*Demokratija*, 2 December 1996)

Nevertheless, the point of all these, to put it mildly, scandalous historical parallels and associations is not to interpret the present demonstrations in Serbia as anything to do with Chetniks or fascism. The more important aim is to link them with something past, old, outlived, failed. The Chetniks and fascists are useful for the regime propaganda only as symbols of so-called defeated historical forces and old, failed ideas. The same purpose can quite well be served also by communists and Marxists. This is confirmed by two examples. The judge of the Constitutional Court of Serbia, S. Vučetić, who joined the protest, is described in *Borba* (10 December) as 'a man who was virtually until yesterday an orthodox communist and member of the Presidency of Serbia', while a commentator on Radio Belgrade attacked Vuk Drašković, in a news broadcast on 9 December, as a man who 'has shown his real face, that he is at heart a communist and a Marxist.'

When it does decide to notice the current demonstrations and protests of the citizens and students of Serbia, the regime propaganda paints them like something moving in a charmed circle, according to 'an organised scenario'. Observing that cheerless picture, a person would say that days, years, decades will not be enough for the citizens of Serbia who credulously accept the opposition's invitation to protest against the government, to break out of that circle, as they stamp, walk, trudge, follow their own shadows. But they could. If only they could see through the pointlessness and falsity of the scenario according to which the opposition directs their path. For there exists a real path: the way of hope, the way of progress, the way of the future, the imperial way. In fact—the motorway.

For the motorway (even a whole network of motorways!) is what the government in Serbia has offered its citizens instead of the circular pedestrian path along which the opposition is trudging through the towns of Serbia. In this way Milošević has refuted the idea that he has no real response to the demonstrations, that he is silent. For days already the response has been there, and for days it has been repeated, although many people have not yet understood that the news of the building of a Trans-Yugoslav motorway, announced by the presidents of Serbia and Montenegro and the most important 'builders' and then joyfully spread further by the regime media, is in fact a direct response to the demonstrations and protests in Serbian towns. It has certainly not happened by chance that it is precisely during the demonstrations that the grandiose building project, which should supposedly begin next year, has been launched with such pomp and from the highest place.

The role of Milošević's promotion of motorways, with special emphasis on the one from Belgrade straight to the sea, as an alternative to the roads trodden every day by the demonstrators in Serbia is well illustrated by a comparison of the reports of two apparently unconnected events in *Večernje novosti* on 10 December. The fourth page carries various bad pieces of news about the demonstrations and opposite it, the fifth page sings of the future Belgrade—Bar motorway under the headline 'To the sea—four lanes'. The situation is repeated when on the sixth page we are startled by the enormous headline 'Scenario against the people', while on the seventh, as consolation and relief, we are greeted with the headline, in equally large letters, of yet another rhapsody about the future motorway: 'Into the Future!'

There is therefore an alternative, there is a choice. All we have to do is decide: shall we continue to trudge in circles through the cold streets, or shall we turn towards the sea, the warm south, open oceans, blue horizons?

26. Piano

'We love you, Slobo!'—'I love you too!' This exchange of declarations of love between the masses and the leader were the main event at a recently held demonstration of the SPS in Belgrade.[1] It came as the apex of the political love story launched with so-called messages of support, which activists of the ruling party have been sending to their leader over the last few days. The content of these messages of love, devotion and loyalty directed to Milošević (in the form of telegrams, but also in letters, slogans on placards and chanting at demonstrations) shows what kind of politics and, particularly, what model of an imagined political community the Milošević regime is currently offering as an alternative to the increasingly strong and increasingly broad movement for a civil and democratic Serbia.

The most important figure in this ritual political communication is the figure of the leader, the subject and recipient of the messages. But he is, above all, the figure of embodied, personified power. Artur Rubenstein liked to say that the piano is an instrument in which the whole of music is contained. Similarly it could be said of Milošević, taken as he is presented in the messages of support of his followers, that he comprises the whole of Serbian politics. Government, diplomacy, the state and its institutions are represented as something which may in its entirety be reduced to Milošević's name and embodied in his person.

---

[1] This was a demonstration held on 24 December 1996 in Belgrade, which the media described as a 'counter-demonstration', because Milošević's party intended, through a mass gathering of its followers, to correct the impression created during the civilian and student protest that it had no support among the people.

Among the qualities which adorn this person is above all wisdom, 'wise politics' or 'state wisdom'. Sometimes this wisdom is more precisely defined as the ability to make 'wise state moves', sometimes it goes in tandem with decisiveness, consistency or dignity. An important feature of Milošević's wisdom is also its alleged rootedness in the people, that is the fact that it appears also as the ability to articulate the popular will politically. Then the president of Serbia is acknowledged in one telegram as having 'correctly articulated the voice of the people', and in another as having replied to a letter from Warren Christopher 'with dignity, with the voice and the heart of the people'.[2] This in fact suggests the conclusion that a wise leader, who knows his people, articulates politically its interests and enjoys its trust, represents an institution of real democracy, a kind that is more effective, cheaper and closer to our people than parliamentary democracy, its parties, conflicts and endless struggles for power.

The wisdom attributed to Milošević in this ritual addressing of the leader was in some cases linked with his exclusive and God-given knowledge of the real truth and real way of illuminating and defending it. We support You, it says in one telegram, because 'you have explained the essence of events in Serbia, in a well-argued and dignified way', because you have 'overcome with the truth all the untruths which keep being repeated about us.' In fact, Milošević is the only one who knows the truth, so his opinion is thereby the only viable one and for the Serbs the only possible one. This is the message from Socialists in Zrenjanin: 'The municipal committee of the SPS in Zrenjanin has received and experienced your reply to the letter of the US State Secretary as the only possible opinion and the attitude of an authentic statesman of the Serbian people.' The like-minded citizens of Kovin add: 'No one in this country can have a different path to this one.' And this is not a path only for today and tomorrow or for the immediate future. The Serbs could follow it for several more centuries! The hope that this is how it will be was expressed at a demonstration in Bor, by a university professor, Dr Milan Janić, and his words were printed without hesitation by *Politika* (22 December 1996): 'May the justice, truth and democracy of our president Slobodan Milošević lead us through the centuries of the third millennium.'

[2] This refers to the reply of Milošević to a letter sent him in the middle of December 1996 by the US Secretary of State Warren Christopher, in which dissatisfaction is expressed at the way the results of the municipal elections in Serbia were altered.

According to the messages of support for Milošević, he personally embodies the accumulation of great political knowledge and authentic Serbian state wisdom, that is to say those values which no parliament and no multi-party system can replace. As a result, it is only the president of Serbia who can successfully administer national affairs, and ensure for his people tranquil sleep and a happy life. All that we have we owe to you, the telegrams say. You have ensured peace and freedom for us, you have united Serbia, you have saved us from war, from internal and external enemies, a foreign boot, chaos. You are the creator of our present happiness. 'There has been enough suffering imposed on us', say the employees of the Rehabilitation Centre in Vrnjačka Banja in a message to Milošević, 'but we are happy, because even then peace was preserved, which is your greatest gift to the Serbian people.'

In view of the President's manifold gifts to the Serbian people, it is not surprising that the words of those who address him in the name of that people are full of love and respect. In addition to direct expressions of love, which can be very simply intimate, such as 'We love you, Slobo', 'You are our pride', 'We are Slobo's, Slobo is ours', messages of support for Milošević have also been presented as expressions 'of the most sincere admiration' and 'the deepest respect', in the form of a desire 'that you should persevere in the struggle', as a plea for him 'to continue as up to now', as a promise of loyalty, or as expressions 'of great gratitude', gratitude 'for all that you have done'. Among these last, the most striking was a message written on a placard which could be seen at SPS demonstrations in Bačka Palanka and Belgrade: 'Thank you for Dayton'.

Judging by these messages of support and dedication to Milošević, allegedly expressing the voice of the people, one would say that the people do not seek for themselves an important role, certainly not an active one, in the political life of Serbia. People want to help, but not in the form of constantly annoying the government and demanding that it take their views into account, of themselves interfering in politics, imagining that they understand affairs of state, aligning themselves with parties, imitating the opposition in its search for 'naked power'. What do they need with all of that, when they have a wise and capable leader who knows what is best for them and who watches over their tranquil sleep and prosperity?

The people know their place: the workers are to work, the farmers to feed the people, pupils and students to learn. The leader and the people have a shared struggle, but it is his business to think and make decisions, while the people work. 'In our Požarevac', says the leader of the local council of that town, 'there are no demonstrations in the streets, for our people are focused on work, aware that our only salvation is work and only work, and that is our greatest contribution to the stability of the state.' A telegram sent to Milošević in the name of the workers of an enterprise from Kraljevo expresses their readiness to contribute to the success of the struggle of the leader and the people, saying that the workers 'will contribute to our shared struggle through our work and dedication'. This is repeated by many others, including a speaker at an SPS demonstration in Pirot: 'The task of the workers is to produce a way out of the crisis.'

This is what the image of good government and a good people in Serbia amounts to in the messages of alleged popular support for Milošević. But the very recourse to such a form of ritual communication of the people with their leader speaks sufficiently clearly about the undemocratic and autocratic character of the present Serbian government and conjures up the memory of some earlier examples of the same political ritual. For example, the messages of support for Milošević in December 1996 do not differ greatly from those which, reached King Milan in May 1894 as we learn from Stojan Novaković, when this king, who in Novaković's opinion was 'a friend only of autocratic personal rule', abolished the democratic constitution of 1888. 'Through an initiative of the police', writes Novaković, 'telegrams reached the king from throughout the country, congratulating him on that move. It was interpreted as the salvation of the country from lawlessness and disorder.' (Novaković, 76) King Milan succeeded in imposing his will on the Serbs two hundred years ago. At this moment, a day after the SPS demonstration in Belgrade, and an hour after the radio carried the news that the police would forcibly prevent further protests in the streets of Serbian towns, I do not yet know whether Milošević will succeed. I am only afraid that for that to happen new telegrams of love will not be enough.

27. Gaudeamus

Things look bad for the regime. The democratic opposition is increasingly well placed. But one would say that the true masters of the situation in Serbia today are the students. Everyone respects them. There is no one who would not agree at least to receive them. They even went to see Milošević and the Minister of the Serbian police and General Perišić. They were received by Patriarch Pavle and several other bishops. They were given a yule log by the monks of Hilandar.[1] They were sent special messages by, among many others, the Prime Minister of Montenegro and the 'Mothers of the Soldiers' organisation. The mayor of Belgrade, Čović, dissatisfied with the policies of his party, allegedly announced that the students were 'the only sincere people in the whole dirty game around the elections.' A group of officers of the Yugoslav Army, concerned about the crisis in Serbia, sent an open letter to three addresses: to their Commander-in-Chief, to the President of Serbia and to the students. Well-known painters, doctors, actors, priests, journalists, writers all come to the feet of the students, i.e. to the square known as Plato beside the Arts Faculty, in order to talk to them.

This general respect for the students is certainly due to the fact that they have presented their protest as something that is not politics in the true sense. Along with open sympathy for the opposition parties damaged by the regime's election thefts and for their protest, the students see their revolt as something that is not confined by the framework of party politics. It came into being as a mark of solidarity with the demonstrations by the citizens of Serbia organised by the

---

[1] The Serbian monastery on Mount Athos. (Transl.)

'Zajedno' Coalition. The student protest of 1996 has not become part of those demonstrations, but is developing alongside them, at a different time and in a different place, it has its own programme and independent public relations. In one statement for the media, the students say: 'We do not support either of the two sides in the struggle for power, but we feel responsible for the future of this country ...'

The students' reserved attitude to politics may be seen also in their distance from political ideologies. They do not wish to choose between Left and Right. 'We are not for either the Left or the Right, we are going straight into the future', says one of the students' leaders. This idea is expressed also by the emblem of the 1996 Student Protest— the word 'straight', defiantly breaking through arrows pointing 'right' and 'left',

Presented as non-party and non-ideological, the student protest of 1996–7 took on the role of an acceptable co-locutor—in any case, more acceptable than the protesting opposition parties—for the government and the Church and many individuals, especially from the world of culture and learning, who believe that to be apolitical or at least to have a certain distance from politics is a virtue of the enlightened and emancipated. The writer M. Pantić interprets the students' protest as a struggle for the respect of 'elementary civil, ethical, therefore pre-political rights'. (*NIN*, 31 December 1996) Turning to the students, the composer V. Kostić explained why every decent person supports them: 'Because your demands to the ruling powers are the clearest and purest, uncalculating and non-party political.' (*Demokratija*, 24 December 1996)

What is it, then, that the students are protesting in the name of— if it is not party political, or ideological, neither left nor right, more pre-political than political? The answer to this question is offered by many statements by the students' leaders and many statements of support for the students' protest. Here the students' resistance is interpreted as a struggle for some of the most important and indisputable social values and national interests, which are on the whole connected with their status of 'class by age', defined as 'young', 'young heads' or 'our children'. The students themselves gladly describe themselves in this way, as young, even as children. Their appeal to the public on the eve of the so-called 'counter-demonstration' of the SPS in Belgrade says: 'The two Serbias do not understand one another today, therefore permit at least your children to be a bridge of understanding.'

The students' demands, regardless of the fact that they fundamentally coincide with the demands of the protesting opposition, have a quite different weight because they are presented as the spontaneous revolt of 'our young people' or 'our children' in the name of the right to life. This point was emphasised by the new mayor of Novi Sad, M. Svilar, when he said of the students that 'their protest is a consequence of their love of truth and justice and the righteousness of their youth.' (*Demokratija*, 13 December 1996) Similarly, Bishop Sava offered his support to the students as support to the young: 'The Church will always be with the young, because it is to them that the Church and the country will be left.' (*Demokratija*, 6–7 January 1997) To accept the demands of the students is to accept the logic of life. 'The changing generations are life itself', explained the President of the Union of Writers of Serbia S. Rakitić, 'which must be joyfully accepted'. (*Demokratija*, 3 January 1997) Similarly, the writer J. Aćin judged that the student protest was 'free of all ideologisation and low politics, non-partisan but still deeply committed: on the side of life and freedom.' (ibid.)

Youth is energy. 'Do not let them break you, you are the energy of Serbia', the actor G. Baletić told the students. 'It will be good if the people realise that you are its energy', added his colleague V. Brajović. Youth is the future. 'You are the youth of Serbia', V. Koštunica told the students. Youth is purity, innocence, honesty, and therefore the students' demands are, in the words of V. Kostić, 'the purest', or, as N. Čović put it, 'the only sincere ones'. But youth means also freshness, clarity of thought, which enables the students to be rational, clever, even wise. That is why the messages sent to them express the hope that 'your consciousness and ideas will prevail' (V. Brajović), the conviction that 'it is only with them that Serbia makes sense' (Lj. Bogdanović), respect for their 'wisdom and spirit' (the actor M. Petrović). Some see the greatest virtue of the present generation of students precisely in the fact that they are 'rational and have an aim', that they are not 'hot-heads' (G. Marković), that is that they have 'a very sober, realistic approach to our problems' (D. Mijač).

Rising up against Milošević, but distancing themselves from parties and from political ideologies, placing 'straight' above 'left' and 'right', giving the consistent impression that what they are doing is something far better, stronger, full of life and valuable than politics, the students represent perhaps a more difficult puzzle and a bigger problem for his regime than the opposition parties. Because they question the legitimacy of the regime on the level of the most important state symbols, on the level of concepts of values and the meaning of life, creating the impression that the survival of Milošević in power and the future of Serbia are two incompatible things.

The majority of the values in the name of which the students are demonstrating and protesting are characteristic also of the other, citizens' protest, but, by all accounts, the economy of symbolic social communication demands that for the symbols, ritual and the whole imaginary which goes along with the protesting democratic and republican drive of Serbia a special stage should be opened, a special jurisdiction. The role of that jurisdiction which symbolically personifies the new liberal, democratic Serbia has been taken over by the 1996–7 Student Protest. It 'plays' and 'carries' it successfully. For instance, the approach of the citizens to the students on Plato Square beside the Arts Faculty has the function of a ritual confirmation of republican values, an emotional and solemn summoning of freedom, justice, peace, a democratic and European Serbia. It is an act of civil and republican baptism or communion; for many an opportunity for purification and repentance, which induced a friend of mine to refer to the ritual on Plato square as a 'laundry'.

But there are signs that the leaders of the student protest are beginning to feel the weight of the role of personifying a new civil Serbia, the weight of symbols, the weight of the words and gestures of people who expect of them and with them deliverance, purification, hope. For some of them it seems that it would be easier if that role could be shifted from the level of profane social symbolism and lay rituals to the religious level, that is if they could be placed under the wing of the authority of the Serbian Orthodox Church, calling, as the students of Niš did in one statement, on 'the unity of the church and the people'.

Those students who think that such unity is the framework in which the idea and shape of a new democratic Serbia should be placed must read once again the Christmas message of one of the currently most influential church dignatories, Metropolitan Amfilohije. They should look particularly at the place where he identifies secular education, such as that of present-day Serbia and all modern states, with training, where he affirms that 'education, if it is not founded on God ... represents the training of people—like the training of dogs.' When they read that, perhaps they will want to sing, in addition to the familiar 'Hymn of St Sava', dear to us all, also the old student song '*Gaudeamus*', which came into being as a parody of church singing, sung to the glory of the joys and liberties of this world.

28. Service

Every Friday, from noon until far into the night, the new chairman of the Zemun municipality, Dr Vojislav Šešelj, receives citizens who come to him asking for his help. As it says in an article published in the local paper *Zemunske novine* (20 December 1996), the chairman of the municipality, who is called 'Mayor' in that article, receives up to 150 citizens daily. They include 'married couples, lonely and decrepit little old ladies, sick people, refugees, young women, young men'. They are all 'troubled souls', 'human fates', 'sad tales', and in addition to their poverty, sickness and the other woes they complain of they have in common also the fact that 'they all believe deeply in Dr Šešelj'. When they enter his office, they are all confused, but they address the Doctor with confidence, even warmth, like someone close, of whom they know that he is on their side, a friend. This can be seen in the fact that they address him simply as 'Šeka' or 'Voja'. The journalist noted some of their words: 'You are our only way out and salvation, Voja. You are the only one we trust, and we know that you will not let us down.'

As a rule, Dr Šešelj cannot solve the problems the citizens bring to him, for the majority of them are looking for somewhere to live or a job, which the municipality cannot provide, or they complain of things which are the responsibility of the court, but nevertheless they always leave him satisfied. At least that's what it says in *Zemunske novine*. People see that the Doctor listens to them attentively, tirelessly, for hours. Till three in the morning. At one moment, exhausted, he went out into the waiting room and asked the citizens to give him a twenty-minute break: 'I'll take a break, if that's all right with you.' People also notice that injustice makes Dr Šešelj angry. That means a lot to them, as do his attention, his kind words, his advice, for 'troubles are easier when they are shared with the leading man in the town.' He listens to them, and then talks to them of love, peace, harmony in the home and happiness in the neighbourhood. He tells them, for instance: 'People are happy when they live in a good neighbourhood and find a common language for their problems with their neighbours.' He advises them against spite, for spite is 'a bad companion', a 'bad business'.

That is why the people's meetings with the Doctor end with a kind of miraculous relief, with the sense that something unusual, joyous and good has taken place. The people leave, writes *Zemunske novine,* 'with new hope granted them by Dr Šešelj'. In the opinion of the deputy chairman of the Serbian Radical Party, Tomislav Nikolić, they take away from their meeting with him the firm belief that the new authorities in Zemun 'have sprung from the people and live with the people', that 'no one has any reason to search on the streets for what he can get as soon as he puts his name down for a conversation with the chairman of the municipality'. While from other quarters comes news of revolt, chaos, demonstrations, good news spreads from Zemun about someone who brings comfort and hope to the desperate, justice to the wronged, who fortifies the discouraged and heals the sick. According to the Doctor himself, 'From Zemun the news travels all over Serbia. In every town in Serbia, in every village people know what good steps we have taken ... The truth can no longer be hidden.' And people come to him 'from all the municipalities' of Belgrade'...

The reception of the people by the 'mayor' on Fridays at noon is one of the steps by which Dr Šešelj and his party wish to show in a graphic way the virtues that adorn their administration in Zemun. The model management of this municipality is an opportunity for them to recommend themselves for more than this, that is for the government of Serbia. Zemun is for them an experiment through which they construct and test a reduced model of a Radical Serbia, a little Greater Serbia. 'For us Radicals', explains the Doctor, 'Zemun is conceived as a demonstration. Through the example of Zemun, we shall show what Radical government in the whole of Serbia would be like.'

In order for the experiment in Zemun to succeed, the leader of the party himself directs it, helped by his party's elite: the deputy leader Tomislav Nikolić, who has taken over charge of the Poslovni Prostor (Business Space) firm; the party spokesman Aleksandar Vučić, the new director of the 'Pinki' hall; Ognjen Mihajlović, the former deputy of the main editor of the radical paper *Velika Srbija* (Greater Serbia), now the main editor of *Zemunske novine*. They have an apostolic function in Zemun, while the Doctor has the role of the Messiah himself. This means that he will be there for a short time, as long as he is needed to establish the foundations of the new government, to awaken people's hope in salvation, to breathe a new spirit into the locality, which will tomorrow be the spirit of Serbia, if, like Zemun today, it has the good fortune to have the Radicals in charge. As T. Nikolić puts it, it is his job to put the affairs entrusted to him in Zemun into good order 'so that afterwards someone else will be able to carry on wherever I leave off.'

The Radicals, with apparent modesty and prosaically, call their experiment in Zemun turning local government into 'a service for the citizens'. In keeping with the idea of service, the municipal civil servants have been given badges with their names and functions and the warning that undue sluggishness in their job, leaving their post during working hours and uncouth behaviour towards the citizens will be strictly punished. 'We shall drive out all those who break the rule that the municipality is the citizens' service,' promises Nikolić. But there is no doubt that working discipline, responsibility towards work and correct behaviour towards clients are not sufficient virtues. They are asked by their own example to show far more: complete dedication to carrying out the tasks assigned them, self-sacrifice, unstinted faith in the new government and the new spirit, a fierce tempo, stamina. In fact the Radical model of good government implies a great deal of revolutionary fervour and the dedication of shock troops. Describing the first steps of the Radical government in Zemun, Dr Šešelj says that the Radicals 'immediately set off at a fierce tempo, that they work 'virtually day and night', and that 'anyone who cannot stand that tempo will have to look for another job'.

The Radical government does not rest, that is why it can be carried out and represented only by people of a particular stamp, special abilities, ready to subordinate everything to the struggle for justice and truth, to neglect their family, their health, not to think of their own interests. Dr Šešelj answers the journalist's question 'When do you spend time at home?' by saying: 'My family is certainly suffering because of all the obligations I have taken onto my shoulders, but they are very understanding of such great obligations.' Besides not resting, the Radical government does not hang about, does not beat about the bush, does not hesitate in carrying out its decisions. The day after taking power in Zemun, the Radicals uncovered a major fraud.

In the course of one day, a 'ruffian' who had moved into the council building was removed. Also in one day a group of singers 'which had café songs in its repertoire' was removed from a building in the parish of the Church of St Nicholas.

All these rapid and effective actions by the new government in Zemun were personally presided over by the leader of the council. And in such circumstances, as on the occasion of the reception of citizens on Fridays at noon, he demonstrated that between himself and the citizens there is no intermediary, that the supreme authority in Zemun, as T. Nikolić put it, 'has not put itself above the people'. All this was recorded by the written word and the camera. As a result, the first two issues of the new series of *Zemunske novine* are largely devoted to the thoughts and acts of Dr Šešelj, and he appears in thirty-five portrait or group photographs.

That is how the Radicals in Zemun, under the falsely modest name of 'citizens' service', have offered Serbia a model of power whose elements are: revolutionary zeal, healing miracle-working, shock troops, employees of a special stamp and—most important of all—populist demagogy with the cult of the leader, whose windows are lit far into the night. Particularly thanks to this last element, the model of Radical government in Zemun in large part coincides with what lies at the heart of the Milošević regime. It could be said that these are variants of the same model. But it seems that today better results, although in a smaller space, are given by the variant we see in the form of Šešelj's 'citizens' service'. That is why it could happen that one Friday at noon, the Doctor's Zemun servicing office may be visited by Milošević himself, crying: 'Voja, you are our only way out and salvation.'

29. Distillation

One would say that everyone in Serbia today agrees that there is no better thing for this country than democracy and that it needs no greater hero than the hero of democracy—the citizen. In discourse on this matter there is also a great deal of enthusiasm, and in that enthusiasm also quite a bit of rhetorical exaggeration. Speaking for *Naša borba* about the effects of the citizens' protest, Dr Čedomir Čupić expressed the opinion that if he once agreed to play the role of citizen, if he only put on the 'citizen's mask', man would fundamentally change, he would experience a kind of miraculous transformation. For a man with that mask, says Dr Čupić, 'feels lighter, it does not hinder or stifle him, it does not close his horizons, it speeds up communication, harmonises human relations, frees people of prejudice. Behind it sourness, anger, fanaticism, stubbornness, hatred, vengefulness, cowardice, anxiety, fear—all melt. The soul opens, the spirit is freed and passion becomes tender.' (*Naša borba*, 1–2 February 1997) This emotion, this poetic rapture in speaking in praise of democracy and the citizen, is understandable in view of the fact that hope in the democratic transformation of Serbia, slender and timorous until yesterday, has suddenly been transformed into the massively and spectacularly expressed will of the citizens that this transformation be carried out as soon as possible. But it is certain that democracy, as the poet Branko Miljković would say, will not know how to sing, at least not the way Dr Čupić sings about it.

Among those who accept democracy in Serbia today, not everyone is enthusiastic about it. There are also many who have reservations. I am not thinking of those people who, in the general turmoil and general excitement, in the midst of the noisy protest and infectious gaiety, in an atmosphere which has been described as 'carnival', try to stay cool and think soberly and critically; I mean those who accept the mass street promotion of democracy and the citizen with big reservations, only under certain conditions, only up to a point, in fact reluctantly and suspiciously. For example, Academician Ljuba Tadić wants democracy, but only on condition that it should not be refined or overcooked, a kind of 'distilled' democracy, as he expressed it in an article in *Književne novine* (1 February 1997). He opposes 'the model of distilled democracy which preaches the incompatibility of democratic and national feeling (consciousness).' Such pure double-distilled democracy is what is poured out, according to Tadić, through the pages of *Vreme, Republika* and *Naša borba*.

The main failing of pure democracy lies in the fact that it does not leave enough space for the nurturing and complete expression of the one value which Tadić cares about above all, and which he most frequently refers to as 'spirit'. The struggle for democracy is only a transitory episode in the political history of Serbia, an occasion for the manifestation and celebration of the 'spirit' that drives it, but which endures independently of historical change. It is older than everything, and therefore also precedes democracy, and, in all likelihood, will one day see its back. Moreover, 'the spirit' can be hampered by democracy, because it is in fact something limited and tight, earthly, a torment to the free 'spirit'. And if the spirit is freely and spontaneously soaring during these winter days in Serbia, surpassing and amazing everyone, then that is happening not because of democracy, but despite it, in defiance of its restriction. 'The current popular movement and its unparalleled spontaneity', says Tadić, in the role of spokesman of the spiritual being which is manifested in this movement, 'the dimensions of which have never been seen before, represents that same spirit which Belgrade demonstrated on 27 March 1941.[1] That spirit is not only democratic, but more than that: it is libertarian, because democracy itself represents a restricted framework for it.'

What is this 'spirit'? Is it the romantic 'spirit of the people'? It is hard to say. In the article the phrase 'popular soul' appears as well, in a sentence which exudes the lust of the good old and—at least for Academician Tadić—never forgotten romantic Eros. The transforma-

---

[1] The day when there were demonstrations against the Pact signed by the Yugoslav government with Hitler's Germany. The demonstration brought down the government and a new one was formed which annulled the Pact. Germany responded by attacking Yugoslavia, bombing Belgrade on 6 April 1941.

tion of 'popular anger' into a 'popular celebration' which, according to Tadić, was the main event on the eve of the new year of 1997 in the centre of Belgrade, showed 'all the rich nuances of the popular soul which could be aroused and excited only by an enormous injustice.' All the nuances? It seems that on that occasion some, nonetheless, were left out. This conclusion is suggested by the fact that, a few lines further on, Tadić corrected and completed this mention of nuances, with the remark that he was referring only to the popular soul of urban Serbia. 'I hope', he added, 'that not much time will pass before it is joined also by rural Serbia and its soul.'

Along with the 'spirit' and the 'popular soul', there appear in this article also other expressions and other metaphors with which the writer tries somehow to anticipate, to bring closer to himself and his reader that ideal figure of the ethnic collective, that being of the people, that essence of the national community which sometimes, as this winter, appears in a spontaneous and spectacular, but nevertheless unclear, incomprehensible way. He uses expressions such as 'the true face of our people', 'divine strength', 'the national identity of the Serbian people', 'the national interest'. But the writer's effort is vain, because how can one name precisely describe something 'unparalleled', and, even more difficult, something blinding?

The dear face of the nation, the bewitching spirit of the people, is always only a dark object of desire. It is hard to talk about it, and if something is nevertheless expressed, then this is not achieved through linguistic means intended for precise description and well-argued discussion, but only through the cunning of rhetoric, which knows how to 'bring to life' phantoms and illusions, shadows and spirits. Among other means, this is done by the repetition of certain combinations of words which, however unreal and unusual they may seem to us at first, through their repetition we begin to accept as an ordinary and, so to speak, neutral means of expression, and so unwittingly accept as something real. We begin to 'see' the ideas and concepts that go with them. For in the struggle of ideas words are not only a means, but an important target of that struggle; one vocabulary strives to drive out the other.

Academician Tadić broaches this aspect of the struggle in the title of his article 'On the occasion of the Serbian Popular Festival'. Here, and further on in the text, the adjective 'popular' stands, one would say, as an essentially synonymous substitute for the adjectives 'civil' and 'democratic', as though it were a matter of synonyms, as though for purely stylistic reasons, for the sake of artistry, what others call 'a civil carnival' or 'a feast-day of democracy' in Tadić's text acquires the name of 'Serbian Popular Festival'. But there is no doubt that this apparently purely stylistic operation has a far more important aim. He uses it in fact to question the widespread practice of calling the current events on the streets of Serbian towns a 'civil protest', 'a civil movement', 'citizens' events' or a 'democratic movement', 'democratic renewal' or even 'a citizens' revolution'. In this way he tries, if not to question, then at least to call a halt to and suppress, undesirable and exaggerated expansion of the ideas which go along with such language. At the same time he seeks to preserve space for other, to him more important, decisive and enduring values, images and tales for that being, for that figure, for that 'spirit' which his pen serves. That is why in this article it is not only the festival which is popular; we also find 'popular anger', 'a popular movement', 'the stirring movement of the Serbian people', 'popular mockery', 'the people's soul', 'popular maxims', 'popular celebration', 'the people's voice', 'the people's interests'.

But today not even Academician Tadić can avoid any reference to the boring citizen. He mentions him twice. First in the expression 'the mature democratic and free-thinking consciousness of the citizen', where 'free-thinking' serves to dilute the overly distilled phrase 'democratic consciousness'. The other time the citizen appears is in the expression 'civil disobedience'. But not even this phrase, which is used today as a technical term, allows one to strut disobediently through the text: it is accompanied by the explanation that this is 'an act whereby the people, by natural rights, express disobedience to a prevailing injustice'. Thus, in each case, when he decides to use in his article what is perhaps the key word in a democratic political vocabulary—the word 'civil'—Academician Ljubomir Tadić endeavours to drown it well and truly with 'popular', so that its authentic meaning can never again be reached by any process of transformation or distillation.

30. Horseshoes

Whenever the Serbs were engaged in democracy, their enemies conspired against them unhindered. That is why dedication to democracy and the struggle for it—an otherwise absolutely positive and modern political orientation—should be kept within reasonable bounds. If it is not, the main thing will be neglected. And that is the definitive struggle for the survival of the Serbian nation, which is today perhaps under greater threat than ever before. Aggressive neighbours, merciless international powers and worldly brokers menace our survival also in what remains of our ethnic space, stunted and disconnected as it is. And, worse than that, they call into question our fundamental national interests, our traditions, our dignity, our freedom, the sovereignty of the Serbian state. That is why we must be extremely watchful, cautious and wise and put our trust in skilful and decisive people, capable of taking on our enemies on an equal footing and without pardon. For that, our democracy will not be of much use. The job will not be done either by civil rights, or respect for electoral law, or the freedom of the media, or by overthrowing Milošević's regime, or by the resignation of the Vice Chancellor. Democracy can wait a little while, and it is not good if it prevents us from seeing what is essential: that our enemy is covertly sharpening his teeth, assessing the moment when he will exploit our disunity, inter-party strife and discord, and, in that weakened state, pounce on us.

Whose words could these be? Who speaks to the Serbs about the Serbs in this way today? Who scares them with a hostile world? Someone will recognise the voice of the regime in these words, that same voice which announced that the citizens' and students' protests against electoral theft were instigated by 'foreign factors', that they were organised by a 'fifth column', with the aim of 'destabilising' and then subjugating Serbia. We and our people, says that voice, will not be deceived by stories about so-called democracy and civil rights. We know who is behind that. Serbia will not be governed by a foreign hand.

Those who recognise in the warning that the democratic protests are actually weakening Serbia's strength the thought or pain of Vojislav Šešelj, are right. It pains Šešelj that the Serbs who are protesting against Milošević in the name of democracy—blowing whistles, capering to the rhythm of the samba and rock music, carrying the flag of Serbia along with the flags of various democratic states and the placard 'Belgrade is everything'—all forget who are their real enemies. It is as though their defensive instinct had slackened, degenerated. 'We are badly hurt by that wound', says Šešelj in an interview, 'inflicted on us by the people demonstrating in Belgrade, carrying the flags of hostile countries: the USA, Germany and several others, those same countries which bombed Republika Srpska, Serbian villages and towns, Serbian children.' (*Zemunske novine*, 1 February 1997)

But the story about the dangers brought by democracy when it is taken in unmeasured doses has other sources as well. We may recognise other authors too. Among those who enrich it with their contributions there are even some sympathisers and participants in the current civil protests in Serbia. This makes it more interesting than it would otherwise be. For instance, it is interesting to see the historian Milan St. Protić, in a conversation carried by *Književne novine* (15 December 1996), giving a variation on the theme of the meagre benefit from democracy and civil awareness in this real, true, decisive struggle for the Serbian national thing. In his opinion, to talk of truth and justice in politics is out of place. Politics is a dirty game and in politics it is not the honest and truth-loving fighters for democracy and civil rights who win, but skilful people unburdened by moral scruples. For example, 'in order to fight this regime,' says Protić, 'we shall have ourselves to do things that we would not otherwise do, but only in order to achieve our aim.' This is even more true of international politics, where the dirtiest methods of struggle for one's own interests are not only permissible, they are the only effective ones. There 'matters are resolved', explains Protić, 'by methods which people would not use in their private life and personal relations ... There people hit out, bribe, lie, accuse in order to achieve a particular effect.'

For example, this was also done by the people who were most responsible for the successes of the foreign policies of Serbia from 1804 to 1914: Prince Miloš, Jovan Ristić and Nikola Pašić. 'Those are', in Protić's judgment, 'three lying, hypocritical, dishonest, insincere, skilful men, who, through diplomatic machinations and all possible means in their relations with the international community of their time contributed respectively to: the recognition of an autonomous principality, the recognition of an independent state, and bringing Serbia into the European scene.' Such people and such national politics are what are needed today as well. For the essential position does not change. On the other side of historical and political fluctuations, relations between peoples and states are reduced to an uncompromising struggle for survival and expansion. Thus Serbia is today struggling with 'a hypocritical, two-faced, deceitful international community', and that is why 'there is no choice but to adapt to that fact, and to outwit them'.

But success in that measuring up, out-deceiving and outwitting of the hostile world by the Serbs is jeopardised by some over-sensitive and feeble intellectuals, who do not have the heart for great ideas and great deeds, but take at face value all the tales about democracy, about international cooperation, about a Europe without frontiers, about civil awareness. They are taken in by the haranguing of our enemies against the project of a greater Serbia, as though it were something aberrant, sinful. However, for all peoples an extensive state is more urgent than extensive democracy. No one will abandon power to the Arabs out of civil awareness. 'All peoples', Milan St. Protić assures us, 'dream of their own extensive state. It is a lie and illusion that there are peoples who do not have that dream and that there exists anywhere a society in which civil awareness is developed to such an extent that it would allow Arabs, or who knows who else, to govern them. Those are the tales of our spoiled intellectuals who, let me put it crudely, are like the frog in the folk tale which sees the horse being shod so lifts up its foot as well.'

The struggle for democracy and insistence on electoral justice drive into the background that main issue, the defence of the national space, Pan-Serb solidarity in resistance to a hostile world. That is the opinion also of Bishop Atanasije Jevtić, which he expressed in a speech at a gathering held in Priština. The Bishop was vexed with the 'little Belgrade gentlemen' who 'protest about local elections, but did not react when the *krajinas* fell'. They do not understand that the Serbs are threatened with destruction by democratic America, which is 'an enormous international tyrant', that Clinton is 'a man with an angelic face, and a demonic soul', that the West is indifferent about who rules here, if only it can achieve its aims, and now they are 'interrogating these opposition people, weighing them up to see whether they can realise through them what the communists began.' That is why, in the opinion of this bishop as well, if we cannot avoid the outside world, we must handle it cautiously, cunningly. Cunning requires that 'we watch what the world is doing and involve ourselves in it. If for no other reason, then to spy on it.' (*Demokratija*, 28 January 1997)

As they struggle for democracy, the Serbs often do not see that they are playing someone else's game. At the launch of the first issue of the new magazine *Slovenski glasnik* (Slav Herald), in Belgrade, reported in *Politika* (24 February), the editors announced that for them 'there was no question of the value of maxims such as democracy, individual liberties, human rights and the rights of minorities.' However, they had noticed that it was 'in recent years, the greatest world power' that insisted most on these 'maxims', and they expressed the anxiety of the 'bearers of the Slav idea' that, under the excuse that it was defending democracy, it was in fact carrying out 'global unification' and 'threatening the sovereignty of individual Slav countries'. Are those democratic 'maxims' really worth such a risk?

There are other examples of this kind of discourse, this fear that because of democracy the Serbs will lose their soul and their empire. The three months of protests by the citizens and students of Serbia have shown that one fear along the road to achieving democracy has been largely overcome—the fear of a change of regime. The other fear on that road—fear of the outside world—appears to be more deeply rooted, to have more people interested in its maintenance. The paranoid tale about democracy as a gift from the Greeks which the Serbs have stupidly accepted into the fortress of their sovereignty is still offered in many places as the discourse of patriots concerned for the fate of national selfhood. The struggle for democracy, which means including the Serbs in the community of democratic countries, is described in that tale as the business of irresponsible weaklings, for whom it would be better if they did not interfere in serious matters. The only Serbs who have the qualities necessary to be involved in national affairs, and therefore to determine the real price of democracy, are—as Milan St. Protić put it so picturesquely—those who let themselves be shod, so that the leader may ride them and, if necessary, harness them to drag artillery or supplies.

31. Mantle

The political language of Serbia today is beginning to turn to prose. And a particularly dry kind of prose at that. Instead of epic and lyric strains, we find more and more often the discourse of calculation and interest. There are more and more of those who would like to speak soberly, steadily, to calculate precisely, to predict accurately, to judge realistically, to remain within the limits of the possible, to find effective and practical solutions. The voice of prosaic sobriety has not been hushed even during three months of noisy, 'carnivalesque', at times dramatic protests of the citizens and students. It could even be said that these protests have been marked by, among other things, the rational curbing of uncontrolled outpourings of fury and enthusiasm.

Among the values which these protests have driven into the foreground there is one quite prosaic one—pragmatism. It has been said of the students that they are witty, brave, tenacious, but, also that they know what they want, that they are pragmatic. According to D. Mijać, they bring 'a very sober, realistic approach to our problems', so that 'with this generation we shall not have the phenomenon of politicians' giving fiery speeches which rely on emotion, rather they will rationally explain to the citizens what are the possibilities of something being done.' (*Demokratija*, 12 December 1996)

It turned out that the protests, demonstrations and conflicts with the police could be an opportunity for the affirmation of a politician whom many see as the personification of pragmatism. In discourse about the 'pragmatic Djindjić' there is not much enthusiasm, perhaps not even much sympathy, but far more rational approval, far more agreement with someone who appears to take account of the realistically possible. In fact, that discourse is itself inspired by a certain model of pragmatic reasoning, a kind of ideal of the practical mind, and Djindjić is less its subject than its embodiment. And however much it is a matter of a prosaic, unattractive, perhaps even ambivalent value, it seems that Djindjić's political rating has not been at all adversely affected by his having become its symbol.

The gradual shift towards political prose, discourse of accurate perception and realistic assessment is a sign that the time has come when Serbia is beginning to look for itself more on the earth than in the sky, more in reality than in a dream, more in political society than in an ethnic community, more in pragmatic politicians than in charismatic leaders. But this sign could be deceptive. Often 'unspellbinding' political discourse, discourse in the registers of dry facts and the measured tone of prose, is simply the rhetorical propaganda cunning of a policy based on spreading fear of the world, the cult of the forebears, death, the leader and—something by no means pragmatic—'what cannot be'.[1] Often what appears to be sober political prose is in fact a prose transcription of programmes which are better known, to our cost, in their 'poetic' versions.

For example, although the government in Serbia still bases its survival on spreading fear of both internal and external enemies, it likes to refer nowadays to banal economic and political reality. Thus the recently signed agreement between Milošević and Krajišnik about their so-called 'parallel relations' was described in the press as an act of 'practical significance', as 'an expression of the strategic interests of the Serbian people', as a document which 'does not promote anything unknown, any adventures, or anything that has not ever been seen in these regions'. This agreement, as was said in *Politika* (1 March 1997), respects 'reality in our part of the world and as a result, it promotes economic pragmatism'.

The so-called great national projects and great historic aims of the Serbian people, whose realisation has so far brought Serbia nothing but defeat, shame and poverty, are adapted to the current new realistic and pragmatic political language. Thanks to such an adaptation, even the psychiatrist Jovan Rašković, known as the first leader of the revolt of the Serbs in Croatia, with its tragic outcome, and the author of what is, to put it mildly, an extravagant psychoanalytical interpretation of the character of the Yugoslav peoples, has now become a man of carefully measured action. Professor Vasilije Dj. Krestić describes him,

---

[1] A reference to a line in *The Mountain Wreath* by Petar Petrović Njegoš: 'Let what cannot be occur!'

in the last issue of the paper *Zbilja* (*Reality*, 31 January 1996), as 'a pragmatic politician in the vortex of events which have followed one another with the speed of film.'

Krestić's colleague Milorad Ekmečić, in an article in *Književne novine* (15 January 1997), finds the causes of our current failures to realise 'the historic aims of the Serbian people' in the fact that they were not 'proportionate to the real state of their powers to achieve and defend them.' Ekmečić also understands 'the strength of the people' 'realistically', by looking to Ilija Garašanin as the military force at the heart of state policy. The national policy aims of 1990 and 1991 were 'an historical error', because they did not correspond to 'the mantle of state power which would have been able to cover them'. Much was improvised. 'Public opinion', Ekmečić reflects, 'in its centres, academies, assemblies, pan-Serb assemblies, congresses, round tables and public speeches, was greatly entertained by the production of new ideas which were in the majority of cases nothing but radical improvisation.' That is why, in the next attempt at realising the great national idea—and there is no doubt that Ekmečić is convinced that this idea merits renewed sacrifice—more realism and pragmatism are required. We must, first and foremost, 'assess how extensive our mantle is'.

Ekmečić expects that it will be possible to arrive at an exact assessment of the extent of the Serbian mantle through 'new national opinion sounding in all areas where Serbs live'. However, today such a task can also be assigned to a specialised institution—the recently established Institute for Geopolitical Studies. Its founder, Milivoje R. Reljin, explained that the Institute would 'study themes that are a priority for our state and national interests'. As it was expressed by a member of the Institute's staff, General Radinović, its aim was to 'offer some answers to challenges so that this should serve as the analytical base of appropriate state strategies'. That is why, according to *Politika* (9 February 1997), employees of the Institute expect that its first clients will be the governments of Serbia, Montenegro and the Federal Republic of Yugoslavia. That is entirely in keeping with Renan's scientist credo: 'Great deeds will be accomplished by science and not democracy'.

The Institute's coat of arms was also presented to the public. Its elements are the Nemanjić shield, a pattern taken from the clothing of St Sava, an owl and the inscription: 'The Foundation of Future Endurance'. But, despite this unconcealed weakness for tradition and heraldry, the first announcements of researchers at the Institute suggest that deep and eternal questions are posed there in dry scientific prose. For example, a conversation with an associate of the Institute, T. Kresović, published in *Demokratija* (3 March 1997), discloses that in the vocabulary of that prose the main role is given to words and phrases such as 'space', 'power', 'interest', 'vital interest', 'strategic interest', 'strategic way', 'geostrategic', 'control', 'system', 'logistic', 'locate', 'plan', 'dominant impression'.

But, nevertheless, this 'analytical' vocabulary does not mean that those who use it question the credibility of mythic concepts of the nation, enemies, war and peace, which are on the whole familiar to us in the form of the epic variants of Serbian political mythology. Ostensibly erudite and scientific presentations about the struggle of the nation and the state for existential space do not say anything that cannot be found in other, more folkloristic and literary versions of the national myth, where there is no mention of strategy, interests, powers or space, but of hearths, roots, forebears and graves. That is why one is not surprised by the ease with which some Serbian geopoliticians sometimes combine a pseudo-scientific vocabulary with the commonplaces of folkloric-literary-mythic discourse. One of them (M. Knežević) gave a picturesque description of Serbia as 'what is left when all the geopolitical jackals die out' *(Demokratija,* 18 February 1997), and another (R. Radinović) spiced the *topos* about 'challenges and threats to our survival' with the scientific assertion that they are 'of a politico-strategic nature' (*Demokratija*, 13 February 1997). Dr M. Marković, a participant in a scholarly conference organised in Petrovaradin by the Institute for Geopolitical Studies, abandoned himself completely to the charms of political folklore. As was reported in *Demokratija* (ibid.), on that occasion he said: 'I think that in recent days among us something has awoken, if not been born, and it is essential that we should preserve this newborn power and develop it, by placing ourselves at the service of the salvation of the Serbian people.' Such is the extent of the mantle.

Coat of arms of the Institute of Geopolitical Studies, Belgrade.

32. Moloch

What was the nature of the recently ended war in Bosnia? Did it end with the defeat or the victory of the Serbs? How can the participation of Orthodox believers and priests in the war be justified? These are the most important questions addressed by the authors of the contributions to the collection *Jagnje božije i zvijer iz bezdana, Filosofija rata* (Lamb of God or Beast from the Abyss: The Philosophy of War), which was recently published in the journal of the Metropolitanate of Cetinje, *Svetigora*.

On the subject of the nature of the Bosnian war and its main features, the authors represented here have on the whole offered mutually concordant answers. In essence, they amount to the opinion that for the Serbs this war, like all the others in which they participated, was a defensive war for physical and spiritual survival, imposed on them by others. And that on this occasion, as always before, the aim of the Serbs' enemies was, as Dr Mirko Zurovac expressed it, 'the final defeat of the Serbian people and its complete destruction', that they were waging a 'genocidal war against the Serbian people under the protection of the UN'. The majority of the authors emphasise the international, planetary and epochal significance of the war in Bosnia, and especially the role of the Serbs in it. In the introduction by the editors of the volume (R.M. Mladenović and Archdeacon Jovan Ćulibrk), what happened to the Serbs in this war is presented as a 'paradigm of the fate of the whole of the contemporary world'. The Serbs found themselves in the difficult and thankless, but glorious role of opposing, in the words of Bishop Atanasije Jevtić, 'international injustice and hypocrisy', and especially the 'perfidious Americans who are the offspring of the eternally perfidious English' and the Germans and

Moloch

Austrians 'who have always hated and attacked us'. The Serbs were left virtually alone in their heroic fight for the defence of the authentic values of their spirituality, and thereby of European civilisation, for, in the opinion of the same author, 'we are Europe before Europe, and civilisation before their civilisation.'

The meaning of the struggle of the Bosnian Serbs against their eternal enemies and the hypocritical world is not only historical. That struggle brings to life once again the biblical, mythic conflict of Good and Evil, and activates archetypal forms of the search for meaning and the mystic purity of the spirit. Dr Radovan Karadžić, represented in this collection by a kind of literary note entitled 'Was this War?', puts forward the opinion that what happened in Bosnia was not an ordinary war, of the kind discussed by Clauzewitz, but a conflict which unfolded according to a bloody, fatal scenario, unchanged over the centuries, according to which the Bosnian Serb, for God knows how long, has suffered at the hands of his scheming neighbour. That is why that Serb, like his leader Karadžić, never has time to wonder whether things could have been done differently, whether war could have been avoided. 'He is prevented', explains Karadžić, 'by his neighbour, a murderer and butcher, who has had his eye on him for centuries.' What the Serbian fighter in Bosnia knows will always remain hidden from the Westerner in incomprehensible and impenetrable depths. 'Clausewitz does not know this story', says Karadžić; 'it is not historical. It is biblical.'

The timeless, mythic dimension of the war in Bosnia and the figures of Serbian warriors is also emphasised by Dr Zurovac. He writes: 'the heroes of that war, General Mladić and President Karadžić,' are not only certain people, who were in certain positions in the course of their people's struggle for survival, but mythical giants through whom a threatened people sought to be understood in its heroic-tragic situation.' Similarly, in the opinion of Mateja Arsenijević, for the Orthodox Serbs the war in Bosnia, like every other war in which they had taken part, meant a return to the deepest, mystical roots of the national being, to 'the Serbian holy-warrior archetype, to that language of the sanctified decasyllabic verse which speaks to us mystically in our bones, even before our birth, from our mother's womb.'

But why should it be the Serbs who have so many enemies, why do they provoke so much hatred? Precisely because of their qualities, because of the strength of their love and the firmness of their belief, because of the depth of their memory. Their neighbours and other

254   *Characters and Figures of Power*

Bishops of the Serbian Orthodox Church, Atanasije Jevtić and Amfilohije Radović. (Caricature by Predrag Koraksić Corax, published in the weekly *Vreme*, 15 August 1994)

peoples, especially those in the West, sunk in vice, in the thrall of vanity and hypocrisy, cannot bear that there should exist a nation which proudly resists that vice and bravely bears the standard of good and truth. In the opinion of Tihomir Burzanović, Muslims kill Serbs because that represents the 'conscious or unconscious destruction of witnesses of their deceit, their conversion'. In the same way, Metropolitan Amfilohije Radović explains why it is that the great Western powers also long to destroy the Orthodox Serbs. That longing has as its conscious or unconscious base the realisation that somewhere here a priceless treasure, the deepest memory is preserved, and that memory has to be wiped out in order for people to be able to live calmly, undisturbed in this rotten world, nourished with the spirit of necrophilia, in the earthly mortuary.'

The Serbs are the victors of the war in Bosnia. That is affirmed by all the authors in this volume who deal with the question of the outcome of the war. But at the same time, they are thinking predominantly about spiritual, moral victory. For example, when successful cleansing is mentioned, then it refers not to territory but to the soul. 'The five-year long Fatherland War in Srpska and the Krajinas', writes M. Arsenijević, 'cleansed our national soul, enlightened our Christian mind.' The editors of the collection stress 'the collective conviction of all the participants in this act that something which resembled tragic defeat is beginning to be transformed into a profound inner victory, whose dimensions, no less than at the time of Kosovo, can be cosmic.' It is interesting that the interpretation of the success of the Serbs in the war in Bosnia as more spiritual than a material, military victory is close also to that of the commanders of the Serbian army there. According to the evidence of Colonel Milovan Milutinović, the command of that army had strategically decided on aims of a higher, moral order of value, so that one can speak of the 'Kosovo choice of the military leadership' of the Bosnian Serbs, 'where physical defeat in battle does not exclude the possibility of spiritual victory.'

One would expect that the 'Kosovo choice' in the war would be closest to the Orthodox priests. But in this collection it is precisely they who are most reserved about such a choice. For example, Archdeacon Jovan Ćulibrk prefers to speak about the cleansing of territory of enemies and false friends, about the political and military victory of the Bosnian Serbs, than about the heavenly kingdom. In his opinion, that victory is reflected in the fact that the Serbs destroyed and cleansed at least part of multiethnic Bosnia, at least part of the Sarajevo the Serbs so hated, that city where they had to live in the false, fictitious peace of a multinational community which, after Tito, was imposed on them by the West and its pop-culture. 'Finally', writes Ćulibrk, '*Serbian* Sarajevo is also the symbol of a town cleansed by fire. Its survival (through Republika Srpska) is the ruin of the *political* charge of pop-culture: proof of the impotence of the West to realise its fiction through the tools of politics.'

Philosophical and theological arguments in support of such a 'nationally correct' and 'realistic' attitude towards the so-called 'Kosovo choice' as that of Ćulibrk is offered in this collection by Metropolitan A. Radović. When the nation and state are in danger, priority must be given to physical survival, to the earthly kingdom. The suffering of the people obliges all Serbs, including the Church and clergy, to come to its aid, to prepare it for war and to defend it themselves with the sword. The Metropolitan is aware of the fact that such an outlook does not accord with Christian morality, that the participation of the clergy in war, 'seen through the prism of Christ's crucifixion and His attitude towards the knife, would be hard to justify.' That is why he does not look for justification but prefers to settle for the relativisation of Christ's example as a signpost which cannot be followed in historical reality, as a model which is irrelevant to that reality, something that 'does not belong to historical man'. As a result, he frees the Serbian warrior, and the warrior-priest, of the obligation of following Christ, reassuring him that, when the survival of the nation is in question, he should hold to the ethic of implacable revenge and vengeful anger. 'That is not', he says, 'a New Testament principle, it is clearly an Old Testament principle, but one that is so present and realistic in life that it is inseparable from Christian history.'

So it happens that some of the pieces published in this collection also confirm that the secular 'religion of the nation', its myths and its mysticism, are exceptionally attractive precisely to people, like some of our Orthodox priests, who serve religion in the true sense. Many of them endeavour somehow to reconcile the cult of the nation with the Christian cult and sometimes, as the examples quoted show, they are even prepared, for the sake of serving the Moloch of the nation, that beast from the abyss of nationalistic madness, temporarily to suspend the basic principles of Christian morality, if not to renounce them forever.

PART IV
The Age of the Crowd

'Various elements in democracy have as their aim the removal of every magical and idolatrous means of exerting power which gives it, in the eyes of the masses, the appearance of omniscience and omnipotence. The magical form of exerting unlimited power has never been so widespread. It has never had so many methods at its disposal. That is why the choice for or against such power has become in our century as serious as the choice for or against the atomic bomb.' (Serge Moskovici, *The Age of the Crowd*, 1981)

1. Football, Hooligans and War

The story of the collapse of Yugoslavia, in a frenzy of hatred and war, in honour of the gods of ethnic nationalism and pre-modern militarism may also be described as a story of the evolution of violence in Yugoslav sport, especially among hooligan football supporters, and of the gradual transference of that violence, at the end of the 1980s and beginning of the '90s, on to the terrain of inter-ethnic conflicts and 'greater-nation' politics, and thence on to the battlefield. It is a story of the ostensible opposition of sports reporters to the raging of nationalism among fans, of the consecration of the Red Star football club in the role of one of the most important symbols of 'Serbdom', of the 'spontaneous' organisation of the supporters of that club into a group under the name of 'the Valiants' and then of their transformation into volunteer soldiers and their despatch to war. It is an unfinished story, but one of its possible ends may be glimpsed: the victory of the hooligan tribes and the founding of a new, vandal-warrior tribalism.

'At the gates of hell'

Judging by articles published in the sports press, from the middle of the eighties on, the violent behaviour of supporters in Yugoslavia (football fans, above all) was increasingly manifested as insults, incidents and conflict on a so-called national basis. Through the expression of adherence to their clubs or independently of that, supporters increasingly demonstrated a sense of national allegiance, just as, on the other hand, the greatest aggression was shown towards teams and supporters from different national centres. In the years which preceded the outbreak of armed conflict in Croatia, in sports stadia, and most of all at football grounds, among the supporters' paraphernalia there began to appear placards bearing political messages, portraits of national leaders and saints, national coats of arms and flags, Chetnik songs, the Ustashe initials and greeting.

Such an increasingly obtrusive and increasingly radical transformation of the supporters' zeal into nationalistic hatred and aggression was met with the unanimous condemnation of the sporting press of former Yugoslavia. Between 1989 and 1991, the Belgrade press printed a large number of commentaries full of dramatic warnings of the danger presented by the spread of chauvinistic passions in sports stadia and appeals that something should be done to put a stop to such a development.[1] The titles of some articles convey the tone in which they are written, for example the titles of commentaries published during 1990 and the first half of 1991 in the organs of the Red Star (*Crvena zvezda*) and Partizan clubs: 'Politics as a Pollutant', 'Nationalistic War Games', 'Spectators Outplay Politics', 'The Championship and War Games', 'No Politics in the Stadium!'(*ZR*); 'At the Gates of Hell', 'Distorted Support', 'Demons of Evil', 'Love instead of Hate', 'The Abuse of Sport', 'Falangists among Sportsmen', 'Supporters Turn Wild', 'National Valiants', 'Threat to the Principles of Decency and Strength of Spirit'(*PV*).

The sports journalists start from what is for them the indisputable idea that 'sport is one of the most exalted activities of human creativity, understanding and communication between people' (*PV,* 3 February, 1990), that 'sport is a synonym for exalted ethical principles' (*PV,* 30 March 1990), that 'sportsmen were always harbingers of conciliation, connection and not division, harbingers of tolerance and not dark forebodings of war' (*ZR*, September 1990), that 'whoever loves sport does not tolerate violence' (*PV,* 17 March 1990), that 'throughout history, sport was always the ambassador of peace and understanding' (*T,* 2 July 1991). United in the defence of sport, and especially football, understood in such a way, these journalists do not hesitate to condemn the outpourings of destructive instinct, hatred and chauvinism among fans.

In these texts, the sports journalists' tone ranges from moral indignation to didacticism and ideological judgment. 'Nationalism', writes one of them, 'is the greatest ill that could befall a multinational com-

---

[1] The examples quoted here are taken from the following sports papers: *Sport* (hereafter S), *Sportski žurnal* (Sports Journal, SŽ), *Tempo* (*Te*), *Partizanov vesnik* (Partizan Herald, PV) and *Zvezdina revija* (Star Review, ZR).

munity' (*PV*, 3 March 1990). Another considers that the word 'chauvinism' is more appropriate, describing it as 'an expression of impotence, behaviour which has nothing to do with education and intellect. But it is precisely with that vice that young men arm themselves when they go to the stadium with the desire to break, burn and beat.' They are 'destroyers of everything progressive'. (*ZR*, June 1990) A colleague laments that 'we are living at a time of the unbelievable raging of almost all the irrational delusions of the past, in which—in our Yugoslav space—the "vampirisation" of national-chauvinism has become so rife that we are threatened not only with general civilisational disintegration, but a return to a time when the guillotine, the knife and harassment were in everyday use.' (*PV*, 3 February, 1990).

In these articles both sportsmen and sports officials were accused of nationalism, because 'in all of this the people who occupy positions of responsibility in sports organisations are not at all innocent.' (*ZR*, September 1990) What is more, some sports commentators do not refrain from criticising political leaders, that is 'the nebulous politics of Nazi-chauvinists and the ruling political bureaucracy'. For this dangerous 'cry of the blood of the nation ... is launched by no small number of current power-holders in our country' (*PV*, 3 February 1990). What is at stake is the 'bestial abuse of sport on the part of people who are powerless to respond to the challenges of the contemporary world, exchanging creativity for the callous struggle for bare power, based on intrigue and international manipulation.' (*PV*, 17 February 1990)

For nationalist politicians, 'sporting events serve as a mask for the public testing of the reality of their dark, national-chauvinistic aims', and so sports stadia and halls have become 'a vestibule for the unhindered action of forces already historically overcome and beaten' (*PV*, 17 February 1990).

The true picture of the moral value, pedagogical effect and political meaning of such condemnation of violence with a nationalistic tone in Yugoslav sport, and especially among fans, expressed by sports journalists in Belgrade on the eve of the outbreak of armed conflict emerges when one takes into account the choice of examples (place, protagonist and inspiration) of the chauvinistic behaviour of fans.

As a rule, the main cause for sounding the alarm in texts about 'the demons of evil' and the 'bestial abuse of hatred' was the behaviour of supporters outside Serbia. So in one article, examples of the 'aggressive and fascistic behaviour of the spectators' occurred exclusively in

Trogir, Mostar, Dubrovnik, Split, Zagreb and Ljubljana (*PV,* 17 February 1990). 'Pro-fascist cries' were loudest in the stadia of Maksimir in Zagreb and Poljud in Split, and there was even a reference to 'the twilight of Maksimir nationalistic rampaging' (*ZR,* June 1990).

As a rule, Belgrade sports commentators found examples of the worst 'rampaging' among supporters of Dinamo (Zagreb) and Hajduk (Split). According to one journalist, at the Dinamo-Partisan match in Zagreb on 25 March 1990, the supporters of Dinamo were overcome by a real 'bestial madness'. 'Like beasts, they smelled blood in the air, they wanted it to be spilled so that their basest instincts could be satisfied' (*PV,* 9 June 1990). The picture painted of Hajduk supporters is no better because 'in them the instinct of the wild beast has superseded human reason.' (*PV,* 6 October 1990)

Among the sportsmen cited as bad examples of abandonment to nationalistic passions there is not a single one from a Belgrade club in the corpus we are analysing here, the worst offenders are the Cibona basketball player Arapović, from Slovenia (*PV,* 31 March 1990) and the Dinamo football players Boban, Šalja and Škerjanc (*PV,* 26 May 1990).

In the unanimous opinion of Belgrade sports commentators, the cause of the distortion of support for sport into nationalistic outbursts and conflicts occurred first and in its most extreme form in 'the northern republics', above all in Croatia: 'In pursuit of their egotistical aims, obsessed with nationalistic hysteria and unbridled hatred of everything Yugoslav, the power-holders in Croatia and Slovenia have now encroached on sport.' In the same place, the commentator attacks 'the organic national arousal and nationalistic blustering of the leadership of the ruling parties—DEMOS in Slovenia and HDZ in Croatia' (*PV,* 24 August 1990).

One of the most frequent targets of journalists who in 1990 and 1991 spoke out against nationalism and its transference to sport was Tudjman and his HDZ party. In the opinion of one commentator, 'Tudjmanism carries with it international hatred and the destruction of Yugoslavia' (*PV,* 31 March 1990). The journalists of *Partizan Herald* were particularly concerned to dispute the opinion that Tudjman had an important role in the founding of the 'Partizan' Sporting Society. In an article entitled 'Tudjmanism among us', Tudjman was called 'one of the most obscure personalities of our political milieu', and the HDZ was described as 'by all accounts a pro-fascist party'. It was also said that he could not possibly be the 'intellectual instigator of our Sporting Society' and could not decide any important questions (*PV,* 17 March 1990).

As a rule, sports journalists in the role of critics of nationalism in sport stress that the blade of such criticism should be aimed also at 'our own'. 'The phenomenon of irresponsible behaviour exists also in the Yugoslav National Army stadium', writes another journalist. However, he immediately adds that this 'refers to a small, almost negligible section of the spectators.' (*PV,* 31 March 1990). In another place there is an estimate that such 'irresponsible elements' amount to some 150 to 200 Partizan supporters (*PV,* 26 May 1990).

When there are chauvinistic eruptions among 'our' supporters, those responsible are 'imposed groups of so-called supporters' or 'the extreme element among supporters' (*PV,* 12 May 1990). 'Our' fans are not nationalist in themselves but become so by watching 'other' fans. 'It would be wrong', writes one commentator of the *Partizan Herald*, 'to affirm now that it is only "their" fans who are ugly, evil and prepared for anything. [...] We must face the facts. There is little distinction between "ours" and "theirs", and some Partizan fans have been infected. But that is the work of "provocateurs", outsiders, people from other environments. Someone is dragging them into the mire, they want to be the same as many hordes in our stadiums. [...] We would like to believe that the Partizan fans would escape the noose which others are placing round their neck.' (*PV,* 9 June 1990)

At the end of a commentary devoted to 'nationalistic raging' after the Dinamo–Red Star match of 13 May 1990, the author mentions also 'an element of Star supporters, who did not lag behind their Zagreb contemporaries in their chauvinist delusions and actions.' But they were not real Red Star supporters (as suggested by the title of the article 'They are not all Valiants'), but are described as 'Groups of varying size which demonstrate that they they do not come to football grounds in order to watch a competition, but in order themselves to compete in hooliganism.' (*ZR,* June 1990)

When the nationalism of Belgrade supporters is not an imitation of other people's nationalistic 'raging', it is the work of provocateurs from the ranks of some Serbian nationalistic opposition parties. 'In Serbia too there are parties', writes the author of 'They are not all Valiants', 'which threaten with daggers, which seek to erect monuments to war criminals on Ravna gora,[2] which respond to nationalism with nationalism.' These parties endeavour to infiltrate into sport 'political marketing, particularly of an ill-fated and bloody spirit that once raged through Serbia. In the Second World War the Chetniks were the

---

[2] A reference to the monument to the Second World War Chetnik leader, Draža Mihailović, erected at the instigation of Vuk Drašković. (Transl.)

national disgrace of the freedom-loving Serbian nation. [...] Red Star has taken on a difficult task. It has publicly distanced itself altogether from such mad political ideas and political marketing.' (ZR, September 1990)

Among the politicians whom the commentators of *Partizanov vesnik* and *Zvezdina revija* accuse of chauvinism in 1990 and 1991, in addition to Tudjman, Rupel, Rugova, one Serbian politician is also mentioned: Vuk Drašković. There is not the slightest allusion to the role of the ruling SPS party or its leader (Slobodan Milošević), and there is no attempt to connect the atmosphere in sports stadia with the similar atmosphere at political rallies in Serbia and Montenegro in 1988–9, nor is there any mention of the striking similarity of slogans, songs and placards which were appearing both in the stadia and at political rallies, the main hero of which—in both cases—was Slobodan Milošević, to whom supporters in the stadia and participants in rallies would frequently chant: 'Serbian Slobo, Serbia is with you.'[3]

'Serb-haters and football-haters'

When armed conflict began in Slovenia and Croatia, the sports journalists took over from their political commentator colleagues the main *topoi* of war-propaganda discourse. The reasons for the collapse of Yugoslavia and the outbreak of war and the consequences of such a situation in the realm of sport, it was suggested, can be explained with the help of 'arguments' offered by the state media. One article devoted to the cancellation of the start of the football league championship in Yugoslavia in 1991 begins like this: 'The national football championship did not begin as expected on the first Saturday of August. In Croatia, with the Ustasha-like policies of Tudjman's HDZ party, vicious war games are being played, in which the Serbian population is suffering. It is suffering precisely because it is—Serbian.' The article also mentions 'Croatian fighters in Slavonia and Krajina' who 'keep attacking the Serbian inhabitants... who are defending their homes'. (ZR, August 1991)

Similarly, the decision of UEFA, taken in August 1991, banning matches in European competitions from being held in stadia in Yugoslavia, is interpreted as part 'of the general hypocrisy towards Yugoslavia, and it seems particularly towards Serbia.' (ZR, September

---

[3] *'Slobo Srbine, Srbija je uz tebe!'* On Milošević as a hero of folklore dating from the time of mass political rallies (1988–9), see Čolović, 1993: 28–37 and 1994: 23–7.

1991) It is explained by one commentator in *Sport* as 'a Serb-hater and football-hater's whim'. He attributes the main role in dismantling Yugoslav football to 'the German lobby'. 'UEFA, obviously German-led, is doing all it can to destroy Yugoslav football,' writes this author, adding that this was increasingly reminiscent of a return to 'the marches of 1933, 1939 and 1941.' This fundamental idea of his commentary is suggested by its title: 'A slap in the face for the Germans' (*S*, 14 December 1991). In another place, the role of the 'fiercest and most frenzied destroyers' is attributed to Austria (*ZR*, January 1992). This 'anti-Serb lobby' includes also Hungary, which, in an article about the Red Star-Anderlecht match, played in October 1991 in Szegedin instead of Belgrade, is referred to as 'a country which is in any case ill-disposed to the Serbian nation in Croatia.' (*ZR*, November 1991).

The exclusion of Yugoslav teams and clubs from international competitions is also interpreted through the explanation of the international isolation of the Serbian regime offered by the state media. According to their interpretation, Milošević's Yugoslavia was exposed to international isolation and an economic embargo and other United Nations sanctions, because the main voice in the international community was that of enemies of the Orthodox Serbian nation, and above all the influential German and Vatican lobbies. The enemies of the Serbian nation hate it because it is in every way better and more righteous than they are and so, in accordance with this logic, they imposed sanctions in sport in order to disable a nation that was far in advance of all others in this field. As the author of an article entitled 'Europe's petty spite' put it succinctly: 'They want to spite us because we are the best'. (*SŽ*, 21 December 1991).

Such an explanation for the introduction of sporting sanctions against Yugoslavia was put forward by Milan Tomić, the general director of Red Star, in a statement for *Zvezdina revija* (September 1992): 'We represented a particular kind of danger for world sport. [...] We would have found ourselves in the centre of events at the Olympics, and that means that we would have been on the victors' podium in every team sport. The world could not bear that. Especially those who have pretensions to be powerful. For example, in team sports Germany means nothing. And nor does Britain. And if individual sports represent the civilisational premise of a nation, team sports are its spirit, which, however, those nations lack. [...] For all of these reasons I am convinced that many of the pretentious sporting nations could not tolerate our increasingly obvious domination in sports which form the backbone of the contemporary media sports phenomenon... and that it is a matter exclusively of the desire to deliver a blow to Serbian sport where it has attained the highest international achievements. That is an appalling strategy.'

This alleged endeavour of Western sport to eliminate Serbian competitors is only the latest episode in a war that has lasted for two millennia. 'Besides', Tomić continues, 'As early as the time of Cornelius Sula in the first century AD, the West had already reduced the Olympic spirit to its lowest, circus level, to the level of gladiators and blood. The nobility of Athenian athletes and Olympic victors was lost for a long time thanks to the Latin need for games soaked in blood.'

The coming of footballers as refugees from Croatia into Belgrade clubs was also an opportunity for sports newspapers to reach for imagery from war propaganda. So one former player from Osijek was quoted as saying: 'I could not remain in a city where people were killed just because they were Serbs and Orthodox.' It seemed to the journalist conducting the interview with him that 'all the evil suffered by the Serbian nation in Slavonia could be seen in his eyes.' Another of the footballer's statements was chosen as the title of the article: 'I always crossed myself with three fingers.' (SŽ, 5 December 1991).[4]

Their adherence to 'Serbdom' and the Orthodox church is also the reason why our coaches suffer innocently in various Catholic countries. At the end of 1991, the football club Español in Barcelona broke off its contract with the coach Ljupko Petrović, and somehow at the same time the basketball coach Bozidar Maljković also found himself out of work. 'Both of them', explains the author of an article, 'paid the price of their adherence to Orthodoxy. The Catalans could forgive them all their successes and failures but not their origin. Is that the reason why yet another Serb, Radomir Antić, is even today working at Real with a knife at his throat?' (SŽ, 31 December 1991).

Serbian Star

In the circumstances of the international isolation of war, involvement in sport, playing and supporting football, particularly abroad, acquires an exceptional patriotic value. In the opinion of sports journalists, Red Star and its fans participate in the defence of 'Serbdom' and Serbia whenever they go to matches played by our cup-winners outside Belgrade, in Szegedin or Sofia. In one report of a match between Red Star and Panathinaikos played in Sofia in March 1992,

---

[4] The Orthodox way of making the sign of the cross. (Transl.)

the fans are praised for their exemplary patriotism, comparable to that shown by the Serbian army in the most glorious moments of our history. 'The Army of the Valiants', states the report, 'was as numerous as the Serbian army led by the Mrnjavčević brothers* ... A team which was persecuted and cursed by UEFA did something that no one else has ever succeeded in doing ... In the international 1991–2 football season, the miracle called FC Red Star can be compared only with the Serbian army in the First World War. That army, also despised and humiliated by its allies, and driven out of its homeland by a more powerful opponent, survived and was victorious on a front that was always "away" ... "There is no hope for us, we must win." That sentence, spoken by Nikola Pašić* in 1915, appears to have become the way of life of FC Red Star.'

To follow Red Star on this thorny road represents the supreme act of patriotism: 'Star's supporters display unparalleled patriotism. They clutch that one bright national and internationally acknowledged phenomenon, FC Red Star, as a drowning man does a straw, regretting neither time nor expense, neither effort nor unjustified absences from school nor the reprimands of their bosses nor threats of the directors of their firms.' To be with Red Star in these difficult times is a real education for the young, far more important than that imposed on them by their teachers. The author of the article quotes several examples in support of this opinion, including the following: 'One father from Belgrade took his 11-year-old son to the Star-Panathinaikos match in Sofia, the child missed two days of school, and then the father went to see his son's teacher and said: "Madam, I took my son to the Red Star match in Bulgaria in order to give him some pratical lessons in patriotism, and it is up to your conscience to decide whether to consider those lessons administratively justified or not."' (*Te*, 25 March 1992)

In the sports press, in the course of 1991 and 1992, particularly in *Zvezdina revija,* the idea became firmly established that the greatest value of this club was its Serbian identity, and that supporting Red Star meant in fact supporting 'Serbdom' and Serbia. So one article in *Zvezdina revija* in August 1991 stated that Red Star was 'a European club in its results, but in its origin and the allegiance of its fans supremely—Serbian'. It is particularly emphasised that 'For Serbs from Croatia, Red Star is practically a part of their national identity! Until recently they did not dare to say aloud what they were by nationality, but they could say who they supported—always! "Red Star is more than a football club, it is a symbol of the Serbian being" is a quotation from one of the last issues of *Naša riječ* [Our Word], the paper of the Serbian nation in Croatia. "In Cetina, near Knin, every single child and young man knows the Red Star anthem, but few of them know the Orthodox Lord's Prayer," was recently reported in *Slobodna Dalmacija* [Free Dalmatia]. In the reception centre for refugees from Tenj, Borovo, Mirkovci, Bršadin and Vukovar some fifty youngsters, boys and girls, accommodated in Kula, asked for balls as they chanted "Zvezda, Zvezda!" directly into the television cameras.'

The article is illustrated with two pictures of the 'Valiants'. On one they are holding a flag with the initials SER, on the other a flag with the old Serbian coat of arms. They are accompanied by the captions: 'Among the Valiants: at every match something new' and 'The arsenal of supporters' props is expanding: at the present time the club sign is inadequate'.

In addition to the journalists, the club's officials also participated in the definitive shaping of the Serbian character of Red Star, its consecration in the role of one of the most important symbols of 'Serbdom', that is the Serbian national identity. So Vladimir Cvetković, the general manager of FC Red Star (later also a minister in the Serbian government), in an interview published in August 1992, was at pains to deny any connection whatsoever of his club with communism and the previous Communist régime in Serbia. 'First of all', said Cvetković, 'the Star is not a symbol of communism, we have no hammer and sickle in our coat of arms ... If we were to roll the film back a little, it would be clear that we were never a club that was closely connected with the government.' (*Te*, 12 August 1992)

Had Cvetković really been inclined to 'roll the film back' he would have found in the monograph *Crvena Zvezda*, published in 1986, at the time when he was secretary of the club, information about the fifteen political and military leaders who were presidents of the club between 1948 and 1992, from the first, Mita Miljković, to the last, Miladin Sakić. He could also have remembered that the introduction to this official publication was written by Dragoslav-Draža Marković, one of the most influential people in the Serbian government of the time, and he could have read in that introduction that the name of Red Star 'was associated with the five-pointed star, under which we spilled our blood in the course of the revolution.'

Writers of a political bent also came forward to bear witness to the Serbian identity of Red Star. The literary critic Petar Džadžić recalled in 1989: 'In the seventies, my friends and I identified only four important institutions in the current social life of the Serbs: the Serbian Academy of Science and Arts, the daily paper *Politika*, the publisher Prosveta and Red Star.' (*Politika*, 30 January 1989) In an interview in *Sport*, the writer Brana Crnčević said something apparently contradictory about himself, namely that he was 'a Partizan fan, who supported Red Star'. But in fact there was no contradiction, because for Crnčević too Red Star was a symbol of Serbian identity. 'Star's successes', added Crnčević, 'meant a great deal both to Serbs in the diaspora and to Serbs here.' (*S*, 26 December 1991). The poet Matija Bećković once explained that he had begun to support Star because 'national allegiance was expressed through support' for that club (*ZR*, March 1992).

Hooligans or patriots?

Before the crisis in Yugoslavia, the collapse of the federal state and the outbreak of armed conflict in some parts of the country, the most fanatical Yugoslav supporters, especially of football, belonged to the great international family of hooligan-fans. For them, as for groups of other European fans, which began to attract public attention through their violent behaviour, their models were English and Italian fans. Following their example, our fans also chose provocative names, gathered round belligerent leaders, came to matches equipped with the requisite props for supporting their club but even more for fighting, throwing firecrackers onto the pitch, lighting Bengal fires, making enormous flags, and above all they came to settle scores with the supporters of opposing teams and to cause havoc in the towns where they went to encourage their club.

What is striking is the mutual association of these hooligan-fans, their hostile attitude to society and its official representatives, which usually extends also to the club's officials.[5] Defying the established order, overturning the hierarchy of official social values, the fans develop a kind of subculture, or more precisely, a counter-culture.[6] They practise—or at least praise—alcoholism, barbarity, vandalism, madness, free sex and a pornographic vocabulary.[7]

[5] Milan, 18 years of age, a Partizan supporter: 'I am not particularly interested in those organisations of fans, or meetings with the club officials. Because as soon as they start to hold forth, it's all over, they launch into politics and that's nothing to do with me.' (Questionnaire, 17 January 1990) Zare, 25, 'Red Star' supporter: 'I don't go to the Club or to any kind of meetings. That's where the boot-lickers go, the people who let these buggers rabbit on about God knows what, give them passes and pay for their tickets if they are needed to go somewhere. Incidentally we take those passes and tickets off them.' (Questionnaire, 16 May 1989)
[6] The person who has paid most attention to this aspect of supporters' meetings is Benjamin Perasović (Perasović, 8–19).
[7] In December 1990, a photographer from *Politika* observed the appearance of

It seems then that the real target of the hooligan-fans' provocations is the ruling authorities in their immediate social environment. When they are aggressive towards visiting supporters, they provoke above all the local community leaders and organs of public order, and when they behave destructively at away matches, they are competing with the local hooligans rather than currying favour with the chauvinists back home.

A substantial part of the supporters' folklore consists of songs of a 'hooligan' character, that is songs in which, in order to be provocative, the fans consciously take on the role of antisocial types, social dropouts, alcoholics, madmen. This hooligan defiance of the 'Gypsies' (Red Star fans) and 'Gravediggers' (Partizan fans) is expressed in the following lines:

> *As long as the Earth revolves round the Sun*
> *Star's hooligans will never settle down.*
>
> *Thousands of Gravedigger hooligans*
> *will lay down their lives for Partizan.*

Following the example first of English, then of Italian fans, they usually give themselves names which emphasise that role: Vandals, Maniacs, Bad Boys, Evil Hordes. One group of Red Star supporters called themselves BAH (Belgrade's Alcohol Hooligans). Their anthem goes:

> *Alcohol, alcohol, that's the real thing,*
> *If you don't like to drink, you're not all there.*

Hajduk (Split) favoured this little song:

> *Dawn is breaking, the day grows light,*
> *the whole of the north is laid out, blind drunk,*
> *everything is drunk, everything is drugged,*
> *and we are all supporters of Hajduk.*

Taking on the role of social outcasts and rebels, the fans develop forms of 'war-like' behaviour and discourse. One group of Star supporters called themselves 'Zulu Valiants'. The fans are 'at war' not

---

'a new kind of folklore' at a 'Rad'/'Hajduk' match. 'At a given moment, a group of young "Rad" supporters, who called themselves Blue Wolves, stripped to the waist (and some even "lower").' The published photograph is more eloquent than this description. (*Politika*, 12 December 1990).

only with foreigners or their neighbours, with 'other nations', but most readily with rival local clubs. Partizan and Star supporters exchange threats full of death, blood, axes and slaughter. The first shout: 'If you're happy kill a Gypsy.' The 'Gypsies' have a ready response:

> With an axe in the hand
> and a knife in the teeth,
> there'll be blood spilled tonight,
> the Gravediggers' red blood.
> Oh Gravediggers, Gravediggers,
> Now you are nothing,
> you'll end up like the Frogs[8]
> playing against Liverpool.
> Thirty-eight met their death then,
> hurry home, hurry home,
> there'll be dead now too.

The vocabulary and phraseology of confrontation with an opponent, used by the hooligan-fans, consist equally of elements from the repertoire of the language of violence and death and from the arsenal of obscene, pornographic words and sentences of abuse. Here, if 'slaughter' and 'fuck' don't mean precisely the same thing, they are at least equally offensive. In one example there are two characteristics of the hooligan fans which became unacceptable at the time when inter-nation hatred and preparations for war were beginning to flare up: offending the 'same-nation' opponent, combined with solidarity with a club of a 'different nation', and a pornographic vocabulary unworthy of a disciplined national fighter.

> Oh Star, you fucked-up tart,
> Let Hajduk fuck you, let them all,
> especially the Gravediggers.

For the fans, coming to the stadium and supporting their team means 'release', liberation, throwing off restraints and rules. At least that is how some of them answered the direct question as to what they got out of supporting their teams at matches. 'Dad started taking me to matches as a kid', says Mihajlo (22, Partizan supporter), 'and I simply began to like that experience of a crowd, that's a special kind of release. There's a kind of beauty in hating the others, those who don't support

---

[8] Pejorative term for Italians (not for the French, as in English). (Transl.)

the team you support. Also, you can shout your head off... I like that, everything else in life has rules.' (Questionnaire, 20 January 1990)

But, at the time of the 'national happenings' in Serbia and Montenegro, there began increasingly to appear among the fans those who looked for a kind of patriotic justification for their provocative and aggressive behaviour, especially at matches where their team was playing against clubs from 'different centres'. So Goran, 23, leader of the 'Vandals' group of Partizan supporters, said that 'one should give the fans due recognition, because they were the first to support Serbia in these changes.' 'I think', he added,'that it all began in the stadium. People always knew that Star and Partizan were Serbian teams, and Hajduk and Dinamo Croatian, and that's all there is to it. End of story.' (Questionnaire, 8 May 1989)

From the mid-1980s, the supporters' folklore in Serbia (songs, slogans, placards, flags, coats of arms, etc.), was dominated by the theme of ethnic identity, until then sporadic and proscribed. And at the same time that theme began to appear in political communication and propaganda, especially at the populist mass political rallies which gave the tone to political life in Serbia and Montenegro in the course of 1988 and 1989. And the supporters wanted, above all, to present themselves as belonging to 'their nation', Star and Partizan supporters as Serbs, and at the same time to see opposing clubs as representatives of different nations, inimical to them.

According to one Red Star fan, preparations for going to Zagreb for the Star-Dinamo match of 21 May 1989 included one feature, obligatory for all. All supporters, including Partizan fans, had to have tattooed on their arm the four letter 'S's from the Serbian coat of arms.[9] 'Imagine the scene', he said, 'when we all roll up our sleeves and begin to wave our arms!' (Questionnaire, 7 May 1989). At the same time there was a similar evolution towards the national self-determination of supporters in Croatia too, also under the influence of the development of political circumstances there, i.e. the establishment of a nationalistic regime.[10]

---

[9]The Serbian coat of arms consists of 4 Cyrillic letters: 'c' ('s') arranged in a cross. [Transl.]

[10]A real little history of sports support and hooligan supporters' groups in Yugoslavia was written by the Split sociologist Dražen Lalić. Particularly interesting for us are the places where the author reconstructs the changes which took place in the early and mid-1980s, when the behaviour of the supporters became ever more openly violent, 'losing its earlier symbolic character' and turning into serious mutual conflict and confrontation with the police, i.e. ever since that kind of support

Star supporters, especially when they found themselves in the stadium of their opponents' team, emphasised above all their allegiance to Serbia and its leader Milošević, as these lines from various songs show:

> *We are the Valiants from proud Serbia ....*
> *Come on to the terraces, greet the Serbian race ....*
> *From Kosovo to Knin, Serbs stand shoulder to shoulder ....*
> *Serbian Slobo, Serbia is with you ....*
> ....
> *Who says, who lies that Serbia is small,*
> *It's not small, it's not small, it gave us Slobodan!*
> ....
> *Manastirka, manastirka, Serbian brandy.*
> *that's what warms the Serbian army, Slobodan!*

Sometimes, at the beginning of 1990, Star supporters would also shout the name of Vuk Drašković, as this example shows:

> *Star, Star, in one voice now,*
> *Vuk Drašković supports us.*

But, equally, Star's greatest urban rival Partizan, and particularly its supporters, did not want to stand aside from this movement towards national identification. Among the supporters' slogans and songs, the following lines could be heard:

> *Partizan, Partizan, that's a Serbian team.*
> *Slobodan Milošević is proud of them ....*
> ....
> *The whole of Yugoslavia dances rock-and-roll,*
> *Only a true Serb supports Partizan.*[11]

Nor did Partizan fans want to leave the name 'Valiants' to Star supporters:

'virtually lost any connection with the game itself'. According to the author, that trend continued also at the end of the 1980s, with the difference that 'the basic model of excess became political.' (1990: 124–9)

[11] This couplet, a variation on the text of a famous number by the Belgrade rock-group 'Electric Orgasm', was taken up also by supporters of Hajduk: '*The whole of Yugoslavia dances rock-and-roll, only a true Dalmatian supports Hajduk.*' (Ivo, 23, Hajduk supporter, Questionnaire, 14 May 1989)

> *Partizan loves only Valiants,*
> *warrior heroes of proud Serbia,*
> *may their name shine forever,*
> *long live Partizan and mother Serbia.*

The Star fans would not have that, and responded to such words from the 'Gravediggers':

> *Partizan, Partizan, well-known Muslim team,*
> *Azem Vlasi, Azem Vlasi, is proud of them.*[12]

But still, this folklore bears witness to the overriding endeavour among supporters of both these clubs to establish ethnic solidarity, so that at some matches they chanted 'Serbia, Serbia!' together. The equivalent in Croatia was the sense of fraternity between Dinamo and Hajduk supporters, who were able to forget their internal conflicts and sing together:

> *Dinamo and Hajduk are of the same blood*
> *it doesn't matter which of them is first,*
> *Dinamo and Hajduk are two brother clubs,*
> *the whole of Croatia is proud of them.*[13]

In the years preceding the outbreak of war in Croatia, Star and Partizan supporters often found their inspiration and material for slogans and songs in Chetnik folklore, which reappeared in general circulation at that time, especially in the form of records and tapes freely sold by street vendors in Serbia. Since one of the main demonstrative functions of supporters' folklore is to achieve the maximum degree of provocation and to touch the 'opponent' with the worst possible insult, in the supporters' variations on the lines of Chetnik songs there is more blood and slaughter than in the texts of the 'originals' on which these variants are based. This is confirmed by these examples:

> *The emblem on my beret*
> *is shaking, shaking,*
> *we will murder, we will kill*
> *all who are not with Star.*

---

[12] Azem Vlasi was a prominent Albanian politician from Kosovo. (Transl.)
[13] Perasović, 18–19.

*Prepare yourselves, Gravediggers,
it will be a fierce battle,
heroic heads will fall
we'll slaughter our brother Ustashas [Gypsies].*

*The Serbian army is on the move
heading for Zagreb, heading for Zagreb,
we will murder, we will kill
all who are not with us.*

These examples show that the Chetnik folklore from the Second World War offered suitable material for supporters' slogans and songs. For this purpose bellicose, threatening cries were particularly useful, as was also the theme of sacrifice. This is borne out by the fans' reworking of a line from a folksong, which is best known in its Partizan version:

*We two brothers are both fans,
Don't weep, mother, if we are both killed.*

At the end of 1990 the sports press, and particularly *Zvezdina revija*, began to write about positive changes in the behaviour of Red Star supporters, which were attributed to the influence of their leader Željko Ražnatović Arkan, a man who was imposing himself increasingly on the attention of the broader public. He was credited with reconciling the management of Red Star with a section of the unruly supporters, with establishing order and harmony between mutually antagonistic groups of fans, and most important, with separating support of the club from political passions and interests.

In the first article about Ražnatović, published in *Zvezdina revija*, he is described as 'a man close to Star, with an excellent understanding of events in the Marakana stadium, who was helping the Valiants to leave politics in the political arena.' It also said that 'Star's management proclaimed him its saviour when he succeeded through his personal authority in reconciling the warring factions.' (*ZR*, December 1990) Beside this article there appeared a photograph of a group of supporters—the Valiants with Željko Ražnatović wearing, like all the others, a supporters' cap and trainers.

The coming of Ražnatović among the Valiants appears to have reduced the danger of their displaying 'political intoxication in general, particularly of the Chetnik type' (*ZR*, September 1990), to which *Zvezdina revija* had previously drawn attention, because from that time on the paper wrote about Star supporters in a different way, praising their behaviour. The club itself hurried to repay the Valiants' obedience to the supporters' commissar Ražnatović, paying for some eighty of the most passionate supporters to go to Glasgow for a match against Glasgow Rangers, with Ražnatović as the leader of the expedition. (*ZR*, December 1990).

Another commentary in *Zvezdina revija* from December 1990, 'Spectators Get the Better of Politics', is devoted to the Valiants. Here it states that in Belgrade there had been 'aggressive attempts to politicise sport', although 'significantly less than in other places', for the simple reason that 'Belgraders were traditionally great lovers of true sporting contests.' There was nevertheless a danger because 'it is not difficult to poison the souls of these young people' and 'party leaders strive to imitate only what is worst in the arsenal of Western democracy'. So it happened that 'Belgrade did not escape the attempt to introduce national paraphernalia, and at one time relations between a section of these misguided young men and the Red Star management became strained.' But then Ražnatović came on the scene or rather, as it states here, the Valiants reorganised themselves.

There is no doubt that in these articles it is not so much the introduction of various items of 'national paraphernalia' and everything else associated with them into the stadia that is in dispute as the question of whose hands held them—that is, who was in control of aggressive chauvinistic passions, and therefore had a monopoly over their use for political or military ends. And the war in Croatia and Bosnia was on the horizon.

Ražnatović made the decision to begin preparing Star supporters for real war, as he said himself, after the Dinamo-Star match of 13 May 1990 in Zagreb. 'The match took place on the thirteenth', he was to say some years later. 'We began to organise immediately after that. [...] I could see war coming because of that match in Zagreb, I foresaw everything and knew that Ustashe daggers would soon be slaughtering Serbian women and children again.'[14]

At the end of 1990 Ražnatović attracted the attention of the public when he was arrested in Dvor on the Una (in Croatia) and spent six months in prison accused of coming to Krajina in order to help the Serbs there, who had begun to offer armed resistance to the new Croatian government in a protest known as the 'log revolution'. Just before his arrest, Ražnatovic had founded the Serbian Volunteer Guard, although not much was known about it publicly.

---

[14] *Srpsko jedinstvo*, organ of the Serbian Unity Party (Stranka srpskog jedinstva), no.1, November 1994.

Fighters of the Serbian Volunteer Guard in March 1992, somewhere in Slavonia, reading the magazine of their favourite football club. (Published in the magazine *Zvezda*, March 1992. Zoran Dimic)

When he came out of prison, the leader of the Valiants and commander of the Serbian Volunteer Guard became involved in armed conflicts in Slavonia which, in the course of the summer of 1991, turned into real war. The core of his volunteer army consisted of Red Star supporters. In an interview for *Srpsko jedinstvo* (November 1994), reminscing about those war days in Slavonia, Ražnatović talked about the way he and his fighters prepared: 'Well, remember that, as supporters, we had trained first without weapons ... From the beginning I had insisted on discipline. You know what football fans are like, they're noisy, they like drinking, clowning, I put a stop to that at a stroke, I made them cut their hair, shave regularly, stop drinking and—it all took its own course.'

In December 1991 *Zvezdina revija* published a short 'note from the front' about 'the legendary Željko Ražnatović-Arkan, leader of the Star 'Valiants' and commander of his Tigers who distinguished themselves in the liberation of Vukovar', but it was only from the March 1992 issue that this paper began to write more extensively about the Star supporters on the Slavonian battlefield. A report 'Rifles on their racks, flags in their thoughts' described 'a day with the Valiants in the Serbian Volunteer Guard':

All with neatly cut hair under their black military berets, they set off to the song 'We are the Serbian Army, Arkan's Tigers, all to a man volunteers, we'll let no one have Serbian land'. The beat of their marching feet seemed to give rhythm and strength to the melody. They disappeared into a wood, but it rang with the words: 'To battle, to battle, to battle, rise up my Serb brothers, do not leave your hearth, Serbs are protected by glory and by God! I wind back the film of my memories and distribute these brave boys through all the stadia of Europe. I know exactly where each of them stood, who first started the song, who first unfurled his flag, who first lit the torch. Arkan's Valiants. [...] They occupy every line of the new issue of *Star*. The best supporters in the world. [...] The Valiants have left their supporters' props somewhere under the arches of our Marakana stadium and set off to war with rifles in their hands. Fearless fighters, heroes to a man.' (ZR, March 1992)[15]

The Red Star footballers did not forget their supporters at the front. The captain, Vladan Lukić, was praised in one issue of *Srpski žurnal* (Serbian Journal) for having gone 'in his Mazda 323 four times to Erdut to visit the wounded', and for the fact that he was planning to spend New Year's Eve with them. He was quoted as saying: 'Many of our loyal supporters from the north end of Marakana are in the most obvious way writing the finest pages of the history of Serbia.' (SZ, 25 December 1991) His team mate Siniša Mihajlović complained that thinking about the war stopped him from concentrating on football: 'Our supporters are at the front ... my people are dying and bleeding, and how can I play? I even caught myself thinking that it was actually indecent for us to play and enjoy ourselves when there are so many casualties.' (Te, 11 December 1991)

The fighter-fans did not forget their clubs or their songs. It turned out that supporters' songs and war songs could easily exchange themes and other essential elements. Many of the supporters' songs, which had come into being through improvisation on the basis of Chetnik and patriotic folklore, were simply restored to their original form. But, some were 'authentic' supporters' songs—i.e. they had no iden-

---

[15] After Slavonia, in the summer of 1992, Arkan and his Valiants (*Delije*) participated in the military campaign in Bosnia. Rade Leskovac, one of the commanders of the Serbian paramilitaries, remembers those days nostalgically: 'Always now in my dreams about what once was I see a dusty village road and the Serbian flag carried by Ražnatović and his boys together with the Star supporters' flag. They always trumpeted their way through our villages, shouting one after another "Arkan, Arkan!".' (*Svet*, 6 September 1993)

tifiable external model; there were only supporters, their antisocial violent behaviour and the requisite props. These 'hooligan' texts were the shared heritage of various groups of supporters, who improvised adaptations. They included the two following verses:

> *Tonight there's going to be trouble,*
> *tonight will be a madhouse,*
> *the hooligans are moving*
> *through the streets of Belgrade [Zagreb, Split].*
>
> *Let axes ring out,*
> *let chains rattle,*
> *here come the Gravediggers [Gypsies]*
> *the greatest madmen of all.*[16]

As they went to war, into paramilitary volunteer units, supporters from Serbia adapted their 'hooligan' songs to their new function, turning them into patriotic and war folklore. That is how this song, published in the Pale weekly *Javnost* in October 1993, came into being:

> *There will be hell again,*
> *there'll be a madhouse again,*
> *the specials are on the move,*
> *from the streets of Foča.*
>
> *The Chetniks are on their way,*
> *the fighters are on their way,*
> *Ćosa's men are on their way,*[17]
> *Serbian volunteers.*
> *They do not fear Allah,*
> *they do not fear the faith*
> *they do not fear Alija [Izetbegović]*
> *and all his Turks.*

Sport as military training

The example of the orderly departure of a group of supporters to the war, combined with the fact that in so doing they did not lose their supporters' identity, casts new light on the question of the relationship

---

[16] The variant *'Tonight there's going to be trouble, tonight will be a madhouse, the hooligans are moving through the streets of Zagreb'* is quoted in Perasović, 19.
[17] Brana Ćosović, 'Ćosa', leader of a unit of specials. (Transl)

between violence, sport and society. Over the last two decades, this question has usually been posed as the problem of the anti-social, destructive and violent, but often also the criminal behaviour of extreme groups of hooligan football fans. In peacetime, in countries faced with the growth of aggression among supporters' groups, appropriate (political, police, sporting, educational etc) measures are sought to end their destructive behaviour as 'a social evil',—in other words, the supporters have to be pacified.

However, the episode of the Valiants going to war demonstrates that in a country where, as in many others, supporters' hooliganism had become a serious problem the fans' aggression becomes a valuable 'capital of hatred' for the state in war,[18] and the fans themselves are welcome as 'cannonfodder'. The state does not then need to repress the violence of the fans, partly because wartime conditions provide little opportunity for it to be manifested in the usual way. On the contrary, it is in the interest of the state that the supporters' 'capital of hatred' should be conserved to be used for the realisation of war aims.

Those who study the state in the twentieth century have already noted that it is interested in sport and physical culture on the whole as a kind of military training. That is particularly true of states with totalitarian features or that are preparing for war. On the eve of the First World War, Henri Degrange, editor of the French sporting paper *Auto* and creator of the famous Tour de France bicycle race, proposed the thesis that 'in the end war is just sport, a big match between two states'. In his country, right up till 1926, the teaching of physical education was the responsibility of the Ministry of War.

Nor is the idea that the creation of national sporting idols and supporters' adherence to sports clubs can be of use to the state at moments when psychological or military mobilisation of the citizens is needed a recent discovery. 'Between the wars', writes Eric Hobsbawm, 'international sport became, as George Orwell soon recognized, an expression of national struggle, and sportsmen representing their nation or state, primary expressions of their imagined communities. [...] The imagined community of millions seems more real as a team of eleven named people. The individual, even the one who only cheers, becomes a symbol of his nation himself.' (Hobsbawm, 143)

Fascist Italy is quoted as the first state to use football for political purposes. It was above all the Second World Cup, held there in 1934, that was exploited in this way; Mussolini called the members of the Italian team 'soldiers in the service of the nation' (Milza, 164).

---

[18]For the 'capital of hatred', see Čolović, 1993: 93–8.

In the opinion of some authors, this historical connection between football and fascism is not coincidental, but rests on a deep affinity between sport and fascist movements. Thus Michel Caillat, in the conclusion of his book *L'Idéologie du sport en France* (1989), which analyses the language, institutions and development of sport over the last centuries, writes that he is 'profoundly convinced that sport is imbued with fascism'. The traits which confirm this, in his opinion, are: celebrating competitiveness and selection among people, glorifying suffering and heroism, the expectation of renewal of the social body threatened by decadence, anti-intellectualism, the cult of the leader and chauvinism, parades and props resembling military ones, the manipulation of the masses and sportsmen, encouraging the irrational.' (Caillat, 210)

In recent years researchers into sport and spectators, and particularly the violent behaviour of fans at football matches—which led during the 1980s to a series of bloody incidents of which the worst, with the greatest number of casualties, were at the Heisel stadium in Brussels (29 May 1985, 39 dead) and Hillsborough in Sheffield, England (15 April 1989, 95 dead)—have drawn attention to the connection of the most aggressive groups of supporters in Europe with the extreme Right. 'It seems that in all European countries', writes Didier Pagès, 'groups of fascists are increasingly often in action at football grounds. All the big European clubs have little groups of fascist supporters. [...] These fascists have understood that football is the activity which is most similar to war, and they abandon themselves to it with enthusiasm. [...] Every week, the stadia are full of potential fascists, so much is the spectacle based on hatred of the other. To attend an important match means to offer oneself two hours of ordinary and legal fascism ... It appears that the extreme right has understood the problem of support better than the moralists from sports institutions. Football is war and football stadia are ... terrain for training little Nazis who dream of wider spaces.' (Pagès, 137–9)

The connection between football hooliganism and the political Right in Europe has also been discussed by the Belgian criminologist Kris van Limbergen. In his words, 'Football vandalism is, it seems, a seductive field for recruiting members of the extreme Right.' He describes conditions in Belgium above all, where the 'football scene is characterised by many manifestations of racism, sexism, extreme regionalism, anti-semitism.' (Limbergen, 80–1)

In communist states as well, the main motive for their great interest in sport was the conviction that it is an important means of political propaganda and preparation for potential war. That is how it was perceived in former Yugoslavia. In a paper prepared for the founding meeting of the Red Star Sports Club, held on 4 March 1945, Zora Zujović defined two main tasks for sport in the new communist state: 'First, to strengthen the body for the forthcoming reconstruction of the country, and secondly, accessible to all, it should gather and unite all our young people, regardless of their age or position. Its greatest and most sacred duty is wholehearted and fraternal help to the front.' (Ršumović, 37)

The idea that support for sport was a preparation for war (should it be necessary) was also to be found in Yugoslavia in the period after Tito's death. In a book of patriotic-sporting songs by Nedeljko Neša Popadić, *Srce na travi* (Heart on the Grass), which was published in 1982 by Sportska knjiga (Sporting Books) in Belgrade, there is a poem entitled 'The Fan'. The character of the fan includes the following features:

> *I am one of those*
> *who sings far into the night after a victory.*
> *And who will punch the nose*
> *of my opponent's supporter,*
> *one of those who will go tomorrow to the front*
> *and swap my club's flag*
> *for a rifle in my hand ...*

These patriot-fans, together with their favourites—footballers—make up Tito's army:

> *And therefore ... before the well-known whistle blows*
> *and the signal to start the match is given,*
> *remember the land of the Partizans*
> *and know: now it is you*
> *who are Tito's army!*
> *.....................*
> *Forward for the homeland ... for the House of Flowers ...*[19]
> *Forward for the tricolour ... Forward, forward, for Tito!*

The hooligan revolution

On the eve of armed conflict breaking out in former Yugoslavia, war propaganda on the Serbian side, above all through sports journalists,

---

[19]Tito's mausoleum in Belgrade. (Transl.)

succeeded in directing the aggressive energy of supporters towards the battlefields, giving to the new forms of its manifestation the meaning and value of patriotic sacrifice—if not for Tito and the House of Flowers, then certainly for the new or renewed symbols and ideals of the national collective. In other words, unlike peacetime endeavours to pacify hooligan-supporter groups, here was an example of their militarisation.

The well-documented significant presence of sports hooligans and others who in peaceful conditions would be seen as anti-social and criminal groups, among the 'heroes' of today's wars on the territory of former Yugoslavia is one reason why these wars can be described as the vandalistic, destructive campaigns of hooligan-fans, taken over by the state for the aims of its war policy, disciplined, supplied with 'props', (i.e. arms, and sent to fight with the 'enemy' as though it were a confrontation between rival supporters at some football match.

But how is it possible to transform unruly hooligan-fans so quickly into disciplined soldiers ostensibly fighting for the state and nation? Is the essence of hooligan-fan behaviour, as some believe, the testing of unbridled, excessive freedom, 'rampaging', and chaotic abandonment to 'basest instincts'? If so, the transformation of fans into soldiers (through military drill, cutting their hair, 'coming off' drugs and limiting alcohol) would mean that they undergo a fundamental metamorphosis in order to be transferred forcibly from the chaos of unbridled freedom to the cosmos of military order.

There is reason to dispute such an explanation. Thanks to some new sociological and ethnological research, we know now that in the apparently ungoverned, chaotic world of extremist fans there are in fact elements of order. Their behaviour is full of unwritten rules, codes, protocols, hierarchy and discipline.[20] Hence it is possible to

---

[20] This is one of the conclusions reached by, among others, the French ethnologist Christian Bromberger, studying the behaviour of supporters of Olympic of Marseilles and Juventus of Turin (1987: 13). His description of the 'scenario' expressing support for Juventus against its urban rival Torino is particularly eloquent. 'Twice a year', he writes, 'the derby between FC Torino and Juventus represents one of the peaks of the Italian championship. On those days, the two enormous curves of the Stadio Communale represent two territories, clearly defined by symbols: "Marathon" is the collecting point for fans of "Toro", while "Philadelphia" is filled with the black and white Juventus *tifoseria*. In each arc, groups of fans are arranged from the centre towards the ends according to their importance and on the basis of an agreed protocol. [...] Three hours before the beginning of the match, the "troops" are in place, singing and shouting slogans in honour of their favourites or mocking their opponents. Gestures, words, songs, the unfolding of flags and banners, the release of balloons ... all

explain logically why it is precisely some supporter groups which lend themselves most easily to transformation into volunteer military units: such groups are already imbued with the spirit of organisation and subordination. The transformation of fans into soldiers is only a reinterpretation of the already existing structure of their group, and that is why the essential identity of the group, as fans, can be retained (Arkan's volunteer Tigers did not cease to be Valiants) and also, as in the example quoted, for the supporters' folklore to be preserved.

But, even if that were not the case, and one accepted that, as they say themselves, hooligans really did revel in crime, drunkenness, chaos and madness, their involvement in war would not have entailed any fundamental change; no one says that short-haired, disciplined supporter-volunteers are forbidden to hate the enemy passionately, nor are they prevented from revelling to their hearts' content in that hatred and destructive and murderous revenge. And that means that the taming of the unrestrained behaviour of the hooligans, now soldiers, is only illusory, and that it is perhaps only in war that they can taste to the full the pleasure of freely transgressing fundamental human prohibitions imposed on them in peacetime, including even the most aggressive behaviour in the stadium. However, the grim stories from the war in Croatia and Bosnia about sadistic orgies orchestrated by people in military uniforms engaged in military actions suggest that the freedom of abandonment to the most gruesome forms of violence made possible by war are on a different level altogether from what is tasted by sports fans even at their 'wildest'.

The phenomenon of fighter-fans in the war in former Yugoslavia calls into question the thesis of the positive socio-psychological functions of supporters' violence. Authors who promote this thesis seek to distinguish between the ritual, symbolic, carnival or spectacular manifestation of violence and 'real' violent behaviour, explaining those instances when supporter violence becomes real as isolated incidents and extreme phenomena. According to this interpretation, sporting events, especially football matches deflect the manifestation of mass aggression on to a symbolic plane and transform it into a spectacle, ritual, an image of violence, and thus have the prophylactic function of catharsis. A football match is war, but 'ritualised war',—not only

---

of this is orchestrated to the last detail in each group by the *capo tifo* (chief supporter), who is also called *carismatico*. The movements of the mass in each are finely directed by a choreographer. It is interesting that the Torino choreographer is a fresco restorer by profession.' (Bromberger, 13)

because journalists use military terminology to describe it but because the supporters' props—flags, drums, uniforms—suggest that it is a question of a kind of symbolic warfare. According to Alan Ehrenburg, it is in fact only a 'desire for show' (Ehrenburg, 1986: 148–58).

Michel Maffesoli attributes to contemporary sport the function of ritualising violence—i.e. the channelling of intensity, and a way of expressing it, analogous to the function of ancient bacchanalia and medieval tournaments and duels. In his opinion, ritualised eruptions of violence in sport 'help to prevent the social body as a whole from being contaminated by the aggression which in fanaticism or other forms of integrism acquires a dangerous direction. These eruptions of violence—favouring fusion, and confusion, around one ephemeral god: some sporting star or emblematic team—prevent violence crystallising around some exclusive god with truly bloodthirsty demands. [...] In any case it is less damaging than slaughter on the field of honour in the name of the nation-state.' (Maffesoli, 1990)

Some authors consider the phenomenon of ritually controlled violence in sport and among supporters as a product of modern industrial society. Starting from Herbert Spencer and his followers (for example Norbert Elias), according to whom, by contrast with pre-modern, militaristic society, modern society is characterised by the constant transformation of open, uncontrolled violence into regulated and controlled violence, P. Marsh came to the conclusion that violence in sport appears in just that modern, controlled, ritualised form, and that it is actually an illusion of violence, apparent violence. In the words of Krešimir Popović, from whom we adopt his review of this 'Spencerite' approach to the problem of violence in sport: 'In the behaviour of contemporary football supporters, Marsh sees at work a certain humanising trend. [...] He suggests that the ritualisation of violence is beneficial.' (Petrović, 1990: 35)[21]

However, our example reveals that it was in fact one group of hooligan-fans that showed itself particularly susceptible to recruitment and re-qualification into a war unit, and that they had no difficulty in exchanging the stadium and conflict with the supporters of rival

---

[21] The ritual aspect of football and its support has been discussed in our country, among others, by Ivan Kovačević and Vera Marković. V. Marković quotes some interesting examples of the ritual behaviour of supporters at Belgrade stadia, observed there in the spring of 1987: singing the club anthem, greeting the state flag, waving flags and passing them from hand to hand across the stands, greeting groups of supporters, throwing live hens on to the ground, kneeling and bowing. (Marković, 142–3)

teams for the battlefield and slaughter in the name of the nation-state. The ritual, symbolic warfare in sports stadia, which after all sometimes becomes bloody confrontation between groups of fans, does not appear to offer effective protection from the flaring-up of violence 'in real life'.

Does this mean that war could be the solution to the problem of hooligan violence? It certainly creates the possibility of transfer, that is to say it offers a good opportunity to channel that violence so that its target is no longer authority and established social values, against which the aggression of hooligan-fans is usually directed in peacetime, but external enemies of the nation. The regime in power acquires fighters, demonstrably fierce and fanatical, who, according to a widely-held belief, are better able to carry out the 'dirty' business of war than the regular army, and at the same time it offers an opportunity for such hooligan-fan-fighters to redeem their peacetime transgressions and, sacrificing themselves for the Fatherland, to return under its wing and earn the love reserved for the penitent Prodigal Son. This would mean that, thanks to war, the state redeems the aggression of hooligan-fans (and, on the same model, other anti-social groups) by giving them a chance to become socially useful—or, as it would be put today, 'positive energy', the foundation of postwar life.

Or is it perhaps closer to the truth to say that war—particularly the kind in which the Red Star supporters stood out, becoming first Valiants and then Tigers—is an opportunity for the ultimate victory of the hooligan revolt, a continuation and conflagration of destruction directed, ultimately against the fundamental values of civil society? Thus, the hooligan subculture (as B. Perasović would say), by transforming the leaders of hooligan-fans into national heroes, seeks to become the dominant culture of the social elite. History knows of several examples of the successful realisation of such projects, whose creators, whether on the left or the right, are usually called revolutionaries. Today we are on the way to granting it yet another fine example of the realisation of the hooligan-revolutionary dream.

2. The Rhetoric of Peace

In my contribution to this discussion of the language of peace,[1] I start from the point of view that its promotion requires three sober steps to be taken: first, criticism of the language of war; then, criticism or self-criticism of anti-war language; and, third, the development of a model for the language of peace.

Criticism of the language of war

The outbreak of armed conflict on the territory of former Yugoslavia, which was prepared and then encouraged by the propaganda of hatred and war, was accompanied by the first attempts at the criticism of the language of war. Among the opponents of the war there is today a widespread conviction that the war began first of all in ideas and words, that—as it was put by one of the authors represented in the collection *Intelektualci i rat* (Intellectuals and War)—the whistle of a bullet was first heard in the head (Avramović, 100). The people responsible for the war sit at their desks, said another author, suggesting that the name for them should be *Schreibtischtete* (Reljić, 8).

The person who has written most on this subject from a sociolinguistic point of view is Ranko Bugarski, and it is to him also that we owe the first attempts at a systematic description of the language of war and hatred. In addition to Bugarski, I would mention here also the significant contribution to the criticism of the language of war

---

[1] This refers to an international conference "Towards a Language of Peace', held in Belgrade, 17–18 March 1995, organised by Dr Božidar Jakšić. The conference papers were published in a collection with the same title in 1996.

of an author who, for obvious reasons, is less familiar to the public in Belgrade than he deserves to be. I refer to Ivo Žanić, to his book *Smrt crvenog fiće* (The Death of the Red Fiat), Zagreb 1993, and other essays which he is publishing today, mainly in the journal *Erasmus*.

Like Bugarski, Žanić is concerned with analysing the discourse of political and war propaganda. He too writes about the formula 'either-or', which Bugarski quotes as an example of the linguistic expression of the will to war. His starting-point is the familiar phrase 'Either Serbia will be a republic, or it will not exist'. In it, suggests Žanić, 'the choice between two political and historical possibilities is posed radically and highly suggestively, almost hypnotically.' Žanić reminds us that the 'either-or' formula was used by Hitler: 'Either Germany will be a world player, or it will not exist'. Similarly, Eva Perón: "Peronism will either be revolutionary, or it will not exist.' There are examples also from Stalin's speeches. But here is a statement by Kučan (first President of independent Slovenia): 'In ten years' time either Yugoslavia will be a federal democratic state, composed of free nations, or it will not exist.'

Žanić sees the reason for the general usefulness of this and other similar formulae in the fact that the politicians want 'to gain as many followers as possible and make the strongest possible impression on public opinion, and when that is the desire, many recipes for hearty rhetorical dishes will be found in the great political cookbook. One of these explains that it is essential to suppress the clear meaning of words and to remodel one's statement into a 'suggestive rhythm and pure sound', for that is what arouses strong feelings in the mass audience and stimulates its imagination, while the sentence acquires a liturgical-ritual meaning and is remembered exclusively as an affective form. Since it is used to simplify reality fundamentally, it will not be without effect, because simplicity is the most intoxicating mode.' (Žanić, 158–60) That, in Žanić's opinion, is why 'either-or' and similar formula should on no account be used by a politician in a tolerant democratic society. It should be left to the general on the battlefield.

Criticism of the language of war remains relevant, not only because this language, together with armed conflict, is still being reproduced, but also because it is an enduring component in the promotion of the language of peace and of forms of social communication appropriate to a democratic civil society. As Bugarski rightly says: 'The language of peace means an increased awareness of the deadly action of war rhetoric, achieved through its thorough analysis.' (Bugarski, 184)

Criticism of anti-war language

The experience of criticism of war and criticism of the language of war has also required that criticism itself be examined, its effects assessed, and above all that it too should be examined as language. The organisers and participants in anti-war demonstrations and actions, such as those which began in Belgrade in the summer of 1991 were on the whole disappointed by the inadequate public response to their appeals and messages. The relative ineffectiveness of anti-war messages, speeches, slogans and other verbal and non-verbal means of anti-war campaigning certainly had various causes. One of them is the power of the propaganda machine, in the service of war, to inflame hatred and spread fear. But it is necessary also to ask whether and how far the ineffectiveness of the anti-war actions was due to their language.

Useful ideas in seeking answers to this question may be found also in the experience of the several years of struggle against racism and xenophobia in West European countries, which in recent years has been increasingly exposed to critical assessment. In this process appropriate attention has been given to the criticism of the language of anti-racism and anti-fascism, with the aim of making it more effective than hitherto.

In France today the philosopher Pierre-André Taguieff often appears in the role of critic of the strategy of anti-racism, including its language. In one text with the characteristic title 'The Struggle against Racism, from the Other Side of Illusion and Disappointment' he warns, among other things, that it is unacceptable to reduce anti-racist discourse to the rhetoric of indignation and condemnation by means of the simple demonising labels 'racism', 'fascism' and 'Nazism'. Taguieff especially stresses the damage caused to the struggle against racism by the peremptory use of certain ambivalent words to denote indisputable values. Such are, for instance, 'pluralism', 'multiculturalism' and 'the right to difference'.

In our country, even before the outbreak of the new Yugoslav wars, these 'placard-words in the political slang of the opposition ideologies', such as 'man', 'humanism', 'freedom', 'democracy' and 'human rights', were discussed by Ivan Ivas, the author of *Ideologija u govoru* (Ideology in Speech). Ivas reinforced his critical opinion of such terminology with a sentence from Adorno's *The Jargon of Authenticity*: 'Thanks to its abstraction, such a concept may be injected, like lubricating oil, into the same machine which had once been used to attack.'

(Ivas, 88) But, as Adorno explains in the same place, 'one cannot confirm any *index verborum prohibitorum,* or index of noble nouns which do well in the marketplace, on the contrary, one must examine their rhetorical function in jargon.' (Adorno, 54)

The prevalence of label-words, placard-words and slogan-words in the language of anti-racism transforms its struggle into the sorrowful spectacle, as Taguieff says, of 'a polemic between "racists" (who insist that they are not) and "anti-racists" (who affirm and stress that they are): stereotype against stereotype, dogma against dogma, slogan against slogan, and sometimes myth against myth.' (Taguieff, 39) Taguieff also says that he does not seek to avoid 'a difficult question', namely whether anyone who is satisfied with the language of struggle, the language of conflict, a language which is reduced to that 'anti', is not condemned to suppress hatred with hatred. His idea is backed up by a German grafitto: 'Fighting for peace is like screwing for virginity.' (Lalić, D., 1991, 213)

A model of the language of peace

In shaping a model of the language of peace, that is the language of communication in a democratic civil society, we can follow the path suggested by Bugarski, notably that of the 'inversion of the language of war'. That he says, is, 'the scrupulous avoidance of the worst features of the language of war'. One should avoid, for instance, insulting labels, all hate-speech incitement to war, lies and ambiguities, and false symmetries. (Bugarski, 177) However, it will indisputably be easier to achieve agreement on the features which ought to appear in such a list in some circumstances than in others. Everything depends on the basis for the criteria on which the choice is made.

Some authors would have everything irrational excluded from the language of peace. For instance, in his book *The Strategy of Non-Violent Action* Jean-Marie Muller, the follower of Emmanuel Mounier, Erik Weil and Paul Ricoeur, states that 'revolutionary speech can be rational ... it must be based and developed in a register from which any kind of violence is excluded.' He draws on Erik Weil's definition of non-violent revolution, whereby it is an action 'undertaken by rational people against the power of people who do not use reason.' (Muller, 198–9)

Muller blames philosophers for the victory of the discourse of the powerful, which is contrary to the arguments of reason, because it is their 'political role to remind people, and particularly the administrators of the state, of the demands of reason, in both convenient and inconvenient times.' (ibid., 200) Therefore, the problem of the ascendancy of the speech of hate and war does not lie for him so much in the theoretical ineffectiveness, or indeed the unpopularity, of speech based on rational argumentation and respect for facts, and the impotence of such speech to overcome the seductive voice and suggestive lies of the demagogue as in the inadequate involvement of philosophers. The speech of reason contains in itself the power of action. That is why Muller concludes: 'The first step of non-violent action is to speak so that the truth is proclaimed: so that the word becomes power.' (ibid., 201)

Other writers prefer to avoid what they call, with Taguieff, 'the intellectualistic illusion which consists of faith in the omnipotence of critical reason'. Taguieff describes the space of political argumentation in modern pluralistic democracies as 'a collection of polemical places where more or less sincere opinions come face to face before a public which allows itself to be won over, disappointed or persuaded. But that heterogeneous public can never be transformed into a tribunal of reason: if it has to judge, that is to choose, to give priority, to decide, then it does so in accordance with various mutually incompatible or opposed systems of values and norms, but also on the basis of heterogeneous blocks of the affective and the imaginary, of what are called passions.' Taguieff concludes that one must then, 'accept the existence of a firm core of ideological convictions which resist all argumentation.' Nevertheless, he does not reject rational discussion as a basic measure of the language of democracy and peace, but his awareness of how limited is the effectiveness of a political language based on reason leads him to give such speech the task of assisting 'people of good will' rather than of persuading the masses. 'To accept the limits of rational argumentation', he writes, 'means not losing all hope, but realising that not everything is possible: in the field of opinion and conviction, where all the siren songs can be perfectly heard, the stern voice of proof and submission of evidence is barely audible.'

From this it follows that one should not seek to convince all 'racists' that they are mistaken and that we are freeing them of their pathological illusions. The aim is more modest: 'to give "to people of good will" who lack arguments (and are not satisfied with slogans) the necessary data and elements for reflection'. (Taguieff, 37–9)

In addition to the illusion of the omnipotence of the speech of reason, we should also resist the illusion of the omnipotence of the speech of facts. Henri Poincaré's warning is still valid today: 'People keep saying: let the facts speak for themselves, but unfortunately facts do not speak.' (Muller, 8)

A rhetoric of peace?

Finally, there are authors convinced, like Taguieff, of the limited effectiveness of the language of peace reduced to rational argument. Like him, they do not wish to deny themselves the possibility of influencing a broad public. These authors endeavour to justify, from an ethical and political viewpoint, the use of various means of achieving that influence, including methods of rhetorical persuasion, which are otherwise considered inextricably linked to the type of communication characteristic of an anti-democratic and authoritarian society. The most frequently quoted example of such methods is the political-propaganda slogan.

Olivier Reboul, the author of a book on slogans, starts from the thesis that slogans of hatred, war, racism and the like can be stamped out only by other slogans. Propaganda can be beaten only by counter-propaganda. In his opinion 'a slogan is not only a useful weapon, but an essential one; it is the only thing that can gather the masses around one truth, doubtless approximate, but vital; it is the only thing that gives struggle an immediate meaning, acceptable to all. If it is accepted that essential values, such as democracy, truth, peace, socialism, ought to be adopted through a great struggle, and that this struggle has constantly to be waged, then the slogan ought also to be accepted.' (Reboul, 127)

This means that one should accept that there are good slogans, i.e. ones that are both good and effective: such slogans make a strong impression on an audience, but do not deter them from reflection. But how does one recognise them? As Reboul puts it, they are ones which do not hide their nature as slogans. The people who use them and those for whom they are intended should know that slogans do not contain self-evident truths, that there is no such thing as a 'genuine' statement which 'goes without saying'. And 'to know that the formula we are using is not a self-evident truth but a slogan means to stand outside it, to think.' Therefore, what needs to be demystified above all in the slogan is its tendency to conceal itself.

However, the difficulties which Reboul is confronting here are reflected in the fact that he sees the characteristics necessary for a slogan to have a place in the language of peace and democratic society as being altogether far removed from the slogan in the true sense:

they are to be found in a form of slogan which he calls anti-slogan. This is a slogan which invites reflection and critical distance, and counts on our maturity and sense of humour. Examples, are 'Black is beautiful', 'We are all German Jews', '*La culture est un bouillon*', '*Il est interdit d'interdire*'. As Reboul writes, 'the anti-slogan is not contrasted to any specific slogan (as a counter-slogan), but to every slogan—to what is the essence of the slogan. Instead of enslaving thought which would stimulate action, it stops action in order to stimulate thought.' (ibid., 129)

The problem lies in the fact that in a slogan defined in this way little remains of what makes it such an effective, 'intoxicating' medium of propaganda: its suggestiveness and mobilising power. But regardless of these and other possible problems of the theoretical definition of slogans acceptable to the language of peace, we can at least agree with Reboul that slogans should not be too hastily written out of the language of peace—here Reboul's examples are perhaps more eloquent than his arguments. I would add to these examples a few of our anti-war slogans or, if you like, anti-slogans. One came into being as a radio-grafitto: 'One solitary hothead can cool millions:' (Jevtović, 59) Others are, so to speak, erotic-pacifist, constructed on the model of the anti-Vietnam war slogan 'Make love not war'. This is echoed by one thought up by a Belgrade rock-group in 1992: 'Better lay than slay' and a Zagreb grafitto from the same time: 'Better pull a bird than a trigger'. (D., Lalić, 1991, 218)

Lionel Bellenger, the author of *La Persuasion,* allows for the possibility of 'healthy persuasion'. He proposes elements for a de-ontology of persuasive communication in a democratic society. It has to satisfy one main condition, namely, to allow those to whom it is addressed a free choice whether to accept the attitude being offered or not.

Bellenger's de-ontology of persuasion demands of the persuader that he should (1) accept that the measure of efficacy and influence is the freedom of the other; (2) be aware of the social responsibility of all persuasive behaviour; and (3) accept that the quality of acquiescence is at least as important as its result. On the other hand, the persuaded must: (1) be aware of the intention of the persuader; (2) respect a person's democratic right to exert influence; and (3) understand his own interest in reacting positively to an influence or rejecting it. (Bellenger, 92)

In the opinion of Ivan Ivas, the language of a democratic society—or, we would add here, the language of peace—implies a speech culture, a speech design, i.e a rhetoric. One should not permit rhetoric to be the monopoly of the demagogue. Starting from the existentialist image of human society—proposed by Gerard A. Hauser—as a world which is 'the product of symbols and arguments, susceptible to interpretation and changes', where 'truth is probable and subjective', Ivas concludes that in such a world 'rhetoric has a certain future'. Today, in his opinion, its main task would be 'to supply effective techniques for carrying out public affairs, which include the will and ability to establish relations of dialogue (co-operative relations, without subjugation). By fostering the *for and against* of every subject, it would drive the focused mind to become accustomed to the rights of various points of view (truths). It would strengthen the awareness of shape, by means of which it would increase the quantity of discourse as (trans)formation and reduce the use of ready-made ideological and linguistic forms.' (Ivas, 247)

By all accounts, the rhetoric of peace need not be a single monolithic lesson about the correct use of verbal and other communication in a democratic society. It can develop also in divergent directions, towards the culture of rational argumentation or the culture of suggestive speech. It may also include in itself both strategies of speech intended for communication in a limited circle of participants and the strategy of discourse *urbi et orbi*. It can therefore accept various criteria—the rationality of argument, the effectiveness of output, the truthfulness of testimony, the transparency of persuasive techniques and intentions, the justice of aims—without having to reconcile them into a coherent whole. It is sufficient, that the rhetoric of peace, like the culture of language in a democratic society, should succeed in the case of the participants in social communication, and especially of the receivers of its messages, in increasing their ability to perceive language, i.e. to notice the procedures of production and diffusion of social meaning. This brings us to a theme beyond the scope of the present chapter: education for peace, which includes education in the language of peace.

3. Palm-reading and 'The Little Serbian Fist'

For nearly four months, from the second half of November 1996 to mid-March 1997, the citizens and students of Serbia protested against the regime of Slobodan Milošević, sending out a large number of messages. These took the form of various statements to the public, appeals, announcements, decisions and such like, but the most important and interesting of them were part of the symbolic communication which took place in the course of peaceful demonstrations on the streets of Belgrade and other towns in Serbia against the regime of Slobodan Milošević and election fraud. These were the messages conveyed in slogans, catch-phrases on placards or badges and lines of verse, or they took the form of non-verbal communication, like a gesture, a performance, a caricature, a puppet, a sculpture or a mask, the blowing of tin whistles, the sounding of horns or making a din by banging pots and pans. They were addressed above all to the regime, its leader and the leader's advisers and assistants. But many of them were at the same time addressed to Europe and the 'world'. The addressees included the opposition parties and their leaders, and the messages were also exchanged among individual participants in the protest. Finally, the protest was a stage for mass auto-communication—hence the senders of the messages were themselves also their recipients.

What were the messages conveyed by the protesting citizens and students of Serbia? What convictions and aspirations inspired them? The first striking thing is that many of them called for respect for democracy and democratic values, such as freedom for the citizen, the possibility of changing the government, and the right to be heard. For example: 'Belgrade's right to a voice stolen. Contact B 92', 'I am a student of rights without the right to a voice', 'Democracy is when you are not shut up for being open', 'We want the rule of law, not of mad cows'. Similar to them are messages against the lies of state television 'Switch off the television, switch on your brain', 'I think, so I don't watch RTS'—and those against fear of the regime: 'Submission is rooted in fear!' or 'Don't be a sheep, oppose!'

What this kind of message expresses is the fundamental theme of the protest, which broke out because of the decision by Milošević's regime to alter the results of the local government elections, which had been won by the opposition. The citizens and students rebelled, above all, against electoral theft, lack of respect for their political will, the autocratic and undemocratic regime, the regime media, the allegedly corrupt Vice-Chancellor of Belgrade University, and the police and judiciary being in the service of the ruling party. But at the same time as supporting democratic values in opposition to Milošević and his undemocratic regime, messages appeared at the same time which stressed the principled nature of the choice of democracy. Among these were warnings to 'our people', i.e. to a future democratic government, that it must respect the will of the citizens: 'All will fall if they're seen to steal.' Some messages emphasise that the demonstrations did not break out because of support for individual leaders of the opposition, but because of resistance to the regime which does not respect the most elementary of democratic rights: the right to vote. 'We're not here because of Vuk [Drašković], or Zoran [Djindjić], but because of Slobo' is the message on one placard. The students constantly repeated that their protest was not motivated by sympathy for any party or any political orientation. The emblem of the Student Protest is dominated by the word 'straight': 'Neither left. Nor right. But straight! Not lawlessness. But law!'[1]

The personal is political

The protests affirmed the citizen's position as a free, lucid and disobedient individual. He was protesting in his own name and because he understands that bad politics affect him personally, that he cannot run away into some private world protected from politics. This understanding is expressed in the slogan of a participant in the protest well grounded in theory: 'The personal is political!' Further, the disobedient citizen is a person who, among other things, resists the

---

[1] This slogan is particularly difficult to translate: the word '*pravo*' can mean 'straight' and 'right' (as in 'human rights') also 'law'. The succinct original goes: '*Ni levo. Ni desno. Već pravo! Ne bezakonje. Već pravo!*' (Transl.)

'Look! The handful's on its way!', placard at the demonstrations against the Milošević regime in Belgrade, November 1996.

pathos of collectivist demogogy. Laments over the sorry 'fate of our children', 'the flower of our youth' inspired one exceptionally daring slogan: 'We love you, children. Belgrade Paedophiles.' The frequent personal 'love' and 'sexy' messages can also be understood as springing from the aversion of a rational, independent-minded individual towards the heavy artillery of political rhetoric, which speaks of history, the people, destiny and such things: 'I love you, Ivana!', 'Manipulated student seeks girl for the same purpose', 'I'm looking for a girl', 'I'm looking for a husband', 'I'm here with my mother-in-law', 'Hang on a little longer! I've nearly pulled a bird!', 'Girls! You will do a lot for this protest if you smile at the boy next to you!', 'We're collecting girls' phone numbers' and 'Here are the best legs in Belgrade! Marchers.' Someone thought of making a badge with a text in the form of an offer to one of the most popular student leaders, Čedomir Jovanović: 'Marry me, Čedo!'

Messages of this kind are partly based on the tradition of the pacifist celebration of love as opposed to war. In the protest of the citizens and students in Serbia they served also as a means of expressing the citizens' disobedience to the autocratic regime, not in the form of a celebration of brotherhood and love between people, but as merciless mockery by the sceptical and free individual. That is why communication in the protests in Serbia had less the tone of moral condemnation of the regime, or a warlike summons to a showdown with it, than that of satirical ridicule, which did not baulk even at some pornographic solutions: 'An impotent leader gets the people up!' Throwing eggs at the buildings of state institutions and the media which marked the beginning of the protest in Belgrade (the 'yellow revolution') offered an exceptionally gratifying theme for slogans of this kind:[2] 'Serbia has eggs [balls]!' 'Why eggs [balls]? Let's give the comrades the thing in between.'

The citizen who protests as a responsible and sceptical individual is also suspicious of communication through slogans, because it is a form of communication aimed at suggestiveness, at 'beguiling', and is therefore characteristic of the language of political demagogy and advertising. This suspicion may be seen in a number of anti-slogans or, more exactly, empty slogans,—ones without a message: 'From tomorrow I promise a better placard', 'This is my slogan', 'Dare we carry this slogan?', 'It doesn't matter what it says here, what matters is what it's for', 'I am a living placard', 'Have you come here to protest or to stare at the placard?', 'This slogan doesn't name anyone'. Graphic solutions are also used: 'Little slogan, BIG SLOGAN'.

In addition to a commitment to democratic values, demand for respect for citizens' rights, and fostering a satirical, sceptical and individualistic style of political engagement and political communication, the messages 'broadcast' here also contain a strong aversion to nationalism, and its populist 'folklore' variant, and to political isolation, xenophobia and hatred. This aversion is expressed, above all, as a rejection of the main means of communication and its main themes at mass political demonstrations organised in 1988–9 as a sign of popular support for the then new star of Serbian politics, Slobodan Milošević.

'Serbia has risen. Put on the coffee!'

The demonstrations of that time—known as 'happenings of the people'—were dominated by communication inspired by folklore

---

[2] The word for egg, *'jaje'*, is also the word for 'ball' (testicle). (Transl.)

topoi (heroism, Kosovo, sacrifice, revenge, betrayal, Serbdom, graves, hearths, etc.) and forms (the decasyllabic line, archaic vocabulary and syntax), the proverb. But, during the protests of 1996–7 references to the folklore tradition appeared exclusively as parody—'Whoever is a Serb and of Serb blood and does not come to the fight on Plato, let him never get more than 5, may he rot as long as he studies'; and 'Cure Marko and send him to the army, Serbia cannot be pacified!' One of the main slogans of Serbian nationalism ten years ago was 'Serbia has risen!'. The current demonstrations produced the parodic variant: 'Serbia has risen. Put on the coffee!' For the protesting Serbian citizen of today, not even the old Serbian motto 'Only unity saves the Serb' was sacred, and he composed the slogan 'Only strolling saves the Serb'.[3]

Aversion to populist folklorism did not extend to supporters' folklore because, unlike the newly composed 'folk' songs, it was accepted as an integral part of urban youth culture. One of the most popular slogans of the protest was adopted from supporters of football and other teams: 'Come on! Let's go! All attack!' By contrast with the political folklorism at former Milošević populist demonstrations—the function of which was to advance the political solutions offered in 'popular speech' and thus legitimise the performances as something close to the people—symbolic communication in the 1996–7 protest fostered a new kind of urban political folklore, open to various influences. Among the elements from which slogans were composed, by means of 'bricolage' there were some from cartoon films, as in the cry 'Hey, Boss! Give us back our gains!', which undoubtedly imitates the Road Runner. Another cartoon hero, the Great Smurf, surfaced in the Belgrade demonstrations: 'You've out-smurfed yourself, Great Smurf!' The main character of a popular American TV series also had the honour of appearing on the Belgrade students' placards: 'Slaughter Nick for President!' However, the authors of the slogans, especially the students, did not find the stimulus for their creativity only in popular culture, but often turned also to the great figures of world literature. So in the streets of Belgrade democracy was defended by appeals to Shakespeare, Shelley, Dante ('Slobo, see you in the ninth circle. Dante.'), Orwell or Kafka ('I'm not Kafka, but I feel a trial coming on!').

This reaching out to a cosmopolitan pop-culture and world-famous writers was one of the most striking ways of manifesting one of the main desires of the protesting Serbian citizens and students, the desire

---

[3] See Calvet, 26–33, on parodic slogans and the 'kidnapping' of slogans.

to return to the world, from which Milošević had virtually excluded Serbia and the Serbs. Demonstrating that Serbia is Europe, that Belgrade is the world, that 'we' are a civilised democratic milieu, that we are able to cope with a dictator and his police in a peaceful and dignified way, was one of the most important messages that the participants in the protest in Serbia exchanged with each other, with the regime and with the world. As their main slogan the students did not choose any of those which spoke about the regime, electoral theft, or Milošević. Nor was it a slogan celebrating revolt, democracy or the law. Instead they gave priority to the message 'Belgrade is the world'. It was written on a large canvas banner which the students carried at the head of the column during every protest march through the Belgrade streets.

That Belgrade is the world was shown also by the numerous flags of foreign countries, car manufacturers (Ferrari, Fiat, Alfa Romeo, Opel) and football clubs (Inter) which fluttered, along with Serbian flags, over the mass of the demonstrators, particularly in the first weeks of the protest. The desire to show that they belonged to the world was demonstrated also by the abundance of placards and badges with texts in English: 'So, Slobo must go!', 'We are the champions!', 'Game over!', 'Students against the Machine!', 'Slo be or not Slo be, that is the question!' There was also at least one slogan in German: '500 + 50 *Was denn noch? Hilfe!*'

How important it was for the demonstrators in Serbia to send into the world an impressive picture of mass revolt, though of a non-violent character, against the Milošević regime may be seen also in their disappointment that it took more than ten days for the foreign media and politicians to take an interest in the events in Serbia. Placards immediately appeared expressing their anger at that indifference: 'Fuck you, deaf Europe!' or 'Europe sleeps, the media are silent, Serbia awakes ... God help us!' The same 'street media' registered satisfaction and pride in the images from the Belgrade streets which, accompanied by flattering commentaries, finally found their way on to the main CNN programmes and the front pages of the world's press, and when messages of support began to reach the organisers of the protests from abroad. Europe was no longer deaf to the Serbs and Serbian students, but smiled joyfully at them: 'The Student protest: the joy of Europe'. Sometimes, this support from the outside world grew into an image of 'cosmic' delight at the new democratic Serbia: 'We won't freeze this winter. The whole Solar System is with us.'

'I love you too'

The swift daily reactions to the regime's actions, to commentaries in the media it controlled, to international news, to statements by the opposition and student protest leaders, and to individual slogans and mottoes gave the communication which developed on the streets during the protest the character of an open tribune, a great debating club. On the same evening that transmission by the independent Radio B-92 was temporarily interrupted, allegedly, because 'water had got into the underground cable', slogans appeared on the street: 'Long live the underground cable', 'Long live aqua-Radio B-92'. A similar thing happened with the announcement by the regime functionary Dragan Tomić that the demonstrations had a fascistic character. Responses in the form of mock-fascist slogans on placards appeared immediately, the art of 'Halt, Tomić!', 'Herr Tomić, I am a manipulated fascist marcher'. The anti-German pronouncements of the regime propaganda were greeted with: 'Everything I have is German, on my Marks!' Milošević's wife travelled to India during the demonstrations, and the slogan—comment was: 'Go back to India. They don't kill cows there!' The constant attempts by the state media to play down the number of demonstrators by referring to them as a 'handful' (in the original a 'little fist') gave inspiration too: 'Don't play with a handful, you'll get the middle finger' or 'Don't let me beat my little fist on the table'.

When Milošević came out with his famous *Lex specialis*[4] the students immediately organised a 'Progamme specialis' at the Arts Faculty, and when at a demonstration of his supporters organised in Belgrade on 24 December Milošević responded to a voice from the audience 'We love you, Slobo!' by shouting 'I love you too', that was for days almost the only greeting among the demonstrators: 'I love you', 'I love you too'.

Current affairs also provided inspiration for the authors of slogans. Anything that could be used to ridicule the regime was seized upon. Everything was 'politicised' and 'Miloševićised'. That included sporting events as well. The defeat of Mike Tyson in his match with Holyfield inspired one of the 'walkers' to appear the next day with the words: 'Slobo, Tyson, you'll get your Holyfield!' The result of the football

---

[4] A special law without which there was allegedly no legal basis for recognising the results of the local elections in Serbia.

match between Spain and Yugoslavia, won 2:0 by Spain, engendered a slogan in which, as at the local elections, the will of the court transformed defeat into victory: 'Spain-Yugoslavia 0:2, Supreme Court of Serbia!' On the international day working the fight against AIDS (1 December), the students threw a heap of condoms onto the building of the Supreme Court of Serbia, and placed a large placard in front of it saying: 'Rubbers for robbers, so they can get it up without coming down with something'.

A kind of slogan debate was carried on among the participants in the demonstrations. For example, the message 'Slobo, go back to Loch Ness!' on one placard provoked the response, 'Don't dump any old rubbish in me. Loch Ness' which appeared in one of the following protest 'walks'. Likewise there was a response to one of the most popular slogans against Milošević, used in the demonstrations of 1992, 'Slobo, Saddam'. The response was 'Don't insult Saddam!' One 'debating' placard even had an address: 'A message to the creator of the placard: Better a pigeon in the hand than a sparrow in the bush'. It was followed by the explanation that the drawing illustrating this message, featuring Meštrović's statue 'The Victor', did not go with the text, because Meštrović had depicted a falcon, not a pigeon.

In this winter of Serbian discontent the hundreds of messages sent by the participants to the public, to Milošević's regime or 'the world' were extremely varied, and in many of them the political 'colour' could not easily be figured out. Indeed, a certain vagueness and ambiguity is characteristic of mass symbolic communication, as some of the participants in the protest knew. There was even one 'hermeneutic' slogan which spoke of the problem of understanding the meaning of communication at a protest: 'No one can describe us, we have to be experienced. The Students.' But, despite this ambivalence, many messages simply revealed ordinary disagreements and contradictions, because the people who had gathered at these demonstrations were all opponents of Milošević and supporters of a democratic Serbia, but at the same time often held very different views. However, as if by some tacit agreement, these differences were pushed into the background, and priority was given to manifesting the anti-regime unity and democratic choice of the protesters. This explains how the two great political themes—the Kosovo problem and Serbia's responsibility for the recent war—were largely ignored during the protest.

The few references to Kosovo and the war show just how much even those Serbs who seek and foresee a new, modern, democratic

Palm-reading and 'The Little Serbian Fist' 303

and European Serbia are divided or at least undecided over those questions. For instance, one student leaflet about the war speaks of a 'national catastrophe' because it ended in 'loss of territory' (*Republika*, 1–15 February 1997). By contrast, there were slogans which threatened Milošević with 'The Hague', such as 'We're off to democracy! You choose, mate: exile, asylum, The Hague'. Radically contrasting viewpoints are expressed also in connection with Kosovo. On the invitation of Vuk Drašković, the demonstrators observed a minute's silence in honour of the teacher of Albanian nationality, Feriz Blyachkori, who died from a beating in a police station in Kosovo. That was an exceptionally important event, an indication that even in Kosovo

A rock-climber flashes the traditional Serbian three-finger sign on top of the Belgrade City Hall as climbers remove the Communist star. The opposition took the capital from the Serbian President Slobodan Milošević's neo-Communists in December 2000. (AP photographer Srdjan Ilic)

better days may come. But, such optimism was spoiled by demonstrators who often shouted at police brought from all over the country to protect the government against them: 'Go to Kosovo!'

At the end of this attempt to interpret the symbolic communication that took place during the protests in Serbia—to read the palms of the 'handful' of Serbian citizens and students who protested against Milošević, I shall repeat my answer given in a questionnaire (*Vreme*, 18 January 1997) to the question: what awaits us after the protests? I said that the carnival would come to an end, and so too would solidarity generated by the revolt against a hated regime, and a less euphoric and far more difficult process of forging democracy, would begin. That would not entail a search for a mythic lost national slogan, offered by totalitarian systems which usually smell of gunpowder or incense or both at the same time, but the beginning of something less seductive, and more prosaic: the beginning of democratically articulated conflicts, friction and political battles. I completed my response with the perhaps startling announcement: 'I look forward to the time when there is no need, as there has been in recent weeks, for me to tolerate any fools just because they are against Milošević.' But, in those days of general euphoria, to which I myself gave in from time to time, I felt a need to acknowledge that among those brave and united fighters for democracy in Serbia there were numerous people who would be its future enemies.

Epilogue (November 2000)
Heavenly Serbia comes down to Earth

In driving Milošević out Mr Koštunica, Mr Djindić and the others have done a great thing. And they have refrained and continue to refrain from grand words and grand gestures. It seems that they do not wish to be 'great people', or to address their nation as a 'great nation'. The inauguration of the new head of state was brief, without pomp, fanfares, church bells or gun-salutes. His oath of allegiance to the Constitution bore no resemblance to a marriage between the leader and the people. The ceremony was more reminiscent of the muted ritual of a civil wedding. The new president did not kiss anything— the earth, an icon, or the flag. He did not give us a formal speech about heroes, victory and glory. Instead, for his first address to the citizens as head of state, Koštunica chose a so-called 'contact' programme on television, and his 'messages to the people' came in the form of answers to questions from the programme's presenter and its viewers. Among them was a lady who congratulated the new president with the remark that 'the last one wasn't all that bad either'. Never before has a Serbian leader conversed in this way with the citizens. This is one reason for believing that Serbia has set off along the road of democracy, or at least that its new government intends to take that road. As Napoleon's mother said on hearing the news that her son had become an emperor, 'Long may it last [*Pourvu que ça dure*]!'

It is not easy to entrench imperial power, to oblige the people to worship one man as a god. But it seems that it is no easier to realise the opposite aim, to break people of the habit of living and dying in the shadow of an untouchable leader, bewitched and lulled by his sweet and poisonous words. The people in Serbia have on the whole taken the fall of the Milošević regime easily, many with relief and enthusiasm. The news 'He's finished!', 'It's over!', 'Slobo's dead!' was greeted joyfully, with almost unanimous approval. But for many it was not sufficiently good news, because it was incomplete, not having been fully articulated. It announced the death of a leader, the end of a figure, a name, a story. But it left out the announcement of a new name. The picture of the new boss was not immediately placed in the empty frame left for the president's portrait. More precisely, a certain Mr Koštunica began to appear here and there in the function of the newly-elected president of the Federal Republic of Yugoslavia. But not only did this person not look like a great untouchable leader, but it was evident that he himself did not think that he could fill the enormous void which Milošević had left behind. He announced that he did not intend to move into the vacated presidential residence.

There are quite a number of people in Serbia who find it hard to reconcile themselves to this. Many hurried to complete the announcement of Milošević's political death on their own initiative with the announcement of the arrival of a new messiah, shouting: 'Slobo's dead! Long live Voja!'[1] They would like once again to have before them and above them someone great and wise, who would occupy the White Palace and from there tell them everything they needed to know. Speaking of the difficulty of adjusting to democracy and life without a great leader, the psychologist Mikloš Biro describes the panic reaction of one of his relatives who, on hearing the new president's statement that he did not intend to stay in office for more than eighteen months, said: 'What's this man thinking of, saying he'll be President for only a year and a half? We've only just found him!' *Politika*, the daily newspaper which faithfully served Milošević, and is now trying to ingratiate itself with the new authorities, published an open letter from a reader addressed to our new president, in which the writer described him as a great man who has 'a special intellect which may be discerned through the shaft of his sincere, but steely gaze, through the gesture of his firm hand and through the power of his warm, human words.' I felt like saying: 'For god's sake, woman, have you forgotten that someone just like that—of steely gaze and warm words—has been sucking our blood for more than ten years?'

I hope that the new democratic authorities in Serbia will refuse

---

[1] Short, informal version of Koštunica's first name, Vojislav—the equivalent of 'Slobo' for Slobodan. (Transl.)

various invitations, proposals and wishes to continue Serbian politics in the grand style, whatever the cost. And proposals of this kind are coming from all directions. We hear that these politics have to be the work of a great leader and generally of a great people, but even more often we hear that Serbia must continue to be administered like the country of a proven great people—indeed, from many points of view the greatest. Who knows when that story came into being, but in the propaganda of Milošević's regime it experienced a new youth. It served to present the misery and shame in which we were living as the dignified suffering of the Serbian people, a righteous people among terrible, unduly strong enemies, suffering which the Serbian people accepted as a sacrifice ordained by providence for the salvation of all of mankind. They explained to us that the world, mired in sin, could not for the moment see or understand this sacrifice of ours, but one day it would come to its senses and give us our due recognition.

Judging by some statements and commentaries published since 5 October, that moment has arrived! They describe the destruction of Milošević as an event without precedent, as an exploit of planetary dimensions, through which our people gave an example to the whole world of how to love and achieve freedom. 'The world is amazed at the Serbs' love of freedom and expresses its readiness to help,' one believer explains. The world now 'admires' us, but without knowing why, just as, previously it 'hated us'—also without knowing why. In the words of the so-called Serbian patriots—harnessed till yesterday to Milošević's carriage, but now presenting themselves as champions of democracy—there may be reason in the outside world, but there is no soul or heart. These organs of feeling, faith and fairness may be found only in Serbian breasts, and perhaps in those of some other Balkan peoples—hence, our 'patriots' explain, the uninterrupted lack of understanding that prevails between ourselves and the world. It endures even when the world likes and admires us, as it does today when we are once again demonstrating our greatness.

This is equally true of the foreign journalists who followed the 'Serbian democratic revolution'. It was said in a newspaper report devoted to them that these journalists, seeing with their own eyes what the Serbs achieved on 5 October 2000, experienced the miraculous feeling, described in her time by the English writer Rebecca West, that 'they were suddenly irrationally in love with the Serbs'. 'This will not last, of course,' added the author of this report, 'nor will they be able to explain it to themselves when they return to their rational countries.' Not even Prince Alexander Karadjordjević, who hurried to Serbia to great the victory of democracy, could resist the cliché of pseudo-patriotic rhetoric: he announced that he had come 'to greet a people who have once again amazed Europe and the world'. It was not clear to which earlier amazing Serbian exploits Prince Alexander was referring—I trust he was not thinking of events over the last decade.

There is a long list of dangers, problems, trials and obstacles which the new democratic powers in Serbia will have to confront. Somewhere near the top of the list I see the problem of liquidating political rhetoric based on images and characters which can hardly survive in democratic political discourse. Among them are the figures mentioned here of the great leader and the great people. The democratic authorities must refuse to allow their ideas, their thoughts, their words to move into the vampires' house of so-called Heavenly Serbia, just as Mr Koštunica has refused to move into the residence of its deposed leader and take his place on the empty throne. This is a question not of modesty but of meaning.

Appendixes

A. *Key Characters and Concepts*

Arkan, see Ražnatović

Baja Mali Knindža. Stage name of the contemporary Serbian folk poet Mirko Pajčin, who attracted attention with his patriotic songs about the recent wars in Croatia and Bosina.

Branković, Djuradj, Despot (c. 1375–1456). Ruler (Despot) of Serbia, 1427–56. He founded the city of Smederevo on the Danube and made it his cpaital.

Branković, Vuk (?–1389). Son-in-law of Prince Lazar, died at the battle of Kosovo. In the songs about that battle he is represented as a traitor responsible for the Serbian defeat, which is historically inaccurate.

Čaruga. Nickname of Jovan Stanisavljević (1897–1924), an outlaw who operated in Slavonia after the First World War. A legend grew up around him in which he emerged as the Slav Robin Hood.

Ćosić, Dobrica (b. 1921). Serbian writer and member of the Serbian Academy of Science and Arts, credited with an important role in the formation of contemporary Serbian nationalism. He was elected as the first President of the Federal Republic of Yugoslavia in 1992, but replaced soon afterwards.

Cvijić, Jovan (1865–1927). Professor of Geography, Vice-Channcellor of the University of Belgrade, and president of the Serbian Academy of Sciences. He wrote many important works about the geography of the Balkan peninsula.

dahia (Turkish). A commander of the Janissaries. At the beginning of the nineteenth century, a group of *dahias* who had cut their ties with the Porte took power in the Belgrade *pashalik*. The terror they perpetrated aginst the population provoked an uprising of Serbs, which at first was directed against the *dahias*, but later became a revolt against central Turkish power.

Dušan, Tsar (*c.* 1308–55). King of Serbia from 1331 proclaimed Tsar in 1346. In 1349 he promulgated a code of laws, known today as 'Dušan's Code'. Under his rule, the medieval Serbian state attained its greatest territorial extent.

Fighters' Day (4 July). Holiday introduced after the Second World War by the Communist government in Yugoslavia to commemerate the decision of the Communist Party of Yugoslavia on 4 July 1941 to rise against the German occupation. It has remained in the calendar of the Federal Republic of Yugoslavia.

Giška. Nickname of Djordje Božović (1955–91), a criminal with a European police record. At the beginning of the war with Croatia, in 1991, he became commander of the Serbian Guard, a voluntary unit supported by the Serbian Movement of Renewal, and died in the fighting around Gospić.

gusle. Traditional one-stringed musical instrument played with a bow, widespread in the Balkans, probably originating from Asia.

hajduk (Turkish). Outlaw, bandit. In Balkan lands under Turkish rule a legend came into being about the *hajduks* as fighters against Turkish violence and national avengers. This is how they are presented in the songs collected and published in the nineteenth century by Vuk Karadžić.

Hajduk Veljko. Popular name of Veljko Petrović (?1780–1813), a *hajduk* from eastern Serbia who became one of the most prominent leaders and heroes of the First Serbian Uprising against Turkish rule (1804–13).

Kapetan Dragan. Wartime name of Dragan Vasiljković, a military instructor and commander of a unit of Serbs in western Croatia (Knin) at the beginning of the war in Croatia in 1991.

Karadjordje. Nickname of Djordje Petrović (1768–1817), leader of the first uprising against the Turks (1804–13). Founder of the Karadjordjević dynasty.

Karadžić, Radovan (b. 1945). Medical doctor and writer, from 1992 leader of the Bosnian Serbs and first president of Republika Srpska. In 1996 he was placed on the list of those charged with war crimes by the International Tribunal for War Crimes on the Territory of Former Yugoslavia in The Hague.

Karadžić, Vuk Stefanović (1787–1864). Philologist, ethnologist and historian, who laid the foundations of the modern Serbian language and literature.

Karić brothers. Four brothers born in Peć, Kosovo, who became successful businessmen after Milošević came to power. Bogoljub Karić in particular is, among other things, the founder and proprietor of the large Karić Brothers

Key Characters and Concepts 311

company, which includes a bank of the same name. Today he is one of the wealthiest people in Serbia.

Lazar, Knez/Tsar or Prince Lazar Hrebeljanović (c. 1329–89). Ruler of Serbia from 1371, he led the Serbian army in the battle of Kosovo (1389), where he died. He is the subject of many works of medieval Serbian religious and traditional literature.

Majka Jugovića (the Mother of the Jugovići). Figure from Serbian traditional songs about the battle of Kosovo, which describe among other things the heroic death of her husband Jug and their nine sons.

Maritsa. River in Bulgaria, on the right bank of which, by the town of Černomen, a battle was fought in 1371 between the Turkish army and King Vukašin and Despot Uglješa, ending in the defeat and death of the Serbian landowners.

Marko, Kraljević or Prince (c. 1335–1395). Son of King Vukašin, who ruled after his father's death in 1371 as a Turkish vassal. South Slav traditional literature celebrates him as a great and indomitable hero.

Marković, Mira (Mirjana). Professor of Sociology and founder of the Yugoslav United Left party (1995). She is the wife of the former president of the Federal Republic of Yugoslavia, Slobodan Milošević.

Marković, Svetozar (1846–75). Politician and writer, founder of the socialist movement in Serbia.

Mrnjavčević brothers. Vukašin and Jovan Uglješa Mrnjavčević, medieval landowners, who died in 1371 in a battle against the Turks on the river Maritsa, now in Bulgaria.

Mujo. Diminutive of the name Muhammad, which served a a colloquial ethnonym for a Bosnian Muslim (Bosniak) in former Yugoslavia.

Musa Kesedžija. Turkish outlaw in the traditional song. 'Kraljević Marko and Musa Kesedžija'.

Nemanja, Rastko. See Sava, Saint

Nemanja, Stefan (1114–1200). Ruler of the medieval Serbian state of Raška (1168–96), founder of the Nemanjić dynasty, and father of Saint Sava. He became a monk in 1196 under the name of Simeon, and founded the Chilandar monastery on Mount Athos.

Njegoš, Petar Petrović (1813–51). Montenegrin head of church and state, author of the epic *The Mountain Wreath* (1847), which is seen today as one of the most important nineteenth-century works of Montenegrin and Serbian literature.

Obilić, Miloš. Hero of Serbian medieval and traditional literature; according to legend, at the battle of Kosovo (1389) at the cost of his own life he killed the Turkish Sultan Murat.

Obradović, Dositej (1742–1811). Writer and pedagogue who strove to introduce the heritage of European culture and education into Serbia. First Minister of Education in Serbia (1811).

Obrenović, Milan (1854–1901). Prince (from 1868) and King (1882–9) of Serbia.

Pašić, Nikola (1845–1926). Serbian and Yugoslv politician; one of the founders (1881) of the Popular Radical Party. He served several terms as Prime Minister or minister in the government.

Pavelić, Ante (1889–1959). President of the Indepedent State of Croatia (1941–4), the fascist state founded under Nazi aegis.

Plavšić, Biljana. Professor of biology and politician, who during the war in Bosnia (1992–5) was one of the closest aides of the former leader of the Bosnian Serbs, Radovan Karadžić, and after the end of the war, became for a time president of Republika Srpska.

Princip, Gavrilo (1894–1918). On 28 June 1914 in Sarajevo assassinated the heir to the Austrian throne, Archduke Franz Ferdinand, and his wife Sophie.

Ranković, Aleksandar (1909–83). Yugoslav Communist leader and head of State Security in Tito's Yugoslavia until 1966, when he was dismissed from all his functions and expelled from the Communist Party.

Ražnatović, Željko 'Arkan' (1955–2000). Criminal with a police record in several European countries. In 1990 he became leader of the supporters of the Red Star Belgrade football club, and in 1991 founded the Serbian Voluntary Guard, which participated in the war in Croatia and Bosnia and Herzegovina (1991–5). He was gunned down in a Belgrade hotel on 15 January 2000.

Sava, Saint. Rastko Nemanjić (c. 1174–1235), youngest son of Stefan Nemanja, first Archbishop of Serbia and writer. He became a monk in 1192, under the name of Sava.

Serdar Janko Vukotić (1866–1927). Prominent officer in the Montenegrin amry and from 1919 general in the Yugoslav army; he made his name in the Balkan Wars (1912–3) and the First World War.

sevdalinka. Traditional love-song of oriental origin, most widespread in Bosnia.

Skerlić, Jovan (1877–1914). Serbian literary historian and critic.

Key Characters and Concepts

štafeta (baton). The first *Titova štafeta* (Tito's baton) was organised on 25 May 1945 in honour of Josip Broz Tito's fifty-third birthday. The baton was carried by schoolchildren through all the Yugoslav republics and on 25 May formally handed to the President. From 1957 the ritual became part of the celebrations of Youth Day (*Dan mladosti*).

Starčević, Ante (1823–96). Croatian politician and writer, founder of the Party of Rights.

Starina Novak. Legendary bandit (*hajduk*) leader on Mount Romanija in Bosnia.

Tesla, Nikola (1856–1943). Physicist and electrical engineer, originally a Serb from the Lika region (Croatia), who later worked in the United States and attained world renown.

Uroš, Tsar. Serbian ruler 1355–71, son of Tsar Dušan.

uskoci. Refugees from Bosnia and Herzegovina after the Turkish conquests in the fifteenth century, who secretly returned and crossed into occupied territory and attacked the Turkish forces (their name comes from the verb '*uskočiti*', 'to jump into'). Their exploits are the subject of several traditional songs.

Vidovdan. St. Vitus Day, 28 June, the day of the battle of Kosovo (and of the assassination of Franz Ferdinand), originates in the name of the old Slav god Vid. In 1892 Vidovdan was incorporated into the calendar of feast days of the Serbian Orthodox Church.

vila, a female being of supernatural powers who appears in South Slav mythology and traditional literature.

Vrbica, or Lazar's Saturday, a spring festival in Serbia. On that day children go to church in their best clothes wearing little bells round their necks, and they are handed *vrbice* (birch twigs) which have been blessed.

B. Main Political Parties of Serbia

Civic Alliance of Serbia (GSS). Founded in 1992. Promotes a civic and pro-European orientation in home and foreign policy. The leader was first Vesna Pešić, and from 1999 Goran Svilanović.

Democratic Party (DS). Founded in 1990. Defines itself as a party of the centre. The leader was first Dragoljub Mićunović, followed in 1994 by Zoran Djindjić. In the 1966 elections it gained control of several municipalities in Serbia.

Democratic Party of Serbia (DSS). A party of the conservative nationalist Right which came into being in 1992, with the departure of several members of the Democratic Party, who did not accept the decision of the leadership of the DS not to participate in DEPOS (Democratic Movement of Serbia), a coalition formed at that time. The leader is Vojislav Koštunica.

Serbian Party of Renewal (SPO). Founded in 1990. The leader of the party since its inception is Vuk Drašković. The most influential opposition party in Serbia. It criticised the warmongering and nationalist policies of the regime in Serbia from populist and traditionalist positions. In 1996, the SPO took control of the city council of Belgrade.

Serbian Radical Party (SRS). Founded in 1991. The leader of this ultra-nationalist party is Vojislav Šešelj. At first the party was in opposition, but after 1998 it became the coalition partner of SPS and JUL in the so-called 'government of national unity' in Serbia.

Socialist Party of Serbia (SPS). Came into being as a fusion of the League of Communists of Serbia with the Socialist Union of the Working People of Serbia (SSRNS) at the 'Congress of Unification' on 16 July 1990. The leader of the SPS is Slobodan Milošević. The strongest party in the coalition of three parties which formed the government of Serbia until October 2000. Proclaiming itself a left-wing party, in political practice some of its procedures are characteristic of the extreme nationalist Right.

Yugoslav United Left (JUL). Founded in 1995 as an alliance of several small Communist and left-wing parties and organisations. The President of the Directorate of JUL is Mirjana Marković, wife of Slobodan Milošević. JUL participated in the 'government of national unity'. According to the results of elections, the party did not have support among the electorate, but it was well represented in the government.

Bibliography

Adorno, Theodor, *The Jargon of Authenticity*, London, 1973.
Arsenijević, Matej, 'Pravoslavlje i rat' in *Jagnje božije i zvijer iz bezdana. Filosofija rata*, Cetinje, 1996.
Avramović, Zoran, 'Fijuk metka najpre se čuje u mislima' in I. Čolović, and A. Mimica, (ed.), *Intelektualci i rat*, Belgrade, 1993.
Baczko, Bronislaw, *Les imaginaires sociaux. Mémoires et espoirs collectifs*, Paris, 1984.
Bandić, Dušan, *Narodna religija Srba u 100 pojmova*, Belgrade, 1991.
Barjaktarević, Mirko, *O zemljišnim medjama*, Belgrade, 1952.
Bastide, Roger, *Le Rêve, la Transe et la Folie*, Paris, 1972.
Bećković, Matija, *Lele i kuku*, Belgrade, 1978.
——, *Kaza*, Belgrade, 1989.
——, 'Srbija nema prečih zadataka nego da je ima', *Književne novine*, no. 772, Belgrade, 1989.
Begić, Midhat, 'Jovan Skerlić i njegovo doba', introduction in Jovan Skerlić, *Odabrani kritički spisi*, 1950.
Bellenger, Lionel, *La Persuasion*, Paris, 1985.
Bielefeld, Uli, 'L'état-nation inachevé, xénophobie, racisme et violence en Allemagne à la fin du vingtième siècle' in D. Juteau. M. El Yamani (eds), *Le racisme à la fin du XXe siècle. Une perspective internationale*, Montreal, 1993.
Bielefeld, Uli, 'Existence et image de l'étranger en Allemagne' in B. Falga *et al.* (eds), *Au miroir de l'autre*, Paris, 1994.
Bonazzi, Tiziano, 'Mito politico' in *Dizionario di politica*, Milan 1980.
Braudel, Fernand, *L'identité de la France*, vol. I: *L'espace et l' histoire*, Paris, 1986.
Bromberger, Christian, Alain Hayot, Jean-March Mariottini, 'Allez l'OM! Forza Juve! La passion pour le football à Marseille et à Turin, *Terrain* 8, April 1987.

Buden, Boris, *Barikade*, Zagreb, 1996.
Bulat, Petar, *Mati Zemlja*, Zagreb, 1930.
Bulić, Vanja, *Tunel*, Belgrade, 1996.
Caillat, Michel, *L'idéologie du sport en France*, Paris, 1989.
Čajkanović, Veselin, *Mit i religija u Srba*, Belgrade, 1973.
Cassirer, Ernst, *Le myth de l'état*, Paris, 1992.
——, 'Iz srpske religije i mitologije, I: Majka Jugovića', Zabavnik, Dodatak *Srpskih novina*, 15 September 1918.
Čolović, Ivan and Aljoša Mimica, *Druga Srbija*, Belgrade, 1992.
——, and Aljoša, Mimica, *Intelektualci i rat*, Belgrade, 1993.
——, *Bordel ratnika*, Belgrde, 1993.
——, *Pucanje od zdravlja*, Belgrade, 1994.
Cvijić, Jovan, *Osnovi jugoslovenske civilizacije*, Zagreb, 1922.
Desnica, Gojko, *Borba Srba za opstanak države 1300 godina (690–1900)*, Belgrade, 1990.
Ditchev, Ivaylo, 'Balkans, le complexe des ancêtres', *Libération*, Paris, 14 November 1994.
Djordjević, Tihomir, *Iz Srbije Kneza Miloša*, I: *Kulturne prilike*, Belgrade, 1922; II: *Stanovništvo-naselja*, Belgrade, 1924.
——, *Naš narodni život*, I–IV, Belgrade, 1984.
Djurdjević, Ratibor and M., Rajko, *Srbin povratnik medju Novosrbima*, Belgrade, 1996.
Djuretić, Veselin, 'Sistematizovati istorijska iskustva, pa se na njihovoj osnovi odredjivati prema budućnosti', in *Srpsko pitanje danas*, Drugi kongres srpskih intelektualaca, Belgrade, 1955.
Djurić, Vojislav, *Antologija narodnih junačkih pesama*, 12th edn, SKZ, Belgrade, 1989.
Durand, Gilbert, *Structures anthropologiques de l'imaginaire*, Paris, 1969.
——, *Introduction à la mythodologie*, Paris, 1995.
Ehrenberg, Alain, 'La rage de paraître' in 'L'amour foot', *Autrement*, no. 80, 1986.
Eliade, Mircea, *Histoire des croyances et des idées religieuses*, I, 1976.
Garde, Paul, *Vie et mort de la Yougoslavie*, Paris, 1992.
Gezeman, Gerhard, *Čojstvo i junaštvo starih Crnogoraca*, Cetinje, 1968.
Girardet, Raoul, *Mythes et mythologies politiques*, Paris, 1986.
Gojković, Drinka, 'Trauma bez katarze' in Nebojša Popov (ed.), *Srpska strana rata*, Belgrade, 1996.
Hobsbawm, Eric, J., *Nations and Nationalism since 1780. Programme, Myth, Reality*, Cambridge, 1990.
Ivas, Ivan, *Ideologija u govoru*, Zagreb, 1988.
Iveković, Rada, 'Femmes, nationalisme et guerre', *Peuples Méditerranéens*, Paris, October–December 1992.
Janković, Djordje, 'O jedinstvenom pristupu našoj arheološkoj baštini' in *Srpsko pitanje danas*, Belgrade, 1995.

Jevtić, Atanasije, 'Kosovsko opredeljenje za carstvo nebesko u istorijskoj sudbini srpskog naroda' in *Sveti knez Lazar. Spomenica o šestoj stogodišnjici kosovskog boja 1389–1989*, Belgrade, 1989.
Jevtović, Vladimir (ed.), *Neposlušni bumerang*, Belgrade, 1989.
Kalajić, Dragoš, 'Ka Slovenskoj imperiji', *Naše ideje*, Belgrade, July 1993.
Kalajić, Dragoš, 'Srbi brane Evropu', *Duga*, 15 June 1995.
Kara-Pešić, Živojin, 'Naličje reči' in I. Čolović and A. Mimica (eds), *Druga Srbija*, Belgrade, 1992.
Kerényi, Ch., 'De l'origine et du fondement de la mythologie' in K.K. Jung and Ch. Kerényi, *Introduction à l'essence de la mythologie*, Paris, 1968.
Kinglake, A.V., 'Od Zemuna do Niša' in *Britanski putnici o našim krajevima*, selected, translated and introduced by Branko Momčilović, Novi Sad, 1996.
Kiš, Danilo, *Čas anatomije*, Belgrade, 1978.
Kleut, Marija, 'Srpski mit: opasan i dvosmislen', *Letopis Matice srpske*, October 1993.
Knežević, Miloš, 'Vizantizam u tumačenju zla', in *Srpska Vizantija*, Belgrade, 1993.
Komnenić, Milan, 'Glas praštaoca', *Književne novine*, 1. X 1989.
Koljević, Nikola, *Otadžbinske teme*, Belgrade, 1995.
Korać, Maksim, 'Rasrbljivanje—veća tragedija od kosovske pogibije', in *Srpsko pitanje danas*, Belgrade, 1995.
Kovačević, Ivan, 'Fudbalski ritual', *Gledišta*, nos 5–6, Belgrade, 1987.
Krajina, Mile, *Vukovare, hrvatski viteže*, Čakovec, 1994.
Lacoue-Labarthe, Philippe, Jean-Luc and Nancy, *Le mythe nazi*, Strasbourg, 1991.
Lalić, Dražen, 'Nasilništvo nogometnih navijača. Geneze fenomena u Jugoslaviji', *Kultura*, no 88–90, Belgrade, 1990.
Lalić, Dražen, A., Luburić, and N., Bulat, *Grafiti i subkultura*, Zagreb, 1991.
Lalić, Lazar, *Tri TV godine u Srbiji*, Belgrade, 1995.
Lauer, Reinhard, 'Od ubica postaju junaci—o herojskoj poeziji Srba', translated by Zlatko Krasni, *Zbilja* (Belgrade), 31 May 1994.
Lavalée, Théophile, *Les Frontières de France*, Paris, 1864.
Limbergen, Kris van, 'Fudbalski vandalizam', edited and translated from the Flemish by Mira Bogdanović, *Kultura*, no. 88–90 (Belgrade), 1990.
Losonczy, A.-M., and A. Zemleni, 'Anthropologie de la *patrie*. Le patriotisme hongrois', *Terrain*, no. 17 (Paris), 1991.
Lovrenović, Ivan, 'Bosna u ljudima', *Erasmus*, no. 15 (Zagreb) 1996.
Lukić, Radomir, 'Značaj boja na Kosovu, kosovska epika i kosovski mit—simbol očuvanja srpske nacionalne svesti', *Politika*, 28 June 1989.
Maffesoli, Michel, 'Hooligans', *Globe*, no. 49, 1990.
Markov, Madan. *Smutnoe vreme*, Belgrade, 1976.
Marković, Mihailo, *Izabrana dela*, vol. 8: *Osporavanja i angažovanja*, Belgrade, 1994.

Marković, Vera, 'Zašto su samo navijači u napadu?', *Kultura* no. 88–90 (Belgrade), 1990.

Mićković, Radoš and Aćim Višnjić, *Komandant Srpske garde Gižka Plamen*, Belgrade, 1992.

Mihailescu, Vintila, 'Nos frères d'au-delà. Voisinages, passages et frontières en Roumanie', *Civilisations*, vol. XLII, (Bruxelles), 1994.

Mihović, Dragan, *Rat su započeli mrtvi*, Belgrade, 1993.

Milosavljević, Olivera, 'Jugoslavija kao zabluda' in Nebojša Popov (ed.), *Srpska strana rata*, Belgrade, 1996.

Milošević, Predrag, *Sveti ratnici. Borilačke veštine Srba*, Gornji Milanovac, Priština, 1989.

Milza, Pierre, 'Le football italien', quoted from Ignacio Ramonet, 'Le football, c'est la guerre', *Quel Corps?*, Paris, July 1990.

Mišić, Zoran, *Kritika pesničkog iskustva*, Belgrade, 1976.

Mladenović, R.M. and J. Ćulibrk (eds), *Jagnje božije i zvijer iz bezdana*, Cetinje, 1997.

Muller, Jean-Marie, *Strategija nenasilnog djelovanja*, translated by Stipe Bagarić, Zagreb, 1986.

Nedeljković, Dragan, *Reči Srbima u smutnom vremenu*, Belgrade, 1996.

——, 'Podvišnici i pravednici', *Letopis Matice srpske*, July–August, 1997.

Negrišorac, Ivan, 'Srpsko pesništvo i pitanje opstanka', *Letopis Matice srpske*, October, 1992.

Nenadović, Aleksandar, '"Politika" u nacionalističkoj oluji' in Nebojša Popov (ed.), *Srpska strana rata*, Belgrade, 1996.

Nogo, Rajko Petrov, 'Grbavi od istorije', afterword to Koljević Nikola, *Otadžbinske teme*, Belgrade, 1995.

Novaković, Stojan, *Dvadeset godina ustavne politike u Srbiji*, 1883–1903, Belgrade, 1912.

Ognjanović, Dragutin, 'Celovitost nacionalnog duhovnog i kulturnog bića, njegova obnova i preporod' in *Srpsko pitanje danas*, Belgrade, 1995.

Pagès, Didier, 'Football. Ceux qui vont mourir te saluent ou à qui profite le crime?', *Quel Corps?* (Paris), July 1990.

Perasović, Benjamin, 'Sportsko huliganstvo kao subkulturna pojava', *Pitanja*, nos 5–6 (Zagreb), 1988.

Perović, Latinka, 'Rusija i Evropa N.J. Danilevskog i njeni odjeci u Srbiji, special number of the paper *Republika*, January 1994.

——, 'Beg od modernizacije', in Nebojša Popov (ed.), *Srpska strana rata*, Belgrade, 1996.

Petrović, Krešimir, 'Nasilje i sport', *Kultura*, no. 88–90 (Belgrade), 1990.

Plumyène, Jean, *Histoire du nationalisme*, I: *Le XIX siècle. Les nations romantiques*, Paris, 1979.

Poliakov, Léon, *Le Mythe aryen. Essai sur les sources du racisme et des nationalismes*, Brussels, 1987.

Popov, Nebojša (ed.), *Srpska strana rata*, Belgrade, 1996. English translation: *The Road to war in Serbia: trauma and catharsis*, Budapest, 2000.

Popović, Justin, *Filozofske urvine*, Munich, 1957.
Prošić-Dvornić, Mirjana, 'Modeli retradicionalizacije: put u budućnost kroz vraćanje u prošlost', *Glasnik Etnografskg instituta SANU*, 1995.
Prpa-Jovanović, Branka, 'Izmedju Istoka i Zapada. Kulturni identitet i kulturno-civilizacijska uporišta', *Tokovi istorije*, 3–4 (Belgrade), 1997.
Radić, Radmila, 'Crkva i "srpsko pitanje"' in Nebojša Popov (ed.), *Srpska strana rata*, Belgrade, 1996.
Radović, Amfilohije, 'Vaskrsenja ne biva bez smrti', *Pobjeda*, 19 October 1991, in *Vraćanje duše u čistotu*, Podgorica, 1992.
Reboul, Olivier, *Le Slogan*, Brussels, 1995.
Reljić, Dušan, 'Zločinci za pisaćim stolom' in I. Čolović and A. Mimica (eds), *Intelektualci i rat*, Belgrade, 1993.
Rex, John, 'Stratégies antiracistes en Europe' in Michel Wieviorka (ed.), *Racisme et modernité*, Paris, 1993.
Rougemont, Denis de, *La part du Diable*, Paris, 1982.
Ršumović, Lj. R. Stanojević, and M. Tomić, *Crvena zvezda. Monografija*, Belgrade, 1986.
Samardžić, Radovan, *Ideje za srpsku istoriju*, Belgrade, 1989.
———, *Kosovsko opredeljenje. Istorijski ogledi*, Belgrade, 1990.
Saratlić, Rada, *Intelektualac u smutnom vremenu*, Belgrade, 1996.
Schmaus, Alois, 'Miloš Obilić u narodnom pesništvu i kod Njegoša' in *Gesammelte slavistische und balkanologistiche Abhändlungen*, 1970.
Skerlić, Jovan, *Svetozar Marković*, Belgrade, 1910.
———, *Istorija nove srpske književnosti* (A History of New Serbian Literature), Belgrade, 1913.
———, *Eseji o srpsko-hrvatskom pitanju* (Essays on the Serbo-Croatian question), Zagreb, 1918.
———, *Jakov Ignjatović*, Belgrade, 1922.
———, *Srpska književnost u XVIII veku* (Serbian Literature in the 18th century), Belgrade, 1923.
———, *Omladina i njena književnost* (The Serbian Youth Movement and its Literature), Belgrade, 1925.
———, *Književene studije* (Literary Studies), Book One, edited by Svetislav Petrović and Miodrag Ibrovac, Belgrade SKZ, 1934.
———, *Odabrani kritički spisi* (Selected Critical Writings), Belgrade, 1950.
———, *Feljtoni, skice i govori* (Feuilletons, sketches and speechs), Belgrade, 1964.
———, *Kritički radovi* (Critical works), edited by Predrag Palavestra, Belgrade, 1976.
Striković, Jovan, *Doba ravnodušnih*, Belgrade, 1996.
Subotić, Dragan, 'Pravoslavlje iznad Istoka i Zapada u bogoslovskoj misli Nikolaja Velimirovića i Justina Popovića' in *Šta nam nudi pravoslavlje danas?*, Niš, 1993.
Taguieff, Pierre-André, 'La lutte contre le racisme, par-delà illusions et désillusions' in *Face au racisme*, Paris, 1991.

Tassin, Etienne, 'Identités nationales et citoyenneté', paper given at the colloquium 'European Identities', Faaborg, June 1993.
Thompson, Mark, *Forging War: The Media in Serbia, Croatia and Bosnia-Herzegovina*, London 1994.
Todorov, Cvetan, *Mi i drugi*, translated by B. Jelić, M. and M. Zdravković, Belgrade, 1994.
Tonnies, Ferdinand, *Communauté et société*, Paris, 1944.
Velimirović, Nikolaj, *Vidovdanski govor*, Kragujevac, 1939.
———, *Rat i Biblija*, Belgrade 1993.
Velmar-Janković, Vladimir, *Pogled sa Kalemegdana. Ogled o beogradskom čoveku*, Belgrade 1938. (References are to the 1991 edition.)
Vujović Sreten, *Grad u senci rata*, Belgrade, 1997.
Vukotić, Bojana, 'Srpski fašizam i umetnost', *Sociološki pregled*, Belgrade, vol. XXVI, nos 1–4, 1992.
Wieviorka, Michel, (ed.), *Racisme et modernité*, Paris, 1992.
Wilpert, Czarina, 'Les fondements institutionnels et idéologiques du racisme dans la République fédérale d'Allemagne' in Michel Wieviorka (ed.), *Racisme et modernité*, Paris, 1993.
Žanić, Ivo, *Smrt crvenog fiće*, Zagreb, 1993.
———, 'Zvonimir na remontu. Politika kao pučka književnost', *Erasmus*, no. 15, Zagreb, 1996.

Index

Aćin, J. 234
Adorno, Theodore 149; *The Jargon of Authenticity* 289–90
Aksakov, Ivan Sergeyevitch 90
Albanians 171
Alexander the Great 76
Amfilohije, Metropolitan 168, 235
Andrić, Ivo 126, 184
Antić, Hadži Dragan 222
Antić, Radomir 166;
Arapović (basketball player) 262
Arkan *see* Ražnatović, Željko
Arsenijević, Mateja 253
Atanasije, Bishop 168

Baczko, Bronisław 81
Baja Mali Knindža 309
Bakunin, Mikhail 95
Baletić, G. 234
Balkan Wars 12
Balkans, Secret of 133–6
Basara, Svetislav 187–90
Bastide, Roger 80
Bataille, Georges 85
Baudrillard, Jean 77
Bećković, Matija: at Chilandar charnel-house 19; on Kosovo 27, 66; on European roots in Serbia 41; on Serbs as 'remnants of a slaughtered people' 55; and Serbian political myth 71; and 'spiritual honour' 125; as 'Prince of Serbian Poetry' 180; in Budva 182; and Red Star Belgrade 269
Bellenger, Lionel 293
Bielefeld, Uli 78
Biro, Mikloš 306
Blyachkori, Feriz 303
Boban (football player) 262
Bogdanović, Lj. 234
Bonazzi, Tiziano 81
book, cult of the 211–14
Bosnia: nationalist cartoon strips in 62n; Serbs 13; Serbs in 24, 38, 42; war in 31, 175–6, 276, 284; folklore in 33; as centre for Serbian thoughts and deeds 34; and division 35; Muslims in 69; as frontier with Europe 77; sevdainke poems in 103; Clinton visits 129; and creation of ethnically pure state 130; and Serbian holy relics 132; foreign commentators on war in 137; as land of hatred 183
Božović, Djordje *see* Giška
Brajović, V. 234
Branković, Djuradj 309
Branković, Vuk 100, 152, 309

Branković-Hebski, Despot Djordje 100
Brkić, Boško 158
Bromberger, Christian 283n
Budva 179–82
Bugarski, Ranko 287–8, 290
Bukmirović, Dragana 159
Bulatović, M. 181
Bulatović, Pavle 63
Bulić, Vanja, *Tunnel* 183–6
Byzantine civilisation 190

Caillat, Michel 281
Čajkanović, Veselin 60
cartoon strips 62n
Caruga 37, 309
Chamfor 105
Chernishevsky, Nikolai Gavrilovich 95
Chetniks 14, 53, 131, 185, 225–6, 260, 263, 274–5, 279
Christopher, Warren 229
church, the, and 'Serbian question' 5; see also religion; Serbian Orthodox Church; theology
Ćirilov, Jovan 216
Civic Alliance of Serbia (GSS) 313
Clinton, Hillary 213
Clinton, President Bill 129–30, 247
Combat (magazine) 175–8
Ćosić, Dobrica 130–1, 309
'countries in transition', development of democracy in 1
Čović, Mayor of Belgrade 232
criticism, of Serbian political mythology 80–5
Crnčević, Brana 269
Croatia: nationalist cartoon strips in 62n; political myths in 66n; folklore in 33; as centre for Serbian thoughts and deeds 34; war in 44, 48, 175–6, 264, 276, 284; poem to 55; political myths in 74; 'Greater' 75; and creation of ethnically pure state 130; foreign commentators on war in 137; hatred of Yugoslavia in 262
Croatian Army of Defence (HVO) 53
Croats, as different to Serbs 42
Ćosović, Brana 279n
Culibrk, Archdeacon Jovan 252, 255
Čupić, Čedomir 240
Cvetković, Svetozar 180
Cvetković, Vladimir 268
Cvijić, Jovan 115, 121, 133, 309

Dačić, I. 225
dahia 144, 309
Danilevski, N.J. 89
Dayton Peace Accord 17
Degrange, Henri 280
democracy: in 'countries in transition' 1; requirements of 2
Democratic Party (DS) 313
Democratic Party of Serbia (DSS) 313
demonstrations 224–7, 295–304
Despić, Aleksandar 171–4
Dichev, Ivailo 76
Dimitras, Panayotis Elias 76
Djindjić, Zoran 248–9, 296, 305
Djordjević, Tihomir 112–21
Djordjević Vojislav 153
Djordjević, Živorad 151–2, 226
Djukanović, M. 181
Djurdjević, Ratibor M. 203–6
Dodik, Milorad 198
Dokić, Branko 195
Dragan, Kapetan 178, 310
Dragojević, S. 183
Drašković, Vuk: on graves as frontier-markers 36; on relationship between war 46; on Giška 51; and Milošević 223; attacked 226; instigates erection of monument to Chetnik leader 263n; omitted from attack on chauvinist leaders

264; lauded by Red Star Belgrade supporters 273; demonstrators and 296, 303
Dugin, Alexander 134
Durkheim, Emile 81
Dušan, Tsar 14, 59, 91, 107, 132, 310
Dvorniković, V. 121

Ehrenburg, Alan 285
Ekmečić, Milorad 250
Eliade, Mircea 55
Elias, Norbert 285
Engels, Friedrich 94
epic, Serbian 150
Europe: as political symbol 39–47; Serbia as defender of 48; and Balkans as boundary 75; and ethnic cleansing 77; as 'Devil' 137; and 'heartless Westerners' 209; see also 'Rotten West, The' 'exotic East', the 207–10

Fichte, Immanuel Hermann von 90
Fighters' Day 310
First Serbian-Turkish War 199, 201
First Uprising 12
First World War 12, 51, 84
folklore 119–20, 298–9
frontiers, political symbolism of 29–38

Gandhi, Mohandas Karamchand ('Mahatma') 178
Garašanin, Ilija 250
Garde, Paul 13n
Garibaldi, Giuseppe 94
Gauss, Karl Friedrich 171–4
Girardet, Raoul 80
Giška, Djordje Božović 51, 178, 310
Gligorić, Velibor 65
Goethe, Johann Wolfgang von 96
graves: symbolism of 27; as frontier markers 36
gusle 310

hadjuk 310
Hadjuk Veljko 310
Hague War Crimes Tribunal 303
Hajdjuk Veljko (Veljko Petrovic) 14, 178
hatred, and Serbian political mythology 157–60
Hauser, Gerald A. 294
Haushofer, Karl 133–4
Hegel, Friedrich 90, 96
Herder 90
Herzegovina: and perceived impossibility of territorial divisions 35; nationalist cartoon strips in 62n; Muslims in 69; Clinton visits 129
Hitler, Adolf 134, 226, 241n
Hobsbawm, Eric 280
Hussein, Saddam 302

identity, national 64–73
Ignjatović, Jakov 108
Isaković, Antonije 154
Islam 114
Islamism, opposition to 78–9
Ismić, Admira 158
Ivanić, Mladen 198
Ivas, Ivan 289, 293–4
Ivošević, Milorad P. 196
Izetbegović, President Alija 49, 159, 209, 279

Jakšić, Božidar 287n
Jakšić, Djura 104
Jevtić, Bishop Atansije 215, 246, 252, 254
Jovanović, Čedomir 297
Jovanović, I. V. 225
Jovanović, Vladimir 93–4
Judaeo-Masonic conspiracy 204

Kafka, Franz 299
Kalajić, D. 135–6
Kapetan, Dragan 16
Karadjordjević, Prince Alexander 308

Karadjorje (Djordje Petrović) 14, 62, 118, 150, 178, 310
Karadžić, Radovan 17, 19, 34, 49, 130, 167, 184, 253, 310
Karadžić,Vuk Stefanovic 17, 60n 91, 99, 102, 115, 187–90, 310
Karavelov, Ljuben 93
Karić, Marinka 213
Karić brothers 310
Kasirer, Ernst, *The Myth of the State* 3
Katsikis, Dimitrios 134
Khomyakov, (Russian Slavophil) 90
Kinglake, A. W. 207
Kiš, Danilo 92
Kleut, Marija 84n
Knindža, Baja Mali (Mirko Pajcin) 127
Koljević, Nikola 126
Kollar, Jan 90–2
Konrad, George 74
Konstantinović, Radomir 12, 65–6
Kosovo: Battle of 8, 10–11, 12n, 27, 43, 60, 70–1, 132; myth of 10; and 'genetic determination' 16; symbolism of Serbis in 27; and Serbian ethnic space 31; and renewal of Serbian nation 34; Prince Lazar and 37; and defence of Europe 43; Striković on and 65; Bećković on 66; Muslims and 69; and 'call of Serbian culture' 70; difficulty of replacing myth of 84; Skerlic on 99; and Branković's treachery 100; and 'spiritual honour' 125; and sense of ethnic community 162; Gauss and 171; and common Serb-Albanian state 172–3; 'scientific solution' to problem of 172; epic of 190; and the 'Kosovo choice' 255; folklore of 299; lack of mention of 302
'Kosovo option' 10–12, 15
Kosovo pledge *see* 'Kosovo option'
Kostić, Laza 106

Kostić, V. 233–4
Koštunica, V. 234, 305–6, 308
Kovačević, Ivan 285n
Kozić, Goran 154, 159–60
Krajina 33, 37, 42, 104
Krajina Republika Srpska 34
Krajišnik, Momčilo 198, 249
Krestić, Vasilije Dj. 249
Krsmanović choir 180
Kučan, (Milan), President of Slovenia 288

Lacoue-Labarthe, Philippe 82
Lakićević, Ognjen 211–13
Lalić, Dražen 272n
land, and Serbian political ethnomyth 7
language, and Serbian political ethnomyth 7
Lassalle, Ferdinand 94
Lauer, Reinhard 82–3
Lazanski, Miroslav 175–7
Lazar, Prince 11, 14, 37, 59, 61, 69, 310–11
Lazarević, S. 169
Leskovac, Rade 278n
Letica, Slaven 75
Lika 37
Lilić, President Zoran 179–82, 213–14
Limbergen, Kris van 281
Ljotić, Dimitrije 51
Ljubiša, Stevan Mitrov 180–1
Lovrenović, Ivan 155–6
Lukić, Vladan 278
lyric verse 149–52

Maffesoli, Michel 285
Maljković, Božidar 266
Maritsa, Battle of 17, 311
Marjanović, Mirko 169
Marko, Kraljević 59–61, 311
Markov, Mladen 215
Marković, Dragoslav-Draža 268

Marković, Mihailo 6n, 71–2
Marković, Mirjana (Mira) 213, 221–2, 311
Marković, Ratko 199–201
Marković, Svetozar 94–5, 97, 99–102, 311
Marković, Vera 285n;
Marović, S. 181
marriages, ethnically mixed 25
Mars, Tex 191
Marsh, P. 285
Marx, Karl 94n 95
Matić-Marović, Darinka 180
Mazzini, Giuseppe 94
Meštrović, Ivan 163n 302
Michnik, Adam 85
Mihailescu, Vintila 74–5
Mihailović, Draža 131, 263n
Mihailović, Ognjen 237
Mihajlović, Siniša 278
Mihiz, Borislav Mihailović 180
Mijać, D. 248
Milan, King 231
Milašinović, Jasmina 137–9
Mileusnić, Slobodan 127
Miljanov, Marko 102, 108
Miljković, Branko 240
Miljković, Mita 268
Miloš, Prince 118, 246
Milošević, Slobodan: as embodiment of mythical heroes 14; takes power 18–19; on Serbia as defender of Europe 43; and 'historical' aspirations of Serbian people 130–2; and régime's need for relics 169; and attacks on SDS 195; rhetoric of followers of 197; and cultural-artistic gatherings 202; increasing insecurity of hold on power 219–23, 235, 239, 244–5; and popular demonstrations 226–32 264–5; and Red Star Belgrade supporters 273; fall from power 295–308
Milutinović, Colonel Milovan 255

Mladenović, R.M. 252
Mladić, General Ratko 42, 253
Montenegro: symbols of politics in 2; as 'daughter' of Mother Serbia 32–4; Skerlic on 99–100; cult of 103; and sense of ethnic community 162–3, 165; symbolic importance of weapons in 164
Mother of the Jugovici, the 59–60, 311
Mounier, Emmanuel 290
Mrnjavčević, Jovan Uglješa 267, 311
Mrnjavčević, Vukasin 267, 311
Mujo 311
Muller, Jean-Marie 291–2; *The Strategy of Non-Violent Action* 290
Murko, Matija 90
Musa Kesedžija 311
Mussolini, Benito 280

Nancy, Jean-Luc 82
Napoleon Bonaparte, Emperor of France 305
nation: and Serbian political ethnomyth 7; as body 26; as living being 35
national heroes: construction of 58; popularisation of 61
'natural' life 98
Nature, as political symbol 21–8
Nazis, mythology of 82
Nedeljković, Dragan 12, 19–20, 145–8, 215, 217
Nedić, Ljubomir 102
Negrišorac, I. 125–6
Nejgoš, Petar Petrović 249n
Nemanja, Stefan 311
Nemanjić dynasty 62, 147, 250
Nenadović, Ljubomir P. 92
'NeoSlavism' 96
New Age 191–4
Nikolić, Tomislav 237
Njegoš, Petar Petrović 14, 62, 69n 91, 107–8, 163–5, 311

Nogo, Rajko Petrov 21, 40, 71, 126, 217–18
Novaković, Relja 67–8
Novaković, Stojan 231
Obilić, Miloš 4, 14, 59–61, 132, 162–3, 178, 311
Obradović, Dositej 97, 101, 311–12
Obrenović, Knez Milan 201, 312
Obrenović, Miloš 112, 116
Ognjenović, Vida 179–80
'Old Maid Europe' see Europe
Operation Storm 42
Orwell, George (ps. Eric Blair) 280, 299
Ottoman Empire 75

Pages, Didier 281
Pan-Serbism 216
Pan-Slavdom 89–97
Pantić, M. 233
Pašić, Nikola 89, 246, 267, 312
Pavelić, Ante 35, 312
Pavle, Patriarch 168, 232
peace, rhetoric of 287–94
Penezić, S. 169
Perišić, General 232
Perišić, M. 217
Peròn, Eva 288
Perović, Latinka 89
Petković, Gordana 155
Petronijević, Branislav 188
Petrović, M. 234
Petrović, Archpriest Ljubodrag 138, 191–4
Petrović, Ljupko 266
Petrović, Veljko 108
Plavsić, Biljana 24, 196, 198, 312
Poincaré, Henri 291–2
Popadić, Nedeljko Nesa 282
Popović, Justin 45
Popović, Kresimir 285
preachers, and Serbian national vision 145–8
Princip, Gavrilo 14, 312

Protić, Milan St. 245, 247
Radić, Stjepan 95
Radinović, General 250
Radišić, Živko 196–8
Radmanović, Nebojša 196
Radović, Metropolitan Amfilohije 39–40, 68, 180, 182;
Radović, Bishop Amfilohije 254–5
Rakić, Milan 103
Rakitić, S. 234
Ranković, Aleksandar 169, 312
Rašković, Jovan 249
Ražnatović, Željko (Arkan) 14, 178, 275–8, 284, 312
Reboul, Olivier 292–3
Red Star Belgrade football club 84, 259–86
relics, political symbolism of 166–70
religion, Rousseau on 1; see also church, the; Serbian Orthodox Church; theology
Reljin, Milivoje R. 250
Renan, Ernest 250
Renan, Georges 105, 108n
Republika Srpska 34, 52, 146, 169, 195–8, 245, 255; see also Serbia
Rex, John 78
Ricoeur, Paul 290
Risojević, Ranko 196
Ristić, Jovan 246
Ristić, Ljubisa 222, 226
'Rotten West, The' 89–98, 101; see also Europe
Rousseau, Jean-Jacques 1, 210
Rugova, I. 264
Rupel, D. 264
Ruvarac, Ilarion 100

St Cyril 76
St Methodius 76
St Sava see Sava, Saint
St Vasilije Ostroski 166–9
St Vitus' Day see Vidovdan
Šakić, Miladin 268

Šalja (football player) 262
Samardžić, Radovan 67
Šantić, Aleksa 51, 54n 108–9
Šapćanin, M. 91
Saratlić, R. 216
Sava, Saint (*orig*. Rastko Nemanjić) 14, 45, 59, 61–2, 127, 163, 166, 192, 203, 250, 312; Bishop 234
Schiffer, Daniel Salvatore 207–10
Second World War 131, 134
Serbdom, significance of rivers to 150
Serbia: ethnographic myth in 3–85 passim; Europeanisation of 23n; political mythology of 22n; symbols of politics in 2; discourses in 5–6; as nation 7; political ethno-myth of 7–12, 80; 'Heavenly' 31, 37, 308; as 'Mother Serbia' 32, 52; Greater 34; political mythology of 38; political discourse in 41; as defender of Europe 48; intrepretation of political myths in 74; political myths in 98–111; 'Devil' in 137–40; as modern state 141; and 'de-Serbianisation' 147; lyric verse in 149–52; and sense of identity 153–6; and 'genes of the tribe' 161–5; and sense of national identity 164; and desire for national state 200; and sense of mission 203–6
Serbian Aquarian paganism 193
'Serbian National Myth and Europe, The' (newspaper article) 59n
Serbian Orthodox Church 127, 166–70, 193–4, 235; *see also* church, the; religion; theology
Serbian Party of Renewal (SPO) 313–14
Serbian Radical Party (SRS) 314
Serbian Uprising, Second 118
Serbianisation 117–18
Serbo-Turkish Wars 200; *see also* First Serbian-Turkish War

Serbs: as different to Croats 42; as inhabitants of villages under Turkish rule 113; and conversion to Islam 114; Orthodox 70; Muslims as 69; Roman Catholic 70; and uprisings against the Turks 114
Serdar Janko Vukotic 312
Šešelj, Vojislav 236–9, 245
sevdalinka 312
Škerjanc (football player) 262
Skerlić, Jovan 12, 65, 89–111, 121, 312
Slavophiles 90, 100
Slovenia: political discourse in 41; hatred of Yugoslavia in 262; war in 264
Socialist Party of Serbia (SPS) 314
Spencer, Herbert 285
spiritual, the 125–8
Srebenica 42
Srpska, Republika *see* Republika Srpska
štafeta 312
Stanković, Borisav 103
Starčević, Ante 104, 109, 313
Starina Novak 59, 313
states, modern, and popularisation of national heroes 61
Steuckers, Robert 134
stories, and construction of myth 5–12
Striković, Jovan N. 15, 65, 139, 161–2, 164–5
Štúr, Ljudevit 90, 92
Svilar, M. 234
symbols, nature of 1–2
Szeczenyi, Istvan 107

Tadić, Ljubomir 241–3
Taguieff, Pierre-André 289–92
Taine, Hippolyte, 108n
Tenies, Ferdinand 110
Tesla, Nikola 197, 313
theology: Serbian Orthodox 44–5; Orthodox 127; *see also* church,

the; religion; Serbian Orthodox Church
time, politics of 129–32
Tito, President (*orig.* Josip Broz) 169–70, 255, 282–3
Todorov, Tsvetan 208, 210
Tomić, Dragan 226, 301
Tomić, Milan 265–6
Town and Country 112–21
tribe, genes of 161–5
Tudjman, Franjo 19n, 32, 75, 262, 264
Tunnel see under Bulic, Vanja
'turbo-folk' 193
'turbulent times' 215–18
Turks: arrival of 24; hatred of 103; uprisings against 113; withdrawal of from urban centres 116

United Serbian Youth *see* 'Youth Movement', the
Uroš, Tsar 100, 313
uskoci 313
Ustashas 14, 16, 37, 225–6, 260, 264, 275–6

Velimirović, Bishop Nikolaj 44–5, 51, 66, 166
Velmar-Janković, Vladimir 22, 39–40
video, and political symbolism 141–4
Vidovdan (St Vitus' Day) 12, 14, 131–2, 313
vila 313

virility 48; *see also* warrior
Vlasi, Azem 274
Vojvodina 34
Volkov, Vladimir 213
Vučetić, S. 226
Vučić, Aleksandar 237
Vučurević, Bozidar 169
Vukotić, Serdar Janko 63

war, language of 160
warrior, the, as political symbol 48–56
Weil, Erik 290
West, Rebecca 306
Wierhof (German thinker) 96
Wieviorka, Michel 111
Wilpert, Czarina 78
woman-warrior, as political symbol 49; *see also* warrior, the
World War I *see* First World War
World War II *see* Second World War

'Youth Movement', the (United Serbian Youth) 94
Yugoslav People's Army 48, 175, 178, 199, 263
Yugoslav United Left (JUL) 314
Yugoslavia, 'peace process' in 150
Yugoslavism 96

Žanić, Ivo 83–4, 288
Zujović, Zora 282
Zurovac, Mirko 252

Zvonimir, King 83